Promoting Economic Cooperation in South Asia

Promoting Economic Cooperation in South Asia

Beyond SAFTA

Edited by

Sadiq Ahmed
Saman Kelegama
Ejaz Ghani

THE WORLD BANK

SAGE www.sagepublications.com
Los Angeles • London • New Delhi • Singapore • Washington DC

First published in 2010 by

SAGE Publications India Pvt Ltd
B1/I-1 Mohan Cooperative Industrial Area
Mathura Road, New Delhi 110 044, India
www.sagepub.in

SAGE Publications Inc
2455 Teller Road
Thousand Oaks, California 91320, USA

SAGE Publications Ltd
1 Oliver's Yard, 55 City Road
London EC1Y 1SP, United Kingdom

SAGE Publications Asia-Pacific Pte Ltd
33 Pekin Street
#02-01 Far East Square
Singapore 048763

Published by Vivek Mehra for SAGE Publications India Pvt Ltd, typeset in 10/12pt Minion by Star Compugraphics Private Limited, Delhi and printed at Chaman Enterprises, New Delhi.

Library of Congress Cataloging-in-Publication Data
Promoting economic cooperation in South Asia: beyond SAFTA/edited by Sadiq Ahmed, Saman Kelegama, and Ejaz Ghani.
   p. cm.
   Includes bibliographical references and index.
1. South Asia—Foreign economic relations. 2. South Asia—Economic policy. 3. South Asia—Economic integration. I. Ahmed, Sadiq. II. Kelegama, Saman.
III. Ghani, Ejaz.

HF1586.5.S67P76   337.1'54—dc22   2010   2009049003

ISBN: 978-81-321-0311-0 (HB)

The SAGE Team: Elina Majumdar, Anupam Choudhury and Trinankur Banerjee

Contents

List of Tables

List of Figures

List of Boxes

List of Boxes

List of Maps

List of Abbreviations

ACIS	Advanced Cargo Information System
ACP	Aviation Cooperation Programme (US–India)
ADB	Asian Development Bank
AFTA	ASEAN Free Trade Agreement
AH	Asia Highway
ALTID	Asian Land Transport Infrastructure Development
AMS	Aggregate Measure of Support
APEC	Asia-Pacific Economic Cooperation
APTA	Asia Pacific Trade Agreement
APTMA	All Pakistan Textile Mills Association
ASEAN	Association of Southeast Asian Nations
ASYCUDA	Automated Systems for Customs Data
ATA	Admission Temporaries/Temporary Admission
BATNA	Best Alternative through Negotiated Approach
BG	Broad Gauge
BIMSTEC	Bay of Bengal Initiative for Multi-sectoral Technical and Economic Cooperation
BLA	Bilateral Labor Agreements
BMET	Bureau of Manpower, Employment and Training
BOESL	Bangladesh Overseas Employment and Services Ltd.
BOO/BOT	Build, Own, and Operate/Build, Own, and Transfer
BR	Bangladesh Railway
CAM	Customs Administration Modernization
CASA	Central Asia-South Asia
CAT	Convention against Torture and Other Cruel, Inhuman or Degrading Treatment or Punishment
CEC	Committee on Economic Cooperation
CEDAW	Convention on Elimination of All Forms of Discrimination against Women
CEPA	Comprehensive Economic Partnership Agreement

CFS	Container Freight Station
CGE	Computable General Equilibrium
CII	Confederation of Indian Industry
COMESA	Common Market for Eastern and Southern Africa
CPI	Consumer Price Index
CTH	Change of Tariff Heading
CWE	Co-operative Wholesale Establishment
DVA	Domestic Value Addition
EBA	Everything But Arms
ECO	Economic Cooperation Organization
EDI	Electronic Data Interchange
EEC	European Economic Community
EIRP	Emergency Irrigation Rehabilitation Project
FATA	Federally Administered Tribal Areas
FDI	Foreign Direct Investment
FICCI	Federation of Indian Chambers of Commerce and Industry
FTA	Free Trade Agreement/Free Trade Area
GCC	Gulf Cooperation Council
GD	Goods Declaration
GDP	Gross Domestic Product
GFRP	Global Food Crisis Response Program
GMS	Greater Mekong Sub-region
GNI	Gross National Income
GSDP	Gross State Domestic Product
GTAP	Global Trade Analysis Project
HS Code	Harmonized Commodity Description and Coding System
HTS	Harmonized Trading System
ICA	Investment Climate Assessment
ICCPR	International Covenant on Civil and Political Rights
ICD	Inland Container Depot
ICESCR	International Covenant on Economic, Social, and Cultural Rights
ICRIER	Indian Council for Research in International Economic Relations
ICT	Information, Communication, and Technology
IDA	International Development Association
IFPRI	International Food Policy Research Institute
IISD	International Institute for Sustainable Development
ILFTA	Indo-Lanka FTA

ILO	International Labour Organization
IMF	International Monetary Fund
IOSCO	International Organization of Securities Commissions
IPA	Integrated Programme of Action
IPR	Intellectual Property Rights
ISACPA	Independent South Asian Commission on Poverty Alleviation
ISFTA	India–Sri Lanka Free Trade Agreement
IWT	Inland Water Transport
JSG	Joint Study Group
LCC	Low-cost Carrier
LDCs	Least Developed Countries
LNG	Liquid Natural Gas
LTTE	Liberation Tigers of Tamil Eelam
MDG	Millennium Development Goals
MFA	Multi-fibre Arrangement
MFN	Most Favored Nation
MNC	Multinational Corporation
MoU	Memorandum of Understanding
MRA	Mutual Recognition Agreements
NAFTA	North American Free Trade Agreement
NBIPs	Nonbinding Investment Principles
NIACL	National Indian Aviation Company Limited
NRP	Non-resident Pakistani
NSP	National Solidarity Program
NTB	Nontariff Barrier
NTTFC	National Trade and Transport Facilitation Committee
NWFP	North West Frontier Province (Pakistan)
ODA	Official Development Assistance
OECD	Organization for Economic Co-operation and Development
PACCS	Pakistan Customs Computerized System
PIA	Pakistan International Airline
PIM	Participatory Irrigation Management
PPP	Public–Private Partnership
PSI	Preshipment Inspection [Agreements]
PSLFTA	Pakistan–Sri Lanka FTA
QR	Quantitative Restrictions
RMG	Readymade Garment
RMS	Risk Management System

ROO	Rules of Origin
RTA	Regional Trading Agreement
SAARC	South Asian Association for Regional Cooperation
SACEP	South Asia Co-operative Environment Programme
SACEPS	South Asia Center for Policy Studies
SACODiL	SAARC Consortium of Open and Distance Learning
SAD	Single Administrative Document
SADF	SAARC Development Fund
SAFMA	South Asian Free Media Association
SAFTA	South Asian Free Trade Agreement
SAGQ	South Asian Growth Quadrangle
SAPAP	South Asia Poverty Alleviation Program
SAPTA	South Asian Preferential Trade Agreement
SARTUC	South Asia Regional Trade Union Congress
SASEC	South Asian Subregional Economic Cooperation
SAVE	SAARC Audio-Visual Exchange
SCCI	SAARC Chamber of Commerce and Industry
SDC	SAARC Documentation Centre
SDF	SAARC Development Fund
SDG	SAARC Development Goals
SEBI	Securities and Exchange Board of India
SEBON	Securities Board of Nepal
SIPA	SAARC Integrated Programme of Action
SLBFE	Sri Lanka Bureau of Foreign Employment
SME	Small and Medium Enterprise
SMEC	Snowy Mountains Engineering Corporation
SPAF	SAARC Poverty Alleviation Fund
SPEI	Strategic Plan for Economic Integration
SPS	Sanitary and Phytosanitary Standards
SRILPRO	Sri Lanka Trade Facilities Committee
SRMTS	SAARC Regional Multimodal Transport Study
STOMD	SAARC Terrorist Offences Monitoring Desk
SYVOP	SAARC Youth Volunteers Programme
TAR	Trans-Asian Railway
TLP	Tariff Liberalization Program
TRQ	Tariff Rate Quota
TTFP	Trade and Transport Facilitation Project
UNCTAD	United Nations Conference on Trade and Development
UNDP	United Nations Development Program

UNESCAP	United Nations Economic and Social Commission for Asia and the Pacific
UNFPA	United Nations Population Fund
UNIFEM	United Nations Development Fund for Women
USAID	U.S. Agency for International Development
USTDA	U.S. Trade and Development Agency
WGTF	Working Group on Trade Facilitation
WIPO	World Intellectual Property Organization
WTO	World Trade Organization

Preface

South Asia has attracted global attention because it has experienced rapid GDP growth since 1980, averaging nearly 6 percent per annum. Yet, it faces many challenges. There are two faces of South Asia. The first South Asia is dynamic, growing rapidly, highly urbanized, and is benefiting from global integration. The second South Asia is largely agricultural, land-locked, exhibits high poverty, suffers from many conflicts, and is lagging. The divergence between the two faces of South Asia is on the rise. Many policy and institutional constraints contribute to this dichotomy. One important constraint is regional conflict that has made South Asia one of the least integrated regions of the world. While progress has been made in reducing trade barriers with the rest of the world, intraregional trade is a mere 5 percent of total official trade as compared with over 50 percent in East Asia. Capital flows through legal channels are negligible, transit arrangements are cumbersome and expensive, and the physical connectivity is limited and restrictive. Additionally, lack of effective cooperation has constrained progress on a range of public goods including climate change, water management, HIV/AIDS control and disaster management.

The cost of weak regional cooperation tends to hurt the poor more than the other segment of the population. Two of the poorest South Asian countries are Afghanistan and Nepal; both are land locked. Several lagging regions in the larger South Asian countries of Bangladesh, India and Pakistan are located in the border areas and suffer from lack of market integration. Over 500 million people, most of them very poor, live in the Indus and the Ganges–Brahmaputra river basins. These great basins are shared by six nations and are characterized by almost no cooperation and, instead, marked political sensitivity and tension. Several attempts to promote cooperation have failed. Climate change is predicted to have serious impacts on the monsoon, on river flows, and on the rising sea level, with increased incidence of floods and droughts in areas where current shocks already regularly and severely affect the lives and livelihoods of large numbers of people.

In addition to policy and institutional reforms aimed at removing domestic constraints to growth and job creation, market integration and regional cooperation ought to be key elements of a regional strategy for removing the dichotomy between the two faces of South Asia and eliminating poverty over the longer term. South Asia needs two types of market integration—providing countries, especially the land-locked ones, with a broader access to regional and global markets; and integrating the lagging regions within each country with the growth centers without regard to boundaries. The geography of South Asia is such that both types of market integration will require regional cooperation. After Europe, South Asia has the second largest number of cities in the border region. Most countries share a common border with India.

The unique geography of South Asia—distance and density—has the potential to raise growth through increased trade. South Asia has the highest population density in the world. Distance of cities from the border is low. These features naturally propel trade between countries, but presently this is hindered by policy barriers. For example, currently at US$1 billion, trade between India and Pakistan could jump to US$9 billion if trade restrictions are removed. Similarly, estimates suggest that intraregional trade in South Asia could increase from US$5 billion to US$20 billion if restrictions on trading with neighbors are removed.

The benefits of scale economies could be even bigger, particularly to the small land-locked countries. As in Africa, the smaller countries in South Asia do not have the necessary scale economies to invest in infrastructure (energy, telecom, transport). Regional market integration could provide the benefit of scale economies to the smaller countries to invest in infrastructure. Nepal, for example, could double its GDP if it could export hydro-based electricity to India, an energy thirsty country.

Benefits of cooperation on water and climate would be immense. From the Himalayas, where glacier melt is already changing water flows in ways that remain to be fully understood, to the coastal floodplains of Bangladesh and Pakistan, South Asian countries need to adapt to climate change. This can provide the much-needed trigger for opening a dialogue on regional water cooperation. For example, cross-border cooperation on water between India, Bangladesh, and Nepal offers the only long-term solution to flood mitigation, and would benefit over 400 million people.

The benefits of regional cooperation for South Asia are obvious. Yet a range of political constraints prevent cooperation from happening.

The political dynamics will need to change as the opportunity cost of non-cooperation for South Asia's poor is large. A part of this change will come from leadership from the civil society in terms of much more informed knowledge and debate of the underlying opportunities, issues, and constraints.

The objective of the First South Asia Economic Summit was to provide a forum for this public debate on economic cooperation in South Asia. The South Asia Economic Summit was held in Colombo during 28–30 August, 2008, as a follow-up to the 15th SAARC Heads of State Summit, also held in Colombo. This was organized by the Institute of Policy Studies, Sri Lanka, and the Federation of Chambers of Commerce and Industry of Sri Lanka in partnership with RIS (Research and Information Systems, New Delhi, India), SACEPS (South Asia Center for Policy Studies, Kathmandu, Nepal), SAWTEE (South Asia Watch on Trade, Economics, and Environment, Kathmandu, Nepal), World Bank, Commonwealth Secretariat, UNDP-RCC (United Nations Development Program-Regional Center of Colombo), and Asian Development Bank. The Conference brought together academics, private sector, civil society, and policy makers from Afghanistan, Bhutan, Bangladesh, Pakistan, India, Nepal, Maldives, and Sri Lanka.

This book draws selectively from the range of papers and presentations made at the Economic Summit. In selecting the papers, we looked at both the quality and direct relevance to the theme of this collected volume. We also thought it useful to include a few hitherto unpublished papers that were prepared for another conference on regional cooperation sponsored by the World Bank. These concern the private sector's perspectives on cooperation. The Colombo Summit did not have a large participation from the private sector and as such the other conference papers helped meet this gap and thereby enrich the story on regional cooperation presented in this book.

The book is organized into three parts. Part I talks about the imperative for cooperation in terms of the development context of why cooperation is necessary for South Asia. Part II then looks in some depth at a number of specific areas of options and opportunities for cooperation, including trade, trade facilitation, transport, financial and food crises, migration, and tourism. Part III provides the private sector's perspectives on regional cooperation based on contributions from business leaders of Bangladesh, India, Pakistan, and Sri Lanka. Finally, Part IV deals with a number of political economy issues relating to distribution of gains from cooperation among participating countries and how to make SAARC more effective in implementing agreed programs.

We would like to convey our special thanks to all the sponsoring institutions for their support in making this Summit successful. We would also like to thank all the individual authors for their contributions to the book. Thanks are due also to Marjorie Kingston (World Bank) and Sharmini De Silva (IPS) for their help in processing the book.

Sadiq Ahmed
Saman Kelegama
Ejaz Ghani

Part I

The Imperative
for Cooperation

A Perspective on Peace and Economic Cooperation in South Asia

Akmal Hussain

1. INTRODUCTION

This is the moment of reckoning in South Asia. The economic dynamism and innovativeness of its people is catapulting the region into a leadership position as the seismic change in the global economy shifts its center of gravity from the West to Asia. Yet at the same time, the region is threatened by the specter of a nuclear holocaust, the rupturing of the social fabric by religious extremism, persistent poverty of the masses amid the affluence of elites and the destabilization of the life support systems of its ecology. In this context, regional cooperation has become an important framework for addressing the grave challenges and utilizing the great opportunities. In this chapter, we begin in Section 2 by indicating the economic opportunity now available to South Asia and its rich cultural tradition that can be brought to bear to build a better world. In Section 3, we discuss the need for a new policy paradigm to address the multiple challenges of peace, poverty, and environmental degradation in a holistic fashion. We discuss the need to bring to bear a new sensibility rooted in the South Asian tradition of human solidarity, harmony with nature, and the values of sharing and caring. We also discuss a new policy paradigm of cooperation for economic welfare and ecological survival. This paradigm is an alternative to the existing policy paradigm of competition and conflict to achieve economic welfare and power over other states. In Section 4, we analyze the relationship between the peace process, development, and human security. In Section 5, we analyze the constraints to the peace process between India and Pakistan, the nature of path dependence, and some of the short- and medium-term initiatives that can be undertaken to catalyze the peace process and to achieve regional cooperation.

2. CAN SOUTH ASIA LEAD THE WORLD?[1]

South Asia is likely to play a key role in the global economy in this century. In doing so, the people of this region could help address the challenges of poverty, peace, and environmental degradation that confront the world. In this chapter, we will indicate the economic, political, and cultural issues involved in addressing these challenges.

South Asia is at a historic moment of transforming the economic conditions of its people and playing a leadership role not only in the global economy but also in the development of human civilization in the twenty-first century. For the first time in the last 350 years, the global economy is undergoing a shift in its center of gravity from the continents of Europe and North America to Asia. If present trends of gross domestic product (GDP) growth in China, the United States, and India continue, then, in the next two decades, China will be the largest economy in the world, the United States the second largest, and India the third largest. If South Asian countries develop an integrated economy, however, then South Asia could become the second largest economy in the world after China. Given the geographic proximity and economic complementarities between South Asia, on the one hand, and China, on the other, this region could become the greatest economic powerhouse in human history.

Yet the world cannot be sustained by economic growth alone. Human life is threatened by the environmental crisis and conflicts arising from the culture of greed, endemic poverty, and the egotistic projection of military power. Societies in this region have a rich cultural tradition of experiencing unity through transcending the ego, of creative growth through human solidarity and a harmony with nature (Nehru 2004; Perry 1995; Schuon

1995; Syed 1968, 9–22). In bringing these aspects of their culture to bear in facing contemporary challenges, the people of this region could bring a new consciousness and institutions to the global-market mechanism. In so doing, South Asia and China can together take the twenty-first-century world on to a new trajectory of sustainable development and human security. It can be an Asian century that enriches human civilization.

3. CHANGING THE POLICY PARADIGM: HUMANITY, NATURE, AND ECONOMIC GROWTH

As South Asia acquires a leadership position in the global economy over the next two decades, a change is required in the policy paradigm of nation-states: from conflict to cooperation, from the production of new weapons as the emblem of state power to the nurturing of a new sensibility that can sustain life on earth.

We will suggest that if sustainable development is to take place in the global economy—indeed, if life itself is to survive on this planet—a new relationship will have to be sought between human beings, nature, and economic growth. South Asia with its living folk tradition of pursuing human needs within the framework of human solidarity and harmony with nature may be uniquely equipped to face this challenge.

3.1 The Global Ecological Crisis

In perhaps the largest collaborative scientific effort in the world history, some of the leading environmental scientists recently worked together to produce the United Nation's Intergovernmental Panel on Climate Change (IPCC) assessment report (IPCC 2007). Earlier, a similarly comprehensive audit was conducted on the state of the life support systems of planet Earth by the Millennium Ecosystem Assessment. Both reports present evidence that indicates an ecological crisis. The results show that over the past 50 years, humans in the process of economic growth have caused "substantial and largely irreversible loss in the diversity of life on Earth": 25 percent of the species living on earth have gone extinct in the last 50 years. The crisis is made even graver by the fact that "60% of the ecosystem services that were examined in the study are being degraded ... including fresh water ... air and the regulation of regional and local climate" (Millennium Ecosystem Assessment Report 2005).

The IPCC assessment of the impact of global warming and associated climate change provides evidence that the adverse changes in the life support systems of the planet have been directly caused by human intervention (IPCC 2007). It can be argued that this intrusion into the ecosystem is associated with the levels and forms of production and consumption associated with the economic growth over the last three centuries within the framework of capitalism.

The IPCC report projects with a high degree of confidence that the increased global average temperatures will result in major changes in "ecosystem structure and function," leading to "negative consequences for biodiversity and ecosystem goods and services e.g. water and food supply" (IPCC 2007, 11). It is projected that climate change associated with global warming could decrease crop yields in South Asia by 30 percent by the mid-twenty-first century. This could result in an increase in the intensity and extent of the food crisis and sharply increased poverty that is already being observed.

The IPCC assessment shows that approximately 20–30 percent of plants and animal species are at increased risk of extinction (IPCC 2007, 11). The consequent reduction in biodiversity would make the ecosystem more fragile and therefore more susceptible to exogenous shocks.

The existing process of production and consumption of goods involves releasing toxic gases and materials into the air, land, and water systems. Since the Earth's ecology has a maximum-load capacity, it is clear that the present consumerist culture, patterns of economic growth, and underlying institutional structure cannot be sustained indefinitely into the future without undermining the life support systems of the planet. *For sustaining life on Earth, a new relationship will have to be sought between human beings, nature, and economic growth. Thus, we may be on the threshold either of ecological disaster or the construction of a new human civilization. In this situation, for South Asia to lead the world means introducing new cooperative forms of social and interstate relations to achieve sustainable development, human security, and freedom from hunger. This will require new forms of social organization, technologies, and institutions underpinned by a new consciousness that can sustain life on earth.*

3.2 The New Sensibility

Today, the market is being apotheosized as the mythical space in which the individual can be free and yet provided with plenty by the hidden hand of the market. Yet, inherent in the capitalist accumulation process is the systematic inculcation of an insatiable desire to possess goods (Hussain 2002). As Marx (1990), writing in the nineteenth century, pointed out, "The capitalist system not only produces goods that satisfy needs, but also the needs that these goods satisfy." The subliminal language of advertisement does not *represent* goods, but rather *fantasizes* goods such that they appear to us not in terms of their material attributes, but as magical receptacles of such qualities as beauty, efficacy, and power (Barthes 1973). Thus, qualities that we actually possess as human beings are transposed into goods, and the individual gets locked into an endless pursuit of acquisition (Hussain 2002).

The culture of consumerism, which the market systematically inculcates, is inconsistent with conserving the environment. The life support systems of our planet cannot be sustained beyond a certain limit in the levels of global output growth despite any foreseeable development and adoption of green technologies. As Mahatma Gandhi said, "There is enough in the world for everybody's need but not for everybody's greed."

Contemporary market culture is marked by the atomization of society, the inculcation of greed, egotism, and the estrangement of the individual from his humanity. A new, more humane sensibility must form the basis of a sustainable process of economic growth, forms of production, distribution, and societal as well as interstate relations. Perhaps South Asia can contribute to the contemporary world by weaving from the golden threads of its folk cultures the tapestry of a twenty-first-century sensibility.

In South Asia, the interaction of diverse civilizations across millennia has brought to the surface certain fundamental features of each civilization, which while being rooted in its specific linguistic, religious, and cultural *form*, are essentially of a universal nature. Underlying the diversity of religious beliefs is a universal spiritualism of love, beauty, and truth. Associated with this sensibility is a set of values of caring and sharing. In this context, three characteristics of a South Asian sensibility can be articulated:

- The *other* constitutes the essential fertilizing force for the growth of the self. The *other*, when brought into a dynamic counterposition to the *self*, helps to transcend the ego and thereby enlarge the experience of the *self*. To recall the words of Shah Hussain, the Punjabi Sufi poet, "You are the woof and you the warp, you are in every pore, says Shah Hussain Faqir, I am not, all is you." In the tradition of the Sufis, or the Bhaktis, or the Buddhists, or the Christians, it is through the act of giving that the self is enhanced.

- In the South Asian tradition, whether the Muslim Sufis, the Bhaktis, or the Buddhists, the self is detached from the *desire* for commodities, which are seen as merely *useful*. The Greek philosopher Aristotle held a similar view when he observed in his *Nichomacean Ethics* that goods cannot have value since they are merely useful. It is human functioning that is of value (Aristotle 1998). The voice of the Sufis still echoes in contemporary South Asian folk culture: "Those who have accumulated millions that too is mere dust" (Shah Hussain); and the Tamil poet Kambar in describing a good society says, "There was no one who did not have enough, there was no one who had more than enough" (Wignaraja et al. 1991).
- Nature in the South Asian tradition is treated not as an exploitable resource but as a reference point to *human* nature. Nature is the context within which we experience our connection with the eternal, and sustain economic and social life. The Bishnoi community in Rajasthan and the peasants of Bhutan still conduct their production and social life in harmony with nature, as part of their spiritual beliefs. Najam Hussain Syed, the contemporary Sufi poet of the Punjab, writes, "Plant the moonlit tree in your courtyard, nurture it, and thereby remain true to the beloved."

Amid its diversity, South Asia has shared civilizational propensities of transcending the ego as a means of fulfillment, of locating the need for goods in the context of human responsibility, and of harmonizing economic and social life with nature. It is this South Asian sensibility and the associated human values that could be brought to bear in building a new relationship between humans, nature, and production to sustain life in the twenty-first-century world.

3.3 South Asia and the New Policy Paradigm

All great epochs of economic and cultural achievement are associated with a critique of the received wisdom of the day and a rediscovery of a universal humanity that lies at the root of specific ideological and religious traditions. So must it be for South Asia as it faces the prospect of a leadership role in the twenty-first century. Let us begin with a critical examination of the theoretical postulates that have formed the basis of economic and foreign policy of modern nation-states.

The policy paradigm underlying the last three centuries of economic growth within nation-states and political relations between states has been characterized by two propositions that are rooted in conventional social science theory:

- Maximization of individual gains in terms of continuous increases in production and consumption within a competitive framework ensures the maximization of social welfare at the national as well as global levels (Gilpin 2001).
- The economic and political interests of a nation-state are best achieved by translating economic gains into military power.[2] The assumption here is that a state can enhance national welfare by initiating, or being part of an initiative for projecting, hegemonic power over other states.

These propositions now need to be questioned because of the increased interdependence of people and states on each other and on the ecology within which they function. As this region develops a leadership role in the world, let us briefly critique the following propositions as the basis for an alternative policy paradigm:

- First, the idea that competition alone ensures an efficient outcome may not be necessarily true in all cases in view of the work by Nobel laureate, economist John Nash, who proved mathematically that in some cases the equilibrium, which maximizes individual gains, could be achieved through cooperation rather than competition (Nash 1996).

  The Nash equilibrium solution may be particularly relevant in the context of India–Pakistan relations. Consider. India, if it is to sustain its high growth rate, will require sharply increased imports of oil, gas, and industrial raw materials from West and Central Asia, for which Pakistan is the most feasible conduit. Similarly, India's economic growth, which has so far been based on the domestic market, will, in the foreseeable future, require rapidly increasing exports for which Pakistan and other South Asian countries are an appropriate market.[3] Thus, the sustainability of India's economic growth requires cooperation with Pakistan. Conversely, peace and cooperation with India is essential for Pakistan if it is to achieve and sustain a GDP growth rate of about 8 percent, overcome poverty, and build a democracy based on a tolerant and pluralistic society. It is clear that governments in India and Pakistan will need to move out of the old mind-set of a zero-sum game, in which gains by one side are made at the expense of the other. Now the welfare of both countries can be maximized through joint gains within a framework of cooperation rather than conflict.[4]

The missing dimension of the relationship between competition and welfare in conventional economic theory is that of institutions. The recent work of another Nobel Prize-winning economist, Douglass North, has shown that if competitive markets are to lead to efficacious outcomes, they must be based on a set of underlying institutions (North 1990). He defines institutions in terms of constraints to behavior for achieving shared objectives within an appropriate combination of incentives and disincentives. We can apply North's principle to suggest that emerging economic powers need to seek a broad framework of cooperation for the efficient functioning of a competitive global economy.

Our proposed logic of locating competitive markets within broader institutional structures of cooperation at the regional and global levels is necessitated by the integrated ecology of the planet. Global cooperation in environmental protection, poverty reduction, and defusing the flash points of social conflict and violence will become the essential underpinning of sustainable development and human security in this century.

- The second proposition in conventional social science theory and political practice is that the economic welfare and political influence of a nation-state can be best achieved by translating economic gains into military power. This is also questionable. In the new world that is now taking shape, the influence of an emerging power will be determined not by the magnitude of the destruction it can wreak on other countries but by its contribution to enhancing life in an interdependent world. Thus it is not the military muscle of a state that will be the emblem of status, but its contribution to meeting the challenge of peace, overcoming global poverty, and protecting the planet from environmental disaster.

Meeting these challenges will require a deeper understanding of the processes that shape nature and human societies, as well as a deeper awareness of our inner self and our shared civilizational wellsprings. Thus, as South Asia pursues a leadership position in the global economy, it will also have to strive to reach the cutting edge of human knowledge in the natural and social sciences. At the same time, it will have to bring to bear its value system rooted in the experience of humanity that is evoked in its diverse literary and philosophical traditions (Nehru 2004; Pallis 1995; Syed 1968).

4. HUMAN SECURITY, DEVELOPMENT, AND THE PEACE PROCESS

4.1 Peace: A Question of Life and Death

South Asia today stands suspended between the hope of a better life and fear of cataclysmic destruction. The hope emanates from its tremendous human and natural resource potential: the rich diversity of its cultures that flourish within the unifying humanity of its civilization. The fear arises from the fact that South Asia is not only the poorest region in the world but also one whose citizens live in constant danger of a nuclear holocaust. At the same time, the structures of state and the fabric of society are threatened by armed extremist groups who use hate and violence to achieve their political goals.

It can be argued therefore that interstate peace in the region rather than enhanced military capability is the key to national security, indeed, to human survival. We will propose in this chapter that peace between India and Pakistan not only is necessary for sustaining economic growth but also is vital for building pluralistic democracies and thereby sustaining the integrity of both states and societies in the region.

4.2 Militarization, Human Security, and National Integrity

States in South Asia have primarily pursued "national security" through the building of the military capability for mass annihilation of each other's citizens. It is not surprising that South Asia is the poorest and yet the most militarized region in the world (Haq 1997). It contains almost half the world's poor and has the capability, even in a limited nuclear exchange, to kill more than 100 million people immediately, with many hundreds of million more dying subsequently from radiation-related illnesses (Barry and Hirsh 1998).

The arms race between India and Pakistan (two countries that account for 93 percent of the total military expenditure in South Asia) is responsible for this cruel irony. India, which is ranked at 142 in terms of per capita income, ranks first in the world in terms of arms imports. Pakistan is not far behind, being ranked 119 in terms of per capita income and 10th in the world in terms of arms imports (Haq 1997). These military expenditures whose scale is unprecedented in the developing world are being undertaken in the name of achieving national security in a situation in which the majority of the population in South Asia is living below the international poverty line (US$2 a day) (Haq 2006, 51), 46 percent of the children are malnourished (Haq 2006, 70), and 35 percent of the population is suffering from health deprivation (measured in terms of lack of access to safe water and undernourished population) (Haq 2006, 68). The trade-off between military expenditures and the provision of basic services is worth considering. For example, a modern submarine with associated support systems costs US$300 million, which would be enough to provide safe drinking water to 60 million people. These figures call into question the logic of increasing military expenditures to achieve national security.

The deadly nuclear dimension that since 1998 has been added to the India–Pakistan arms race is seen by the respective governments to reinforce national security through a presumed "deterrence." In this context, it can be argued that three features define the India–Pakistan strategic nuclear environment, which imply a high probability of an accidental nuclear war, thereby making nuclear deterrence unstable: *(a)* the flying time of nuclear missiles between India and Pakistan is less than five minutes; *(b)* the unresolved Kashmir dispute fuels tensions between the two countries, making them susceptible to disinformation about each other's intentions; and *(c)* intrastate social conflicts in each country feed off interstate tensions.

Apart from the danger of an accidental nuclear war, the current structure of the India–Pakistan tension is such that a terrorist attack can induce military mobilization and repeatedly bring both countries to a point at which the nuclear button could be deliberately pressed by one, then the other side. Consider the elements of the structure: First, armed militant groups continue to conduct what they see as a war of liberation in Kashmir. Pakistan's government claims that such groups are not under its control, while India continues to accuse it of being involved in "cross-border terrorism." Second, when a high-profile terrorist attack occurs in India, Pakistan is held responsible, as occurred following the outrageous attack on the Indian Parliament (December 2001) and the barbaric train bombings in Bombay (July 2006). In the former case, India actually mobilized its military forces in a warlike deployment on the India–Pakistan border. Third, in the case of an Indian incursion into Pakistani territory following a terrorist attack, if the territorial gains of Indian forces reach an unspecified critical level, Pakistan has made clear that it will use nuclear weapons to defend itself. At the same time, the declared Indian nuclear doctrine involves, in response, an all-out nuclear attack on Pakistan. As the Indian Defense Minister George Fernandes clarified in December 2002, such an all-out nuclear retaliation will occur even if Pakistan drops a nuclear bomb on Indian forces operating within Pakistani territory (Global Security Newswire 2002).

These elements of the Pakistan–India problem could spark a military confrontation between the two states at any time. Moreover, given the relative lack of geographic depth in the Pakistan case, a conventional war could quickly reach the nuclear threshold. That this prospect is terribly real was illustrated on at least three occasions: The first occasion was India's Operation Brass Tacks in 1986. This military exercise, which Pakistan saw as a prelude to an Indian invasion, led to a threat of nuclear war by the then Pakistani Foreign Minister Sahibzada Yaqub Khan, given explicitly to his old college mate I. K. Gujral, the Indian foreign minister, during a meeting in Delhi. The second illustration is the Kargil conflict in 1999. This conflict quickly escalated to a mobilization of military forces along the international border. The danger of an all-out war became so grave that Prime Minister Nawaz Sharif had to rush to Washington to get President Clinton's support to avoid it. Bruce Reidel,[5] who was present during the Nawaz–Clinton meeting, claims the United States had information that Pakistan was preparing its nuclear arsenal for possible use. Furthermore, he claims that Clinton actually asked Sharif, "if he knew how advanced the threat of nuclear war really was" (Reidel 2002). The third occasion came after the attack by armed militants on the Indian Parliament in 2001. India mobilized its military forces along the international border with Pakistan and tension rose to a point at which Pakistan threatened "unconventional" military retaliation if war broke out.[6] Thus the very structure of the India–Pakistan situation suggests that wars between the two countries cannot be localized or conventional.

With the stakes of catastrophic destruction as high as they are in the region, any nonzero probability of nuclear war should be unacceptable. Yet, as we have argued, the defining features of the nuclear environment in South Asia make the probability of an intentional or accidental nuclear war perhaps higher than in any other region of the world.

In contrast to the preoccupation of governments to achieve "national security" within a paradigm of conflict, the citizens of even adversarial states share a common concern for human security: They seek security from the threats of war, religious extremism, economic deprivation, social injustice, and environmental degradation. Bridging this gap between the preoccupations of state and civil society is necessary to maintain the social contract that underlies the writ of the state and sustains national integrity.

Thus, establishing a new framework of lasting peace for the provision of human security to civil society is essential for the stability of states in South Asia. The questions are, what are the constraints to such a lasting peace and what factors can drive the peace process? These questions are addressed in the following section.

5. THE CONSTRAINTS AND DRIVERS OF THE INDIA–PAKISTAN PEACE PROCESS

Let us start with the strategic dimension of the political economy of India and Pakistan, respectively, within which both the constraints to and the drivers of the peace process can be examined. India's economic strength lies in the fact that having established a heavy industrial base during the Nehru period in the 1950s, and reconfigured India's policy framework in the 1990s to play a role in a globalized economy, India's economy has been launched on a high-growth trajectory. With a domestic technological change capability, international competitiveness in selected cutting-edge sectors like software and electronics, and large capital inflows, India has achieved impressive GDP growth over the last two decades. Yet it has been predominantly based on the home market, with India's exports as a percentage of world exports still less than 1 percent. Continued growth in the future will require acceleration in export growth. To sustain GDP growth, India will need to establish (a) markets for its manufactured exports in South Asia and abroad and (b) an infrastructure for the supply of oil, gas, and electricity. It is in this context of sustaining GDP growth that three strategic imperatives for India become apparent: (a) achieving a regionally integrated economy through an early implementation of the Islamabad South Asian Association for Regional Cooperation (SAARC) Summit Declaration on the South Asian Free Trade Agreement (SAFTA) in January 2004; (b) securing oil and gas pipelines and rail and road transportation routes from Central Asia to India through Pakistan; and (c) overcoming political disputes with Pakistan and other South Asian neighbors to establish a political framework of lasting peace that would be integral to economic union.

Peace and economic cooperation with Pakistan are necessary for India not only to secure its strategic economic interests but also to maintain its secular democratic polity. A high-growth, open economy framework for India today is inseparable from a liberal democratic political structure.

Therefore, the existing social forces of Hindu nationalism, intolerant of minorities, will undermine India's secular democratic structure as much as its economic endeavor. Continued tension between India and Pakistan will only fuel extremist religious forces in both countries, to the detriment of their economy and polity.

Pakistan, by contrast, is faced with an economic crisis whereby it is unable to sustain high GDP growth due to an aid-dependent economic structure, inadequate export capability, and recurrent balance-of-payments pressures. The persistent high levels of poverty and continued tension with India fuel the forces of religious extremism. Armed militant groups have now emerged as rival powers to that of the state within its territorial domain, thereby threatening the structure of the state as well as the fabric of society. Peace with India will mean a substantially improved environment for the much-needed foreign and domestic investment. This could play an important role in accelerating and sustaining GDP growth and poverty reduction in Pakistan.

It is clear that through peace, both India and Pakistan can reap economic benefits for their people and secure their respective democratic structures against the forces of religious extremism. The national security of both countries is threatened not by the neighbor across the border but by internal social forces of intolerance, violence, and poverty. A new structure of peace would reduce the danger of cataclysmic destruction from nuclear war and also provide the two nations with economic and political stability. Thus, by providing increased security of life and livelihood to both countries, national security in their respective nations will be enhanced.

Trade and investment historically has been both the cause and consequence of institutional change. So it can be for Pakistan, India, and indeed South Asia as a whole. Thus, with respect to SAFTA, implementation of the Islamabad SAARC Declaration (SAARC 2004) would be another strategic step toward achieving regional economic integration and peace and strengthening the institutional structures of democracy in the region.

Pursuant to SAFTA, Pakistan ought to quickly establish free trade and investment with India and other South Asian countries, together with an easing of travel restrictions within the region for the people of South Asian countries. Free trade and investment within South Asia and particularly between India and Pakistan could be a driver of change in the institutional structure of the economy, polity, and society: (a) it would be a powerful economic stimulus; (b) it would create stakeholders for peace and the demilitarization of the polity in Pakistan, which would strengthen the struggle for civilian supremacy in Pakistan; and (c) it would help build a tolerant and pluralistic democratic culture. Let us briefly examine each of these dimensions of institutional change resulting from an India–Pakistan peace settlement.

5.1 Economic Cooperation

5.1.1 Free Trade and Sustainable Growth with Equity

An economic opening up with India would sharply accelerate GDP growth in Pakistan through increased investment by Indian entrepreneurs. Moreover, import of relatively cheaper capital and intermediate goods from India could reduce capital-output ratios in Pakistan and thereby generate higher GDP growth for given levels of investment. At the same time, the import of food products during seasonal shortages could reduce food inflation and thereby improve the distribution of real income in Pakistan. Easing of travel restrictions would give a massive boost to Pakistan's tourism, services, and retail sectors, which could stimulate growth. It also would increase employment elasticities with respect to GDP growth (since the tourism sector is labor intensive), thus increasing employment and improving income distribution. Thus, free trade relations with India would enable Pakistan to achieve a higher and more equitable GDP growth.

5.1.2 Free Trade and Civilian Supremacy

As free trade and investment bring substantial economic dividends to the middle and lower middle classes, a large constituency will be created in Pakistan to change the existing perspective of Pakistan as a "national security state," which is presumed to be "threatened by India" and hence requires the dominance of the military in the polity and national policy. Shifting from the ideology of a national security state to a democratic perspective will make it possible to acknowledge that the security and welfare of citizens is primarily achieved through peace and development. This change in the national perspective can be an important factor in achieving civilian supremacy within the polity.

5.1.3 Free Trade and Democratic Culture

An important constraint to building a democratic polity and indeed the principal threat to state structures in South Asia arises from internal conflicts such as religious extremism; ethnic, communal, and caste conflicts; and linguistic sub-nationalism. Containing these conflicts requires institution building for a pluralistic society. In such a society diverse identities between individuals can coexist, and at the same time, multiple identities can be maintained by each individual.[7] For example, Muslims and Hindus not only should be able to live in peace, but also a particular individual could be a Muslim, a Balochi, a Karachite, a Pakistani, a South Asian, and a Commonwealth citizen concurrently.

Underlying the cultural diversity in South Asia is the unity of shared wellsprings of human civilization. It is a unity that is nurtured by its diversity. Thus national integrity is strengthened not by the denial of multiple identities but by creating a democratic polity within which they can blossom. Essential to the building of pluralistic democracies in India and Pakistan, respectively, is the opening up of new economic and cultural spaces within which the people of the two countries can encounter the "other." In so doing, citizens of the two countries can experience the diversity and richness of the self. In the past, state-sponsored mutual demonization has sustained interstate conflict. Demonization involves a narrowing of the mind and a constriction of the identity that places the self and the other into a mutually exclusive and conflicting dichotomy. Nurturing one's richness requires a human relationship within which the other is experienced as a vital fertilizing force in the growth of the self. Liberating the dynamic of such a human contact between erstwhile "enemies" could be vital to the enrichment of identities and the building of pluralistic democracies in Pakistan and India.[8]

5.2 The Dialectic of Cooperation and Confrontation

The constraints to the peace process can be understood in terms of the dialectic between the strategic political and military imperatives for peace on the one hand and the pressures for path dependence within the military establishment on the other. We will briefly discuss this dialectic within the power system to explain the stop–go nature of the peace process and to review the opportunities now available for triggering medium-term change.

5.2.1 The Strategic Imperatives for the Peace Process

The decision by the Musharraf government to engage with India in a peace process was predicated on three power system imperatives:

- Reducing tensions with India in order to focus on economic growth was seen by the new military regime as a means of achieving political legitimacy.
- After 2001, when Pakistan joined the West in the war against terrorism in Afghanistan, closure of the front (at least temporarily) was a rational military necessity to avoid a two-front situation.
- The military government thought it politic to accede to what had now become a popular demand for peace with India.

These strategic military and political imperatives induced General Musharraf to engage with India on the basis of a new and innovative policy formulation constituted by three elements:

- A shift away from the traditional Pakistani position of making a plebiscite in Kashmir the precondition for normalizing economic relations with India was replaced by a new position: a *composite* dialogue was to be conducted within which economic relations with India were to be discussed side by side with the resolution of outstanding political and territorial disputes, including Kashmir.
- The dynamics of each of these two tracks were different: the potential for trade relations produced results relatively rapidly, while the process of resolution of the Kashmir dispute, given its intractable nature, was expected to be much slower. It was initially thought that success in economic relations and the resultant peace dividend would not only create constituencies for lasting peace in both countries but also would help build confidence between the two contending states, resulting in a positive synergistic effect on the political dispute resolution process.
- There was a significant and innovative change from Pakistan's traditional "plebiscite or nothing" Kashmir position in which a plebiscite was seen as the "unfinished business of partition" and hence essentially a bilateral dispute. This was replaced by a more rational policy whereby General Musharraf proposed that the following:

  o Both Pakistan and India should set aside their traditional rigid positions and seek common ground.
  o The resolution of the dispute should be acceptable to India, Pakistan, *and* the people of Kashmir, making the earlier bilateral dispute a trilateral one.

5.2.2 The Power System Constraints to Peace

General Musharraf's stated policy initially produced encouraging results, with a substantial increase in trade volumes between India and Pakistan and confidence-building measures, including increased visa permits for a larger number of travelers across the border. The structural restrictions to trade and, indeed, to investment could be overcome only if Pakistan granted Most Favored Nation (MFN) status to India. This status would enable trade, instead of being restricted to a few officially negotiated items, to be opened up for a free flow of goods and capital, as in the case of other countries under the World Trade Organization (WTO) regime. These structural constraints to freer trade persisted even as Pakistan under the SAARC umbrella signed the Islamabad Declaration making a SAFTA a national objective.

It is at this point that the power system constraints to the peace process kicked in. Influential elements in the establishment regarded a rapid improvement in economic relations and a permanent peace with India as ultimately a threat to the raison d'être of a large military establishment. The military was getting a lion's share of the budget on the basis of the "Indian threat" and the ideology of a national security state. Fears of Pakistan's economy being swamped by India began to circulate, as did the notion that the very identity of the state would be threatened by normalization of relations with India.

These considerations acted as a brake on the peace process, and Prime Minister Shaukat Aziz pointedly declared that improvement in economic relations was dependent on progress on the Kashmir dispute. Thus, the policy of delinking the economic and political tracks was reversed and progress in economic relations once again made hostage to the intractable Kashmir dispute. This setback in the peace process was reinforced as President Musharraf's political position weakened and his reliance on support from his military constituency increased amid the gathering storm of the judicial crisis. The peace process went on hold as President Musharraf faced the double threat to his government from the democratic opposition on the one hand and the intensified attacks from militant extremists on the other.

The new democratic government in Pakistan, which emerged after the February 2008 elections, holds promise to pursue what Foreign Minister Shah Mahmood Qureshi recently called a "comprehensive settlement" with India. Earlier the co-chairperson of the People's Party of Pakistan, Asif Ali Zardari, declared the government's intentions to accelerate the peace process and focus on economic cooperation.[9] The imperatives of peace for building a dynamic economy and a democratic polity are clearly apparent to the leadership of Pakistan's fragile democracy.

5.2.3 Path Dependence and the Short-term Triggers for Accelerating the Peace Process

The concept of path dependence was conceived by Douglass North as a tendency of individuals and groups to resist institutional change where such a change threatens their interests. Such individuals and groups are willing to invest their energy, resources, and time to resist institutional change (North 2005, 51). Thus, as North points out, path dependence is "the constraints on the choice set in the present that are derived from historical experiences of the past" (North 2005, 52).

The problem of path dependence in this context is located in the mind-sets of the respective bureaucracies in the two countries that have emerged through many years of mutual demonization. These mind-sets were reinforced by the wars between India and Pakistan in 1965 and 1971, the more limited Kargil conflict in 1999, and the protracted insurgency in Indian-occupied Kashmir. The recurrent military confrontations and the perception of each other as adversaries in a zero-sum game have bred attitudes of mutual mistrust and suspicion among the military establishments, the bureaucracies, and to some extent the political leadership of the two countries. The attitudes of the political leadership in Pakistan and India have changed significantly during the last decade as a result of the popular pressure to pursue peace. "The trust deficit," however, in the respective military and bureaucratic establishments remains unchanged.

The problem of path dependence in this context is illustrated by an observation made by Prime Minister Manmohan Singh in August 2004, when he graciously invited members of the South Asia Center for Policy Studies to his house in New Delhi for a discussion over tea. When it was suggested that the gains of peace were great for both India and Pakistan and that history had placed the prime minister and the Pakistani leadership in a position to make history by actualizing these potential gains for the people of both countries, the prime minister responded with an incisive remark: "The gains from peace are immense, yet old attitudes of strife, mistrust, and suspicion could lead us to a sub-optimal solution." He went on to say that he is willing, however, to make a "new beginning." Any ideas for peace would have his "fullest support, and I hope that of my government,"[10] he said, turning hesitantly to his National Security Adviser (at that time Mr Dixit).

These "old attitudes" are evident in the power system constraints to peace, which primarily are located in the bureaucratic and military establishments of the two countries. These constraints are locked in the "old attitudes" not only because of the persistence of modes of thought now considered obsolete but also because of their present economic power and influence over the political leadership based on what are regarded as "national security considerations," which may depend on maintaining the status quo. The possibility of overcoming "old attitudes" and taking initiatives for peace is located in the space available to democratic governments within the power structures of the bureaucracy and military and their ability to translate the will of their people for economic welfare and peace into policy action.

Clearly, free trade between Pakistan and India would be an important medium-term objective that could sustain and substantially accelerate the long-term political process for institutionalizing a lasting peace between the two countries. In the context of the power system discussion above, it can be argued that the short-term initiatives required for the medium-term objective in the Pakistan case are integrally linked with the initiatives for strengthening and deepening democracy that are proposed in the preceding section. Achieving free trade essentially would be an act of persuasion, whereby a popular consensus is created among civil society organizations, think tanks, and a responsive parliament. Free trade also would involve persuading the military establishment that such trade would be in the best interest of Pakistan and therefore of the military. Moreover, it would enlarge the corporate gains of the military within its economic sphere.

Four specific short-term initiatives could be undertaken to trigger the process of achieving economic cooperation between India and Pakistan:

- **Host a Conference of South Asian Parliamentarians.** Host a conference focused on the issue of regional economic cooperation.[11] The issue of free trade and implementation of SAFTA ought to be the main item on the agenda. The participants of the conference could include representatives from regional think tanks, experts who have worked on regional cooperation, representatives of civil society advocacy organizations for peace and economic cooperation, civil servants involved in the peace process, lawyers, the media, and representatives from the faculties of the Command and Staff College and the National Defence University.

- **Establish a Network of South Asian Institutes for Regional Cooperation.** Create a network of regional institutes in South Asia that are devoted to policy research and advocacy for peace and economic cooperation through a series of workshops. These workshops would bring together the latest thinking on issues of peace and economic cooperation in South Asia and specifically the dynamics of the peace process.
- **Establish an Advocacy Program for South Asian Parliaments and Governments.** Establish an institutional base to unite representatives of civil society organizations in Pakistan and India as well as representatives from regional think tanks to undertake a short-term advocacy program with their respective parliaments and governments to create the basis for a definitive decision on SAFTA implementation in the SAARC Summit of 2010.
- **Ease Travel Restrictions for Tourism in South Asia.** Ease travel restrictions for South Asians traveling in South Asian countries to enable greater economic, cultural, and social interaction among the citizens of India and Pakistan, in particular, and South Asia, in general. The sharp increase in the magnitude of tourism following an easing of travel restrictions would be a powerful economic stimulus to the economies of the region, and tourism could become one of the largest industries in Pakistan and some of the smaller South Asian countries. Moreover, the secondary multiplier effects of tourism would be to increase incomes of wide strata of the population as porters, restaurant and hotel staff, and transporters.

5.2.4 Medium-term Drivers of Peace and Economic Cooperation

The following medium-term initiatives could be undertaken by the private sector and civil society in South Asian countries with support from SAARC and could help overcome path dependence:

- **South Asia Health Foundation.** Establish a South Asia Health Foundation (SAHF) to make the benefits of peace and cooperation in South Asia palpable to people through improved health care. The objective of the SAHF would be to establish high-quality model hospitals, together with satellite clinics and outreach programs for preventive health care, in selected districts in each of the countries of South Asia.[12]

- **South Asia Education Foundation.** Create a South Asia Educational Foundation (SAEF) on the basis of contributions by individual SAARC member countries, individual philanthropists, and (more substantially) multilateral donor agencies. The purpose of SAEF would be to create a network of high schools at an international standard in every *tehsil* (at least one in each *tehsil*) of each of the countries of South Asia. These SAARC schools could act as role models and set the standards for both the private sector and the individual governments to follow.

  An important dimension of setting up the SAARC network of schools in Pakistan would be to counteract the growing influence of *madrassa*s and militant religious groups that are enlarging their dragnet of indoctrination, particularly in the rural areas and small towns of the North West Frontier Province (NWFP) and the Punjab. One of the factors that attract students to the *madrassa*s is that, in most cases, they get free lodging and board, with the parents having to pay only nominal fees. The SAEF schools, which would provide a broad-based liberal education, ought to have a differential fee system wherein children from affluent families pay higher fees to partially subsidize those from poor families. An endowment fund for scholarships could be created to provide free education to students from poor families. Additionally, the schools should have a residential facility for out-of-town students and a provision for free lunch to day scholars.

- **Energy Cooperation in South Asia.** Establish a system for energy cooperation in South Asia through the following initiatives:

  o In the context of developing energy markets of these resources, power trading in the region calls for establishment of high-voltage interconnections between the national grids of the countries of the region. India, Pakistan, and Bangladesh should cooperate in establishing a gas pipeline for transporting gas from Iran, Qatar, Turkmenistan, and even Myanmar.

  o The precondition to create a competitive power market is to allow freedom for generators to produce electricity and distributors to sell in the market. In this context, the joint development, trading, and sharing of energy should be pursued.

  o Apart from electricity production and distribution through large hydroelectric projects, it is time to undertake joint efforts to develop innovative new technologies, such as solar and wind energy and single turbines on the canal system, for use in both the national and regional grids as well as at the village and *tehsil* levels.

- **Investment within South Asia through Joint Venture Projects.** Increase regional investment and growth through the following key joint venture projects:

  o Facilitate joint private sector projects to build a network of motorways and railways to international quality standards throughout South Asia. These modern road and rail networks would connect all the major commercial centers, towns, and cities of SAARC countries with each other and with the economies of Central Asia, West Asia, and East Asia.

  o Facilitate regional and global joint venture projects to develop new ports along both the western and eastern seaboard of South Asia, and at the same time upgrade existing ports to the highest international standards.

  o Facilitate regional investment projects to build a network of airports, together with cold storage facilities and warehouses, which could stimulate not only tourism but also the export of perishable commodities such as milk, meat, fish, fruits, and vegetables.

  o Facilitate regional joint venture projects to build dams to utilize the huge untapped potential for energy and irrigation in the mountain ranges of South Asia. These dams should be designed and located strictly in accordance with the existing international treaties, such as the Indus Basin Treaty.

  o Facilitate regional joint venture projects to improve the irrigation efficiency of the networks of canals and watercourses in South Asia.

- **Regional Cooperation for Environmental Protection.** Pursue the following specific areas in which regional cooperation could encourage protection of the environment:

  o Institutionalize cooperation in the face of growing water scarcity to undertake innovative joint efforts for water conservation, and improved delivery and application efficiency of irrigation. This could include constructing medium- and small-size dams for increased water availability in the off-season and water distribution on an equitable basis between countries and provinces, lining the canals and water courses, and improving on-farm water management.

o Pursue joint efforts to reduce emissions of greenhouse gases within South Asia and joint diplomatic efforts to achieve the same objective on a global scale to combat global warming.

o Pursue joint efforts to develop heat-resistant varieties of food grains and to conduct biotechnology research to achieve a new green revolution in South Asia as the old green revolution comes to an end.

o Pursue joint efforts at reforestation of watersheds. The treatment of industrial and urban effluent waste could reduce soil erosion, devastating flash floods, and toxicity of rivers.

o Share biosaline research and technical know-how on controlling desertification of soils (for example, the use of plants such as halogenic phradophytes to control salinity).

o Share know-how on ecologically sound industrial technologies and cost-effective and safe methods of effluent disposal.

o Share information on water flow of rivers, especially flood forecasting.

o Engage in joint projects for the development of Himalayan resources, especially the prevention of deforestation and soil erosion on the mountain slopes.

o Collect, systematize, and subject to scientific evaluation the traditional knowledge systems of South Asian communities, which have experience of innovative techniques to conduct their economic existence in a harmonious relationship with nature.

• **Restructuring Growth for Faster Poverty Reduction.** A rapid improvement in the material conditions of the people of South Asia requires not only a faster economic growth rate but also a restructuring of growth to make it pro-poor.[13] This requires providing the institutional basis and economic incentives to change the composition of investment toward those sectors that generate relatively more employment and that enable increased productivity and incomes of the poor (Hussain 2003b).[14] In this context of achieving pro-poor growth, three sets of measures can be undertaken at the country as well as regional levels:

o Undertake joint venture projects to rapidly accelerate the growth of those subsectors in agriculture and industry, respectively, which have relatively higher employment elasticities and which can increase the productivity and hence put more income into the hands of the poor. These subsectors include production and regional export of high-value-added agricultural products such as milk, vegetables, fruits, flowers, and marine fisheries.

o Facilitate a regional network of support institutions in the private sector to enable small-scale industries located in regional growth nodes, with specialized facilities such as heat treatment, forging, quality control systems, and marketing facilities in country-specific and regional economies.

o Establish a SAARC Fund for vocational training to create a network of high-quality vocational training institutes for the poor. Improved training in market-demanded skills would enable a shift of the labor force from low-skill to higher-skill sectors and thereby increase the productivity and income-earning capability of the poor. At the same time, it would generate higher growth for given levels of investment by increasing factor productivity.

6. CONCLUSION

South Asia in the twenty-first century has an opportunity to lead the world by addressing the challenges of poverty, peace, and environmental degradation through cooperation in a region where these challenges are manifest in their most intense form. Regional cooperation in South Asia could enable a new form of equitable and sustainable economic growth. This would involve new initiatives for restructuring the growth process to make it pro-poor and accelerating the process of peace and economic cooperation. Innovative initiatives are required to develop new institutions and technologies for use at the regional, national, and local levels in the fields of water resource management, energy production, heat-resistant seed varieties, reduced soil depletion, and reduced greenhouse gas emissions. Equally important, this process of achieving sustainable development could be catalyzed by capitalizing on South Asians' rich cultural tradition of seeking unity in diversity, human solidarity, and harmony with nature.

Never before in history was the choice between life and comprehensive destruction as stark as it is today. The question is, can we grasp this moment and together devise a new path toward peace, freedom from hunger, sustainable development, and regional cooperation? There is an urgent need to move out of the mind-set that regards an adversarial relationship with a neighboring country as the emblem of patriotism that views affluence of the few at the expense of the many as the hallmark of development, that sees nature as an exploitable resource, and that embraces individual greed as the basis of public action. We have arrived at the end of the epoch when we could hope to conduct our social, economic and political life on the basis of such a mind-set.

NOTES

1. This section is based on a more elaborate paper presented by the author before the Parliamentarians from South Asian countries at the South Asian Free Media Association (SAFMA) Conference on Evolving a South Asian Fraternity, Bhurban (16 May 2005).
2. "[E]ach of the leading states in the international system strove to enhance its wealth and its power to become (or remain) both rich and strong" (Kennedy 1988, i).
3. India's exports as a percentage of its GDP (at purchasing power parity) are 2 percent. For details, see http://www.cia.gov/cia/publications/factbook/geos/in.html#Econ. India's share in total global exports increased by 0.26 percent—from 0.41 percent in fiscal year 1992–93 to 0.67 percent in 2000–01. In the next 5 years beginning fiscal year 2002–03, India aims to raise the share further by 0.33 percent by 2006–07 to have a 1 percent share of total world exports. For more details, see http://www.indiaonestop. com/tradepartners/indias_trade_partners.html (accessed on 6 October 2009).
4. For a more detailed discussion of this proposition, see Hussain (2008a).
5. Bruce Reidel was at that time President Clinton's Special Assistant for Near Eastern and South Asia Affairs at the National Security Council.
6. President Musharraf was reported to have said that Pakistan was not afraid to use unconventional weapons if attacked according to the daily *The Hindu* (see Global Security Newswire 2002).
7. For a discussion on multiple identities, see Sen 2006, 3–5.
8. This subsection is drawn from Hussain 2006, 233–34.
9. In an interview with CNN-IBN's program *Devil's Advocate*, Asif Ali Zardari said that good relations with India would not be held hostage to the Kashmir dispute. He said that the two countries would wait for future generations to resolve the issue and the two countries should focus on trade ties for now (reported in the *Daily Times*, Sunday, 2 March 2008).
10. This discussion was first reported in my article, "Taking the Peace Process Forward" (Hussain 2004b). Significantly, Prime Minister Manmohan Singh repeated his remark about subsequently making a "new beginning" in the United Nations.
11. A few years ago, SAFMA organized a highly successful conference in Bhurban of Parliamentarians from each of the countries of South Asia in which it was agreed that the peace process should be made irreversible through institutional mechanisms in both government and civil society.

12. For an elaboration of this concept, see Hussain 2004a.
13. For a detailed discussion on pro-poor growth, see Hussain 2003a.
14. For a more recent discussion on the subject, focused on the institutional basis of pro-poor growth, see Hussain 2008b.

REFERENCES

Aristotle. 1998. *The Nicomachean Ethics.* David Ross, J.L. Ackrill, and J.O. Unisom (eds). Oxford World Classics. Oxford: Oxford University Press.

Asian Development Bank (ADB). 2008. *Soaring Food Prices: Response to the Crisis.* Manila: ADB.

Barry, John, and Michael Hirsh. 1998. "Nuclear Litters." *Newsweek*, 8 June.

Barthes, R. 1973. *Mythologies.* London: Paladin.

Food and Agriculture Organization (FAO). 2008. *Food Outlook Global Market Analysis, Rice.* Available at http://www.fao.org/docrep/011/ai474e/ai474e05.htm (accessed on 3 August 2008).

Gilpin, Robert. 2001. *Global Political Economy: Understanding the International Economic Order.* Princeton, NJ: Princeton University Press.

Global Security Newswire. 2002. "Pakistan: Musharraf Cautions Cautions India with Unconventional War," 30 December.

Haq, Mahbubul. 1997. *Human Development in South Asia.* Human Development Center. Karachi: Oxford University Press.

———. 2006. *Human Development in South Asia 2005.* Human Development Center. Karachi: Oxford University Press.

Hussain, Akmal. 2002. "Commodities and the Displacement of Desire." *Daily Times*, Lahore, 28 November.

———. 2003a. "A Policy for Pro-Poor Growth." Chapter in *Towards Pro-Poor Growth Policies in Pakistan, Proceedings of the Pro-poor Growth Policies Symposium*, 17 March 2003, UNDP-PIDE, Islamabad.

———. 2003b. *Poverty, Growth and Governance*, with inputs from A. R. Kemal, Agha Imran Hamid, Imran Ali, and Khawar Mumtaz. UNDP, Pakistan National Human Development Report 2003. Karachi: Oxford University Press.

———. 2004a. "South Asia Health Foundation." Concept Note, 8 November 2004, South Asia Center for Policy Studies (SACEPS), Dhaka.

———. 2004b. "Taking the Peace Process Forward." *Daily Times*, Lahore, 23 September.

———. 2006. "Human Security, Economic Development and the Peace Process." In *Non-Traditional and Human Security in South Asia*, a collection of papers presented at an international seminar, jointly organized by the Institute of Regional Studies and National Commission for Human Development, Islamabad, October 31–November 1.

Hussain, Akmal. 2008a. *Poverty, Power and Peace.* Draft Mimeo.

———. 2008b. "Institutional Imperatives of Poverty Reduction." Paper contributed to the Institute of Public Policy, Lahore: Beaconhouse National University.

Inter-governmental Panel on Climate Change (IPCC). 2007. *Impacts, Adaptation and Vulnerability.* Working Group II Contribution to the Fourth Assessment Report of the Inter-governmental Panel on Climate Change, New York. Cambridge: Cambridge University Press.

Kennedy, Paul. 1988. *The Rise and Fall of the Great Powers: Economic Change and Military Conflict from 1500 to 2000*. London: Fontana Press.

Marx, Karl. 1990. *Capital*. Vol. 1. London: Penguin.

Millennium Ecosystem Assessment Report. 2005. *Ecosystems and Human-Well-being, Current State and Trends*, Vols 1–4. Washington, DC: Island Press.

Ministry of Foreign Affairs, Sri Lanka. 2008. *15th SAARC Summit, Colombo Statement on Food Security*. Available at http://www.slmfa.gov.lk/index.php?option=com_content& task=view&id=1349&Itemid=86 (accessed on 15 October 2008).

Nash, John F., Jr. 1996. *Essays on Game Theory*. Vermont: Edward Elgar Publishing.

Nehru, Jawaharlal. 2004. "The Indian Philosophical Approach," in *The Discovery of India*. London: Penguin Books.

North, Douglass C. 1990. *Institutions, Institutional Change and Economic Performance*. Cambridge: Cambridge University Press.

———. 2005. *Understanding the Process of Economic Change*. Princeton, NJ: Princeton University Press.

Pallis, Marco. 1995. "Dharma and Dharmas," in R. Fernando (ed.) *The Unanimous Tradition*. Colombo: Sri Lanka Institute of Traditional Studies.

Perry, Whitall N. 1995. "The Revival of Interest in Tradition." Chapter 1 in R. Fernando (ed.) *The Unanimous Tradition*. Colombo: Sri Lanka Institute of Traditional Studies.

Reidel, Bruce. 2002. "American Diplomacy and the 1999 Kargil Summit at Blair House." Center for the Advanced Study of India, University of Pennsylvania.

Schuon, Frithjof. 1995. "The Perennial Philosophy." Chapter 2 in R. Fernando (ed.) *The Unanimous Tradition*. Colombo: Sri Lanka Institute of Traditional Studies.

Sen, Amartya. 2006. *Identity and Violence: The Illusion of Destiny*. London: Allen Lane.

South Asian Association for Regional Cooperation (SAARC). 2004. "Islamabad SAARC Declaration." Islamabad: SAARC.

South Asian Regional Department (SARD). 2008. *Regional Summary of Inflation in South Asia 2008*. Manila: ADB.

Syed, Najam Hussain. 1968. *Recurrent Patterns in Punjabi Poetry*. Lahore: Majlis Shah Hussain.

Wignaraja, Ponna, Akmal Hussain, Harsh Sethi, and Ganeshan Wignaraja. 1991. *Participatory Development, Learning from South Asia*. United Nations University. Karachi: Oxford University Press.

Making Regional Cooperation Work for South Asia's Poor

Sadiq Ahmed and Ejaz Ghani[1]

1. INTRODUCTION

South Asia continues to grow rapidly, and its largest economy, India, approached near double-digit growth in 2006–07. This is a remarkable transformation of a region whose countries have been infamously dubbed a "basket case." Well up to the late 1970s, South Asia, which includes eight countries—Afghanistan, Bangladesh, Bhutan, India, Maldives, Nepal, Pakistan, and Sri Lanka—was known for conflict, violence, and widespread and extreme poverty. In the initial years after independence, the South Asian countries adopted import substitution growth strategies with heavy trade protection, curbed the growth of private firms, and introduced restrictive labor laws to protect workers. After some 30 years, the outcome of these policies turned out to be quite different from what the leadership had in mind. South Asia delivered sluggish growth, continued dependence on low-productivity agriculture, low levels of industrialization, weak export performance, and inadequate creation of good jobs. Between 1960 and 1980, South Asia grew at only 3.7 percent per year. Much of the labor force was engaged in low-income activities in agriculture and informal services, and some 45 percent of the population lived below the poverty line.

South Asia's prospects changed in the 1980s as it adopted pro-growth policies. It opened up markets to international competition, replaced the public sector with the private sector as the engine of growth, and improved macroeconomic management (Ahmed 2006). The results were impressive. South Asia's annual gross domestic product (GDP) growth rate climbed to around 5.7 percent during 1980–2000, and further accelerated to 6.5 percent during 2000–07. It is now the second-fastest-growing region in the world, after East Asia. Growth rates in South Asia and East Asia appear to be converging (Figure 2.1). In 2007, India experienced a remarkable GDP growth of 9 percent, close to that of China. Other South Asian countries such as Bangladesh, Pakistan, and Sri Lanka experienced growth rates of 6.5 percent. Private investment has boomed, supported by rising national saving rates in South Asia. The region now attracts global attention because of rapid growth, global outsourcing, and skill-intensive service exports. Rapid growth has been instrumental in reducing poverty in South Asia. Poverty has come down sharply in all countries (Figure 2.2). Progress has been made in improving human development, and social indicators compare favorably with countries in other regions with similar income levels (Ahmed 2006).

FIGURE 2.1 Real GDP Growth

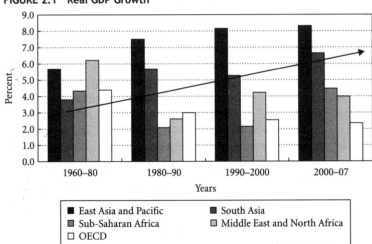

Source   World Bank's World Development Indicators.

Note   Data are averages. South Asia's data include the 2007 growth rate, while the rest of the regions do not.

FIGURE 2.2 Poverty Reduction in South Asia, 1970s–2000s

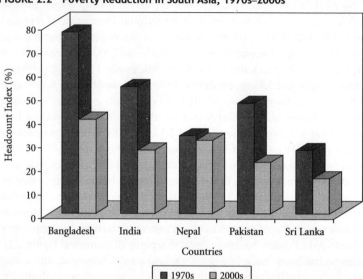

Source World Bank regional database.

Note Poverty estimates use national poverty lines. The respective dates are as follows:
Bangladesh (1975 and 2005); India (1974 and 2005); Nepal (1977 and 2004); Pakistan
(1970 and 2005); and Sri Lanka (1976 and 2005).

While there is much to celebrate, two negative developments have
emerged: *(a)* evidence of growing income inequality in South Asia, and
(b) a growing imbalance among regions within countries and among the
countries themselves. With fairly large and open borders, the growing
imbalances in incomes and opportunities among South Asian countries
present similar social and economic problems to the prosperous neighbors
as the imbalances within these countries.

Poverty, income growth, and lagging regions are interrelated. South
Asia's experience shows that the incidences of poverty and income growth
are strongly and negatively correlated (Figure 2.3). With few exceptions,
lagging regions exhibit a higher than average rate of poverty and lower
than average per capita incomes. The growing divergence between lagging
and leading regions suggests that lagging regions on average are growing
more slowly than leading regions.

So, a substantial part of the poverty and lagging regions challenge is a
growth challenge. Two major development issues face South Asia: *(a)* How
can South Asia grow even faster than in the recent past? *(b)* How can

FIGURE 2.3   Growth–Poverty Correlation in South Asia

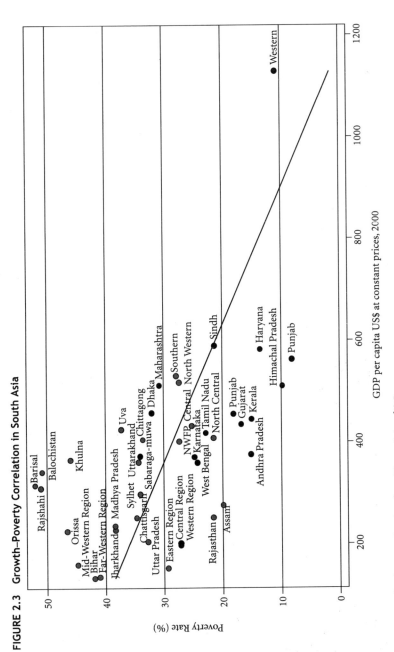

Source   Staff estimates using data from Figures 2.4 and 2.5.

lagging regions accelerate growth to catch up with growth in the leading regions?

The problem of inequality is, however, a more complex challenge. Growth acceleration in the lagging regions might help reduce inequality. But this is only part of the larger task of making growth more inclusive. A pattern of growth that benefits income growth for the poor, higher employment elasticity of growth, and strengthened public service delivery, including better social protection policies, all need to be core elements of a strategy to lower income inequality.

2. GROWTH ACCELERATION, LAGGING REGIONS,[2] AND INEQUALITY: A FRAMEWORK

The experience of East Asia shows that growth supported by factor accumulation as well as productivity improvements can lead to higher growth (Gill and Kharas 2007). South Asia's experience is similarly positive (Ahmed 2006). Additionally, it has two key assets—demography and geography—that have not yet been fully utilized. It has a young labor force. More workers will join the labor force over the coming decades.

Though the small size of the manufacturing sector has prevented the region from converting this demographic dividend into an opportunity, the large and potentially productive labor force could be the catalyst that attracts regional and global production centers to South Asia, as firms move in response to wage differences and globalization benefits low-income countries. South Asia's geography also has the potential to accelerate growth. It has the highest population density in the world, and the second largest proportion of population living in the border areas after Europe. High population density and better access to markets can benefit growth by allowing South Asian firms to take advantage of agglomeration economies.

Despite these benefits of geography—density and distance—South Asia's true growth potential has not been realized because of the lack of market integration within and across countries. South Asia accounts for only 3 percent of the world surface area, but it sustains an extraordinary 20 percent of the world population, nearly 1.5 billion people. It has the highest population density in the world, yet it has one of the lowest urbanization rates. There are indeed large differences across countries in South Asia. In 2005, India (which accounts for 74 percent of the regional population) produced close to 80 percent of the South Asian GDP. Pakistan (13 percent of South Asian population), Bangladesh (10 percent), Sri Lanka (1 percent), and Nepal (2 percent) accounted for 11 percent, 6 percent, 2.3 percent, and 0.7 percent of the regional GDP, respectively. Afghanistan, Bhutan, and Maldives collectively accounted for less than 1 percent of South Asia's GDP. The differences in per capita income are large, ranging from a high of US$2,700 for Maldives (for 2006 measured in current US dollars) to a low of only US$250 for Afghanistan (Figure 2.4). Even if the small economies of Maldives and Bhutan are excluded, the per capita income gaps are quite large.

FIGURE 2.4   South Asia Per Capita Income, 2006

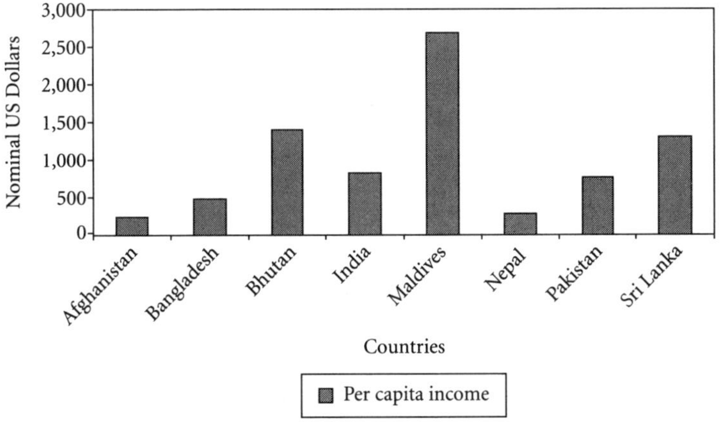

Source World Bank 2008e.

The income gap at the national level carries through at the subnational level (Figure 2.5). During the period 1993–2004, GDP growth in the leading states in India grew at twice the rate of the lagging states. The average annual growth rate for the leading states (Andhra Pradesh, Gujarat, Haryana, Karnataka, Kerala, Maharashtra, Punjab, Tamil Nadu, and West Bengal) was 5.9 percent. The average growth rate for the lagging states (Bihar, Madhya Pradesh, Orissa, Rajasthan, and Uttar Pradesh) was 3 percent per year. In Sri Lanka, the leading regions grew at an annual average rate of 6.5 percent during 1996–2005, while the lagging regions (Sabaragamua, Central, Uva, and North Western) grew at an average rate of 1.5 percent per year. In Pakistan, the difference in the growth rates between the leading and lagging regions is less striking. The leading

FIGURE 2.5 Per Capita Income in South Asia, 2004 (Constant US$)

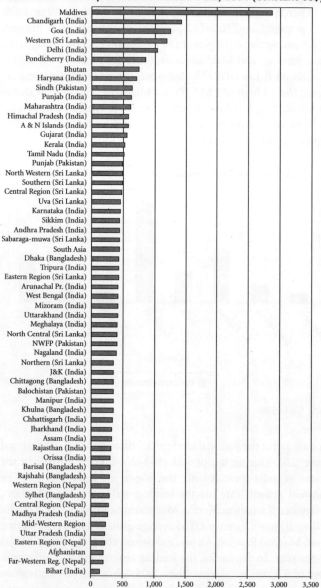

Sources India, Directorate of Economics and Statistics of respective State Governments;
Sri Lanka, Central Bank of Sri Lanka; Bangladesh, *Statistical Yearbook of Bangladesh*;
Nepal (household income per capita), CBS (Central Bank of Sri Lanka) and World
Bank staff calculations using NLSS I and II; Pakistan, World Bank staff; Bhutan,
Afghanistan and Maldives, *World Development Indicators*.

regions of Punjab and Sindh experienced an average annual growth rate of 2.3 percent during 1991–2000, while the lagging regions of Balochistan and the North West Frontier Province (NWFP) grew at an average annual rate of 1.8 percent. In Bangladesh, the leading regions (Dhaka and Chittagong) grew at an annual average rate of 3.15 percent year while the lagging regions (Barisal, Rajshahi, Khulna, and Sylhet) grew at an average annual rate of 2.73 percent during 1990–99. Nepal's growth since 2000 has averaged a paltry 3 percent, around half of the South Asian regional average. Conflict, poor road connectivity, and urban bias associated with earlier growth spurts have resulted in a clear divide between lagging regions and the Kathmandu valley.

The above picture suggests that, despite the differences in economic size and population, South Asian countries face similar development challenges arising from large spatial disparities. South Asia's leading regions are leaving lagging regions behind, as exemplified by the phrase "two South Asias." The leading regions are characterized by rapid GDP growth, urbanization, and integration with the global economy. The lagging regions remain rural, rely on low-value activities, and are not well integrated with the national, regional, and global markets.

The development experience of South Asia, where rapid GDP growth has been accompanied by high regional disparities, contrasts with the regional experience of high-income market economies. There is evidence of strong convergence among regions in the European Union, Japan, and the United States.[3] The income gap between the leading and lagging regions in South Asia is much larger compared with the spatial disparities in industrial countries. In India, GDP per head in the state where it is highest (Haryana) is five times greater than in the state where it is lowest (Bihar). In the United States, the difference is only 2.5 times, and in Japan only two times. Regional disparities are indeed expected to change over time with the level of development. The big issue is whether future developments in South Asia will bring about convergence or divergence between the leading and lagging regions.

Given the strong negative relationship between income and poverty illustrated in Figure 2.3, it is hardly surprising that most lagging regions show higher than average rates of poverty (Figure 2.6). Nearly half a billion people live in the lagging regions of South Asia. Nearly 60 percent of the poor in India live in the lagging states. Every seventh poor Indian lives in Bihar, a lagging state. Sri Lanka shows disturbing regional disparity in poverty rates between the western region (a leading region) and the rest of the country. Nepal's western region (lagging region) has a substantially higher poverty incidence than the more prosperous Kathmandu valley.

FIGURE 2.6 Poverty Incidence in South Asia (Headcount %)

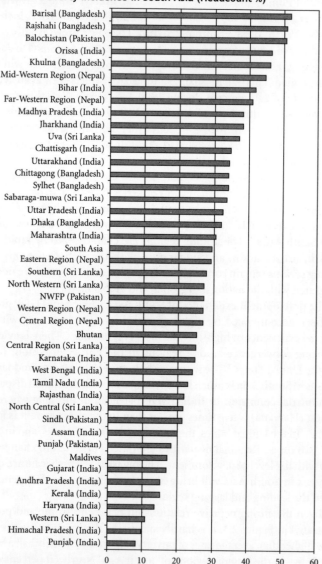

Sources Pakistan, World Bank staff; Sri Lanka, HIES 2002; Nepal, NLLS 2003–04; Bangladesh, HIES 2005; Bhutan, International Monetary Fund; Maldives, Asian Development Bank.

Notes For India, data for poverty headcount rates are based on 2004–05; for Sri Lanka data for poverty are based on 2002; Pakistan on 2005–06; Bangladesh on 2005; Nepal on 2003–04; Bhutan on 2000; Maldives on 2004.

In Pakistan, interprovincial disparities in poverty incidence between the leading regions (Sindh and Punjab) and the lagging regions (NWFP and Balochistan) are huge.

Why some areas develop and others remain underdeveloped is determined by three key drivers: movement of productive factors, transportation costs, and scale economies. These drivers are derived from spatial economics—that is, the study of where economic activity takes place and why (Fujita et al. 1999; World Bank 2008d). Drawing on these works, an ongoing World Bank study is looking at the interactions between geography, institutions, and trade, and how these interactions promote or constrain growth in the lagging regions of South Asia. Geographic, institutional, and trade differences are larger in South Asia than in Europe, Japan, and the United States. In Japan, nearly 97 percent of people live within 100 kilometers of the coast. In Europe, more than half the population lives within 100 kilometers of the coast or an ocean-navigable waterway. The United States is more like India, with a large proportion of the land area away from coast. But because of high labor mobility and efficient agriculture in the United States, a high proportion of the population lives close to the coast. In India, factor mobility has not been able to arbitrage geographic disparities. Disparities between the leading and lagging regions are high not because of geography but because of poor market integration resulting from high transportation costs, poor connectivity between regions and countries, low factor mobility, and regulatory restrictions that prevent firms from taking advantage of the scale economies.

There are two types of geography—first- and second-nature geography. First-nature geography favors some regions by virtue of proximity to rivers, coasts, ports, and borders. Economic activity may concentrate in coastal urban areas because of proximity to the domestic and external markets, and better logistical links between foreign suppliers and customers. First-nature geography explains why some leading regions are located in coastal areas (Maharashtra, Gujarat, and Tamil Nadu in India, and Karachi in Pakistan). Real GDP per capita growth rates for the coastal states in India grew at 4.5 percent per year during the 1990s compared with 2.5 percent for the landlocked states. Second-nature geography is determined by human-made infrastructure. Physical infrastructure influences the interactions among economic agents. Improved infrastructure lowers transportation costs, encourages mobility of labor, goods, capital, and ideas, and increases the size of the market. These interactions give rise to scale economies. As agricultural productivity increases, it releases labor and capital from rural areas, which migrate to urban areas to take advantage of agglomeration forces. Regions with a higher urbanization rate tend to have higher productivity. These forces can generate virtuous circles of self-reinforcing development. Empirical studies identify second-nature geography (physical infrastructure) as a *key* causal factor in explaining levels and trends in regional disparities (Kanbur and Veneables 2005a). Clearly, South Asia has yet to take advantage of the growth benefits of its demography and geography.

In addition to the lagging regions problem, South Asia also exhibits growing income inequality. Figure 2.7 shows economic inequality as measured by the Gini Coefficient.[4] Inequality in South Asia is rising but less than in East Asia.[5] This is apparent when comparing the growing inequality between the rich and the poor in India versus China. Nepal

FIGURE 2.7   Gini Coefficient (the Latest Available) and the Annual Growth Rate of Gini

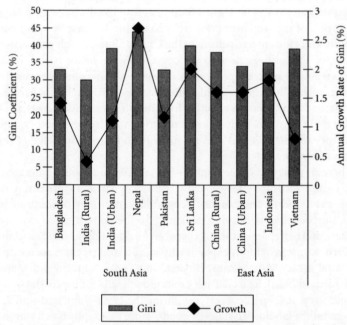

Sources World Bank staff estimation using household income and expenditure surveys of each country. Source data for Bangladesh, HIES 1991–92 and 2005; Pakistan, PIHS 1998–99 and PSLM 2005–06; India, NSSO 50th and 55th rounds; Sri Lanka, HIES 1990–91 and 2002; Nepal, NLLS 1996–97 and 2003–04. Data for all East Asian countries are in the World Bank's data department; and survey years are 1993–2004 for China; 1999–2004 for Indonesia; 1992–2004 for Vietnam.

and Sri Lanka have the highest levels of inequality in South Asia. They also have the highest growth in inequality. Pakistan and rural India have the lowest levels of inequality. Is inequality between regions, that is, spatial inequality, also rising?

For most countries, growth in inequality across leading and lagging regions is rising faster than growth in inequality across individuals. Figure 2.8 reports regional inequality at the sub-national level using the Theil inequality measure.[6] The Figure shows that *regional inequality* is rising at a much faster pace than *pure inequality* in all countries except for Nepal and, to some extent, India. Regional inequality generally increases as an economy shifts from agriculture to manufacturing. Some signs of regional convergence are evident in Nepal and India, as the extremely poor areas in Nepal and India have achieved faster growth rates in consumption. Poorer parts of Nepal and India have benefited from remittance flows as workers have moved to areas of higher economic density either at home or abroad.

FIGURE 2.8   Annual Growth Rate of Regional Inequality and the Pure Individual Effect for Selected South Asian Countries

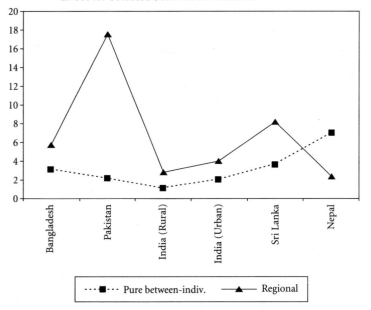

Source   World Bank staff estimates using household income and expenditure surveys of each country.

Can South Asia achieve both high and inclusive growth? Good examples of factors that can contribute to high and inclusive growth include labor mobility, better job creation, skills and education, and resolution of internal conflict. Inclusive growth is not about balanced growth but shared opportunities. Spatial disparities in growth are inevitable when growth accelerates and countries make the transition from being an agricultural to an industrial economy. The challenge for public policy is to identify the growth constraints in the lagging regions and remove them.

The strongest indicator of inclusive growth is poverty reduction. As mentioned earlier, all South Asian countries have reduced poverty. Going forward, however, poverty reduction is likely to be complicated by the fact that growth is increasingly concentrated in the leading regions, while poverty is concentrated in the lagging regions. The large concentration of poor in the lagging regions suggests that public policy must concentrate on raising growth and improving human development in these lagging regions. The evidence that regional inequality is rising also suggests that higher income growth in lagging regions might help reduce income inequality.

3. CROSS-BORDER CONSTRAINTS TO GROWTH AND POVERTY REDUCTION

The lagging regions challenge requires recognition of another factor of geography that has been largely neglected in public policy debates: many of the South Asia's lagging regions are either landlocked countries (for example, Afghanistan and Nepal) or are border districts, states, or provinces of the three larger countries of Bangladesh, India, and Pakistan. This is obvious from Figure 2.5, Map 2.1, and Table 2.1, which show the following results:

o The landlocked countries of both Afghanistan and Nepal are among the lowest per capita income group in the region (Figure 2.5).
o Out of 14 states of India that have borders with neighbors, 12 have per capita income levels that are at or below the national average (Arunachal Pradesh, Assam, Meghalaya, Mizoram, Nagaland, Tripura, Manipur, West Bengal, Bihar, Uttar Pradesh, Jammu and Kashmir, and Rajasthan). The only exceptions are Punjab and Gujarat (Figure 2.5 and Map 2.1).

MAP 2.1   Per Capita Income in South Asia

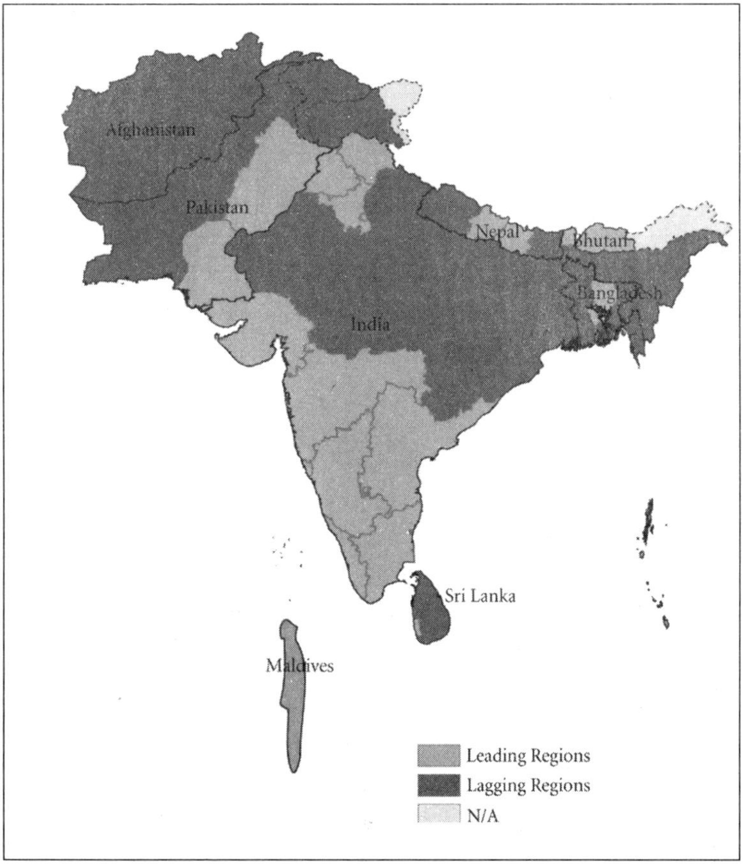

Source   Created by the author. Based on Figure 2.5.

Notes   (a) Leading/lagging regions are defined at the national level based on per capita incomes above or below the national average. (b) Afghanistan, Bhutan, and Maldives show national averages because sub-national data are not available. (c) This map is not to scale and does not depict the authentic boundaries of India.

o In Pakistan, per capita income is lower than average in the border provinces of NWFP, Balochistan, and rural Sindh. As in the case of India, Pakistan's Punjab is an exception. Similarly, urban Sindh is richer than the national average because of the dominance of the port city of Karachi (Figure 2.5 and Map 2.1).

TABLE 2.1 Population Mass, Economic Mass, and Poverty Mass: Bangladesh Districts Bordering India's North-east and West Bengal, 2000

Districts	Population	Per capita income (US$)	Economic mass (US$)	Human poverty index	Poverty mass	Literacy rate (age 7+) Both sexes	Female
Bordering north-east							
Bandarban	298,120	339	101,062,680	39.77	118,562	31.66	23.67
Brahmanbaria	2,398,254	304	729,069,216	37.65	902,943	39.45	36.68
Comilla	4,595,557	266	1,222,418,162	26.72	1,227,933	45.98	42.63
Feni	1,240,384	262	324,980,608	28.15	349,168	54.26	51.18
Habiganj	1,757,665	299	525,541,835	34.45	605,516	37.72	33.62
Jamalpur	2,107,209	277	583,696,893	41.87	882,288	31.80	28.02
Khagrachari	525,664	239	125,633,696	37.58	197,545	41.80	32.65
Kurigram	1,792,073	282	505,364,586	39.42	706,435	33.45	27.55
Lalmonirhat	1,109,343	265	293,975,895	35.63	395,259	42.33	36.25
Maulvibazar	1,612,374	280	451,464,720	32.69	527,085	42.06	38.45
Mymensingh	4,489,726	305	1,369,366,430	34.70	1,557,935	39.11	36.26
Netrokona	1,988,188	303	602,420,964	37.06	736,822	34.94	31.88
Nilphamari	1,571,690	261	410,211,090	38.50	605,101	38.84	32.58
Panchagarh	836,196	277	231,626,292	35.03	292,919	43.89	37.33
Rangamati	508,182	365	185,486,430	35.74	181,624	43.59	34.21
Sherpur	1,279,542	277	354,433,134	42.98	549,947	31.89	28.55
Sunamganj	2,013,738	262	527,599,356	39.44	794,218	34.37	30.47
Sylhet	2,555,566	315	805,003,290	35.06	895,981	45.59	41.51

Bordering West Bengal

Thakurgaon	1,214,376	329	399,529,704	35.87	435,597	40.32	35.87
Dinajpur	2,642,850	311	821,926,350	33.31	880,333	36.24	33.31
Joypurhar	846,696	323	273,482,808	35.70	302,270	37.23	35.70
Naogaon	2,391,355	305	729,363,275	32.32	772,886	36.91	32.32
Nawabganj	1,425,322	255	363,457,110	39.66	565,283	41.68	39.66
Rajshahi	2,286,874	339	775,250,286	33.57	767,704	35.98	33.57
Kushtia	1,740,155	320	556,849,600	35.78	622,627	36.79	35.78
Meherpur	591,436	318	188,076,648	36.01	212,976	36.91	36.01
Chuadanga	1,007,130	305	307,174,650	32.11	323,389	34.02	32.11
Jhenaidah	1,579,490	317	500,698,330	32.37	511,281	35.74	32.37
Jessore	2,471,554	357	882,344,778	28.20	696,978	30.77	28.20
Satkhira	1,864,704	309	576,193,536	31.74	591,857	35.53	31.74
Dhaka	**8,511,228**	**758**	**6,451,510,824**	**26.51**	**2,256,327**		
Bangladesh	**124,355,263**	**355**					

Source Massum 2008.

Note Population data refer to 2001, per capita income data refer to 1999–2000, and human poverty index refers to 2000.

o In Bangladesh, the border districts tend to have per capita incomes
   lower than the national average (Table 2.1). In terms of income,
   most lagging regions are also lagging in terms of having a higher
   than average incidence of poverty or poorer human development
   indicators (Figure 2.6, Maps 2.2 and 2.3, and Table 2.1).

Detailed analyses of these lagging regions indicate the following
socioeconomic characteristics (Government of India 2008; Massum 2008;
World Bank 2005a, 2005b, 2005c, 2007b, 2008a, 2008b):

MAP 2.2   Distribution of Poverty in South Asia

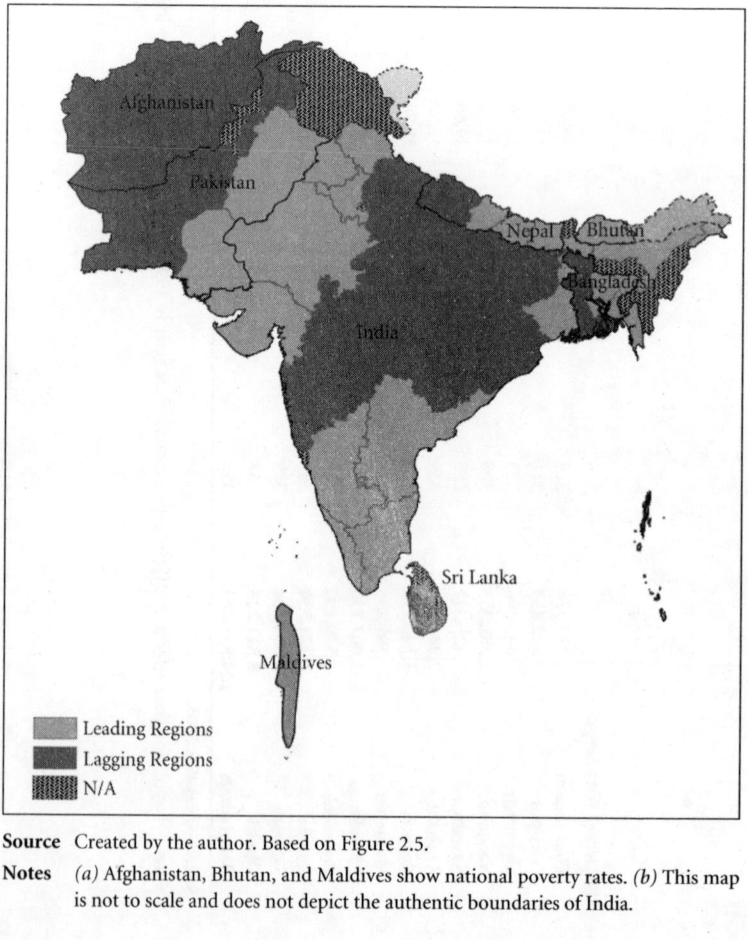

Source Created by the author. Based on Figure 2.5.

Notes (a) Afghanistan, Bhutan, and Maldives show national poverty rates. (b) This map
is not to scale and does not depict the authentic boundaries of India.

MAP 2.3   Distribution of Poverty by Leading and Lagging Regions

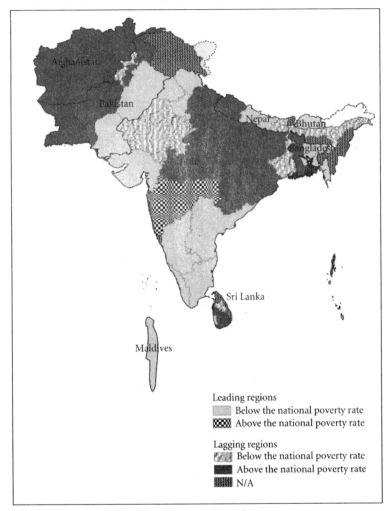

Leading regions
▢ Below the national poverty rate
▩ Above the national poverty rate

Lagging regions
▨ Below the national poverty rate
■ Above the national poverty rate
▥ N/A

Source   Created by the author. Based on Figures 2.5 and 2.6.

Notes   *(a)* Afghanistan, Bhutan, and Maldives show national poverty rates. *(b)* This map is not to scale and does not depict the authentic boundaries of India.

- These lagging landlocked and border countries, states, provinces, and districts have an estimated 400 million people, of whom an estimated 200 million are poor (reference year of 2005). This is about 50 percent of South Asia's estimated total number of poor for the year 2005.

- Much of the population is rural (90 percent), and most are engaged in low-productivity agriculture.
- The human development indicators tend to be below the comparable national average, and many indicators are lower than the average in South Asia.
- Infrastructure is, on average, poorer than the rest of the respective countries and poorer than the average for South Asia.
- The border regions, on average, tend to be more vulnerable to water shortages and flooding problems than other parts.

A review of history suggests that not all areas were lagging and poor all the time. For example, both Afghanistan and Nepal prospered in the eighteenth and nineteenth centuries on the basis of free trade and commerce with neighbors, including Central Asia, the Middle East, the Indian subcontinent, and China. Over the years, conflict and border restrictions removed this key source growth. A more dramatic example is that of India's north-east (the so-called seven sisters). The partition of the Indian subcontinent into Pakistan and India brought havoc to the economies of these seven sisters, especially the booming state of Assam, by cutting off its sea access and sharply increasing the transport distance with the rest of India (Box 2.1). The Kashmir valley was a prosperous and peaceful tourist resort until conflict between Pakistan and India took its toll. The Federally Administered Tribal Areas of Pakistan (FATA) and the NWFP were similarly prosperous and peaceful trading outposts until regional and global conflicts converted many parts of these border areas into conflict-prone, security risk regions with low per capita incomes, high incidence of poverty, and low human development indicators.

Apart from being poor, the lagging regions also share a number of common vulnerabilities. First and foremost is their vulnerability to natural disasters. Figure 2.9 shows the impact of natural disasters in terms of the share of GDP lost. South Asia has lost a significant amount of its GDP because of natural disasters. This loss has been especially significant for Bangladesh, Maldives, Pakistan, and Sri Lanka. The impact of natural disaster is particularly strong in South Asia because of its high population density. The losses typically are not insured in the financial market. It is the poor who are adversely affected by disasters.

FIGURE 2.9 Percentage of National GDP Damaged by Select Natural Disasters

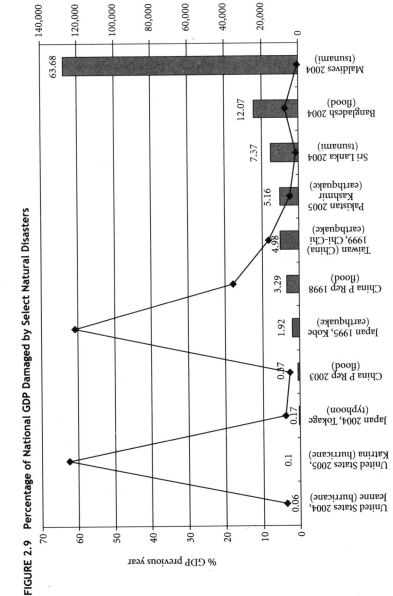

Source United Nations, International Strategy for Disaster Reduction. Available online at http://www.unisdr.org/disaster-statistics/top50.htm (accessed on 17 September 2009).

BOX 2.1 Bangladesh and India: A Tale of Two Border Regions

India's north-east and West Bengal lag behind the rest of India in per capita gross state domestic product (GSDP). So do the Bangladesh districts adjoining West Bengal and India's north-east. India's north-east and Bangladesh districts bordering the above region and West Bengal have considerable similarity, such as being predominantly agricultural, with agriculture accounting for the largest share of employment; having a narrow manufacturing base; and having low levels of consumption of electricity, which significantly constrain their growth prospects. The three hill districts of Bangladesh have large shares of tribal population, as do three states of India's north-east, and people of both sub-regions have been practicing the same low-productivity agricultural technology that featuring shifting cultivation called *Jhum* for generations. The two regions formed a single economic entity under British rule, shared common infrastructure, and developed close links that contributed to the economic growth of both regions. The partition of British India in 1947 into two separate states (India and Pakistan) and the two regions dividing into two countries that did not maintain friendly relations caused havoc to the economy of India's north-east, as a sudden snapping of all economic ties made its economy extremely vulnerable, in addition to converting it into a virtually landlocked region. The adjoining Bangladesh (then East Pakistan) districts also suffered by losing their traditional sources of supplies and markets for their products; however, because they retained most of the common infrastructure, including access to the sea and thereby to the outside world, their situation was not as bad. Their growth performance, however, indicates that they performed relatively poorly compared with most other Bangladesh districts. Bangladesh districts bordering West Bengal also performed relatively poorly. With the emergence of Bangladesh as an independent country in 1971, it was expected that the linkages earlier lost would be restored, but little progress has been made so far in this direction. It is, however, believed that improved economic linkages between India's north-east and West Bengal, and the adjoining Bangladesh districts, would promote development of all these regions.

Source Massum 2008.

A second and related vulnerability is access to water for irrigation and transport. An estimated 400 million people, many of whom are poor, directly or indirectly depend on the water flows of the three mighty rivers of Indus–Ganges–Brahmaputra for their livelihood. Frequent water shortages (and floods) create serious challenges to maintaining the income level of these large numbers of poor.

4. REGIONAL COOPERATION TO SUPPORT DEVELOPMENT OF SOUTH ASIA'S LAGGING REGIONS

Cooperation can be a powerful way to raise growth, reduce the gap between leading and lagging regions, and reduce vulnerabilities for the poor. By focusing on the income of the poor both through the growth mechanism and by reducing vulnerability, regional cooperation can be helpful in lowering income inequality. Specifically, in the context of the framework developed in Section 3, it can be argued that South Asia has the potential to accelerate growth and reduce poverty by exploiting four underutilized spatial features of the region: geography, transportation, factor mobility, and scale economies. Regional cooperation can facilitate this process.

- First, as mentioned earlier, South Asia is densely populated, with a significant proportion of the population living close to the borders between countries. After Europe, South Asia has the largest concentration of people living close to the border. It has the maximum "city pairs" within 50 kilometers with a population of more than 25,000 people.[7] Almost all the South Asian countries share a common border with the largest regional partner (India). Regional integration initiatives will unlock the growth benefit of geography and support income convergence across regions and countries. Regional trade is more sensitive to transport costs, scale economies, and factor mobility than global trade.
- Second, South Asia suffers from high trade and transportation costs compared with other regions because of border restrictions and poor transport. The cost of trading across borders is nearly double for India and Bangladesh compared with China. It is more than three times higher for Afghanistan, Bhutan, and Nepal. The quality of transport infrastructure in South Asia, especially the highway networks, is poor. Truck operating speeds are low, delays at state and provincial check posts are frequent and can be long, and delivery times are consequently subject to significant variation. The regions away from the main trade corridors have the poorest infrastructure and face the greatest constraints. Raising the level of the infrastructure and reducing regulatory barriers to trade, whether international or national, will help integrate the

lagging regions into both the national and global economies, reducing the relative advantages of the coastal states.

- Third, factor mobility, and in particular migration rate, is low in South Asia. Only 2 million people migrate every year in India from rural to urban areas, compared with nearly 20 million people in China. Increased agricultural productivity could reallocate labor and capital from low-value activities (agriculture) to high-value activities (manufacturing and services sectors) and support growth.

- Fourth, South Asian firms are disproportionately small. They are unable to reap the benefits of scale economies because of labor and regulatory restrictions that prevent them from growing. The policy changes aimed at taking advantage of the interactions between geography, transportation, factor mobility, and scale economies not only will lift growth in the lagging regions but also will support higher growth rates at the country level and in South Asia.

These ideas are developed in greater detail next.

4.1 Regional Cooperation for Supporting Growth in the Lagging Regions

In terms of policy focus, the two main ways that regional cooperation can foster higher growth in South Asia, and especially in the lagging regions, are by promoting market integration and by improving infrastructure.

4.1.1 Market Integration

Market integration allows economic agents to interact across spatial scales: local, regional, and international. The extent to which economic agents take advantage of market integration is affected positively by density but negatively by both distance and division (Fujita et al. 1999). A high level of economic density implies "thick markets" in the exchange of goods and services, as well as in the informal exchange of ideas. This creates productivity advantages for firms and welfare advantages for workers. By contrast, a high level of distance to density denies economic agents the opportunity to access these markets with consequent negative impacts on poverty and well-being.[8] Likewise, divisions—created by conflict, transport costs, and both formal and informal barriers to trade—separate economic agents in one country from the advantages of density in other countries.

By reducing distance and division, market integration, both within and between countries, brings economic agents in lagging regions closer to the density of leading regions, promoting positive spillover effects that enhance spatial multipliers.[9] Given that South Asia is the most densely populated region in the world, it is well placed to bring areas close to the market and bolster the value of the spatial multiplier. Market integration (global, regional, and within country) can ignite growth, as countries benefit from increased demand, agglomeration, and scale economies; improved factor mobility; and the free flow of ideas and technology. Market integration can pull weak countries toward income levels that they would be unable to achieve in isolation. Landlocked countries, in particular (Afghanistan, Nepal), can benefit from cross-country growth spillovers and neighborhood effects. Neighboring countries can provide mutually beneficial economic linkages, spillovers, and complementarities that allow groups of countries to increase their incomes.

The region has significantly more room to benefit from market integration globally, across countries within South Asia, and within country. Globally, South Asia's rapid GDP growth benefited from rapid expansion in trade. It has experienced one of the fastest growth rates in trade (Figure 2.10) averaging 10.8 percent in 2007, following growth

FIGURE 2.10   Real Growth in Trade of Goods and Services

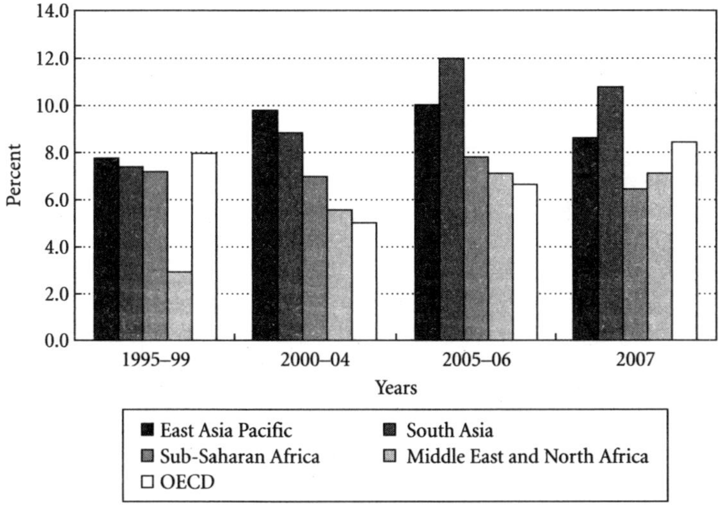

Source   World Bank's World Trade Indicators (World Bank 2008d).
Note   Data for 1995–99, 2000–04, and 2005–06 are averages.

of almost 12 percent during 2005–06, which was the highest among all regions. Yet, the region has more room to benefit from trade. Despite recent reforms, South Asia continues to have the most restrictive tariff policies compared with other regions (Figure 2.11). Among developing countries, South Asia has the most protective agricultural trade policies. South Asia's global integration, measured by trade as a ratio of GDP, was 49 percent in 2007, which although higher than its late 1990s ratio of 20 percent, is the lowest among developing countries (World Bank 2008a).

FIGURE 2.11   Trade Tariff Restrictiveness Index

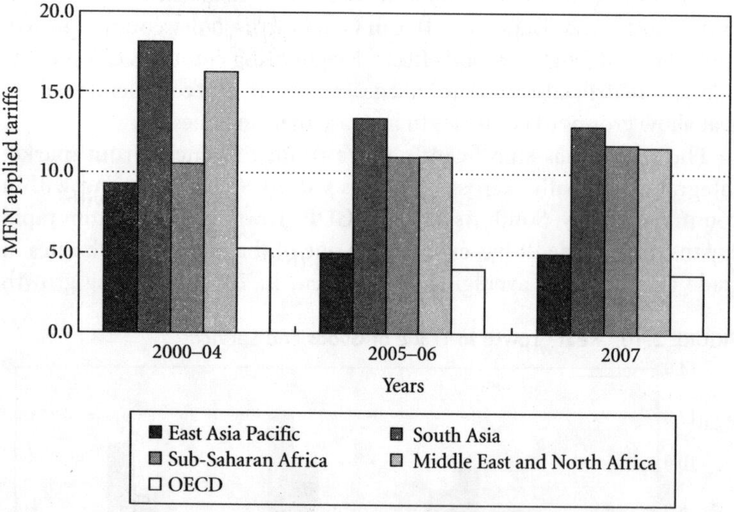

Source   World Bank's World Trade Indicators (World Bank 2008d).
Note   Data for 1995–99, 2000–04, and 2005–06 are averages.

Within South Asia, market integration is the lowest in the world as reflected by intraregional trade between countries being less than 2 percent of GDP for South Asia compared with 40 percent for East Asia. Border barriers to trade and services have mostly disappeared in the rest of the world but not in South Asia. Divisions across countries in South Asia have increased dramatically over the last four decades.[10] In 1948, South Asia's share of intraregional trade as a share of total trade was 18 percent. In 2000–07, it fell to 5 percent of total trade. Cost of trading across borders in South Asia is high. At the Petrapole–Benapole, one of the main borders between Bangladesh and India, trucks wait for more than 100 hours to cross the border. It takes 200 signatures in Nepal to trade goods with India, and some 140 signatures in India to trade goods with Nepal. It is estimated that trade between India and Pakistan, currently at US$1 billion,[11] could jump to US$6–10 billion, if divisions were removed. Divisions in South Asia have been aggravated by conflict.

The geographic configurations of South Asia contain huge agglomeration potential to propel growth.[12] East Asia is an example of a region with a high level of intraregional and intra-industry trade that enabled firms to internalize externalities arising from agglomeration. Firms exporting to the regional markets in South Asia are more constrained by the quality of connectivity and productivity-enhancing infrastructure.[13] It is the seamless interaction of improved trade, better connectivity, and converging institutions that can accelerate growth in the lagging regions and that can benefit the slower-growing and smaller landlocked regions and countries. In Latin America, Brazil's growth creates export opportunities for Bolivia. In Africa, resource landlocked countries piggybacked on the growth of Kenya. In East Asia, Thailand is an important market for Cambodia and Laos People's Democratic Republic.

Growth benefits of market integration are likely to be large but unequal. India, a large country, with a big home market, can get by with more restrictive borders, because the size of its economy and population provides the incentive to importers and exporters to overcome these barriers. It is the small, landlocked countries, like Afghanistan, Bhutan, and Nepal, that will benefit most from improved access to the markets of others. Small countries depend more on openness to overcome the disadvantage of size: small population, small markets, and inability to take advantage of agglomeration and scale economies. Even within India, the peculiar geography that isolates the seven north-eastern states (the so-called seven sisters) from mainland India, with Bangladesh located in between, suggests that market integration requires trade and transit arrangements with neighbors to benefit all regions that are lagging and isolated from the growth centers. Tradable economic activities are inherently scalable in the sense that small economies can expand output without running into diminishing returns (unlike domestic services). Rapid economic growth, associated with modern sector export growth, can be "lumpy" (Venables 2006). Spatially, it can be uneven, with production being concentrated in some countries, regions, or cities. In product space, specialization is likely to increase, with regions specializing in a few tasks rather than production of integrated products. Examples of specialization from South Asia include information and communication technology (ICT) service export from Bangalore in India; shirts, trousers, and hats exported from Bangladesh; and exports of bed linen and soccer balls from Pakistan. Temporally, rapid growth will happen only once some threshold level of capabilities has been reached. Some countries may experience growth before others, resulting in sequential rather than parallel growth. The benefits of market integration, however, cannot be achieved without improving the infrastructure.

4.1.2 Infrastructure

Infrastructure is like second-nature geography, which can reduce the time and monetary costs to reach markets and thus overcome the limitations of physical geography (Kanbur and Venables 2005a). Improved infrastructure that enhances connectivity and contributes to market integration is the best solution to promoting growth as well addressing rising inequality between regions. The Ganga Bridge in Bihar in India is a good example of second-nature geography. The bridge has reduced the time and monetary costs of farmers in the rural areas in north Bihar to reach markets in Patna, the largest city in Bihar. The Jamuna Bridge in Bangladesh is another good example of spatially connective infrastructure. The bridge has opened market access for producers in the lagging north-west areas around the Rajshahi division. Better market access has helped farmers diversify into high-value crops and has reduced input prices.

So far, South Asia has achieved impressive growth rates despite poor infrastructure. This growth may be difficult to sustain in the future. Poor infrastructure and restrictive labor laws (to be discussed later) are among the major factors that have restrained the growth of manufacturing sector and prevented firms from growing (Fernandez and Pakes 2008). Table 2.2 shows that the manufacturing share of value added in India is smaller than that share in other large developing economies, although it is similar to that share in smaller countries with GDP per capita similar to that of India (such as Vietnam). As Table 2.3 shows, however, the growth of value added in manufacturing in India is noticeably lower than that in these smaller similar income countries. Indeed the sectoral growth comparisons in Table 2.3 are rather striking. The growth of value added in services in India is comparable to that in China, and about 10 percentage points higher than that in other countries. In rather stark contrast, the growth of value added in manufacturing in India is only about *half* that in China and Vietnam.

The service sector in India has done well because it relies less on transportation and is less energy intensive than manufacturing. South Asia

TABLE 2.2   Industry and Manufacturing Share of Employment and GDP across Countries

	Employment in industry as % of total employment in 2000	Value added in industry as % of GDP in 2000	Value added in manu-facturing as % of GDP in 2000	2002 GDP per capita (in 2000 US$)
India	18.2	26.3	15.6	480
Brazil	19.3	28	17.1	3,473
China	23	45.9	34.7	1,106
Indonesia	17.3	45.9	27.7	844
Pakistan	18	22.6	14.8	532
Vietnam	12.4	36.7	18.6	444
Low-income countries	12.3	26.6	14.1	
Lower-middle-income countries	18.5	38.3	24.2	

Source   World Development Indicators 2005 (World Bank 2005d).

Note   Industry includes not only manufacturing, but also mining and quarrying (including oil production), construction, and public utilities (electricity, gas, and water). Lower-income countries and lower-middle-income countries are defined based on the World Bank classification.

TABLE 2.3   Growth in Sectoral Value Added across Countries

	Growth in value added in manufacturing (%)		Growth in value added in agriculture (%)		Growth in value added in services (%)	
	1995–2000	2000–05	1995–2000	2000–05	1995–2000	2000–05
India	28.1	38.4	13.7	14.9	48.4	50.3
Brazil	5.7	5.6	17.3	23.7	26.5	31.8
China	57.6	67.4	18.5	21.2	57.3	61.2
Indonesia	14.6	27.5	7.0	17.3	–2.4	35.7
Pakistan	17.1	56.6	26.5	12.0	20.9	29.9
Vietnam	70.3	73.8	24.2	20.7	31.9	40.0

Source   World Development Indicators, various years, World Bank.

has the highest share of services in its exports at 31 percent, which is higher than high-income member countries of the Organization for Economic Co-operation and Development (OECD). ICT exports and global outsourcing have benefited from the use of the Internet, which has reduced information transmission costs dramatically. While other countries can emulate India's successful efforts to boost services export, sustained high growth will require a substantial effort to raise manufacturing growth in all South Asian countries. In general, poor infrastructure has constrained the growth of labor-intensive manufacturing firms in South Asia and has prevented the region from making use of its most important asset, its people.

South Asia suffers from three infrastructure deficits. First, it suffers from a *service deficit*, as the region's infrastructure has not been able to keep pace with a growing economy and population. Power outages and water shortages are a regular occurrence in India and Bangladesh. Rural roads are impassable in lagging regions in India (for example, Bihar, Uttar Pradesh) and Sri Lanka. India has 6,000 kilometers of four-lane highways and China in the last 10 years has built 35,000 kilometers of four- to six-lane highways. Every month, China adds power capacity equivalent to what exists in Bangladesh. Second, South Asia suffers from a *policy deficit*, given highly distorted pricing, poor sector governance and accountability, and weak cost recovery. It is estimated that eliminating the financial losses from the power and water sectors alone would provide a substantial chunk of the incremental funds for infrastructure investment that India needs. Third, South Asia suffers from a *cooperation deficit*. India, one of the energy-thirstiest nations sits next to an immensely energy-rich neighbor, Nepal. Yet, because of inadequate cooperation with India, Nepal has barely exploited its hydropower potential. Similarly, India, which has attracted global attention in ICT, contrasts with other South Asian countries that are lagging in ICT. In South Asia, only 7 percent of the international calls are regional compared with 71 percent in East Asia. South Asia needs to overcome a huge gap in infrastructure. South Asia has invested only 3.5 to 4 percent of GDP per year in infrastructure over the period 2000–05. This is lower than what the East Asian countries have invested: Vietnam and China had investment rates of around 8 percent to 10 percent of GDP. In 1980, India actually had higher infrastructure stocks—in power, roads, and telecommunications—but China invested massively in infrastructure, overtaking India by 1990, and the gap is currently ever widening. It is estimated that for the South Asia region to sustain a growth target of 8 percent, it will require an investment in infrastructure amounting to 7.6 percent of GDP (Harris 2008). To achieve a higher growth rate in the 10 percent range will require an even more rapid pace of investment to modernize the infrastructure.

Much of the infrastructure investment gap has to be financed at the national level along with necessary improvements in sector policies and institutions. Yet regional cooperation can be of great help to meet a significant part of this need. The three priority areas for regional cooperation include telecoms and Internet networking, energy, and transport.

A regional telecom network and a high-bandwidth, high-speed Internet-based network could improve education, innovation, and health. A regional network would facilitate better flow of ideas, technology, investments, goods, and services. It also would facilitate greater interactions between knowledge workers in areas such as high-energy physics, nanotechnology, and medical research. Untapped positive synergies at the regional level would result from information sharing and competition in ideas among universities, non-university research and teaching entities, libraries, hospitals, and other knowledge institutions. It also could aid the building and sharing of regional databases, and could help address regional problems, including multi-country initiatives such as flood control, disaster management, climate change, and infectious disease control. Importantly, such an effort could help spark higher and more sustainable regional growth.

Regional cooperation in telecoms and Internet access could strengthen the competitiveness of South Asia in the services-export sector. India has established itself as a global player in ICT and outsourcing. Other countries in South Asia potentially could benefit from neighborhood and spillover effects. The expansion of services exports would contribute to growth and job creation, and other sectors would benefit from improved technology and management (Hamid 2007). The services-export sector, although less infrastructure intensive than manufacturing, needs different types of infrastructure than the traditional export sectors. For these exports, investment is needed in fiber optic highways, broadband connectivity, and international gateways and uplink facilities. Increased investments in tertiary education and in technical and English proficiency also are needed. South Asia needs to remove barriers to trade in ICT services, eliminate restrictions on the flow of intraregional foreign direct investment (FDI), and remove visa restrictions on the flow of people.

The potential gains from regional trade in energy are substantial. This is best seen by looking at Map 2.4, which shows South Asia's potential sources of hydropower and its demand. Map 2.4 illustrates a powerful story. Afghanistan and Nepal are sitting on water resources that could potentially generate some 24,000 megawatts of electricity from Afghanistan and an estimated 83,000 megawatts from Nepal. These countries together account for 40 percent of South Asia's presently installed capacity. Bangladesh, India, and Pakistan are all power-deficit countries, especially India. The growing electricity constraint is threatening the ability to sustain rapid growth. Yet, less than 1 percent of the region's electricity-generating potential has been used so far. The reason for this

After decades of insignificant cross-country electricity trade and the absence of any trade in natural gas through pipelines, regional political leaders and businesspeople recently have evinced a great deal of interest and enthusiasm in cross-border electricity and gas trade, not only within South Asia but also with its neighbors in the west (Central Asia and Iran) and in the east (Myanmar). South Asia has two regional energy clusters. The eastern market includes India, Bangladesh, Bhutan, Nepal, and Sri Lanka, extending to Myanmar; the western market includes Afghanistan, India, and Pakistan, extending to Central Asia and Iran. India bridges these two clusters. Some activities are under way, including a successful hydropower trade between Bhutan and India in the eastern market and an ongoing project in the western market that will bring electricity from Tajikistan and Kyrgyzstan to Afghanistan and Pakistan.[14]

To promote such energy trade, governments need to continue reducing political and security tensions; consider energy trade as an enhancement of energy security and political and economic cooperation; continue energy sector reforms; improve commercial performance of the utilities; improve the credibility, competence, and accountability of regulation; adopt sustainable (cost-reflective) tariffs and a social protection framework; promote commercial approach to energy trade; encourage private sector participation in the form of public–private partnership (PPP) structures in cross-border investments; help the transit countries (especially Afghanistan) integrate; reach water-sharing agreements; seek accession to international agreements (such as the Energy Charter Treaty); strengthen regional institutions at both political and technical levels; and identify priority trade-oriented investment projects and pursue their implementation. The success of the India–Bhutan electricity trade should offer useful lessons to other countries in the region.

Restrictions in transport border crossings are a major constraint to global and intraregional trade in South Asia. Removing these restrictions would boost trade within South Asia as well as lower costs for international trade in general, as many landlocked countries and regions would benefit from access to the closest ports. Currently, efforts to improve trade facilitation and transport networks are being pursued in a fragmented manner, and where cross-border issues are involved, little cooperation exists. Establishing corridor-based approaches for improving the trade, such as a transport arrangement for intraregional trade, would be essential to improve the efficiency of regional transport and to reduce trade costs.

4.2 Regional Cooperation Reducing Vulnerabilities of South Asia's Poor

South Asia's poor would probably gain most from regional cooperation in water and climate. This is again obvious from Map 2.4. From the Himalayas, where glacier melt is already changing water flows in ways that remain to be understood, to the coastal floodplains of Bangladesh and Pakistan, South Asian countries need to adapt to climate change. The melting of Himalayan glaciers, leading to the disastrous prospect of reduced water availability in the South Asian rivers, the frequency of floods and cyclones, and the evidence of rising sea level, have given South Asia a wake-up call for collective action for managing climate change to reduce vulnerability and poverty over the longer term. Actions only at the national level cannot provide sustainable solutions as much of the water flows from upstream countries of Afghanistan, China, parts of India, and Nepal to Bangladesh, most of India, and Pakistan. Finding sustainable solutions for flood control, irrigation, and river transport will require cooperation with upstream countries. Thus, cross-border cooperation on water between India, Bangladesh, and Nepal offers the only long-term solution to flood mitigation. The benefits of cooperation are clear. For example, watershed management and storage on Ganges tributaries in Nepal could generate hydropower and irrigation benefits in Nepal and flood mitigation benefits in Nepal, India (Uttar Pradesh, Bihar) and Bangladesh; water storage in north-east India could provide hydropower and flood benefits in India and Bangladesh; and both would provide increased and reliable dry season flows. Specific cooperation between Bangladesh, India, and Nepal on the Ganges presents an emerging and promising opportunity.

Similar benefits of water cooperation exist between India and Pakistan and between Pakistan and Afghanistan. The success of the Indus Water Treaty between Pakistan and India has already demonstrated that cooperation that benefits people can withstand all political obstacles. Building on this success, other water disputes and potential water markets could be developed through a similar cooperative solution. Afghanistan sits on the upper riparian of some five water basins that have huge potential for irrigation and hydropower benefits that could well transform Afghanistan's economy. Yet, little of the critical investment required to transform this natural resource into a productive asset for the benefit of the people of Afghanistan has been made thus far. As a result, Afghanistan is a severely water-constrained economy with a serious power shortage as well. A key constraint is a lack of a framework for water-sharing agreements with its neighbors. The Kabul River Water Basin Project is a high-priority project that will yield substantial hydropower and irrigation benefits for both Afghanistan and Pakistan. A key requirement for this project to move forward is a riparian agreement between Afghanistan and Pakistan. Again, a cooperative solution will result in a win–win situation for both countries.

More generally, regional cooperation can be instrumental in facilitating the design and implementation of effective country-level strategies to address a range of global public goods; to improve water management, disaster management, and climate and environmental management; and to combat HIV/AIDS, narcotics and drug trafficking, and security and arms trade. Geographic proximity and common borders mean common action in these areas will eliminate negative externalities, reduce transaction costs of monitoring and implementation, and allow learning from shared best practices.

South Asia needs to strengthen its regional governance institutions. This governance is vital to manage the provision of regional public goods and common pooled resources. South Asia suffers from numerous prisoners' dilemmas, such as free riding and overuse of resources, because of a lack of effective institutions. This problem can be overcome by engaging the government, the private sector, nongovernmental organizations, and communities in formal and informal social institutions (networks, norms, and sanctions) based on collective action.

5. MANAGING THE POLITICS OF COOPERATION IN SOUTH ASIA: THE WAY FORWARD

The potential benefits of economic cooperation are obvious. Global examples of successful cooperation agreements reinforce the point that possible gains for South Asia from effective cooperation and partnerships can be substantial. In particular, the experience of East Asia is illustrative of the potential gains that can be achieved from more and better cooperation. Cross-border physical connectivity has improved tremendously through land-, sea-, and air-based transport networks; private sector–led vertical integration of production networks has spurred industrial productivity and growth; and e-commerce is flourishing. Yet, the actual experience with cooperation in South Asia so far has been rather dismal. Following are the key constraining factors:

- First and foremost is the prevalence of a number of regional disputes. These include the long-standing conflict between India and Pakistan over Kashmir, which has continued to strain relations between these two large neighbors. The Afghanistan–Pakistan relations are constrained by allegations of support for the Taliban from sources in Pakistan. Similarly, securing the immigration and security issues in the India–Bangladesh border areas is another source of concern.
- Second is the lack of good analysis and information in the public domain about the benefits of regional cooperation. Unfounded populist negative perceptions in the smaller countries contribute to the misconception that increased cooperation will simply result in greater domination of India in the political and economic matters of these countries.
- A third factor has been the internal political interests in countries that are divided along nationalistic, religious, and ethnic lines, which substantially complicates policymaking that involves cross-border dialogue and cooperation.
- Fourth, and perhaps most important, the approach to international cooperation has been seriously flawed in that this has been largely seen as a bilateral politically driven agenda rather than a cross-boundary commercial investment. The bilateral political approach has partly contributed to suspicions in smaller countries of India's dominance.

International experience suggests that political constraints and historical conflicts need not be permanent barriers to development cooperation. Neither is the presence of a dominant member country a necessary threat to cooperation and shared gains. For example, the members of the European Union have fought numerous wars in the past, many of them far more intense, long drawn, and expensive in terms of loss of human lives and material resources than conflicts in South Asia. Similarly, member countries diverge considerably in economic strength. Yet these European countries have found it mutually advantageous to come together and formulate a formidable economic union. In East Asia, the economic dominance of China has not prevented effective regional cooperation with the much smaller East Asian countries.

Fortunately, the political environment for cooperation in South Asia is now changing. Historically, the regional cooperation efforts in South Asia culminated in the formation of the South Asian Regional Cooperation

(SAARC) in 1985. Until recently, SAARC has functioned basically as an annual event for heads of governments to meet with declarations of cooperation intentions but with limited implementation because of conflict and political difficulties. Armed with recent economic successes, the political space for better regional cooperation is now growing in South Asia. The last two SAARC meetings have succeeded in bringing the countries closer than ever in recognizing the merits of regional cooperation and taking significant actions to realize these benefits.

The next step is to identify concrete bankable projects in which multi-country cooperation would yield tangible benefits for citizens. The immediate priority areas are well known: promote trade facilitation by removal of all trade barriers; improve regional transport by removing transit restrictions and opening up port facilities for international trade; promote trade in energy in all possible ways, including hydropower, gas pipelines, and regional grid facilities; and pursue water cooperation to resolve flooding and irrigation problems. Cross-border transactions must be depoliticized and pursued on a commercial basis. Enabling national and international private investors to participate in these transactions holds more promise of success than bilateral political deals. International financial institutions can play a useful role by bringing global good practices, by providing technical assistance to smaller countries, and by mobilizing external financing. Where legal agreements are needed, these can be best pursued multilaterally to avoid any perceptions of dominance.

It is not realistic or necessary to expect that all political and social conflicts will have to be resolved first before meaningful cooperation can happen. Indeed, economic cooperation is a powerful means to resolve political and social conflicts. Trust and goodwill at the citizen level also can be a credible way to resolve conflicts. Economic cooperation by raising citizens' welfare can be instrumental in building this trust. Political forces can provide the impetus by reducing policy barriers to regional integration.

NOTES

1. The authors are with the World Bank in Washington, DC. Parts of the analysis of this chapter draw from an earlier paper (Ahmed and Ghani 2009). The views expressed in this chapter are those of the authors and do not necessarily reflect the views of the World Bank Group. Research assistance from Veronica Milagros Minaya is gratefully acknowledged. Errors are the sole responsibility of the authors.

2. A lagging region is defined as a poor region that does not grow as fast as the others, and its per capita income is low compared with national averages.
3. See European Union 2007, which provides evidence on convergence occurring both at the national and regional levels within European Union.
4. We are grateful to Nobuo for this work.
5. Based on their survey of evidence of more than 50 developing nations, Kanbur and Venables (2005a, 2005b) argue that the uneven spatial impact of trade and globalization played a major role in the increase in regional and urban spatial inequalities in developing countries in recent years. Moreover, they argue that, in addition to geographic remoteness, the backward regions and rural areas suffered from an inequitable distribution of infrastructure, public services, and policies that constrained the free migration of peoples from backward places.
6. The Theil inequality measure has a convenient property: it can be decomposed into inequality across areas, or "*regional* inequality," and inequality between individuals, after controlling for the former, or "*pure between-individual* inequality."
7. We are grateful to Souleymane Coulibaly for the data on city pairs.
8. Distance here is to be interpreted as an economic and social concept, rather than a purely physical concept. As such, a location that is physically close to a region of high density can, in principle, still be economically distant. This will be the case, for example, if the quality of spatially connective infrastructure linking the two areas is poor or there are economic, social, and institutional barriers to commuting and the free flow of labor between the areas.
9. A spatial multiplier is a concept that captures the additional beneficial effects that result from a policy change as a result of the feedback from spillovers between neighboring regions.
10. Borders and divisions are not the same thing. Borders define a nation-state whereas divisions influence the flow of people, goods, services, capital, ideas, and technology across borders.
11. Includes both formal and informal trade.
12. For example, given the large economies of scale in services industries (for example, telecoms), incentives to invest are greater if the markets are not segmented from other neighboring countries.
13. Based on data from S. Coulibaly.
14. This is the Central Asia-South Asia (CASA) energy project that seeks to sell 1,000 megawatts of surplus power from Tajikistan and Kyrgyzstan to Afghanistan and Pakistan. The project is being developed in cooperation with a number of multilateral financial institutions, including the World Bank.

REFERENCES

Ahmed, Sadiq. 2006. *Explaining South Asia's Development Success: The Role of Good Policies.* Washington, DC: World Bank.
Ahmed, Sadiq, and Ejaz Ghani. 2007. *South Asia: Growth and Regional Integration.* New Delhi: Macmillan.

Ahmed, Sadiq, and Ejaz Ghani. 2009. "Accelerating Growth in South Asia." In Sadiq Ahmed, and Ejaz Ghani (eds), *Accelerating Growth and Job Creation in South Asia*. New Delhi: Oxford University Press.

Commission on Growth and Development. 2008. *The Growth Report: Strategies for Sustained Growth and Inclusive Development*. Washington, DC: World Bank.

European Union. 2007. *Growing Regions, Growing Europe*. Fourth Report on Economic and Social Cohesion. Brussels: European Union.

Fernandes, Ana M., and Ariel Pakes. 2008. "Evidence of Underemployment of Labour and Capital in Indian Manufacturing." In Sadiq Ahmed and Ejaz Ghani (eds), *Accelerating Growth and Job Creation in South Asia*. New Delhi: Oxford University Press.

Fujita, M., P. Krugman, and A. J. Venables. 1999. *The Spatial Economy: Cities, Regions, and International Trade*. Cambridge, MA: MIT Press.

Gill, I., and H. Kharas. 2007. *East Asian Miracle*. Washington, DC: World Bank.

Government of India. 2008. *North Eastern Region Vision 2020*, Vols 1 and 2. New Delhi: Ministry of Development of North Eastern Region and North Eastern Council.

Hamid, Naved. 2007. "South Asia: A Development Strategy for the Information Age." In Report on the South Asia Department Economists' Annual Conference 2006. Manila: Asian Development Bank.

Harris, Clive. 2008. "Is South Asia Closing the Deficit in Its Infrastructure?" Mimeo. Washington, DC: World Bank.

Kanbur, Ravi, and Anthony J. Venables. 2005a. "Spatial Inequality and Development." In R. Kanbur and A. J. Venables (eds), *Spatial Inequality and Development*. Oxford: Oxford University Press.

———. 2005b. "Spatial Inequality and Development: Overview of UNU-WIDER Project." Available at http://www.arts.cornell.edu/poverty/kanbur/WIDERProjectOverview.pdf (accessed on 6 October 2009).

Massum, Mohammad. 2008. "Bangladesh and the North East Exploring Development Possibilities through Economic Linkages." Draft Paper, South Asia Region. Washington, DC: World Bank.

Sen, Binayak, and David Hulme. 2006. *Chronic Poverty in Bangladesh: Tales of Ascent, Descent, Marginality and Persistence*. Dhaka: Bangladesh Institute of Development Studies.

Venables, A. J. 2006. "Shifts in Economic Geography and Their Causes." *Economic Review* Q IV: 61–85. Kansas City: Federal Reserve Bank of Kansas City.

World Bank. 2005a. *India: Rajasthan: Closing the Development Gap*. Report No. 32585-IN. Washington, DC: World Bank.

———. 2005b. *Bihar: Towards a Development Strategy*. New Delhi: World Bank.

———. 2005c. *Pakistan: North West Frontier Province Economic Report*. Report No. 32764-PK. Washington, DC: World Bank.

———. 2005d. *World Development Indicators 2005*. Washington, DC: World Bank.

———. 2007a. *Agriculture for Development: World Development Report 2008*. Washington, DC: World Bank.

———. 2007b. *Jharkhand: Addressing the Challenges of Inclusive Development*. New Delhi: World Bank.

———. 2008a. *Accelerating Growth and Development in the Lagging Regions of India*. Report No. 41101-IN (draft). Washington, DC: World Bank.

———. 2008b. *Balochistan Economic Report: From Periphery to Core*. Joint World Bank, ADB, and Government of Balochistan Study (draft). Washington, DC: World Bank.

World Bank. 2008c. "World Trade Indicators: Benchmarking Trade Policies and Outcomes." Mimeo. Washington, DC: World Bank.

———. 2008d. *World Development Report 2009: Reshaping Economic Geography.* Washington, DC: World Bank.

Yoshida, Nobou. 2008. "A Note on the Trend of Regional Inequality across Areas in the South Asia Region." Mimeo. Washington, DC: World Bank.

Part II

SAFTA and Beyond
Selected Cooperation Issues

Part II

SAFTA and Beyond
Selected Cooperation Issues

SAFTA

Current Status and Prospects

Dushni Weerakoon

1. INTRODUCTION AND BACKGROUND

South Asian countries, which had open economies in the immediate post-independence period in the 1940s, had become some of the most highly protectionist economies in the world by the 1970s. Tariff and, even more important, nontariff barriers were extremely high, state interventions in economic activity had become pervasive, attitudes to foreign investments were negative, often hostile, and stringent exchange controls were in place. This started to change in the late 1970s, however. In 1977, Sri Lanka initiated a process of policy liberalization, and other countries followed in the 1980s. The liberalization process, however, was often rather hesitant and was uneven across countries. It was from the early 1990s, with the start of a major reform process in India, that the region as a whole really started to liberalize. By the end of the decade, although important policy barriers to trade and foreign investment remained, enormous progress had been made throughout the region in this direction (World Bank 2004).

The changes to the trade policy regime in South Asia have been driven primarily by across-the-board, unilateral liberalization by individual countries. However, a process of preferential trade liberalization also has been ongoing since the establishment in 1985 of the South Asian Association for Regional Cooperation (SAARC). South Asia was fairly late in embracing the concept of regional economic cooperation—it took a decade after the initial establishment of SAARC for the region to turn its attention to the promotion of trade through a regional agreement. Nevertheless, having accepted the concept of regional economic cooperation, SAARC was quick to set itself an ambitious agenda. The proposal to set up a South Asian Preferential Trade Agreement (SAPTA) was accepted and came into formal operation in December 1995. In 1996, SAARC member countries agreed in principle to go a step further and attempt to enact a South Asian Free Trade Agreement (SAFTA) by 2000, but not later than 2005. With the apparent progress of three rounds of negotiations under SAPTA completed by 1998, it was proposed that the date for establishing SAFTA be brought forward to 2001.

The momentum of economic cooperation in South Asia suffered a setback from late 1998, however, with the deterioration in bilateral relations between India and Pakistan that saw the consequent postponement of SAARC Heads of State Summits for the next three years.[1] With the resumption of official contact in January 2002, negotiations on a Framework Treaty on SAFTA were initiated and the framework was adopted in January 2004. Outstanding issues in key areas of the tariff liberalization program, rules of origin, sensitive lists, and so on, were completed on schedule by January 2006 to allow the implementation of SAFTA to begin in July 2006. Under the proposed tariff liberalization program (TLP), SAFTA will become fully effective for non–least developed country (LDC) member countries of SAARC by 2013 (and by 2016 for LDC member states).

To date, the SAFTA process has generated only limited enthusiasm. It suffers from significant shortcomings, primarily on account of a cautious approach adopted to achieve the ultimate objective of free trade within the South Asian region. Concerns about the very usefulness of SAFTA have been mounting in light of more liberal bilateral free trade agreements (FTAs)—as well as preferential access that could conceivably be granted through alternative trading arrangements—among SAARC countries. The dynamics of regional integration in South Asia have also changed with the growing emergence of India not only as an Asian economic power, but also as a rapidly emerging world economic power. With India looking increasingly to strengthen economic relations with the wider Asian region through initiatives such as Association of Southeast Asian

Nations (ASEAN)+3+India, the strategic interests of the smaller South Asian economies are likely to become inextricably linked to successful integration with the Indian economy. The evidence to date suggests that economic integration of the South Asian region is gathering pace, but that SAFTA remains fairly marginal in that process.

2. FROM SAPTA TO SAFTA: WILL "FREE" TRADE IN SOUTH ASIA YIELD BENEFITS?

Despite a number of empirical studies that have looked at the prospects for regional integration in South Asia, the results remain inconclusive. The quantitative assessments have used a variety of methodologies, including gravity models, computable general equilibrium (CGE) models, and partial equilibrium studies. Early studies predicted pessimistic outcomes for the most part. They concluded that most of the preconditions required for a successful trading arrangement were not present in South Asia (De Melo et al. 1993; De Rosa and Govindan 1994; Srinivasan and Canonero 1993; Srinivasan 1994), and that the region would be better off liberalizing trade unilaterally (Bandara and Yu 2003). Others argued strongly that regional trade integration initiatives in South Asia will yield a net welfare loss and slow unilateral liberalization (Baysan et al. 2006; Panagariya 2003). Indeed, it has long been recognized that the fact that South Asian countries share some basic similarities (low income, relatively abundant labor, comparative advantage in similar commodities, such as tea and garments) reduces the potential for comparative advantage–driven trade.

Nevertheless, it has been argued that increased economic integration would carry with it the ability not only to secure new and larger markets for traditional products, but also to enable the diversification of domestic economic structures. More recent studies have highlighted benefits to be had from pursuing economic integration in South Asia, not only in trade in goods but also in services and investment (ADB/UNCTAD 2008).

Notwithstanding the inconclusive nature of empirical assessments, the notion that deeper regional trade integration can create spillover effects that would strengthen economic and political ties between South Asian countries has persisted (SAARC Secretariat 1999). SAPTA was intended as the initial step in the process to support regional economic integration. However, the SAPTA process was rather ineffective. Three rounds of negotiations were completed under SAPTA where the consolidated list of concessions covered 3,857 tariff lines, including special concessions (2,762 tariff lines) offered to LDCs.[2] The most limiting factor of SAPTA was the actual trade coverage of preferential access granted. In fact, it has been estimated that on average only 8.4 percent of tariff lines in the case of imports from non-LDCs (and 6.2 percent in the case of imports from the LDCs) were covered (World Bank 2004). In reality, products imported under SAPTA concessions translated to only 15 percent of total imports between SAARC member countries (Mukherji 2000). Thus, SAPTA had little or no impact in changing the existing trade patterns in South Asia. Intra-SAARC trade continued to stagnate in the region of 5 percent of total trade with the rest of the world—one of the lowest volumes of intraregional trade of any major geographic region.

SAFTA was intended o provide a fresh boost to the integration process. Unlike SAPTA, SAFTA adopted a negative list approach with the intention that South Asian countries would phase out import tariffs to other member countries on all goods apart from those items reserved under a "sensitive" list. The key features of the Agreement related to the modalities of the TLP, the treatment of sensitive goods, and the rules of origin.

2.1 SAFTA: Key Features and Current Status

As far as the TLP is concerned, the approach adopted makes a commitment toward a top–down reduction of tariffs in which non-LDC member states are required to reduce existing tariffs to 20 percent within 2 years of implementation of the agreement, and thereafter to further reduce tariffs to a range of 0–5 percent in the next 5 years.[3] LDC member countries are required to reduce existing tariffs to 30 percent in 2 years and further ensure a reduction to a range of 0–5 percent in the next 8 years (Table 3.1).

One criticism that may be made of this formula is that it may allow back-loading in the tariff-reduction process. That is, those countries whose tariffs are well below 20 percent may not have to commit to substantial reductions until the last minute. The agreement only requires a 10 percent margin of preference reduction in each of the two years and recommends a 15 percent reduction each year in the second phase. However, the formula adopted—unlike the alternative of a progressive linear reduction formula—is not without its benefits. It is likely to be more efficient if convergence is achieved initially by all countries lowering their tariffs to a maximum rate and then proceeding further. An alternative of an annualized percentage reduction, on the other hand, would have meant that countries with high tariffs still continue to benefit in relation to the other regional partners. International experience of regional blocs

TABLE 3.1   Comparative TLP across FTAs in South Asia

	SAFTA	*ISFTA*	*PSFTA*
Immediate 0%	Not applicable	India: 1,351 items Sri Lanka: 319 items	Pakistan: 206 items Sri Lanka: 102 items
TLP for others	Non-LDCs: reduce tariffs to 20 percent over 2 years (LDCs 3 years)	India: duty on balance items to be phased out over 3 years	Pakistan: duty on balance items to be phased out over 3 years
	Non-LDCs: reduce to 0–5 percent over next 5 years(LDCs 7 years)	Sri Lanka: duty on balance items to be phased out over 8 years	Sri Lanka: duty on balance items to be phased out over 5 years
Date of full implementation	2016	2008	2010

Source   Respective agreements.

Note   FTP = Free Trade Agreement; ISFTA = India–Sri Lanka Free Trade Agreement;
PSFTA = Pakistan–Sri Lanka Free Trade Agreement; SAFTA = South Asian Free
Trade Agreement; TLP = Tariff Liberalization Program.

generally finds clauses that favor convergence—as in SAFTA—to be more
successful in ensuring that benefits of tariff reduction are extended to all
member countries.

Another key area is rules of origin (ROO), which is an important
provision in any FTA. Within trade arrangements, ROO have a number
of functions. The most important are to limit the benefit of preferences to
countries within the agreement, and related to that, to encourage industrial
development within the member countries. ROO can have positive as well
as negative effects. Positive effects of properly constituted ROO requirements generally include prevention of trade deflection, facilitating value
addition, and augmenting the volume of intraregional trade. On the negative side, it is often argued that ROO might inhibit intraregional trade and
favor high cost and inefficient production. Ideally ROO should, therefore,
be open, transparent, predictable, and consistent in application, as simple
as possible and leave little room for administrative discretion.

Three criteria are generally used to determine whether 'substantial transformation' of goods—that is, the final product should be distinct from its
constituents—has taken place. Each rule could be applied in isolation, in
the alternative, or in tandem. The rules are:

- a percentage test according to which a minimum percentage of
  domestic value addition (DVA) should be achieved on the basis of
  domestic inputs;

- a change in tariff heading (CTH) test whereby the tariff heading of the final product is different from the tariff headings of its components; and
- specified process tests that require a product to undergo certain stipulated processes.

The SAFTA agreement requires domestic value addition (DVA) of 40 percent for India and Pakistan (as non-LDC member countries), 35 percent for Sri Lanka (as a small economy), and 30 percent for LDCs, in combination with a change of tariff heading (CTH) at classified at the four-digit Harmonized Commodity Description and Coding System (HS) code (Table 3.2). However, derogation from the General Rule has been permitted under SAFTA because some products may undergo substantial transformation and allow the DVA criteria to be met without CTH at the four-digit code and vice versa. Besides the single-country ROO, there is also provision for cumulative ROO with a minimum aggregate content of 50 percent with the proviso that the minimum input from the exporting country should be 20 percent. The SAFTA ROO is more or less the same as those under the bilateral FTAs in the region.

One of the most critical provisions in SAFTA is the one that deals with sensitive sectors. It seems reasonable that each country has some

TABLE 3.2 Comparative Rules of Origin across FTAs in South Asia

	SAFTA	ISFTA	PSFTA
Single-country ROO			
DVA (% of FOB)			
India and Pakistan	40%	35%	35%
Sri Lanka	35%	35%	35%
LDCs	30%		
CTH	4-digit	4-digit	6-digit
Cumulative ROO			
Minimum Aggregate Content	50%	35%	35%
Input from Exporting Country	20%	25%	25%
Derogation from General Rule	DVA: 25, 30, 40, or 60% CTH: at 4- or 6-digit Process: PSR		Not applicable

Source Respective agreements.

Note CTH = Change of Tariff Heading; DVA = Domestic Value Addition; FTP = Free Trade Agreement; ISFTA = India–Sri Lanka Free Trade Agreement; LDC = Least Developed Country; PSFTA = Pakistan–Sri Lanka Free Trade Agreement; ROO = Rules of Origin; SAFTA = South Asian Free Trade Agreement.

sensitive industries that should not face increased competition, even from relatively less competitive neighbors. An improvement in the SAFTA treaty compared with the bilateral FTAs in the region was that it provided room for negotiations to ensure a maximum ceiling on items that can be placed under the negative list by each member country. It appeared in the initial stages of negotiations that a fairly liberal approach would be adopted, perhaps limiting the negative list to 10 percent of tariff lines (of a total of 5,224 tariff lines at the HS six-digit level), but the final decision was to retain a negative list of 20 percent of tariff lines for non-LDC member states and a close approximation of that for the LDC member countries (Table 3.3).

TABLE 3.3   Comparative Negative Lists across FTAs in South Asia

	SAFTA	ISFTA	PSFTA
Bangladesh	1,254[a]		
Bhutan	137		
India	865[b]	419	
Maldives	671		
Nepal	1,335		
Pakistan	1,183		540
Sri Lanka	1,065	1,180	697

Source Respective agreements.
Notes FTA = Free Trade Agreement; ISFTA = India–Sri Lanka Free Trade Agreement; PSFTA = Pakistan–Sri Lanka Free Trade Agreement; SAFTA = South Asian Free Trade Agreement.
[a] For LDCs 1,249.
[b] For LDCs 744.

This means, in principle, that the actual trade coverage of the negative lists of each country could be quite high. Perhaps of more concern is that there is no formal and binding provision in the framework agreement requiring that negative lists are pruned down over time. In contrast, the ASEAN Free Trade Agreement (AFTA) requires explicitly that its negative list products—the corresponding Temporary Exclusion List—be phased out in five equal installments. The only provision that the SAFTA treaty has made is for a "review" of the negative list at least every four years "with a view to reducing the number of items" (Agreement of South Asian Free Trade Area, Article 7(3b), p. 5). The underlying intention may be to prune it, but the provision is vague and has no authority to require any movement from the current position of member countries. Given that SAFTA has left the issue of negative lists fairly open ended—even four years is a fairly long time horizon to wait for any improvement in the agreement—there is always the danger that the agreement will fall short of free trade even in the long term. By comparison to SAFTA, the negative lists of existing bilateral FTAs in the region are more limited.

Indeed, mapping the sensitive list of each country to their imports from the rest of South Asia reveals that nearly 53 percent of total import trade among South Asian countries by value (at the time negotiations were initiated in 2004) is excluded from the liberalization of tariffs proposed under the SAFTA treaty (Table 3.4). The LDC member countries such as Bangladesh, Maldives, and Nepal have sought to "protect" 65–75 percent of their imports from South Asia by excluding them from being subject to tariff liberalization. Sri Lanka (51.7 percent) and India (38.4 percent) also have restricted a fairly high share of imports from being subject to tariff cuts. At first glance, it appears that Pakistan has been fairly generous in restricting only around 17 percent of its current imports to the sensitive list, despite the fact that it has the largest number of items in the sensitive list of non-LDC members. However, Pakistan maintains a positive list of items in regard to its trade with India that, in theory, can limit the potential trade volumes to a great extent.

TABLE 3.4   Trade Restriction under SAFTA

	Value of imports from SAARC subject to SL (%)	Value of exports to SAARC subject to SL (%)
Bangladesh	65.0	22.0
India	38.4	56.5
Maldives	74.5	57.6
Nepal	64.0	46.4
Pakistan	17.2	34.0
Sri Lanka	51.7	47.0
Total	52.9	

Source   Weerakoon and Thennakoon 2008.

Note   SAARC = South Asian Association for Regional Cooperation; SL = Sensitive List.

Another area of concern in the SAFTA treaty is the lack of an explicit commitment to deal with the issue of nontariff barriers (NTBs). In identifying NTBs, a distinction can be made between those that have to be eliminated and those that have to be harmonized, such as measures relating to technical standards, plant and animal health, and environmental protection and safety. If any quantitative restrictions exist, these can more easily be converted to tariffs and subsequently reduced. Generally, the experience of FTAs has been that customs surcharges, technical measures and product characteristic requirements, and monopolistic measures (particularly in relation to exclusive import rights of state-controlled enterprises) are the most difficult to identify and eliminate. While South Asia has made significant progress in eliminating quantitative restrictions (QRs), nontariff measures do exist that can act as a barrier to the free flow of goods between SAARC countries (World Bank 2004).

The SAFTA framework agreement has provisions to deal with paratariffs and NTBs, but no explicit commitment is required of countries. In particular, there is no commitment in the SAFTA framework agreement to eliminate NTBs on items for which tariff reductions are to be made. By contrast, an important feature in AFTA, for example, is that member countries are required to eliminate QRs on products on which they receive concessions, and eliminate other NTBs within 5 years of receiving such concessions. What is contained in the SAFTA treaty appears to be merely an understanding that NTB-related issues will be subject to continuous negotiations.

The SAFTA treaty has been confined to trade in goods, which is viewed as a limiting factor. Globally, the trends governing bilateral and regional trade initiatives are toward implementing broader economic partnership agreements that include trade in services and investment, and areas of economic cooperation. SAARC has taken some initial steps to incorporate services and investment into the SAFTA framework agreement by commissioning a joint study to examine the issues that need to be addressed.

Thus, it is clear that SAFTA as it stands contains certain limitations. Nonetheless, implementation is progressing per the terms of the agreement, subject to the early dispute that arose with regard to the application of Pakistan's Positive List to trade with India regarding the implementation of SAFTA.[4] However, the required initial tariff liberalization (for example, to achieve a threshold of 20 percent) is quite minimal given that most South Asian economies have been unilaterally lowering Most Favored Nation (MFN) tariffs quite substantially over time. For instance, if the liberalization formula is applied to the Sri Lankan context, leaving aside those items in Sri Lanka's SAFTA sensitive list, it is clear that the only commitment required is to reduce tariffs from 28 percent to 20 percent on approximately 300 tariff lines (at HS six-digit) in three installments over a 2-year period.[5]

The other main area of progress is perhaps that of pruning sensitive lists. But here again, it is confined largely to a voluntary exercise, with India taking the initiative with an offer to unilaterally prune its sensitive list ahead of schedule by removing an additional 264 items applicable to LDCs. India has long been viewed as the key to enabling a successful regional economic integration effort in South Asia, given the significantly asymmetric nature of economic power it wields. In light of India's growing economic stature—alongside a rapidly changing pattern of trade and investment linkages across the wider Asian region—the prospects for integration in South Asia have to be viewed from a broader perspective. Such a perspective would include an assessment not only of India's own economic interests and how they relate to the South Asian region, but also how other South Asian economies respond to new challenges.

3. TRENDS IN ECONOMIC INTEGRATION IN SOUTH ASIA: THE ROLE OF INDIA

The current low levels of intraregional trade in South Asia and the limitations of the SAFTA process to provide dynamism to kick-start the process might be taken as an indication that regional economic integration in South Asia is likely to remain a distant dream. However, a key issue that needs to be looked at is whether such integration must necessarily be achieved through the SAFTA process or whether alternative arrangements are, in fact, already paving the way for an eventual approximation to free trade in the South Asian region. In this context, the role and relevance of India is overwhelming.

India remains the dominant trading partner for all South Asian economies (Table 3.5). Indeed, more than 90 percent of regional trade for such countries as Bangladesh, Nepal, and Sri Lanka is confined to a bilateral relationship with India. Even Pakistan finds nearly two-thirds of its total trade with South Asian economies relate to its bilateral trade with India. In effect, economic integration in South Asia can be argued to consist, in principle, of bilateral links to India, bypassing any notable degree of trade with third countries in the SAARC grouping.

Thus, the notion of creating a free trade area within the South Asian region, in practice, involves market access between India and other South Asian economies. In this context, it is also clear that India has played a more proactive role in the bilateral process than in the regional arena with regard to its engagements in South Asia (Box 3.1). India was much more generous in allowing significant asymmetric treatment to Sri Lanka under the bilateral FTA regarding the size of its negative list, additional years for implementation of the tariff liberalization, and so on, than the

TABLE 3.5   South Asia's Bilateral Trade with India

	2000	2001	2002	2003	2004	2005	2006
India's share in total intra-SAARC trade (%)							
Bangladesh	86.6	90.3	91.5	90.2	90.2	89.8	89.5
Maldives	34.7	38.4	35.9	37.0	43.6	57.9	57.9
Nepal	98.4	98.4	98.3	98.9	98.5	99.3	99.5
Pakistan	44.2	54.9	46.4	47.3	58.7	63.3	64.5
Sri Lanka	73.4	77.4	84.3	86.6	88.0	91.2	91.2
India's share in total world trade (%)							
Bangladesh	7.6	9.5	9.5	10.5	9.4	10.3	9.9
Maldives	7.7	9.0	8.7	8.2	8.7	10.0	9.9
Nepal	37.1	43.6	47.2	51.8	56.5	65.8	71.5
Pakistan	1.2	1.6	1.0	1.2	2.0	2.2	2.4
Sri Lanka	5.6	6.2	9.3	11.2	13.3	15.8	17.3

Source   IMF 2007.
Note   SAARC = South Asian Association for Regional Cooperation.

BOX 3.1   Asymmetric Treatment from India: SAFTA versus Bilateral FTAs

SAFTA	*ISFTA*
Non-LDCs maintain 20 percent of tariff lines; LDCs approximately 25 percent.	Sri Lanka maintains 25 percent of tariff lines; India maintains 8 percent.
No such immediate zero-duty concessions.	India offered immediate zero-duty concessions on 25 percent of tariff lines; Sri Lanka offered only about 6 percent.
LDCs get additional three years to implement.	Sri Lanka gets additional five years to implement.

Source   Compiled from relevant agreements.
Note   FTA = Free Trade Agreement; ISFTA = India–Sri Lanka Free Trade Agreement; LDCs = Least Developed Countries; SAFTA = South Asian Free Trade Agreement.

concessions it offered to LDCs at the regional-level SAFTA negotiations. The differences in the level of engagement are clear from a cursory look at the applicability of negative lists at the time of implementation of the two agreements. For example, only 13 percent of Sri Lanka's exports to India were subject to the Indian negative list under the India–Sri Lanka Free Trade Agreement (ISFTA), while nearly 42 percent of Sri Lanka's exports to India were found to be excluded under the Indian negative list under SAFTA (Weerakoon and Thennakoon 2008).

Indeed, the ISFTA is viewed as the most successful bilateral or regional trade initiative in South Asia. Sri Lanka's exports to India have been rising faster than India's exports to Sri Lanka since the implementation of the ISFTA in March 2000. Perhaps even more critical, India has emerged as a significant investor in Sri Lanka, partly in response to the cementing of economic relations governed by the ISFTA (for an evaluation of post-implementation performance, see Kelegama and Mukherji 2007). The perceived advantages of the ISFTA in generating trade in goods between the two countries, in fact, prompted the initiation of negotiations to deepen and broaden the agreement by including trade in services and investment under a Comprehensive Economic Partnership Agreement (CEPA).

Thus, India's stance and approach toward initiatives to promote economic integration in South Asia can be viewed as a crucial component. A possible Indian role has to be looked at not only in terms of the South Asian region but also in terms of India's wider strategic economic relations in the Asian region. These have inevitably evolved since the start of negotiations on the SAFTA framework in 2004, which governed the subsequent terms on which it has since been implemented. India as a rising economic power is increasingly more confident of its demonstrated capacity to sustain a strong growth momentum in the coming decades.

Does India's economic interest lie in South Asia? The recent pattern of import and export trade suggests otherwise. India's exports to South Asia have stagnated in the region at 5–5.5 percent of its total exports, while its imports from the region have consistently hovered around 1 percent of its total imports. By contrast, India trade with the East Asian region (ASEAN+3)[6] has been growing quite sharply: exports have grown from 13.5 percent to nearly 22 percent, while imports have grown from 17.1 percent to 27 percent between 2000 and 2006 (Table 3.6).

The growing trade links with the East Asian region clearly demonstrate why India has enunciated a "Look East" policy (Grarer and Mattoo 2001). The Indian economy is increasingly developing complementarities with East Asian economies in knowledge-based segments such as microchips, information technology, and other areas. Strengthening trade and investment linkages with the region, therefore, makes sound economic sense—a policy reflected in India's recent bilateral and regional trade initiatives in the region (Box 3.2).

It is not only India that appears to strengthening its trade links with East Asia, as opposed to stronger trade flows with the rest of South Asia. Most of the other South Asian economies, too, are witnessing a progressive increase in trade with the East Asian region, while their share of intra–South Asian trade is stagnating (Table 3.7). In addition to India,

TABLE 3.6   Relative Share of India's Trade with SAARC and ASEAN+3

(in percent)

	2000	*2001*	*2002*	*2003*	*2004*	*2005*	*2006*
SAARC							
Exports	4.2	5.7	5.1	6.4	5.6	5.2	5.5
Imports	0.9	1.3	0.9	0.9	0.8	0.9	1.0
ASEAN+3							
Exports	13.5	18.1	16.7	18.2	18.9	20.6	21.9
Imports	17.1	24.9	19.3	21.4	20.6	19.9	27.0

Source   IMF 2007.

Note   ASEAN+3 = Association of Southeast Asian Nations, plus China, Japan, and the Republic of Korea; SAARC = South Asian Association for Regional Cooperation.

BOX 3.2   India's Bilateral and Regional Engagements in East Asia

Country	*Type of Agreement*	*Date*
Singapore	CECA	Signed 2005
Korea, Rep. of	JSG JTF to develop CEPA	Completed 2006 Ongoing
Thailand	Framework Agreement Aim for FTA	Signed 2003 Ongoing
ASEAN	Framework Agreement Aim for CECA	Signed 2003 Ongoing
China	JSG JTF to develop trade agreement	Completed 2005 Ongoing
Malaysia	JSG Aim for CECA	Completed 2007 Ongoing
Indonesia	JSG Aim for CECA	Commenced 2007
Japan	JSG JTF aim for CEPA/EPA	Ongoing

Source   Department of Commerce, India. Web site: www.commerce.nic.in.

Note   CECA = Comprehensive Economic Cooperation Aagreement; CEPA = Comprehensive Economic Partnership Agreement; EPA = Economic Partnership Agreement; FTA = Free Trade Agreement; JSG = Joint Study Group; JTF = Joint Task Force.

Bangladesh, Maldives, and Pakistan have seen their share of trade with ASEAN+3 countries improving significantly, whereas their share of trade with SAARC countries has been stagnating or even declining over time. The exceptions are Nepal and Sri Lanka—interestingly, the two countries that have the most comprehensive bilateral FTAs with India in the SAARC region. Both have seen their share of trade with SAARC increase—indeed, wholly with India (Table 3.5)—while their trade share with East Asia has declined (Nepal) or stagnated (Sri Lanka).

TABLE 3.7   Direction of Trade for South Asian Economies

	2000	2001	2002	2003	2004	2005	2006
India							
SAARC	2.4	3.3	2.9	3.4	2.9	2.7	2.8
ASEAN+3	15.5	21.7	18.1	20.0	19.8	20.2	24.9
Pakistan							
SAARC	2.7	2.9	2.2	2.6	3.3	3.5	3.8
ASEAN+3	18.7	18.3	19.1	19.4	18.9	19.9	26.7
Bangladesh							
SAARC	8.7	10.6	10.4	11.6	10.5	11.5	11.0
ASEAN+3	25.4	25.9	27.4	26.2	23.0	24.6	30.3
Nepal							
SAARC	37.7	44.3	48.0	52.4	57.4	66.3	71.9
ASEAN+3	17.3	21.2	18.7	16.4	16.1	17.2	12.5
Maldives							
SAARC	22.3	23.5	24.3	22.3	19.9	17.3	17.1
ASEAN+3	42.9	40.2	39.9	43.1	42.2	42.1	46.9
Sri Lanka							
SAARC	7.7	8.1	11.0	12.9	15.2	17.4	19.0
ASEAN+3	23.9	22.6	22.2	23.1	21.7	20.7	22.1

Source   IMF 2007.

Note   ASEAN+3 = Association of Southeast Asian Nations, plus China, Japan, and the Republic of Korea; SAARC = South Asian Association for Regional Cooperation.

4. CHALLENGES AND PROSPECTS FOR SAFTA: SOME CONCLUSIONS

What is clear from a cursory examination of current trading patterns of South Asian economies is the progressive strengthening of trade links in a wider Asian context. For India, the priority will be to strengthen strategic links with East Asia. It could well carry other South Asian economies along, in which case India would be the hub that connects South Asian countries and also would be the bridge that connects South Asia to East Asia. Two key issues that arise in this context are whether SAFTA has a meaningful role in this process, or whether it has already lost the opportunity to be the main dynamic force from within South Asia.

Evidence suggests that SAFTA has already lost a great deal of momentum in the evolving dynamics of regionalism in Asia. As previously argued, SAFTA has made only a cautious attempt to enact free trade in the SAARC region. It already has been overtaken by the bilateral process in many instances, and would appear to be in danger of being further upstaged by bilateral and other regional initiatives. As previously argued, India is the key to South Asian economic integration. Bilateral market access is fast providing an environment that could reasonably approximate free trade in South Asia. Bhutan, Nepal, and Sri Lanka have virtual free trade access to the Indian market for their exports despite having a significant share of their exports to India restricted under SAFTA (Table 3.8). India has restricted only a limited share of imports from Maldives (3.6 percent) and Bangladesh (11.2 percent) under SAFTA.

TABLE 3.8 Bilateral Trade Restriction under SAFTA

	Bangladesh	India	Maldives	Nepal	Pakistan	Sri Lanka
% of imports under SL						
Bangladesh		11.2	0.0	29.7	31.3	45.2
Bhutan	69.4	36.8	0.0	15.0	50.4	0.0
India	66.0		65.2	64.2	14.5	53.5
Maldives	72.9	3.6		0.0	0.0	59.2
Nepal	87.8	46.2	0.0		25.4	17.6
Pakistan	54.5	16.4	15.5	30.0		28.4
Sri Lanka	66.6	41.5	85.4	37.6	29.7	

Source Weerakoon and Thennakoon 2008.

Note SAFTA = South Asian Free Trade Agreement; SL = sensitive list.

Alternative regional initiatives in the pipeline will grant Bangladesh opportunities to further its access to the Indian market. These include the proposed transition of the Bangkok Agreement to an FTA under the Asia Pacific Trade Agreement (APTA) and the implementation of an FTA under the Bay of Bengal Initiative for Multi-Sectoral Technical and Economic Cooperation (BIMSTEC). In addition, Bangladesh has indicated interest in negotiating a bilateral FTA with India. Bangladesh and Maldives will both stand to benefit from enhanced access to India with the proposed unilateral reduction of India's sensitive list by a further 264 items applicable to LDCs. This may still restrict some amount of trade, but it is being offered on a nonreciprocal basis and ahead of the scheduled four-year revision of sensitive lists.

Thus, bilateral market access to India for the smaller South Asian economies is evolving at a much more rapid pace than under the SAFTA framework (Box 3.3). The net result of these alternative bilateral and regional agreements in South Asia—with India playing a pivotal role—may eventually become something approximating free trade within the region. However, Pakistan is conspicuously absent in the evolving network of such alternative agreements. In contrast to the other South Asian countries, Pakistan is seeking its own trade arrangements with the East Asian region. To date, it has signed FTAs with China (2006) and Malaysia (2007).[7]

BOX 3.3 Bilateral and Regional Agreements Involving India (except SAFTA)

Country	Bilateral	Other
Afghanistan	PTA (2003)	
Bhutan	FTA (1995)[a]	BIMSTEC
Bangladesh	Trade Agreement (2006)	APTA, BIMSTEC
Maldives	Trade Agreement (1981)	
Nepal	FTA (1991)[b]	BIMSTEC
Pakistan		
Sri Lanka	FTA (1998)	APTA, BIMSTEC

Source Department of Commerce, India, available at www.commerce.nic.in.

Notes APTA = Asia Pacific Trade Agreement; BIMSTEC = Bay of Bengal Initiative for Multi-Sectoral Technical and Economic Cooperation; FTA = Free Trade Agreement; PTA = Preferential Trade Agreement; SAFTA = South Asian Free Trade Agreement.
[a] Renegotiated in 2006.
[b] Renegotiated in 2002.

Thus, there are obvious divergences of interests and strategic interests amongst SAARC countries. These developments pose internal challenges to the SAARC process and the future pace of regional economic cooperation under SAFTA. A multiplicity of alternative bilateral and regional arrangements among SAFTA members would not pose a major constraint, if the SAFTA process was keeping pace with such developments. Unfortunately, the current experience is that SAFTA is, in fact, lagging.

India's attention on issues of regional trade initiatives is spreading rapidly beyond South Asia. India's more accommodative approach to SAFTA—such as the unilateral decision to enhance market access to LDC—as well as its bilateral agreements with South Asian countries can be read as a signal of its growing economic confidence, and a sign of its willingness to carry along the South Asian region as it links up with East

Asia. The onus will be on the other South Asian economies to weigh the advantages and disadvantages of strategically linking with a fast-expanding Indian economy and to take advantage of potential intraregional trade and investment linkages.

For SAFTA to be the catalyst for this process of integration, the two economies that remain the least integrated in the SAARC region (that is, India and Pakistan) will need to enforce an expanded trade liberalization program.[8] This will require not only a relaxation of sensitive lists, but also a means of addressing bilateral trade issues between the two countries. In addition, other South Asian economies will need to consider opening up their economies. At present, most South Asian economies are restricting 55–65 percent of their imports from India under SAFTA sensitive lists (Table 3.8). Although Pakistan appears to have offered more favorable treatment (limiting only around 16.5 percent of Indian imports), this figure has to be viewed in the context of the existing trade restrictions between the two countries. Alongside efforts to broaden the scope of the TLP, moves to incorporate trade in services and investment into SAFTA also need to be advanced to stimulate spillover effects.

In the absence of progress on these fronts—particularly in expanding the scope of the TLP—there is a very real threat that the SAFTA process can stagnate, or worse, that it can fragment, as countries pursue bilateral market access and other alternative regional arrangements. An approximation of free trade in South Asia may be achievable through such means, but it would compromise many of the political and economic goals that were intended to be achieved through regional economic integration that includes all the member states of SAARC.

NOTES

1. In the interim, bilateral free trade agreements (FTAs) among SAARC member countries were negotiated; the India–Sri Lanka FTA (ISFTA) was concluded in December 1998 and negotiations on a Framework Agreement on a Pakistan–Sri Lanka FTA (PSFTA) were concluded in June 2002.
2. A fourth round was initiated but was never ratified by member countries.
3. Sri Lanka is given an additional one year in recognition of its small vulnerable economy status.
4. The notifications issued by Pakistan includes a rider that Indian imports into Pakistan would continue to be as included on the positive list of importable items from India, which at present consists of 1,075 tariff lines.

4

Bilateral Free Trade Agreements in SAARC and Implications for SAFTA

Deshal de Mel

1. INTRODUCTION

Regional economic integration within South Asia had been mooted since the early 1990s. The emergence of the South Asian Preferential Trade Agreement (SAPTA) in 1995 followed by the decision to deepen it to a South Asian Free Trade Agreement (SAFTA) in 1996 suggested that there was limited rationale for bilateral trade agreements within the region to emerge. However, the SAPTA had covered limited product lines of trade interests and, when efforts at regional economic integration came to a deadlock in 1998 following competing nuclear tests by the two largest countries in South Asia, countries looked at bilateralism with greater interest. Sri Lanka is involved in both bilateral trade agreements that have emerged within the region. The first was with India, signed in 1998 and implemented in March 2000, and the second was with Pakistan, which came into effect in June 2005. Although both agreements provided Sri Lanka with important market access to its main trading partners in the region, the fact that the three most developed countries within South Asian Association for Regional Cooperation (SAARC) have entered into bilateral trade agreements threatens the significance of SAFTA. Given the current deadlock in the World Trade Organization (WTO), other South Asian countries (Bangladesh in particular) may consider the bilateral route of trade liberalization more seriously.

Eight years have passed since the commencement of the Indo–Sri Lanka FTA (ILFTA), and it is now possible to have a better idea of the implications of the agreement. Aggregate values show strong benefits for Sri Lanka in terms of export growth, but a more disaggregated analysis shows that the actual picture is less encouraging. The Pakistan–Sri Lanka FTA (PSFTA) has had limited impact on trade thus far, and the efficacy of the agreement and lessons for other countries can be considered in this light. This chapter will examine the structure of each agreement and evaluate their impact on trade between Sri Lanka, India, and Pakistan. The chapter also touches on the position of the two agreements within the context of SAFTA and highlights some lessons that emerge for SAFTA and for other countries looking to sign bilateral agreements within the region. Section 2 will deal with the India–Sri Lanka FTA (ISFTA) with subsections touching on the structure of the agreement, economic impacts, and the moves toward the Comprehensive Economic Partnership Agreement (CEPA) between the two countries. Section 3 will deal with the PSFTA, and subsections will again touch on the structure, economic implications, and the way forward. Section 4 compares the two bilateral trade agreements with SAFTA and highlights lessons for other countries; Section 5 concludes.

2. INDO-SRI LANKA FTA

The ILFTA was the first bilateral trade agreement that was signed by both Sri Lanka and India. The agreement was signed in the backdrop of expanding economic ties between the two countries following liberalization of the Indian economy in the early 1990s. While India had become one of Sri Lanka's major import sources, exports to India remained low. With the deteriorating political relationship between India and Pakistan stalling progress on SAFTA, Sri Lanka and India were keen to forge ahead with a bilateral agreement to cement the improving economic integration between the two countries.

2.1 Structure of the Agreement

Learning from the poor trade impact of the product-by-product approach of SAPTA, the ILFTA utilized a negative list approach to trade liberalization. Thereby, all items would be liberalized except those deemed sensitive by each country. At the foundation of the agreement is that, given the asymmetry between India and Sri Lanka, there would be less than full reciprocity between the two countries. Several special and differential treatment measures were implemented to allow for this asymmetry.

2.1.1 Negative Lists

India's negative list, with 429 tariff lines, was substantially smaller than that of Sri Lanka, which maintained 1,220 items on the negative list. Sri Lanka protected much of the agricultural sector and many other sectors for which particularly small and medium industries were perceived to be vulnerable to Indian competition. These included such sectors as rubber, ceramics, paper, and products thereof. Furthermore, revenue compensation was excluded from the agreement and, in lieu of this, Sri Lanka was allowed to maintain key revenue-earning items in the negative list. Therefore, products such as motor vehicles and parts—key imports from India—were kept in the negative list. Such measures were required to placate Sri Lankan domestic interests with regard to the perceived threat of "flooding" of Indian products and revenue implications. As a result, of the 1,180 items on Sri Lanka's negative list, 712 were traded between the two countries at a value of US$912.3 million. Therefore, around 50 percent of India's exports to Sri Lanka, in terms of value, were subject to the negative list and did not receive preferences under the FTA. On the other hand, 70 of the 429 items on India's negative list were exported from Sri Lanka to India, accounting for 3.3 percent of Sri Lanka's exports to India in value terms in 2006 (Weerakoon and Thennakoon 2008).

2.1.2 Tariff Liberalization Program

While India's tariff liberalization program (TLP) would be completed over a period of three years, Sri Lanka was given eight years to complete its liberalization process, allowing domestic firms time to adjust to the shocks associated with trade liberalization. The TLP for both countries is summarized in Table 4.1.

India's initial preferences to Sri Lanka were larger than Sri Lanka's preferences to India. India provided immediate zero duty for 1,351 tariff lines compared with Sri Lanka's 319 tariff lines and also provided 50 percent preference margins for the remaining 2,870 tariff lines (to be phased out over 3 years), while Sri Lanka did the same for 889 items.

TABLE 4.1   Tariff Reductions ILFTA

Tariff reductions	India	Sri Lanka
Negative List	1,220	429
Immediate Zero Duty (March 2000)	1,351	319
Zero Duty within 3 years (cuts of 50%, 75%, and 100% by March 2003)	2,870	889
Zero Duty within 8 years (cuts of 35%, 70%, and 100% by March 2008)[a]	—	2,802

Source   India–Sri Lanka Free Trade Agreement, available at http://www.doc.gov.lk/web/indusrilanka_freetrade.php (accessed on 4 October 2008).

Notes   ILFTA = India–Sri Lanka Free Trade Agreement; — = not available.
[a] Because of procedural delays, Sri Lanka was only able to fulfill the March 2006 70 percent tariff reduction in September 2006. Accordingly, the March 2008 tariff reduction has not taken place at the time of writing.

The remaining tariff lines exported by India were given a preference margin of 35 percent in March 2003, which was increased to 70 percent in September 2006 and then tariffs would be phased out after a total of 8 years in 2008.

2.1.3 Tariff Rate Quotas

India's negative list included many products of export interest to Sri Lanka, including tea and garments. To provide Sri Lanka with some degree of market access, tariff rate quotas (TRQs) were allowed for these products, with product-specific rules of origin, even though these products remained in the negative list (Table 4.2).

However, due to difficulties for Sri Lankan exporters in taking advantage of the TRQs (Section 2.3), negotiations took place to ease these restrictions. In June 2007, India relaxed the port restriction for tea imports and allowed the import of 3 million garment pieces per year, free of duty and with no sourcing requirement. For tea, the initial notification (26/2000) by India was that a 50 percent margin of preference would be provided; however, a subsequent notification in the same year revised that to a standard tariff of 7.5 percent.

2.1.4 Rules of Origin

Rules of origin (ROO) are required to prevent products of a third country being re-exported to one of the parties to the bilateral agreement, through the other party to the agreement, without substantial value added or

TABLE 4.2   ILFTA Tariff Rate Quotas

Product	Tariff preference	Quota	Other restrictions
Tea	Standard duty rate of 7.5%[a]	15 million kg annually	Entry allowed only to the ports of Cochin and Kolkata
Garments (Chapters 61 and 62)	50%	8 million pieces per year, 6 million of which need to have material sourced from India to receive preferences	—
Textiles (Chapters 51–60 and 63, except few items in Chapters 53–56)	25%	—	—

Source Respective Agreements, available at http://www.doc.gov.lk/web/indusrilanka_freetrade.php (accessed on 4 October 2008).

Notes ILFTA = Indo–Sri Lanka Free Trade Agreement; — = not available.
[a] According to the World Trade Organization (2006), India's average applied Most Favored Nation (MFN) tariff on tea and coffee is 56.3 percent.

transformation in the final exporting country. The ISFTA uses a combination of domestic value addition (DVA) and change of tariff heading (CTH) to adjudicate origin. For products including inputs from third parties, minimum DVA is 35 percent of the freight on board (F.O.B.) value of the product (Table 4.3). If the inputs originate in the importing party (for example, if Sri Lanka is exporting a product to India where some of the inputs to that product originate in India), DVA must be a minimum of 25 percent of the F.O.B. value of the product, provided that the combined value addition of the two parties is at least 35 percent of F.O.B. value of

TABLE 4.3   ILFTA Rules of Origin

Measure	Requirement
Domestic value addition	Minimum of 35% F.O.B. value
Cumulative rules of origin	Exporting country minimum value addition of 25% F.O.B. if inputs from importing country are utilized; subject to the condition that aggregate value addition is 35% F.O.B. value
Change of tariff heading	CTH at four-digit HS classification

Source ILFTA, available at http://www.doc.gov.lk/web/indusrilanka_freetrade.php (accessed on 4 October 2008).

Note F.O.B. = freight on board; HS = Harmonized Commodity Description and Coding System.

the product. In addition to fulfilling the DVA criteria, the final product being exported must have a different classification, according to the Harmonized Commodity Description and Coding System (HS Code) at the four-digit level, from all of its constituent inputs.

2.2 Economic Impacts

Even before the FTA was implemented, India had become a significant source of Sri Lankan imports. In 1999, India accounted for 8.6 percent of Sri Lanka's total import basket and was the second highest source of imports (with Japan being the highest). Sri Lankan exports to India were not substantial before the FTA, with total exports in 1999 being a mere US$47 million, around 1 percent of total exports, and India not even being among Sri Lanka's top 10 export destinations. Furthermore, in 1999 Sri Lanka's trade deficit with India was substantial (US$463 million) with an import–export ratio of 10.5:1. In 1999, Sri Lanka's main exports to India were in primary products—mainly agriculture and unprocessed metals. The major exports included pepper, which made up 20 percent, and areca nuts, which made up 11 percent, while such products as waste steel and waste paper made up 8 percent and 5.5 percent, respectively. It is clear from this passage that before the FTA, Sri Lanka's trade with India was limited in terms of both value and industrial depth. While the trade balance was weighted toward India, this was not compensated by investment flows. Foreign direct investment (FDI) from India to Sri Lanka was limited, with cumulative investment as of 1998 a mere Sri Lankan Rupees (SL Rs)165 million (US$2.5 million[1] or 1.3 percent of total FDI).

The implementation of the FTA had a dramatic impact on trade relations between the two countries (see Figure 4.1). By 2007, Sri Lanka's exports to India had increased to US$515 million (6.6 percent of total exports). India is now Sri Lanka's third largest destination for exports and largest source of imports, making up 23 percent of total imports in 2007. The trade balance between the two countries narrowed until 2006 (when the import–export ratio was 4:1 compared with14.3:1 in 1998), as the rate of growth of Sri Lanka's exports was greater than that of imports. Furthermore, FDI from India followed trade as cumulative FDI expanded to reach SL Rs 9.5 billion by 2005 (US$191.2 million or 8.3 percent of total FDI). India is now the fifth highest investor in Sri Lanka. The number of products exported from Sri Lanka to India doubled from 505 in 2000 to 1,062 by 2005 (Kelegama and Mukherjee 2007), and more important, there was a shift from primary products to processed goods. Vegetable fats and oils, refined copper, wires (copper, aluminum), margarine, rubber, and articles

FIGURE 4.1   Domestic Value Addition of Indian Investment in Sri Lanka

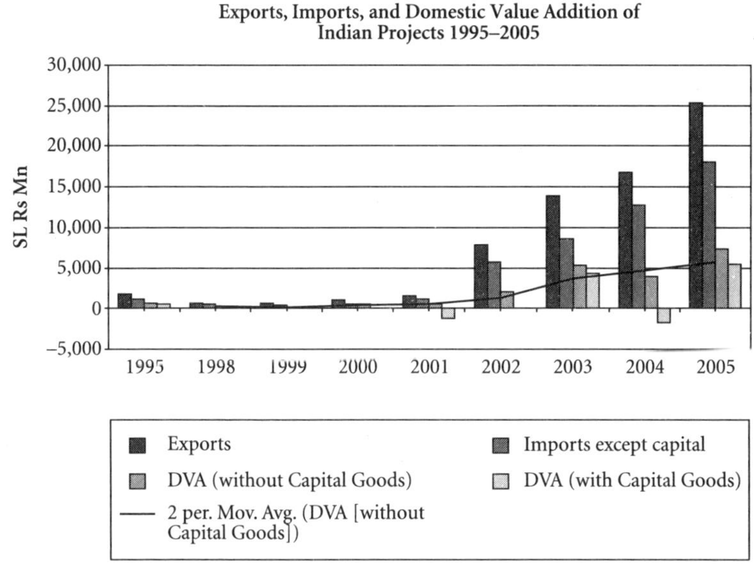

Exports, Imports, and Domestic Value Addition of
Indian Projects 1995–2005

Source   Wickremasinghe 2006.

thereof all come ahead of traditional exports such as pepper and spices. New products such as furniture (exports of which increased from US$1.7 million in 2002 to US$6.4 million in 2006), antibiotics (no exports until 2004 and reaching US$22 million in 2005), and ceramic products (US$0.8 million in 2002 increased to US$22.7 million in 2006) successfully entered the Indian market.[2] The FTA was instrumental in this expansion of trade, as 75 percent of Sri Lankan exports to India received preferential treatment in 2006, compared with 22 percent in 2001.

Thus, bilateral market access to India for the smaller South Asian economies is evolving at a much more rapid pace than under the SAFTA framework. The net result of these alternative bilateral and regional agreements in South Asia—with India playing a pivotal role—eventually may become something approximating free trade within the region. However, Pakistan is conspicuously absent in the evolving network of such alternative agreements. In contrast to the other South Asian countries, Pakistan is seeking its own trade arrangements with the East Asian region. It has signed FTAs with China (2006) and Malaysia (2007) to date.[3]

The benefits of tariff arbitrage had begun to wane since 2007. Copper exports were the first to be hit as earnings fell from US$145 million in 2005 to US$27 million in 2007. A key cause of this reduction in earnings was the change in invoicing methods after India insisted that pricing be done according to London Metal Exchange prices. This addressed the issue of underinvoicing by copper exporters to meet ROO criteria, and eligible exports reduced as a result. Exports of *vanaspati* (vegetable oil) improved in 2007 following a fall in 2006 resulting from the imposition of quotas by India. This progress is likely to be all but completely eroded in 2008, however, with the decision by India to completely slash Most Favored Nation (MFN) tariffs on palm oil imports. As a result, exporters from Sri Lanka lose their preferential margin and will not be competitive in the Indian market. The outcome of these changes will be significant in terms of Sri Lanka's trade with India because export earnings were dominated by copper and *vanaspati* for the last 3 years.

2.3 Factors Inhibiting Growth of Sri Lankan Exports

The dominance of *vanaspati* and copper in the early years of the FTA is partly due to the fact that Indian entrepreneurs invested substantially in these industries and also to the fact that other exports have failed to expand in the same manner. Several factors contribute to the lack of dynamism in the export of other tariff lines to India. The key factor is that India is not a traditional export market of Sri Lanka. Sri Lanka's export basket is dominated by garments, and these items traditionally have been exported to the United States and European Union. This structure has been cemented over several years of developing buyer relationships, establishing markets, and creating supply chains. There is naturally a degree of inertia with regard to producer preferences when these factors are taken into consideration. Nonetheless, even in the garment sector there have been some recent developments in terms of Sri Lankan producers looking to tap the Indian market. MAS, a leading apparel exporter in Sri Lanka, recently launched an intimate wear label Amante, targeting India's upper-middle class. The product is specially designed to cater to South Asian women.

Another important factor is that Sri Lanka's traditional export products (garments and tea) until very recently have been hampered by prohibitive ROOs. Garment exports to India were under the negative list except for a 50 percent margin of preference for 8 million pieces, 6 million of which would need to use Indian fabrics to receive preferences. The sourcing requirement ensured that Sri Lankan garment exports to India were not competitive relative to domestic producers and, as a result, there was less than 1 percent quota utilization. In June 2007, however, Sri Lanka was allowed 3 million garment pieces to enter India free of duty with no sourcing requirement. In the most recent secretary-level meeting of the India–Lanka CEPA in July 2008, it was agreed that Sri Lanka will be allowed to export 6 million garment pieces to India free of duty with no sourcing requirement and an additional 2 million pieces with a margin of preference of 70 percent. This is yet to be implemented as the requisite administrative processes have not been completed. Nonetheless, the most recent indications suggest that garment exports to India have expanded, taking advantage of the 3 million pieces quota. With regard to tea, given the fact that pure Ceylon tea is more expensive than tea in the Indian domestic market, Sri Lanka's primary scope of export to India was realized through the blended tea market. This is why Sri Lanka chose the ports of Kolkata and Cochin as ports of entry—that is, these ports provide easy access to Indian teas to produce a blended tea variety for the Indian market. Unfortunately, with the present agreement, the ROOs are such that blended tea has effectively no chance of penetrating the Indian market. The requirement of a CTF at the four-digit level is not practically possible. As a result, just 2.7 percent of the 15 million kg quota has been utilized by Sri Lanka (Kelegama and Mukherjee 2007). In June 2007, the port restriction on Sri Lankan imports was eased, but there was no change in the ROOs, and therefore it is unlikely that there will be an expansion of Sri Lankan tea exports to India. In order for tea exports to India to take off, a product-specific ROO that allows a CTF at the six-digit level is required.

There have also been concerns about paratariffs, particularly the state-level tariffs imposed on any products entering particular Indian states (even from other states) over and above those faced by domestic state producers. For instance, in Tamil Nadu, local producers pay a state tax of 10.5 percent, while producers from foreign countries and other states pay a tax of 21 percent, thereby eroding the preferences obtained through the FTA (Kelegama and Mukherjee 2007). It is argued that, despite the state taxes, Sri Lanka is provided a preferential advantage with respect to other international trading partners. A state like Tamil Nadu (population 66 million) is substantially larger than a country like Sri Lanka (population 20 million), however, and given Tamil Nadu's geographic proximity to Sri Lanka, it is a major export market (compared to more distant states where Sri Lankan exports are less competitive because of transport costs). Therefore, state taxes in Tamil Nadu substantially undermine Sri Lanka's competitive export potential to the Indian market. Another problem faced by Sri Lankan exporters is that, despite the insignificance of Sri Lankan exports compared to the size of the overall Indian market, Sri Lankan exports have created turbulence within particular states. For instance, Sri Lankan pepper exports are perceived to have had an adverse impact on price in the state of Kerala. Such issues, along with the surge in *vanaspati* exports to India, resulted in safeguard measures being adopted by India. *Vanaspati* imports to India were first capped and then canalized, resulting in a drastic drop in *vanaspati* exports from Sri Lanka in 2006. Similar quotas were imposed on pepper exports.

2.4 A Way Forward

Despite these bones of contention, both countries have been keen to deepen and broaden economic integration to form a CEPA. In 2003 a Joint Study Group (JSG) was commissioned to examine the potential for further economic integration between the two countries. The ensuing report published in 2004 suggested that trade in services, investment liberalization, and economic cooperation should be added to the further liberalization of trade in goods. In February 2005 the first round of technical-level negotiations of the IL-CEPA took place and, since then, 12 more technical-level negotiations have taken place as of July 2008. At the same time, negotiations took place at the domestic level as well between sector-specific stakeholders and the negotiating team. Much progress has occurred with draft offers for legally binding commitments being made in the liberalization of investment, trade in services, and reduction of the respective negative lists in the goods sector.

Trade-in-services negotiations have taken place on a positive list, request-offer approach akin to the General Agreement on Trade and Services. This approach provides Sri Lanka with the flexibility to schedule only those sectors that are within developmental interests and comfort zones. This has been important given the perceptions that services liberalization will result in flooding of the domestic service market by Indian professionals. With the positive list approach, Sri Lanka was able to make draft offers in areas where there are shortages in certain subsectors that have constrained the performance of other sectors. For example, in the maritime services sector certain skilled labor categories were not produced by Sri Lankan training facilities, and Sri Lanka made draft offers to allow the import of Indian labor within certain limitations in these categories. Furthermore, Sri Lanka recognizes the value of a services agreement in terms of attracting investment. A legally binding commitment to a particular level of liberalization provides investors with the confidence that is not available with a unilateral liberalization regime that can be backtracked overnight. Many economies are at present negotiating agreements with India, recognizing the fact that India will undoubtedly become an economic superpower sooner rather than later. The European Union, Association of Southeast Asian Nations (ASEAN), and countries like the Republic of Korea are in the process of negotiating similar agreements and, unsurprisingly, Singapore beat them all to it. Thus, in terms of export interest as well, it is important from a Sri Lankan perspective to secure legally binding market access to the Indian economy. This applies to trade in goods, services, and investment. The current level of liberalization in any country is contingent on both the domestic and international political economic climate. A shift toward a more protectionist regime could reverse the progress made in economic liberalization. In such a scenario, only a legally binding framework could ensure the continuation of at least the present status quo.

3. PAKISTAN–SRI LANKA FTA

Having obtained significant market access in India through the India–Sri Lanka Free Trade Agreement (I–LFTA), Sri Lanka was keen on doing the same with the other major economy in the South Asian region, Pakistan. The framework agreement of the PSFTA was signed in August 2002 and the agreement began implementation in June 2005.

3.1 Structure of the Agreement

Like the ILFTA, the PSFTA takes into account the asymmetry between the two economies. In this case, Sri Lanka has a larger negative list and longer tariff liberalization periods (Table 4.4).

3.1.1 Tariff Liberalization Program

Pakistan offered 206 tariff lines (at the six-digit level) for immediate zero duty, while Sri Lanka offered 102 such tariff lines. The remaining products were liberalized over a 3-year period by Pakistan, which ended in June 2008. Sri Lanka in effect has access to more than 4,000 tariff lines duty free in the Pakistan market. Sri Lanka is to liberalize the remaining products outside the negative list over a 5-year period ending in 2010 at a 20 percent margin reduction each year.

TABLE 4.4 Duty Concessions of PSFTA

Duty concessions	Pakistan's commitments (number of tariff lines)	Sri Lanka's commitments (number of tariff lines)
No Concessions (Negative List)	540	697
Immediate Zero-Duty Concessions	206	102
Tariff Rate Quotas		
Tea: Duty free 10,000 MT	4	
Apparel: 35% MOP 3 million pieces	21	
Basmati: Duty Free 6,000 MT		1
Potatoes: Duty Free 1,200 MT		1
Products entitled for MOP		
Betel: 20% MOP	1	
Cosmetics: 50% MOP	11	
Tariff Liberalization Program	34%, 67%, 100% reduction over 3 years	20%, 30%, 40%, 60%, 80%, 100% over 5 years

Source Department of Commerce of Sri Lanka.
Note MOP = margin of preferences; MT = metric tons; PSFTA = Pakistan–Sri Lanka Free Trade Agreement.

3.1.2 Negative Lists

The Pakistani negative list consists of 540 tariff lines at the six-digit level. This includes many of Sri Lankan export interests such as tea (except for a quota of 10,000 metric tons), several textile and garment items, rubber products, paper products, many dairy products, plastic products, footwear, and certain ceramics. The Sri Lankan negative list consists of 697 items, including the bulk of the agricultural sector, rubber products, paper products, footwear, ceramic products, many metals products, many motor vehicles, and parts for revenue purposes.

3.1.3 Tariff Rate Quotas

The TRQs provided by Pakistan to Sri Lanka are as follows:

- Tea—Sri Lanka can export 10,000 metric tons of tea to Pakistan free of duty per year. Any quantity over and above this amount will be faced by the MFN tariff rate (Appendix 4.1).
- Betel Leaves—According to the initial agreement, betel could be exported by Sri Lanka under a TRQ of 1,200 metric tons betel exports

per year which would receive a Margin of Preference (MOP) of 35 percent per year. However this was revised in 2007 such that the quota was lifted and an MOP of 20 percent will be provided (see below).

- Garments—3 million garment pieces exported from Sri Lanka within 21 tariff lines will be provided with a 35 percent MOP, only for a maximum of 200,000 pieces per tariff line (*Ibid.*).

The Margins of Preference (MOPs) provided by Pakistan are as follows:

- Ceramics—Five tariff lines of ceramic products will receive an MOP of 20 percent on applied MFN rates (Appendix 4.2).
- Betel Leaves—Sri Lankan betel leaves exports will receive an MOP of 20 percent of the MFN applied rate.
- Cosmetics—Eleven tariff lines of herbal cosmetic products exported by Sri Lanka's national brands will receive a 50 percent MOP on the applied MFN rate (*Ibid.*).

The TRQs provided by Sri Lanka to Pakistan are as follows:

- Basmati Rice—6,000 metric tons of long grain Pakistani rice exports will receive zero duty annually.
- Potatoes—1,000 metric tons of potatoes from Pakistan can be exported free of duty provided that two-thirds of this quota is exported during the months of June and July and the remaining one-third is exported during the months of October and November each year.

3.1.4 Rules of Origin

Like the ILFTA, the PSFTA uses two criteria to determine origin for products that are not wholly obtained in the exporting party. The PSFTA's DVA requirement is the same as that of the ILFTA at 35 percent. Similarly, for cumulative ROOs to apply, an aggregate DVA of 35 percent must apply with a minimum of 25 percent value addition in the final exporting country. The major difference between the ROOs in the ILFTA and those in the PSFTA is that for the CTH criterion, the PSFTA adopts a CTH at the six-digit level, which is substantially more favorable to Sri Lanka, particularly with regard to the export of blended tea (Appendices 4.1 and 4.2).

3.2 Economic Impacts

The PSFTA is yet to become fully operational as Sri Lanka is scheduled to complete tariff liberalization on non-sensitive list products in 2010. Pakistan has fully liberalized trade other than items in the sensitive list as of June 2008. Therefore, a complete picture in terms of economic impacts of the agreement will not be available at this stage, although some indications can be obtained. Thus far, the impact of the agreement in terms of Sri Lankan exports to Pakistan has been limited (see Figure 4.2). In 2003, Sri Lanka's exports to Pakistan were US$36 million (0.7 percent of total exports). While in absolute terms, total exports to Pakistan by 2007 had increased to US$56 million, they still accounted for a mere 0.7 percent of total exports. Furthermore, it is clear that Pakistan's exports to Sri Lanka have grown at a much faster rate during this period, increasing from US$71 million in 2003 (1 percent of total imports) to more than US$178 million in 2007 (1.6 percent of total imports) (Figure 4.2).

FIGURE 4.2   Trade between Sri Lanka and Pakistan 2003–07

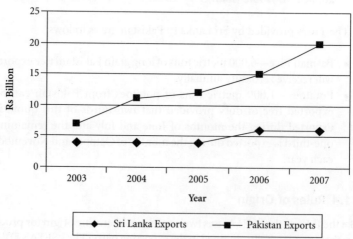

Source   Trade statistics from Department of Customs Trade Statistics Database.

The growth in Sri Lankan exports to Pakistan was largely in similar products to those exported prior to the Agreement (Figure 4.3).

The only notable change between 2002 and 2007 was the increase in exports of coconuts and the decline in exports of tea.[4] In 2006 exports of

FIGURE 4.3   Sri Lanka's Top Five Exports to Pakistan, 2002 and 2007

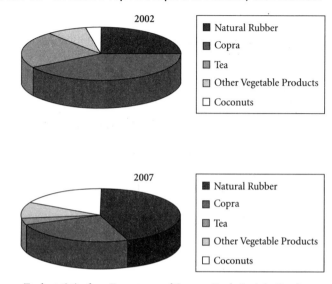

Source   Trade statistics from Department of Customs Trade Statistics Database.

tea did not use even half the quota allocation under the PSFTA and garment exports to Pakistan have thus far been negligible. It is clear that export diversification has been limited, but it remains early in the implementation of the agreement and it will take some time for the full impact of Pakistan's complete liberalization of the market to be felt. Nonetheless, some products have been exported to Pakistan taking advantage of the preferential tariffs. Fresh pineapples, sports goods, tamarind with seeds, and activated carbon are just some of the products that previously were not exported to Pakistan but now are exported using concessions.

Imports from Pakistan have grown significantly since the FTA came into place. The major import item from Pakistan is textiles and fabrics, making up 55 percent of Sri Lanka's imports from Pakistan in 2007. Other items include medicaments, potatoes, rice, and dried fish. The majority of the items imported from Pakistan do not receive benefits under the FTA. Textile and apparel articles receive MFN duty-free rates, as do medicaments. Rice and dried fish fall under the negative list and potatoes are imported under a TRQ, with the state retail firm Co-operative Wholesale Establishment (CWE) being allocated the quota. In 2006, the quota was 10,000 metric tons during Sri Lanka's off-season, and only 25 metric tons was imported by the CWE from Pakistan in that year (State of the Economy 2008). .

3.3 A Way Forward

At the first PSFTA review meeting, both countries agreed to deepen the existing FTA to form a CEPA. Thus far, one round of technical-level negotiations has taken place and the CEPA is due to include trade in services and investment and to deepen commitments in trade in goods by gradually reducing the size of negative lists. In terms of moving forward with economic relations between Sri Lanka and Pakistan, the CEPA is a rational move because it would at least bind existing levels of liberalization between the two countries. As with the case of India, it would take time for Sri Lankan producers to shift preferences and consider new markets such as Pakistan to which certain niche products could be successfully exported.

4. COMPARISON WITH SAFTA

Despite the fact that regional economic liberalization in South Asia (SAPTA commenced in 1995) began a long time before bilateral liberalization took place in the region (ILFTA began implementation in 2000), the existing bilateral agreements have significantly outpaced regional agreements. Furthermore, the depth of preferences available in both bilateral agreements is substantially greater than those of SAFTA. As a result, there is a risk that the relevance of SAFTA is diminished for countries that do enter into bilateral agreements within the region. This is certainly the case for Sri Lanka, as it has deeper access to the two largest markets in the region than what will be possible through SAFTA. This section will examine some of the differences in the agreements and suggest some steps that can be taken in SAFTA to remedy the situation.

4.1 Differences in the Structures of the Agreements

4.1.1 Negative Lists

The negative lists of India, Pakistan, and Sri Lanka in SAFTA are substantially larger than those in the respective bilateral trade agreements (Table 4.5).

TABLE 4.5   Comparison of Negative List Coverage between ILFTA, PSFTA, and SAFTA

	SAFTA	ILFTA	PSFTA
Sri Lanka	1,065	1,180	697
India	885	429	
Pakistan	1,191		540

Source   Respective agreements.
Note   ILFTA = Indo-Lanka FTA; PSFTA = Pakistan–Sri Lanka FTA; and SAFTA = South Asian Free Trade Agreement.

According to Weerakoon and Thennakoon (2008), trade restriction under SAFTA's negative lists amounts to 53 percent of current intraregional imports. A more detailed breakdown of country-by-country restriction is provided in Table 4.6.

According to Table 4.6, 42 percent of Sri Lanka's exports to India are restricted by the Indian negative list in SAFTA. However, only 3.3 percent of Sri Lanka's export value to India falls under the negative list in the ILFTA. Similarly, 44 percent of India's exports to Sri Lanka fall under the negative list in the ILFTA, but under SAFTA, the figure is 54 percent (Weerakoon and Thennakoon 2008). It is clear that the difference in market access between the ILFTA and SAFTA is substantial. With regard to ROOs, SAFTA requires a CTH at the four-digit level, whereas the PSFTA has a more favorable six-digit CTH requirement. Most important are the time frames. Sri Lanka already has complete access to the Indian and Pakistani markets (except for items in the negative list), whereas under SAFTA, this access would be available only in 2013. In the recent past, efforts at rejuvenating the Doha Round of the WTO talks have come to a

TABLE 4.6   Bilateral Trade Restriction under SAFTA

	Bangladesh	India	Maldives	Nepal	Pakistan	Sri Lanka
Percent of imports under NL						
Bangladesh		11.2	0.0	29.7	31.3	45.2
Bhutan	69.4	36.8	0.0	15.0	50.4	0.0
India	66.0		65.2	64.2	14.5	53.5
Maldives	72.9	3.6		0.0	0.0	59.2
Nepal	87.8	46.2	0.0		25.4	17.6
Pakistan	54.5	16.4	15.5	30.0		28.4
Sri Lanka	66.6	41.5	85.4	37.6	29.7	

Source   Weerakoon and Thennakoon 2008, calculated using World Integrated Trade Solution (WITS) data.
Note   NL = negative list.

standstill, and in this backdrop, other South Asian countries, particularly Bangladesh, have been considering the possibility of engaging in Bilateral FTAs with other SAARC members—further threatening the relevance of SAFTA.

4.2 Improvements Required in SAFTA

Despite the identified drawbacks in SAFTA, improvement in the agreement could salvage some degree of relevance. In the TLP, SAFTA could identify some heavily traded products in the region and provide a fast-track liberalization process for these items. In terms of trade coverage, the agreement could incorporate a binding provision to reduce the size of negative lists. As it stands, the agreement only has a vague best endeavors clause to reduce the size of negative lists within a 4-year time horizon; however, there is no binding provision. Nontariff barriers (NTBs) continue to be a problem in the implementation of the bilateral agreements, and SAFTA could score in this area if it incorporates binding commitments for the reduction of NTBs. Trade facilitation is included in SAFTA, but again it is in the form of best endeavors clauses with limited practical realism. It would be more practical to tackle a few key areas of trade facilitation, such as simplification of customs operations, transit procedures, and standards harmonization, and implement binding requirements on these measures, with special and differential treatment for least developed countries (LDCs). Finally, although CEPAs are being negotiated in the ILFTA and the PSFTA, they have not been implemented as yet. SAFTA, as it stands, covers only trade in goods, and to be a meaningful agreement, it must incorporate trade in services more substantially than what will be covered in the India–Lanka CEPA and Pakistan–Sri Lanka CEPA. In this regard, it is important to consider innovative measures to encourage commitments by the respective members, such as the common subsector approach[5] that was adopted in ASEAN. If such steps are adopted, SAFTA could still capture the interest of member countries and provide a useful format for regional economic cooperation.

5. CONCLUSION

This chapter examines the bilateral trade agreements that Sri Lanka has implemented with India and Pakistan, providing analysis on the structure of the respective agreements and their trade impacts. It was found that although the agreements have provided significant market access to Sri Lanka, full advantage has not been taken of this market access for a combination of reasons. Certain impediments to trade remain despite the existence of the FTAs. Furthermore, Sri Lankan entrepreneurs need to be more open to diversifying from traditional export markets in the United States and European Union and need to consider markets in neighboring countries as well. Finally, a comparison of bilateral agreements with SAFTA found that the latter requires much improvement to have an impact on trade within the region.

APPENDIX 4.1

TABLE A4.1   Tariff Lines Exported by Sri Lanka Subject to Tariff Rate Quota under the Pakistan–Sri Lanka Free Trade Agreement

HS Code	Product Description
0902	**Tea**
0902.10	Green tea in packets/bags in immediate packing of a content not exceeding 3 kg
0902.20	Other green tea
0902.30	Black tea and partly fermented tea in immediate packing of a content not exceeding 3 kg
0902.40	Other black tea and other partly fermented tea
Ch. 61	**Articles of Apparel; Knitted or crocheted**
6107.11	Men's and boys' under pants and briefs of cotton
6107.12	Men's and boys' under pants and briefs of MMF
6107.19	Men's and boys' under pants and briefs of other textile materials
6108.21	Women's or girls' briefs and panties of cotton
6108.22	Women's or girls' briefs and panties of MMF
6108.29	Women's or girls' briefs and panties of other textile materials
6108.31	Women's or girls' night dresses and pajamas of cotton
6108.32	Women's or girls' night dresses and pajamas of MMF
6108.39	Women's or girls' night dresses and pajamas of other textile materials
6109.10	T-shirts, singlets and other vests of cotton
6109.90	T-shirts, singlets and other vests of other textile materials
6112.31	Men's and boys' swimwear of synthetic fabrics
6112.39	Men's and boys' swimwear of other textile materials
Ch. 62	**Articles of Apparel; Not knitted or crocheted**
6207.11	Men's and boys' under pants and briefs of cotton
6207.19	Men's and boys' under pants and briefs of other textile materials

(Table A4.1 Continued)

(Table A4.1 Continued)

HS Code	Product Description
6208.21	Women's or girls' night dresses and pajamas of cotton
6208.22	Women's or girls' night dresses and pajamas of MMF
6208.29	Women's or girls' night dresses and pajamas of other textile materials
6211.11	Men's and boys' swimwear
6212.10	Brassieres
6216.0	Gloves, mitten and mitts

Source Department of Commerce, Government of Sri Lanka. Available at http://www.doc.gov.lk/web/pakissrilanka_freetrade.php (accessed on 20 October 2008).

APPENDIX 4.2

TABLE A4.2   Tariff Lines Exported by Sri Lanka Subject to Margin of Preference under Pakistan-Sri Lanka Free Trade Agreement

HS Code	Product Description	MOP
6907.10	Ceramic tiles, cubes and similar articles; unglazed	20%
6908.10	Ceramic tiles, cubes and similar articles; glazed	20%
6911.10	Tableware and kitchenware; (other than of porcelain or china)	20%
6911.90	Other tableware and kitchenware; (other than of porcelain or china)	20%
6914.10	Other ceramic articles; of porcelain or china	20%

Cosmetic products manufactured and marketed by National Brands in Sri Lanka–HS Codes 3303, 3304, 3305, 3306 and 3307.

Source Department of Commerce, Government of Sri Lanka. Available at http://www.doc.gov.lk/web/pakissrilanka_freetrade.php (accessed on 20 October 2008).

NOTES

1. The 1998 exchange rate was US$1 to SL Rs 67.8.
2. Figures from Department of Commerce trade statistics. Available at www.doc.gov.lk/web/tradestatistics.php (accessed on 6 October 2009).
3. Pakistan also entered into an FTA with Sri Lanka in 2002.
4. The likely cause of this reduction is the fact that the price of Ceylon tea increased as global demand (especially from the Middle East and Commonwealth of Independent States countries) increased substantially, making it less attractive compared with Kenyan tea, which did not increase in price to the same extent. It remains to be seen whether

the decline in tea exports is a one-off event or a continuing trend—the former is more likely given the unusually high commodity prices that prevailed through the latter half of 2007.

5. If more than three countries (including at least two LDCs) make commitments in a particular subsector, all countries have to make some commitment in that subsector. This encourages countries to make commitments in sectors that are of real trade interest.

REFERENCES

Department of Commerce. Sri Lanka. Available at http://www.doc.gov.lk/web/index.php (accessed on 6 October 2009).

Institute of Policy Studies of Sri Lanka (IPSSL). 2008. *Sri Lanka: State of the Economy 2008.* Colombo: IPSSL.

Kelegama, S., and I. Mukherjee. 2007. *Indo-Lanka Bilateral Free Trade Agreement: Six Year Performance and Beyond.* Research and Information Systems (RIS) for Developing Countries. New Delhi.

Weerakoon, D., and J. Thennakoon. 2008. "SAFTA: Which Way Forward?" *Journal of South Asian Development* 3 (1) 135–49.

Wickremasinghe, U. 2006. "Indo-Lanka Free Trade Agreement: A Survey of Progress and Lessons for the Future." Paper presented at the Roundtable on Regional Integration, Colombo, 24 November 2006.

World Trade Organization. 2006. *WTO Tariff Profiles 2006.* Geneva: WTO.

5

Connecting South Asia

The Centrality of Trade Facilitation for Regional Economic Integration

Jayanta Roy and *Pritam Banerjee*

1. INTRODUCTION

According to the World Trade Organization (WTO), trade facilitation is the process of "simplification and harmonization of international trade procedures" covering the "activities, practices, and formalities involved in collecting, presenting, communicating and processing data required for the movement of goods in international trade."[1] It relates to a wide range of activities at the border, such as import and export procedures (for example, procedures relating to customs, licensing, and quarantine); transport formalities; and payments, insurance, and other financial requirements. However, the concept of trade facilitation also is intrinsically linked to several factors behind the border. The quality of a country's domestic transport and logistics infrastructure and regulatory policies that affect the flow of goods and services within its boundaries are a vital part of the overall transaction costs of trade. Table 5.1 lists the key trade facilitation issues under two heads: (*a*) gateway issues related to trade facilitation at the border and *(b)* behind-the-border issues related to transaction costs imposed on trade within the border.

TABLE 5.1   Key Trade Facilitation Concerns

Gateway issues	Behind-the-border issues
• Customs and other border formalities like nontariff barriers	• Quality and costs of transport infrastructure
• Transparency of regulations	• Availability of multimodal transport
• Efficacy of regulatory agencies	• Quality of logistical support in the hinterland such as warehousing facilities
• Efficacy and logistical capability of ports, airports, and land border crossings	• Efficacy and transparency of regulations of within-country border crossings (that is, crossing across provincial or municipal lines)
• Cost and quality of international transport linkages	
• Quality of international institutional linkages such as Mutual Recognition Agreements (MRA) and Preshipment Inspection (PSI) Agreements	

Source   Authors' compilation from various sources.

The importance of reducing the transaction costs of trade through better trade facilitation is underlined by the fact that for 168 out of 215 U.S. trading partners, transport cost barriers outweigh tariff barriers (World Bank 2002, 100). Trade facilitation assumes even greater importance now in the arena of international trade given recent trends in the structure of goods (and services) traded and the sophistication of such products. Modern supply chain management techniques and the rapid spread of information technologies and e-commerce have progressively increased the use of just-in-time techniques by manufacturing industries and have encouraged the growth of integrated global supply, production, and distribution systems. In this environment, where manufacturers rely on the uninterrupted reception of the necessary components to meet production contingencies, businesses cannot afford to have imported or exported goods tied up for long periods because of unnecessary or overcomplicated trade procedures and requirements.

The spatial distribution of global production system is no longer simply driven by labor cost arbitrage. The competitiveness of an operation within the global production system is a combined function of cost, time, and reliability. Differences in cost of production, especially those related to labor, are increasingly being overcome through the introduction of automated systems and greater productivity. As the opportunities of differentiation in terms of price diminish, competition within the global production system will be in terms of reliability and time. Thus, countries that ignore the issue of trade facilitation will do so at the cost of compromising their global competitiveness in the long run.

As emerging market economies, including those in South Asia, seek to stimulate growth in trade, it is important for policymakers to understand that trade facilitation plays the pivotal role in this effort. The three crucial trade expansion strategies—diversification, moving up the value chain, and encouraging export-oriented entrepreneurship—all depend to a large degree on the efficacy of trade facilitation measures (Arnold 2007, 191–92). Diversification requires the introduction of new supply chains and complementary improvements in logistic services. Moving up the value chain to more sophisticated products would require participating in and managing a more complex supply chain and undertaking an increasing number of transactions, which by definition would require better logistical infrastructure. Encouraging export-driven entrepreneurship in emerging countries would require that the costs of trading for small and medium enterprises (SMEs) be kept low. Such SMEs are typically involved in niche product segments or work as subcontractors within the global supply chain. However, niche markets and small-scale shipments have more challenging international logistics, while subcontracting requires better domestic logistics, making trade facilitation crucial for such activities (Arnold 2007, 191–92).

Intraregional trade in South Asia, especially through formal channels, remains abysmally low at about 2 percent of total trade. Although a large part of the problem is related to a high level of formal trade barriers and the political unwillingness to liberalize interregional trade, the poor state of trade facilitation, as well as both gateway and behind-the-border issues, also play a critical role in keeping inter-South Asian trade low. The following sections of this chapter present the broad issue of trade facilitation in the South Asian context. Section 1 introduces the current scenario in terms of trade facilitation and transaction costs in the South Asian region in comparison with other parts of the developing world. Section 2 provides a brief overview of some of main trade facilitation issues and policies in a country-by-country basis for the six major South Asian economies. Section 3 discusses the trade facilitation content of the two major regional trade integration initiatives in the region—SAFTA and BIMSTEC. Section 4 provides some concrete policy recommendations and the way forward. Section 5 concludes the chapter.

2. TRADE FACILITATION AND TRANSACTION COSTS IN SOUTH ASIA: AN OVERVIEW

While the concept of trade facilitation can cover a wide array of transaction costs imposed by the entire infrastructure of economic exchange, this chapter will narrow its focus on a few specific aspects. Essentially, the focus will be on the following:

- Regulatory issues at ports of entry.
- Transport and logistical infrastructure supporting both cross-border trade as well as behind-the-border movement of traded goods, including shipping, air, road, rail, and inland water transport.

The centrality of the two above themes to regional integration is highlighted by Table 5.2, which provides Wilson and Otsuki's (2007) estimates on the gains for South Asian intraregional trade accruing from improvements in regulatory and logistical issues.

TABLE 5.2   Gain in Intraregional Trade from Capacity Development in Trade Facilitation (US$ millions)

	Customs modernization	Regulatory reforms	Port efficiency (air and marine)	Services infrastructure	Total gain
Bangladesh	144	71	228	339	782
India	193	123	314	519	1,149
Pakistan	29	42	74	191	336
Sri Lanka	63	41	97	175	376
South Asia	429	278	712	1224	2,643

Source   Wilson and Otsuki 2007.

While the overall gain is a substantive US$2.6 billion in intraregional trade, an increase of more than half of current levels of trade, two important messages need to be drawn from Table 5.2. First, the maximum gains come from improvements in port efficiency and logistical infrastructure, the poor quality of which remains a critical impediment for trade in South Asia. Second, this table does not include the gains to intraregional trade that can accrue from improvements in behind-the-border factors such as quality of roads, railways, and investment in multimodal transport. Given the high incidence of transaction costs from behind-the-border logistics and transport in South Asia, gains from improvements in these factors can be expected to be greater than combined gains of all the four factors in Table 5.2. Keeping these lessons in mind, the following paragraphs of this section will provide an overview of the current state of regulatory and logistical issues related to trade in South Asia. This section provides the regional overview on the main themes, and the following section will take up the country-specific issues related to different aspects of trade facilitation. Section 4, which follows the discussion of regional initiatives on trade facilitation, will address the policy issues and recommendations related to the major trade facilitation themes discussed in this section.

2.1 Regulatory Issues

2.1.1 Documentation Requirements and the Use of Information Technology

Keeping with the global trend of reforms of customs administrations, South Asian countries too have seen improvements in the overall quality of their customs-related bureaucracy. With the exception of Afghanistan and Bhutan, the widespread use of electronic data interchange (EDI) and the increasing use of paperless transactions has become the norm in South Asia's customs administration (Domus 2005, 13). However, the scope of EDI and the use of information technology (IT) are still limited, and there is ample room for improving the level of procedural simplicity and documentation requirements. In all countries, many agencies, apart from customs, involved with the clearance of goods are not yet up to the mark in automation, and hence paper trails remain. It is not so much the absence of an IT infrastructure, which increasingly is less of a concern, but rather the lack of movement in procedural reforms that is holding up further efficiency gains at South Asia's customs gateways. Figure 5.1 presents the average documentation requirements to export, and Figure 5.2 provides the average number of days required for customs clearance.

Figure 5.1 illustrates that South Asian countries have much higher documentation requirements than other emerging market economies and countries such as China. Figure 5.2 shows that major South Asian economies of Bangladesh, India, and Pakistan are below the average for lower-middle-income economies and much below the Chinese average in terms of number of days required for customs clearance. This means that despite the use of EDI, South Asian countries require further reforms in to reduce documentation requirements and to streamline procedures with the use of IT if the region is to reach global standards.

FIGURE 5.1 Number of Documents Required to Export

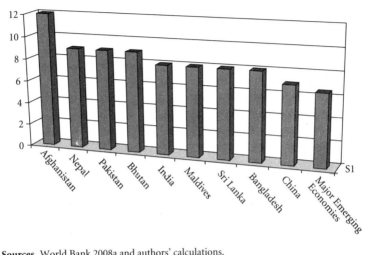

Sources World Bank 2008a and authors' calculations.

FIGURE 5.2 Average Days Taken for Customs Clearance

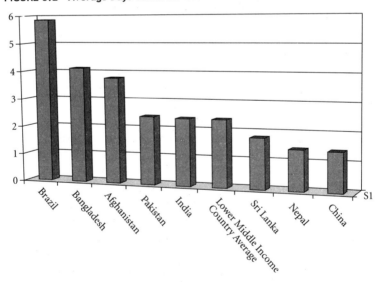

Sources World Bank 2008a and authors' calculations.

2.1.2 Security Requirements: Protecting Citizens and Consumers

Gateways have important security concerns related to protecting the nation's consumers from harm by using stringent quality controls, including sanitary and phytosanitary standards (SPS) that are applicable to food and agricultural products. Given the sensitivity of issues related to cross-border terrorism and narcotics, gateways also need to implement proper policing requirements to protect their citizens from drugs and terror. However, current procedures in the implementation of health and safety certification at the borders of South Asia remain far from efficient. Coordination is lacking between agencies are involved in this process, and the use of IT is limited. Procedural reforms to streamline the verification and certification process and modern risk-management techniques are also lacking. Figure 5.3 compares the average rates of physical inspection in South Asian and some other emerging economies.

FIGURE 5.3   Rate of Physical Inspection of Cargo

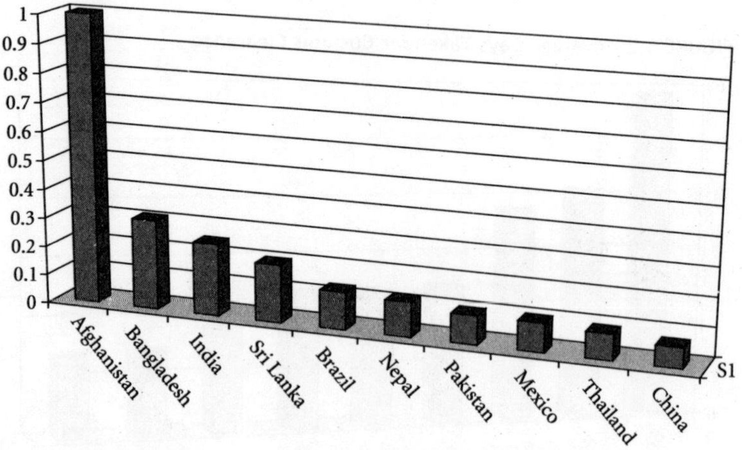

Sources World Bank 2008a and author's calculations.

Figure 5.3 clearly shows that South Asian countries have far higher rates of physical inspection than their counterparts in the developing world, especially those in Southeast and East Asia. This rate of inspection reflects the poor risk management techniques and efficient sampling methods that cut back on the need for physical inspection of goods.

2.2 Logistics and Transport Issues

2.2.1 Efficacy of Ports

Efficient ports (sea and land based) and airports that can handle large volumes of container traffic and that are linked to an efficient network of multimodal transport systems are essential features of a successful modern economy. However, most of the important South Asian seaports are inefficient and face severe congestion and delays. Some ports such as Karachi, Colombo, and the Jawaharlal Nehru Port Trust near Mumbai have seen some improvements in recent years, but their performance remains poor relative to ports in other parts of Asia, not just in comparison with leading hubs like Dubai, Singapore, and Shanghai, but also in comparison with even smaller, less important shipping hubs like Laem Chabang in Thailand and Port Klang in Malaysia (UNESCAP 2002, 2004). Figure 5.4 compares the median lead time to import goods, which is a good proxy for port efficacy.

FIGURE 5.4   Lead Time to Import Lead Time to Import (median days)

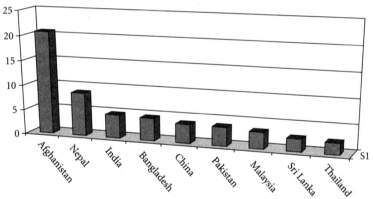

Sources World Bank 2008a and author's calculations.

Figure 5.4 shows that South Asian economies, except Sri Lanka and Pakistan, are behind their leading Asian counterparts in the time taken to import goods, and this relative inefficiency of South Asian ports plays an important role in delaying the movement of goods across borders. The average container dwell time in Chittagong (Bangladesh) is between 18 and 20 days, whereas it is between 10 and 12 days in comparable ports in

Southeast Asia (Domus 2005, 29). The average turnaround time for Indian ports is 4.7 days compared with averages of 1.5 to 2 days in Southeast Asia, while the pre-berth waiting time is almost one whole day. In many Indian ports, the equipment utilization rate is a poor 30 percent as a result of inefficient management (Domus 2005, 45).

The development of South Asian overland points of entry, such as Benapole between India and Bangladesh and Birgunj between India and Nepal, is even more critical to regional integration than seaports. These overland crossings are among the most inefficient in the world, and little effort has been made to improve their conditions. Behind-the-border issues, such as the poor quality of national road and rail infrastructure, are major causes of inefficiency of overland routes. Inadequate infrastructures at the land ports at the border are also to blame. For example, at the Benapole border, lines of 1,500 trucks or more often have to wait for up to five days to get clearance (Subramanian and Arnold 2001, 42). Not just infrastructure, but national policies play an important role in causing such inefficiencies. Bangladesh's policy of not allowing foreign trucks to operate in its territory necessitates transhipment from Indian and Nepali trucks into Bangladeshi trucks, causing huge delays at the border. Some of the key problems common to all South Asian border crossings and land ports are as follows:

- Limited number of designated overland routes between countries and poor ICT and modern infrastructure.
- Congestion.
- Trucks of one country often not allowed into the other, or are allowed only under strict conditions that limit operability.
- Lack of warehousing and proper storage facilities as cargoes await transhipment into trucks from one side to the other.
- Rent-seeking by officials.
- Poor quality of transport connectivity with the hinterland and lack of multimodal transport linkages.

2.2.2 Overland Road and Rail Linkages Connecting South Asian Economies

Despite an integrated road and rail network that connected most of South Asia during the colonial era, overland connectivity between South Asian countries today is suffering and is hostage to the political climate prevailing in the region. This is even more tragic given that India, with its central location in South Asia, has one of the world's largest rail and road systems. Pakistan's refusal to allow overland traffic to India from Afghanistan and Bangladesh's reluctance to open an overland route connecting north-east India to the rest of South Asia and the port of Chittagong has prevented a trans–South Asian road network from emerging. Even where overland routes do exist, such as between Bangladesh and Nepal and Bangladesh and Bhutan through India, behind-the-border issues such as poor quality of roads, rent-seeking officialdom, and poor quality of trucks (largely due to regulatory incentives in the region that keep the trucking sector fragmented and small scale) have prevented such overland road routes from emerging. Such policy oversight in investing in a trans–South Asian road network is tragic, as a Kabul to Chittagong integrated road system could have embedded the South Asian region as the central element within the emergent trans-Eurasian road network stretching from St. Petersburg and Istanbul to Singapore and Busan.

Overland railways in South Asia are also suffering from lack of regional initiatives. A major problem is that different South Asian countries use different track gauges, and unlike other parts of the world, especially in Europe and among Association of Southeast Asian Nations (ASEAN) members, where there is an active effort to harmonize track gauges and other rail-related equipment, South Asia has not begun to create a cohesive policy in this direction. Like roads, railways also suffer from behind-the-border issues that limit their use, even when overland routes do exist (as between India and Bangladesh and India and Nepal). The critical behind-the-border issues are as follows:

- Lack of efficient railway dry ports with logistical support.
- Rent-seeking and theft of cargo while in transit.
- Lack of multimodal linkages with railways.
- Lack of efficient and cheap transhipment facilities between rail hubs and seaports (in some cases).

Like in the case of roads, a trans–South Asian railway network (with a ferry service connecting Sri Lanka) could become the hub for a trans-Asian rail transit system stretching from Iraq to Singapore. Such a network looks improbable right now, but if South Asian countries play the lead, the region could provide the impetus for other parts of Asia to follow suit.

Table 5.3 outlines the importance of behind-the-border overland routes to South Asia's trade integration within and outside the region.

TABLE 5.3   Transport Time via Transhipment Hubs

	From Kolkata	From Colombo
North Europe	25–32 days	13–20 days
U.S. East Coast	36–41 days	26–29 days
Mediterranean	24–29 days	12–17 days

Source   Arnold 2007.

The high monetary and time-related costs of overland routes, a result of inefficient infrastructure behind the border, do not allow a rationalization of transport hubs, especially container-related hubs. As Table 2.3 illustrates, certain hubs such as Colombo have a marked advantage in terms of time (and by association cost) over Kolkata and other ports. Similarly, exports from Nepal headed to Europe or North America would benefit if they could effectively access Mumbai port rather than using Kolkata/Haldia. For example, the cost of exporting a carpet from Nepal to Europe using Mumbai instead of Kolkata would save US$1,300 (Subramanian and Arnold 2001, 58), a substantial amount equaling 30 to 40 percent of the total value of export and would save 7–10 days in terms of time.

An efficient overland infrastructure would have allowed goods to move smoothly across South Asia, reaching out to the most efficient hub using multimodal means. The resultant competition would have led to the emergence of efficient hub and feeder route combinations using rail, road, and regional shipping routes, greatly reducing the transaction costs imposed on South Asia's entrepreneurs. Many of these entrepreneurs are left out of the global and the regional market precisely because they are priced out of it by the incidence of transaction costs on trading.

2.2.3 Cost of Freight

The cost of freight traveling from or into South Asian sea- and airports is relatively high. Figure 5.5 compares the relative cost of a 40-foot container for import to South Asia's major economies and some selected Asian countries.

Figure 5.5, while underlying the relatively higher costs for containers destined for major South Asian economies (exceptions being Bangladesh and Sri Lanka), also highlights the point about poor behind-the-border logistics made earlier. Landlocked countries (Afghanistan, Nepal) and countries with relatively large hinterlands (India, Pakistan) have to depend more on behind-the-border logistical support as the goods move across the hinterland into the ports, increasing costs of trade.

FIGURE 5.5   Typical Charge for a 40-ft Container for Imports (USD)

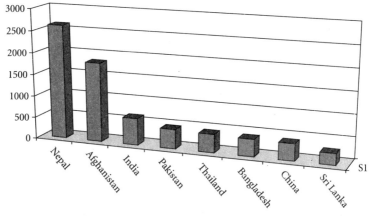

Sources World Bank 2008a and author's calculations.

Both China and Thailand also have significantly large hinterlands, and yet have much lower costs (although the economic centers that do most of the trade in both these countries tend to be near their major seaports). In the case of Bangladesh, however, the Logistics Performance Indicators reports a low figure for import (US$4,396, as reported in Figure 5.5) and exports (US$210). Another source (Domus 2005, 29) reports that the average cost of a container for export exceeds US$600 and that total transport costs for textiles from Bangladesh (its most important export) account for more than 15 percent of total costs and are more than twice (in percentage terms) than those of its competitors such as India, Sri Lanka, and Taiwan, China.

Figure 5.6 shows that the cost of airfreight from South Asia to the United States (a good proxy for airfreight costs in general[2]) is relatively high compared with some selected Asian countries.

Cheap airfreight is important for time-sensitive exports such as high-end agro products and high-end textiles. Given South Asia's great distances, airfreight is bound to play a part in the expansion of interregional trade over the years, and the poor condition of the regions' airports and related freight-handling services do not bode well for the region's exporters and importers (Domus 2005).

The next section will provide a brief overview of some of the country-specific trade facilitation issues, policies, and recent developments.

FIGURE 5.6 Average Cost of Air Freight to the United States (USD per lbs)

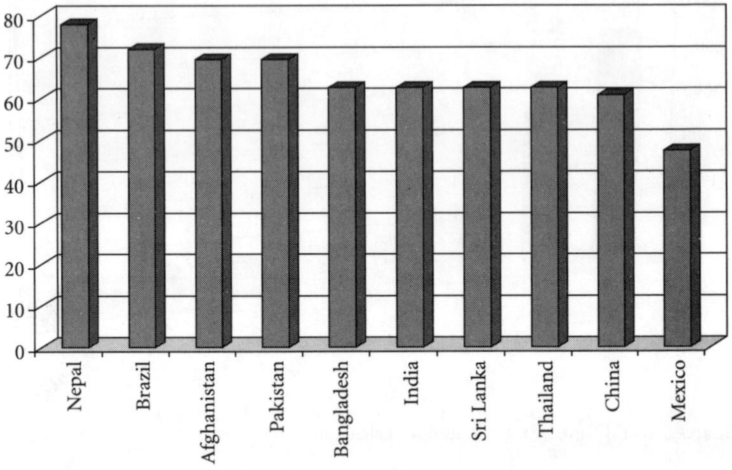

Sources World Bank 2008a and authors' calculations.

3. TRADE FACILITATION ISSUES AND POLICIES IN SOUTH ASIAN COUNTRIES: A BRIEF OVERVIEW

The purpose of this section is not to present a comprehensive report on trade facilitation for each of the South Asian economies, but rather to briefly touch on some of the key concerns and major policy responses with respect to trade facilitation in recent years.

3.1 Afghanistan

The key issues for Afghanistan trade facilitation are the lack of connectivity, lack of trained human resources, and lack of proper equipment. In terms of connectivity, a key concern has been the lack of access to South Asia's largest market, India, because of Pakistani opposition to the development of an overland route between India and Afghanistan via Pakistan. Afghanistan's access to the seaports of Karachi and Gwadar in Pakistan is hampered by the poor quality of roads, security issues, and logistical hurdles, although Pakistan currently remains Afghanistan's only outlet to maritime trade.

Afghanistan, with help from India and Iran, is developing an all-weather double-carriage road between Zaranj on the Iranian border and Dilaram in western Afghanistan. This road will link the Iranian port of Chahbahar to the Herat–Kandahar highway, linking the Persian Gulf to Central Asia and provide the Afghans with a more efficient and secure outlet to the sea. Multilateral and bilateral aid is also helping Afghanistan built crucial logistical linkages between Afghanistan and Tajikistan (Kunduz–Faizabad highway) and Turkmenistan (Herat–Torghundi highway). Besides roads, attention has been paid to the development of air-transport linkages. The World Bank and the Japanese government have been helping Afghanistan develop the Kabul international airport. Three other airports (Herat, Mazar-i-Sharif, and Jalalabad) have been identified as priority development projects.

3.2 Bangladesh

Historically, poor transport facilities and infrastructure have been great impediments to the development of international trade in Bangladesh. Bangladesh's infrastructure also suffers from deterioration caused by periodic flooding and soil erosion. Some of the key issues for Bangladeshi trade facilitation are as follows:

- Inadequate development of a multimodal system that combines roads with railways, and even more important, inland waterways, the proper development of which can go a long way toward increasing connectivity in a riverine geography like Bangladesh.
- Congestion and inefficiency at major ports, especially Chittagong (sea) and Benapole (land).
- A limited role for the private sector in transport and trade facilitation.
- Inefficient coordination and institutional deficit across three major ministries dealing with transport, commerce, and customs administration.
- Limited IT support for basic customs functions.
- Severely constrained customs administration resources (both physical and human resources).

Since 1992, Bangladesh has undertaken substantive reforms in customs administration and has implemented ASYCUDA (Automated Systems for Customs Data) in five ports (Dhaka Customs House, Dhaka Inland

Container Depot, Chittagong, Mongla, and Benapole). In 1999, as part of the reforms process and implementation of ASYCUDA, a customs modernization initiative called Customs Administration Modernization (CAM) funded by the World Bank was put in place. Under the aegis of the CAM initiative, import clearance procedures were simplified by reducing the number of signatures required, and the frequency of physical inspection of cargo was substantially reduced (Khan 2004, 98). Bangladesh still needs to implement substantive reforms in the transport sector, invest in physical infrastructure, and broaden the scope of the customs modernization project. A bilateral understanding with India that allows India overland routes (to north-east India as well as Southeast Asia) has the potential to make Bangladesh a regional trade and transit hub.

3.3 India

India still has several problem areas in trade facilitation, and substantive transaction costs are involved in trading with the nation. While some impressive gains have been made over the last decade in terms of eradicating transaction costs, a lot of work needs to be done to bring India up to the global standards in this area. In India, like some of the other South Asian economies, it was felt that IT-led modernization and automation would lead to huge improvements in trade facilitation. Although introduction of automated processes and EDI did enhance trade facilitation, work done by two specialized policy entities (the Task Force on Indirect Taxes of 2002 and the Working Group on Trade Facilitation [WGTF]) of 2004), chaired by one of the authors of this chapter, clearly has shown that, without accompanying institutional and procedural changes, effective trade facilitation cannot take place (Roy and Banerjee 2007, 310–11).

The WGTF study, which focused on the problems of Indian exporters,[3] found the average dwell time is between one and two hours. An estimated 85 percent to 95 percent of the exports are cleared at sea formations within four hours, whereas in the case of air customs formations, this figure is in excess 98 percent. However, the report also considered the fact that dwell time figures for exports may be understated because they do not take into account the clearances required from several other agencies before goods arrive at customs. Furthermore, work done in 2002 by the Task Force on Indirect Taxes had pointed out that the process of prior clearances involves up to 257 signatures from 30 different agencies that may even take a couple of days to punch in the data. Clearance of goods also is delayed on account of withdrawal of samples or the verification of price of goods falling under various exports incentive schemes (Roy 2002). Progress has been slow since 2005 on several of these fronts.

Unlike Pakistan and Sri Lanka, India has never tried to create an umbrella trade facilitation body that includes all the major public and private stakeholders along the lines of Sweden's or the United Kingdom's governing trade bodies. This is a major policy shortcoming, especially given India's status as an emerging economic power, one that is central to South Asian region, and thus in a position to take the lead in a South Asian regional integration initiative with trade facilitation as its focus. Far too many agencies are involved in the clearance process in India, with leadership and accountability issues not addressed yet. A proper discussion of India's behind-the-border logistical and infrastructure problems, including the poor condition of its overland border crossings with Bangladesh, Bhutan, Myanmar, and Nepal, would require a separate paper; some of the key points are summarized below. It is important to realize, however, that given India's geography, the quality of its behind-the-border infrastructure has enormous bearing on the connectivity between South Asian countries and on access to seaports for the landlocked countries of Bhutan and Nepal.

India faces the following logistical issues:

- Lack of multimodality, and poor use of its extensive rail network
- Congested, inefficiently run ports.
- Lack of nearby air-cargo ports in large parts of the country.
- Near nonexistence of any effective inland water transport system feeding into ports, despite the huge potential.
- Inefficiently run state-level (provincial) border crossings; complaints of rent-seeking and harassment in the name of security abound.
- Overlapping jurisdictions implementing border–related procedures leading to delay, discretionary powers to officials (and associated rent-seeking), and lack of transparency.
- Extremely poor feeder roads in large parts of the country combined with poor warehousing and logistics.

3.4 Nepal

Nepal's mountainous terrain and associated difficulty of connectivity has been a major impediment for effective trade facilitation. Nepal faces an acute shortage of trade facilitation–related equipments such as weigh-bridges, X-ray machines, and even enough computers and faxes (Dahal 2004, 124). Nepal's customs administration also lacks personnel with adequate training and experience to implement modern trade facilitation procedures (Dahal 2004).

The country has implemented ASYCUDA and has introduced a new single custom declaration form (Single Administrative Document or SAD), but the rate of physical inspection remains high,[4] even though it has come down in recent years. Despite the implementation of SAD, documentation requirements also remain relatively high, as do the number of bureaucratic procedures. An important development for trade facilitation in Nepal has been the implementation of the Advanced Cargo Information System (ACIS). The ACIS allows traders to track their shipments and also get advance notice of cargo arrival, which allows for better logistical coordination.

The absence of a direct rail link between Nepal and Kolkata, and the congestion and inefficiency at the Birgunj border with India, are major trade facilitation issues for Nepal. The existing route for most Nepalese exports through Kolkata involves transhipment via Singapore or Colombo, adding to costs of trading. As discussed earlier, better overland connectivity to Mumbai, which has direct shipping facilities to the European Union, Middle East, and the United States, will go a long way toward helping Nepal's trade. Nepal is strategically located between China and India, and adequate investment in trade facilitation infrastructure at its borders combined with investment in roads could allow to the country to emerge as a major trading hub between western China (including Tibet) and India.

This is very much within the realm of possibility, because the relationship between the two Asian giants, China and India, normalizes, and Chinese investment in its western provinces leads to increasing demand for imports (Roy and Banerjee 2005).

3.5 Pakistan

Like other South Asian countries, Pakistan suffers from the lack of an integrated transport network and absence of institutional convergence between the various ministries and departments that regulate, plan, or control its road, rail, air, and maritime transport systems. Pakistan's ports have seen substantive improvements in the recent past, however, especially in the container terminals at Karachi and Port Qasim. Pakistan on average has better roads than other parts of South Asia and one of the lowest road-transport tariffs in the world (Bashir 2007, 4).

Trade facilitation activity commenced in Pakistan in August 2001 with the establishment of a National Trade and Transport Facilitation Committee (NTTFC) and initiation of work on a World Bank–funded Trade and Transport Facilitation Project (TTFP) with technical assistance of the United Nations Conference on Trade and Development (UNCTAD). NTTFC is chaired by the secretary of the Ministry of Commerce, and its membership includes the ministries related to trade transport and finance; public sector organizations dealing with customs, trade, and transport; and private sector bodies representing the industry, trading community, and service providers like insurance companies (Ministry of Commerce, Government of Pakistan 2007, 23–25). The NTTFC's institutional structure should be followed in other South Asian countries. However, the success of the NTTFC has been modest and mostly related, like the trade facilitation efforts across the border in India, to customs reform.

The three major projects achievements under the aegis of the NTTFC are as follows:

- Introduction of a SAD as the standard for the Pakistan Goods Declaration (GD).
- Introduction of an automated customs clearance system based on the Risk Management System (RMS).
- Development of a comprehensive single window for all customs clearance operations called the Pakistan Customs Computerized System (PACCS), a completely paperless, Web-based online system.

Much needs to be done in terms of developing a logistical infrastructure in Pakistan. The country's railways, underfunded and underutilized, need attention. Special attention also needs to be given to the proper development of inland water transport. Overland routes from Afghanistan should be given priority development status and made more secure. Given Pakistan's geography, it can emerge (as the region historically has been) as the center of a trading network connecting Central Asia, Persian Gulf countries, and South Asia. The two prerequisites for that to happen are infrastructure and political understanding with its neighbors.

3.6 Sri Lanka

Sri Lanka is the pioneer of trade facilitation in South Asia. The country set up an umbrella body of private and public stakeholders called the Sri Lanka Trade Facilities Committee (SRILPRO) as early as 1980. The mandate for

SRILPRO was to help the government eliminate superfluous regulatory and procedural mechanisms and make the customs administration more transparent. By the late 1990s, however, lack of proper funding, inability to retain the right kind of interest, and lack of interest on the part of certain important stakeholders led to its demise (Shanta and De Silva 2006).

The country's next major initiative has been the Sri Lanka Automated Cargo Clearance System implemented since 2002, which allows electronic processing of documentation related to imports, exports, transhipments, and e-banking (Dissanayake 2005, 13). However, the assumption that automated electronic processing would necessarily lead to efficiency seems not to have been fully borne out, and recent evidence suggests that the total time requirement for dealing with administrative formalities have not come down significantly (Shanta and De Silva 2007).

The Colombo transhipment hub, despite some problems, remains one of the most efficient ports in the region. The ambitious expansion plans for this port, once completed, will lead to reduction of congestion and better facilities. Sri Lanka's biggest challenges in terms of trade facilitation are behind-the-border problems. The extremely poor quality of Sri Lankan roads makes transport from the hinterland to the ports difficult. The concept of multimodality (that is, using a combination of rail and road) does not exist and, regardless, is difficult to achieve in a country with the size and terrain of Sri Lanka. The ongoing political tensions add security challenges to the transaction costs of domestic movement of goods and services.

4. TRADE FACILITATION MEASURES IN REGIONAL AGREEMENTS IN THE SOUTH ASIAN REGION

This section will briefly discuss trade facilitation measures SAFTA and BIMSTEC, the two trade-related regional agreements currently in place in South Asia.[5] Both SAFTA and BIMSTEC disappoint in terms of their scope, ambition, and commitment to trade facilitation. The failure of both these agreements to proactively take up trade facilitation measures seems especially stark in comparison to initiatives like the Greater Mekong Sub-region (GMS), comprising Cambodia, China, Laos People's Democratic Republic, Myanmar, Thailand, and Vietnam. In 1992, with the Asian Development Bank's assistance, these six countries entered into a program of sub-regional economic cooperation specifically designed to enhance the development of infrastructure and promote the freer flow of goods and people.[6]

4.1 SAFTA

SAFTA, whose stated objective is to create a free trade area in South Asia (that includes all the member states of the South Asian Association for Regional Cooperation [SAARC][7]) by 2016, also incorporates a few modest goals in terms of trade facilitation and trade facilitation cooperation on a regional basis. Some of the specific trade facilitation measures in SAFTA include the following (Chaturvedi 2007):

- A protocol ensuring regular publication of laws and regulations pertaining to trade-related measures by all member countries (transparency measure).
- Notification of any changes to mandatory requirements that affect trade (transparency measure).
- Right of appeal for disputes and disagreements related to eligibility for preferential treatment.
- Recognition of a certificate for rules of origin (ROO) issued by the exporting member by the importing member,[8] and a consultation mechanism in case of disputes regarding ROO.[9]

In addition, Article 8 of SAFTA makes a vague "commitment" by members to "consider" the following trade facilitation measures:[10]

- Simplification and harmonization of standards, customs procedures, and customs classification based on the Harmonized Commodity Description and Coding System (HS coding system).
- Cooperation mechanisms between customs administration, especially with respect to disputes at customs entry points.
- Mutual recognition of tests and reciprocal accreditation of testing laboratories.
- Overland transit facilities for efficient intra-SAARC trade with special regard to the needs of landlocked countries.
- Development of transport and logistics infrastructure.
- Simplification of procedures for business visas.

Although not explicitly mentioned in Article 8, customs cooperation entails the development of protocols to move toward mutual recognition of electronic signatures and digital certificates (Chaturvedi 2007).

Thus, SAFTA steers clear of making any specific, actionable, and time-bound commitments on the critical trade facilitation issues afflicting cross-border transactions in South Asia, such as overland transit facilities, poor administrative quality of customs and other bureaucracies at the border, the lack of harmonization of rules and procedures, the lack of institutional trust between authorities in different countries, and any real movement toward convergence of the IT platforms so that data can move seamlessly between the operating systems of different countries. Furthermore, the agreement, unlike the GMS initiative, offers no mechanism to address the critical logistics and transportation bottlenecks, including the substantive behind-the-border issues, and makes no commitment to the development of efficient overland border crossings.

4.2 BIMSTEC

BIMSTEC is a sub-regional grouping formed with the explicit ambition of integrating the South and Southeast Asian regions. The group's members are Bangladesh, Bhutan, India, Myanmar, Nepal, Sri Lanka, and Thailand. BIMSTEC does not include any formal, explicit agenda on trade facilitation. The agreement identifies transport and communication as a priority subsector for "voluntary" cooperation and makes vague commitments to implement mutual recognition of standards, establish protocols for ROO, and engender institutional cooperation among customs administrations. It also proposes preparatory work on the following three transportation projects:[11]

- Feasibility Study in Short-Sea Shipping Development in Bay of Bengal (Thai Proposal).
- Preparation of BIMSTEC Framework Agreement on Multimodal Transport (Thai Proposal).
- Detailed Design of Three Pagoda Pass Railway line on the Thai-Myanmar border.

The relevance of BIMSTEC as a vehicle for trade facilitation in South and Southeast Asia has declined since the two main drivers (India and ASEAN and Thailand and Myanmar) are negotiating a comprehensive free trade agreement (FTA). India already has an FTA with Sri Lanka, has an economic protocol with Bhutan, and negotiating a comprehensive treaty on economic exchange and cooperation with newly elected government in Nepal. These FTAs and economic protocols all lack an ambitious trade facilitation agenda, however. The final section of this chapter deals with policy recommendations, starting with suggestions on how a reformed BIMSTEC could meet this deficit by becoming a treaty on comprehensive trade facilitation reform.

5. POLICY RECOMMENDATIONS

Given the lack of trust between India and Pakistan that has persisted over the decades, with no prospect of resolution in the near future, it is difficult for SAFTA to emerge as a dynamic institution for regional integration. South Asia's economic integration is too important a part of the regional development agenda to be held hostage to a bilateral political dispute that excludes six of the region's eight countries. A trans–South Asian linkage with Central Asia via Afghanistan also has been made the subject of the India–Pakistan bilateral political dispute. BIMSTEC has emerged as an alternative institutional basis for South Asian integration, as it includes all SAARC countries except Afghanistan, Maldives, and Pakistan. BIMSTEC easily can be extended to include Maldives and, simultaneously a joint protocol between Afghanistan, India, Iran, and Sri Lanka could create an integrated transport agreement linking Afghanistan and rest of Central Asia to South Asia via the Persian Gulf port of Chahbahar.

South Asian member countries of BIMSTEC, in conjunction with Thailand and Myanmar, should consider extending the membership of the group to Cambodia, Malaysia, Maldives, Laos People's Democratic Republic, Singapore, and Vietnam and reorient the focus of this group (again following GMS) as a nodal agreement on trade facilitation. The following paragraphs will outline the agenda for such a nodal agency toward comprehensive trade facilitation for the South and Southeast Asian regions. Such an agenda will have to meet three stringent conditions to have any chance of success: (a) it must have specific targets, (b) the targets must be mandatory for all member states, and (c) the parties must agree to achieve these targets within a specific time frame. These specific trade facilitation targets will have to cover institutional, technological, logistical, and transport-related issues.

5.1 Institutional and Technological Facilitation

5.1.1 Seamless Borders

The following steps should be taken to ensure seamless borders:

- Bilateral protocols on customs and other administrative processes and harmonization of standards and certifications, including reciprocal recognition of standards and laboratories.

- Harmonization of IT operating systems to allow digital transfer of all forms and signatures.
- Availability of adequate modern communication facilities and logistics support at the border.
- Preshipment Inspection protocols with private sector (industry chambers) participation.
- Adaptation of modern risk management techniques, including protocols for capacity building in such techniques for the less advanced member countries such as Bhutan, Laos People's Democratic Republic, Myanmar, and Nepal.
- Simple ROO with private sector (industry chambers) involvement in the ROO certification process.

5.1.2 Technology

The following steps should be taken to facilitate the use of technology:

- Use of standardized containers with a harmonized system of barcodes that provide a unique identification sequence for each container.
- Automated weighbridges at all border crossings.
- X-ray machines compatible for use for large containers.
- Electronic lock systems that prevent or allow detection of tampering with all containers while in transit.

5.1.3 Administrative Protocols

The following steps should be taken to establish administrative protocols:

- Member states must allow the use of their roads by commercial vehicles of other countries, which would eliminate the need for transhipment between trucks at borders and is a necessary condition for seamless border.
- All commercial vehicles that are allowed cross-border travel permit must be issued a special BIMSTEC registration number and must be assigned a unique barcode that allows their identification with all details of origin, cargo consignment, ownership, and point of entry.
- Customs administrations of member states will set the goal of completely harmonizing their product classification systems according to the HS coding system up to a six-digit level of disaggregation within five years of the agreement on trade facilitation coming into force.

5.2 Transport and Logistics Facilitation

A crucial element of the regional trade facilitation agenda would have to be an ambitious transport and logistical development program that creates multimodal linkages between member states, playing special attention to behind-the-border segments of such a transport and logistical network. Key areas of rail, road, and shipping are highlighted in the following paragraphs.

5.2.1 Roadways

Dedicated road transport corridors joining important overland border crossings with main economic centers and ports need to be identified. Based on an agreed-on time frame, these corridors need to be upgraded to international standards, preferably with private sector involvement. Some important corridors are as follows:

- Delhi–Siliguri–Guwahati–Imphal (all India)–Tamu (Myanmar) with feeder linkages from Nepal at Kakarbhitta and Birgunj, and from Bhutan through Phuentsholing.
- Varanasi–Mumbai (both India) with linkages from Nepal via the Nautanwa (India)–Sunali (Nepal) border.
- Birgunj (Nepal)–Kolkata/Haldia (India).
- Kolkata (India)–Dhaka–Chittagong (both Bangladesh)–Sittwe (Myanmar).
- The old "Stillwell Road" linking north-east India with northern Myanmar via Ledo (India).

India, being the central geography of this system, will have to simultaneously integrate its national highways development project linking Mumbai, Kolkata, Bangalore, Chennai, Visakapatnam, and Delhi with all the major overland border crossings with its neighboring member states.

5.2.2 Railways

The South Asian railway system, the bulk of it in India, will have to be linked to Southeast Asia via Myanmar. The first step would be to harmonize track gauges and freight cars, and to integrate the traffic control systems of India, Bangladeshi, and Nepalese railways. The second step would be to develop overland railway routes connecting three key routes:

- Kathmandu (Nepal)–Siliguri (India) via Birgunj (Nepal).
- Kolkata (India)–Chittagong via Dhaka (both Bangladesh).
- Kolkata–Imphal (both India) via Dhaka (Bangladesh) and Agartala (India).

The final step would be to develop railway linkages between Southeast Asia and South Asia at three points:

- Northern Route: via Tinsukia (India) on to Northern Myanmar.
- Dhaka (Bangladesh)–Agartala–Imphal (both India) onto Myanmar.
- Chittagong (Bangladesh)–Sittwe (Myanmar).

The general planning of development of such cross-border railways has already been undertaken as a part of the Trans-Asian Railway projects southern corridor plan.[12]

5.2.3 Ports

South Asian ports, both inland and at sea, will have to be rapidly expanded and upgraded. It is important to use private sector resources and open up the ports for private investment. The development of free ports should be encouraged. Key inland ports for development include New Delhi (India), Varanasi (India), Birgunj–Raxaul (India–Nepal border), Benapole (India–Bangladesh border), Kakkarbhitta (India–Nepal border), Nataunwa–Sunali (India–Nepal border), Phulbari (India–Bangladesh border), Hyderabad (India), Bangalore (India), Ledo (India), Moreh–Tamu (India–Myanmar border), and Teknaf (Bangladesh–Myanmar border).

The key seaports that need to be developed or expanded are Mumbai (India), Tuticorin (India), Colombo (Sri Lanka), Visakapatnam (India), Haldia (India), Chittagong (Bangladesh), Mongla (Bangladesh), Sittwe (Myanmar), and Dawei (Myanmar). Logistical elements such as state-of-the-art warehousing facilities and multimodal linkages should be a part of the port development process.

5.3 Role of the Private Sector

The importance of private sector involvement has been underlined throughout the discussion on priority policies on trade facilitation. The private sector in all member countries, with the industry associations taking the lead, should be encouraged to develop proposals for all aspects of the trade facilitation agenda. The nodal trade facilitation secretariat (as proposed, a reformed, reoriented BIMSTEC) should have a special private sector cell that will engender cross-border private sector cooperation and investment. The private sector will have to take the lead in the development of logistics facilities and ports as well as evolving protocols on ROO and Preshipment Inspection agreements. Private sector inputs and experience will be vital to the development of common IT platforms and cross-border digital information systems. The development of standardized containers and barcodes for trucks and containers will not be possible without the proactive support of private sector stakeholders.

To fully engage the private sector in the development of transport and logistics, some of the behind-the-border regulations on distribution services, transport services, and shipping would have to be revised in member states, allowing for investment and removing regulatory disincentives that prevent effective private sector participation in these sectors. The cross-border flow of capital needs to be allowed so that larger companies can develop integrated cross-border supply chains involving several modes of transport. The interests of small-scale service providers can be protected through in-built local content arrangements for these services, which would require larger companies to integrate the smaller players into their integrated logistics network.

6. CONCLUSION

Section 2 shows the relatively poor state of trade facilitation in South Asia and the high transaction costs associated with cross-border exchange in the region. Sections 3 and 4 highlight the lack of adequate initiatives, both unilaterally on the part individual South Asian countries, as well broader regional trade initiatives. Thus, the future agenda is clear: the need for proactive unilateral trade facilitation (with a focus on behind-the-border issues) that is buttressed by regional initiatives (focused on the border issues that require cooperation across countries). Given current geopolitical realities in South Asia, this chapter suggests that making any regional development agenda subject to the resolution of a long-standing bilateral political dispute is counterproductive. For this reason, the proposed Afghanistan–Pakistan–India–Bangladesh–Myanmar international corridor as a new silk route, although attractive, does not appear to be feasible in the short to medium term. Instead, the policy target should be to use an existing agreement that includes all the South Asian countries willing to commit themselves fully toward a regional economic agenda, like BIMSTEC, as nodal agency for regional trade facilitation.

To be successful, the regional trade facilitation agenda must include measures that are mandatory on the contracting parties and set a specific time frame for achievement of these measures. Focus will have to be on border issues of custom modernization and the development of cross-border rail, road, and ship linkages. Equally important are behind-the-border issues like providing decent logistics and transport networks that feed into the regional transport corridors. While such behind-the-border issues are best handled unilaterally, setting region-specific targets will provide incentives for policymakers to prioritize.

A regional integration agenda can never succeed without proper trade facilitation. As discussed, in many cases it is transaction costs rather than tariff barriers that keep entrepreneurs from taking advantage of opportunities across borders, and this is especially true of SMEs. The South Asia–Southeast Asia regional exports are often driven by such SMEs, and thus trade facilitation is a crucial aspect of any trade integration agenda for this region. Trade facilitation has not received the attention it deserves, but increasingly it is gaining prominence in policy circles as well as in the popular media. It is high time to leverage this new interest in trade facilitation and reduction in transaction costs to push for an aggressive reform agenda for the South Asia–Southeast Asia region with full support of the governments and the private sector.

NOTES

1. From the World Trade Organization (WTO) definition on the scope of trade facilitation discussions under the aegis of WTO.
2. Readers are advised that specific countries might enjoy advantageous freight rates in certain routes because of better connectivity or bilateral efforts by governments. Pakistan enjoys relatively cheap air-freight rates to Saudi Arabia and the United Arab Emirates, while Bangladesh enjoys relatively cheaper rates to China.
3. Data are for June to September 2003 for four sea customs formations (Mumbai, Chennai, Cochin, and Kolkata) and two air customs formations (Chennai and Mumbai) reported by the Working Group on Trade Facilitation (WGTF).
4. Dahal (2004, 125) reports a high number of almost 100 percent for the rate of physical inspection; however, the recent Logistics Performance Index (LPI) data as reported in Section 1 show that Nepal has a low incidence rate of physical inspection of just 12 percent in 2006.

5. The section does not discuss bilateral agreements such as the India–Sri Lanka FTA.
6. Details of this regional initiative are available at http://www.adb.org/GMS/default.asp (accessed on 6 October 2009).
7. Pakistan has refused extend the provisions of the SAFTA to India until the Kashmir dispute is settled.
8. Annexure B of the SAFTA draft available at http://www.saarc-sec.org/data/agenda/ economic/safta/OCPs%20_Anx-B%20of%20Annex-IV.pdf (accessed on 6 October 2009).
9. Ibid., Article 21, p. 7.
10. SAFTA draft available at http://www.saarc-sec.org/data/agenda/economic/safta/ SAFTA%20AGREEMENT.pdf (accessed on 6 October 2009).
11. Details available at the BIMSTEC Web site at http://www.bimstec.org/project_3.html (accessed on 6 October 2009).
12. For details, visit the UNESCAP Web site at http://www.unescap.org/ttdw/common/ TIS/TAR/scorridor.asp (accessed on 6 October 2009).

REFERENCES

Arnold, John. 2007. "Role of Trade Facilitation in Export Growth." In Sadiq Ahmed and Ejaz Ghani (eds), *South Asia: Growth and Regional Integration*. New Delhi: World Bank and Macmillan.

Banerjee, Pritam, and Dipankar Sengupta. 2004. "Economic Growth, Exports and the Issue of Trade Facilitation." In Debashis Chakraborty, Pritam Banerjee, and Dipankar Sengupta (eds), *Beyond the Transition Phase of WTO: An Indian Perspective on Emerging Issues*. New Delhi: Academic Foundation.

Bashir, Shahid. 2007. "Trade Facilitation: Experience of Pakistan." Conference Paper for Expert Meeting on the Regional Integration in Asia, New Delhi, March 28–29.

Chaturvedi, Sachin. 2007. "Trade Facilitation Measures in South Asian FTAs: An Overview of Initiatives and Policy Approaches." Asia-Pacific Research and Training Network on Trade Working Paper Series, No. 28, United Nations, Bangladesh.

Dahal, Navin. 2004. "Cost of Doing Business in Nepal and Trade Facilitation." In *Trade Facilitation: Reducing Transaction Costs or Burdening the Poor*. Jaipur: CUTS-Centre for International Trade and Environment.

Dissanayake, Parakrama. 2005. "Sri Lanka Trade Facilitation Progress and the Way Forward." UNESCAP Trade and Investment Division, Bangladesh.

Dollar, David, Alexandra Micco, and Ximena Clark. 2002. "Maritime Transport Costs and Port Efficiency." World Bank Policy Research Paper No. WPS2781, World Bank, Washington, DC.

Domus A. D. 2005. "South Asia Transport and Trade Facilitation Conference Briefing Book." Prepared for United States Trade and Development Agency, Washington, DC, October 11.

Khan, Mostafa Abid. 2004. "WTO Discussions on Trade Facilitation: Bangladesh's Perspective." In *Trade Facilitation: Reducing Transaction Costs or Burdening the Poor*. Jaipur: CUTS-Centre for International Trade and Environment.

Lakshmanan, T. R., Uma Subramanian, William P. Anderson, and Fannie A. Léutier. 2001. *Integration of Transport and Trade Facilitation: Selected Regional Case Studies*. Washington, DC: World Bank.

Ministry of Commerce. 2007. *National Trade Facilitation Strategy*. Islamabad: Government of Pakistan.

Roy, Jayanta. 1998. "Trade Facilitation: The World Bank Experience." Conference Paper for the Trade Facilitation Symposium, WTO, Geneva, 9–10 March.

———. 2002. *Towards International Norms for Indirect Taxes and Trade Facilitation in India*. New Delhi: Task Force on Indirect Taxes, Government of India.

———. 2004. "Report of the Working Group on Trade Facilitation (WGTF)." Government of India, New Delhi.

Roy, Jayanta, and Pritam Banerjee. 2005. *Nepal at the Crossroads: Implications of an Indo-Chinese Trade Route through Nepal*. New Delhi: Confederation of Indian Industry.

———. 2007. "Trade Facilitation: The Next Big Step in India's Trade Reform." In Suparna Karmakar, Rajiv Kumar and Bibek Debroy (eds), *India's Liberalization Experience: Hostage to the WTO*. New Delhi: ICRIER and SAGE Publications.

Roy, Jayanta, and Shweta Bagai. 2005. "Key Issues in Trade Facilitation: Summary of World Bank/EU Workshops in Dhaka and Shanghai." World Bank Policy Research Working Paper No. 3703, World Bank, Washington, DC.

Shanta, T., and A. De Silva. 2006. "Trade Facilitation National Experiences: Sri Lanka." Conference Presentation for Strengthening National and Regional Trade Facilitation Organizations, Geneva, October 31–November 1.

———. 2007. "Trade Facilitation: Its Implementation in Sri Lanka." *Daily Mail*, Colombo, 15 May. Available at http://www.dailynews.lk/2007/05/15/fin05.asp (accessed on 31 July 2008).

Subramanian, Uma, and John Arnold. 2001. *Forging Sub-regional Links in Transportation and Logistics in South Asia*. Washington, DC: World Bank.

Syed, Irtiqa, and Ahmed Zaidi. 2004. "Research Study on Trade Facilitation in Pakistan." In *Trade Facilitation: Reducing Transaction Costs or Burdening the Poor*. Jaipur: CUTS-Centre for International Trade and Environment.

United Nations Economic and Social Commission for Asia and the Pacific (UNESCAP). 2002. "Selected Port Investments," *Review of Developments in Transport and Communications in Asia and the Pacific, 1996–2001*. Bangkok: UNESCAP.

———. 2004. *Comparative Analysis of Port Tariff Levels in ESCAP Region*. Bangkok: UNESCAP.

Wickramasinghe, Upali. 2007. "Transaction Costs and Trade Facilitation in South Asia." Conference Presentation for Expert Meeting on the Regional Integration in Asia, New Delhi, March 28–29.

Wilson, John, and Tsunehiro Otsuki. 2007. "Regional Integration in South Asia: What Role for Trade Facilitation." World Bank Policy Research Working Paper No. 4423, World Bank, Washington, DC.

World Bank. 2002. *Global Economic Prospects 2002*. Washington, DC: World Bank.

———. 2008a. *Logistics Performance Index*. Washington, DC: Trade Logistics and Facilitation Program, World Bank.

———. 2008b. *World Trade Indicators*. Washington, DC: World Bank Institute.

6

Transit and Border Trade Barriers in South Asia

Prabir De, Sachin Chaturvedi,
and Abdur Rob Khan[1]

1. INTRODUCTION

The world has been witnessing the 25th anniversary of the advent of the South Asian Association of Regional Cooperation (SAARC) in 2009. With the conversion of South Asia Preferential Trade Agreement (SAPTA) into South Asia Free Trade Agreement (SAFTA) in 2006, South Asia is now looking for a Customs Union in 2015 and an Economic Union in 2020. Except Afghanistan and Bhutan, rest South Asian countries are members of the World Trade Organization (WTO) and have been practicing the Most Favored Nation (MFN) principles with an exception of India and Pakistan. It is envisaged that SAFTA will lead the growth in intraregional formal trade from US$11 billion in 2007 to US$40 billion by 2015 (RIS 2008). However, in reality, South Asia is far from realizing its trade potential. One of the critical factors preventing South Asia from achieving its full potential is the absence of regional transit trade.[2] Unlike the European Union, South Asian countries do not have a regional transit arrangement, although partial transit exists for landlocked countries such as Afghanistan, Bhutan, and Nepal.

In order to reduce regional and multilateral trade transportation costs, the South Asian countries have been trying to integrate the region through improved connectivity including a regional transit arrangement. A regional transit means a stronger multilateral transit. However, the challenges are numerous. A number of studies have shown that the economies with geographical contiguity could potentially benefit substantially from higher trade, provided trade and transport barriers are removed through a regional transit arrangement.[3] Some earlier studies identified several challenges related to the implementation of GATT (General Agreement on Tariffs and Trade) commitments in transit and trade facilitation in the context of South Asia.[4] However, the empirical understanding of the relationships between trade barriers and trade flows in context of South Asia remains nascent.

The objectives of this paper are two-fold: first, to review the South Asian countries bilateral, regional and multilateral commitments in transit, and second, to assess the performance of some important land customs stations (LCS) dealing overland trade in eastern South Asia sub-region, that is, Bangladesh, Bhutan, India, and Nepal. The rest part of the paper is organized as follows. The profile of intraregional transit trade is briefly presented in Section 2, while Section 3 discusses the current transit arrangement in the sub-region. Section 4 presents WTO rules on transit and a review of the commitments made by the South Asian countries on transit. To understand whether the border corridors and customs stations are equipped to cope up the changing trade environment, a field survey has been carried out among selected LCSs in both sides of the border in the sub-region. The results of the field survey are briefly presented in Section 5 together with a discussion of the performance of LCSs and the constraint of transit trade in the sub-region. Conclusions are drawn in Section 6.

2. TRANSIT TRADE IN EASTERN SOUTH ASIA

The importance of tariffs as barriers to trade has gradually declined in South Asia. However, high tariffs still exist for certain sensitive products, and there is a strong presence of nontariff barriers (NTBs) including high border transaction costs in the region.[5] In particular, high transportation costs act as a serious constraint to enhancing merchandise trade flow in the region (De 2008, 2009a). In addition, poor institutions (for example, lack of e-filing of trade documents), inadequate infrastructure (for example, lack of a modern warehouse or container handling facility at border), and the absence of a regional transit trade (virtually in the entire region) are prohibiting the growth of trade in South Asia.[6]

In South Asia, Afghanistan, Bhutan and Nepal are landlocked countries and depend solely on transit through neighboring countries. They are confronted with a variety of practical constraints that increase the logistics costs of their international trade. Landlocked developing countries, as a group, are among the poorest of developing countries, with limited capacities and dependence on a very limited number of commodities for their export earnings. About 38 countries are currently landlocked with no access to seaports (Uprety 2006). Lack of territorial access to seaports, remoteness and isolation from world markets have contributed to their relative poverty, substantially inflating transportation costs and lowering their effective participation in international trade (UNCTAD 2005). For example, Bhutan and Nepal rely heavily on India's eastern coast for their international trade. Due to several bottlenecks, including those visible at border-crossing corridors and transit ports, Bhutan and Nepal face substantial trade costs, which otherwise could be avoided if a regional transit trade regime is restored in South Asia (UNCTAD 2004). The trade-reducing effect is strongest for transport-intensive activities (De 2009b). Most, if not all, landlocked countries in South Asia are commodity exporters. The very high transport costs that they must bear constrain export development since that burden limits the range of potential exports and markets in which goods can be competitively and profitably traded. The price of imports tends to increase because of high transit transportation costs (De 2009b). Nonetheless, the present weak and inadequate transit arrangement in South Asia is disappointing.

In eastern South Asia, Nepal and Bhutan depend on India for their regional and international trade. In particular, Nepal is increasingly dependent on India for 68 percent of its exports and 62 percent of its imports per year (Table 6.1a). Relatively larger Bangladesh sources about 13 percent of its global imports from Bhutan, India, and Nepal, but its exports to those countries are low, compared to its imports (Table 6.1b). The interesting development is that Bangladesh's trade with Bhutan has witnessed a steep rise in recent years, with this entire trade being carried overland using the India–Bangladesh–Bhutan transit corridor. India's trade with adjacent countries such as Bhutan and Nepal, with which India has bilateral transit agreements, has also increased, again being carried overland (Table 6.1c). India's trade with Bangladesh has also risen phenomenally, despite the fact that the two countries do not have

TABLE 6.1a   Nepal's Trade with India and Bangladesh

	US$ million		
	1991	2000	2006
Exports to:			
Bangladesh	0.12	1.90	3.24
India	17.45	307.20	562.98
Total (above two countries)	17.57	309.10	566.22
Share in global exports (%)	6.83	42.89	68.25
Imports from:			
Bangladesh	12.70	8.10	1.45
India	85.01	574.20	1,481.51
Total (above two countries)	97.71	582.30	1,482.96
Share in global imports (%)	19.54	37.08	61.85

Source   Calculated based on International Monetary Fund 2008.

TABLE 6.1b   Bangladesh's Trade with India, Nepal, and Bhutan

	US$ million		
	1991	2000	2006
Exports to:			
Bhutan	0.30	0.90	4.08
India	22.8	50.13	146.93
Nepal	11.54	1.32	1.32
Total (above three countries)	34.64	52.35	152.33
Share in global exports (%)	2.05	0.94	1.19
Imports from:			
Bhutan	3.90	4.53	12.95
India	189.49	945.45	2,230.77
Nepal	0.14	3.98	3.16
Total (above three countries)	193.53	953.96	2,246.88
Share in global imports (%)	5.66	10.60	12.56

Source   Calculated based on International Monetary Fund 2008.

TABLE 6.1c   India's Trade with Bangladesh, Bhutan, and Nepal

	US$ million		
	1991	2000	2006
Exports to:			
Bangladesh	324.56	860.33	1,967.8
Bhutan	1.20	2.73	118.03
Nepal	77.28	143.4	1,346.83

(*Table 6.1c Continued*)

(*Table 6.1c Continued*)

	US$ million		
	1991	2000	2006
Total (above three countries)	403.04	1,006.46	3,432.66
Share in global exports (%)	2.25	2.36	2.79
Imports from:			
Bangladesh	5.73	79.85	128.43
Bhutan	0.50	20.33	104.30
Nepal	19.19	238.48	619.28
Total (above three countries)	25.42	338.66	852.01
Share in global imports (%)	0.13	0.67	0.46

Source Calculated based on International Monetary Fund 2008.

any bilateral transit arrangement. In contrast, bilateral trade between Bangladesh and Nepal witnessed a marginal rise between 2000 and 2006, carried overland through a tiny corridor between India, Nepal, and Bangladesh in 2006, amounted to some US$4.5 million.

A trilateral transit understanding between Bangladesh, India, and Nepal is in place in order to facilitate the overland trade between Nepal and Bangladesh through India. Bhutan's trade is again India-centric. Bhutan sources about 75 percent of its imports from India and sells almost 88 percent of its exports to that country (Table 6.1d). To be noted, trade among the countries in the eastern South Asia sub-region is not always a transit trade. For example, India's bilateral trade with Bangladesh, Bhutan, and Nepal cannot be termed as transit trade, whereas the same between Bangladesh, Bhutan and Nepal through India can be seen as transit trade

TABLE 6.1d   Bhutan's Trade with India

	Trade with world		Trade with India					
	Value		Value		Share			
	Exports	Imports	Exports	Imports	Exports	Imports		
Year	(US$ million)		(US$ million)		(%)			
2001	126.23	227.20	118.79	176.62	94.11	77.74		
2002	79.13	253.88	70.50	191.40	89.09	75.39		
2003	90.64	292.32	83.96	258.49	92.63	88.43		
2004	209.03	471.05	196.15	257.62	93.84	54.69		
2005	287.75	430.50	251.95	323.35	87.56	75.11		
2006	350.00	320.00	n.a.	n.a.	n.a.	n.a.		

Source Department of Revenue and Customs 2007.
Note   n.a. = Data not available.

since the trading countries in that particular case are not geographically adjacent. Similarly, the trade of Bhutan and Nepal with the rest of the world through another country (here, India) can also be termed as transit trade.

2.1 Transit Trade Profile

Until recently, transit trade in South Asia was not in the forefront of regional and multilateral cooperation. However, increasing trade volume in recent years has forced the countries in South Asia to be more lenient with transit trade, regional and otherwise. The transit trade in the eastern South Asia sub-region can be grouped into two categories: *(a)* intra-sub-regional and *(b)* extra-sub-regional. Tables 6.2a and 6.2b show the

TABLE 6.2a   Intra-sub-regional Transit Trade

Exporting country	Partner	Transit through	US$ million		
			1991	*2000*	*2006*
Bangladesh	Bhutan, Nepal	India	11.840	2.220	5.400
			(0.232)	(0.015)	(0.018)
Bhutan	Bangladesh, Nepal	India	5.110	5.530	13.230
			(3.060)	(1.565)	(1.975)
Nepal	Bangladesh, Bhutan	India	0.260	2.960	5.440
			(0.034)	(0.129)	(0.169)
Total			17.210	10.710	24.070

Sources   Calculated based on International Monetary Fund (2008) and Bhutan's Department of Revenue and Customs (2007).

Note   Numbers in parentheses are the shares of individual countries in their respective world trade.

TABLE 6.2b   Extra-sub-regional Transit Trade

Exporting country	Partner	Transit through	US$ million		
			1991	*2000*	*2006*
Nepal	Rest of the world[a]	India	654.98	1,409.60	1,182.79
			(86.47)	(61.53)	(36.65)
Bhutan	Rest of the world[a]	India	25.09	49.17	98.72
			(15.02)	(13.91)	(14.73)
Total			680.07	1,458.77	1,281.51

Sources   Calculated based on International Monetary Fund (2008) and Bhutan's Department of Revenue and Customs (2007).

Note   [a] Rest of the world excluding India. Numbers in parentheses are the shares of individual countries in their respective world trade.

volume of intra-sub-regional and extra-sub-regional transit trade for Bangladesh, Bhutan, and Nepal that passes through India. The following observations are worth noting.

First, intra- and extra-sub-regional transit trade in eastern South Asia increased substantially from 1991 to 2006 (Figure 6.1), where extra-sub-regional transit trade grew much faster than intra-sub-regional transit trade. Currently, about 2 percent of transit trade in eastern South Asia is conducted within the sub-region, while the remaining 98 percent is extra-sub-regional.

Second, the volume of intra-sub-regional transit trade is much smaller than extra-sub-regional transit trade in eastern South Asia. In 2006, countries in eastern South Asia recorded a total of US$24.07 million intra-sub-regional transit trade, which was about 1.88 percent of total extra-sub-regional transit trade (US$1.28 billion in 2006) of the sub-region.

Third, countries in eastern South Asia have very limited intra-sub-regional transit trade, compared with extra-sub-regional transit trade. In terms of their global trade, intra-sub-regional transit trade has been miniscule. Bhutan is the only country which has more than 55 percent of intra-sub-regional transit trade, contributing about 2 percent of

FIGURE 6.1   Trends in Intra- and Extra-sub-regional Transit Trade

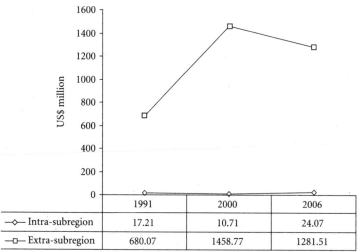

	1991	2000	2006
—◇— Intra-subregion	17.21	10.71	24.07
—□— Extra-subregion	680.07	1458.77	1281.51

Sources   Calculated based on International Monetary Fund (2008) and Bhutan's Department of Revenue and Customs (2007).

Bhutan's international trade (US$13.23 million in 2006). The remaining two countries, that is, Bangladesh and Nepal, have negligible transit trade within the sub-region.

Fourth, compared with intra-sub-regional transit trade, extra-sub-regional transit trade of eastern South Asia is very high. Extra-sub-regional transit trade is driven by Nepal. About 37 percent of Nepal's global trade (US$1.18 billion) is transit trade, conducted outside eastern South Asia, whereas in the case of Bhutan it is about 15 percent. The falling shares of extraregional transit trade (as a percentage of global trade) of both those countries (down from 86.47 percent in 1991 to 36.65 percent in 2006 in the case of Nepal, and from 15.02 percent in 1991 to 14.73 percent in 2006 in the case of Bhutan) indicate that bilateral trade with neighboring India is not only growing rapidly but is also replacing the extra-sub-regional transit trade of Bhutan and Nepal.

Therefore, despite an absolute rise in intra- and extra-sub-regional transit trade in eastern South Asia in recent years, intra-sub-regional transit trade is still miniscule, compared with the extra-sub-regional transit trade volume. At the same time, India's bilateral trade with Bhutan, Bangladesh and Nepal is not only growing fast but is also replacing the extra-sub-regional transit trade volume of Bhutan and Nepal.

3. REVIEW OF TRANSIT ARRANGEMENT IN EASTERN SOUTH ASIA

Cross-border infrastructure alone would not facilitate the movement of goods and vehicles between countries if non-physical impediments are not removed (Subramanian and Arnold 2001; UNCTAD 2007). Trade facilitation can only serve its purpose if based on harmonized legislation, institutions, and practices, at sub-regional, regional and international levels. In spite of consistent efforts and achievements over the years, significant differences continue to exist between South Asian countries in terms of their legislation, institutional arrangements and practices. Operational standards that differ between neighboring countries lead to lack of traffic and transit rights and barriers to the movement of goods and people, having a negative impact on countries' trade and economies. As goods begin to move along international transport corridors, the need for harmonization of laws and processes amongst a larger group of countries becomes clear. International conventions related to transport are essential in facilitating the movement of goods, especially at border crossings, by reducing procedures and formalities and time required.

3.1 Bilateral Understandings

In eastern South Asia, all countries except Bhutan are members of WTO. Trade in eastern South Asia is conducted on an MFN basis, following multilateral (GATT), regional (SAFTA), and bilateral trade agreements. As Table 6.3 shows—with the exception of trade between India and Bangladesh, and between Bhutan and Nepal—bilateral trade agreements among the remaining countries in the sub-region offer mutual understanding on transit. The movement of goods and vehicles is controlled through national legislation as well as a series of bilateral transit and trade agreements and, in certain cases, from "ad-hoc" arrangements deriving from intent between certain country pairs for mutual cooperation.[7] An example of this mutual cooperation is the movement of Bhutanese goods through Indian territory, which is governed by the stipulations contained in the "Agreement on Trade and Commerce" between the two countries and an attached Protocol.[8]

TABLE 6.3   Trade and Transit Arrangements in Eastern South Asia

Agreement	Type	MFN trade	MFN transit	GATT signatories
India–Bangladesh	Bilateral	Yes	No	Yes
India–Nepal	Bilateral	Yes	Yes	Yes
India–Bhutan	Bilateral	Yes	Yes	India—member; Bhutan—observer
India–Pakistan	Bilateral	No	No	Yes
Pakistan–Afghanistan	Bilateral	Yes	Yes	Pakistan—member; Afghanistan—observer
Bangladesh–Nepal	Bilateral	Yes	Yes	Yes
Bangladesh–Bhutan	Bilateral	Yes	Yes	Bangladesh—member; Bhutan—observer
Bhutan–Nepal	Bilateral	Yes	No	Nepal—member; Bhutan—observer

Source   Compiled by the authors.

3.1.1 Bangladesh–India Agreements

Bilateral trade between India and Bangladesh is conducted under the provisions of the prevailing India–Bangladesh Trade Agreement, which was first signed on 28 March 1972. Under the agreement, both countries provide MFN treatment to each other except in the case of transit trade. India and Bangladesh signed a bilateral agreement entitled "Protocol on Inland Water Transport and Trade" on 4 October 1999, and which was renewed in 2007, for bilateral and transit trade between the two countries. This agreement derives directly from the provisions of the aforesaid India–Bangladesh Trade Agreement. Besides, they also signed agreements related to the operation of railways for the purpose of trade in goods and services between the two countries. Under these agreements, both countries agree to operate trains (goods/passengers) through three specific border routes.[9]

3.1.2 India–Nepal Agreements

India and Nepal signed a bilateral trade agreement, the "Treaty of Trade," on 6 December 1991. The validity of this Treaty of Trade in its existing form stands extended for until 5 March 2012. A Protocol attached to this Agreement defines the operational modalities including the list of bilateral trade routes. They also signed an Agreement on 6 December 1991 to control unauthorized trade, which sets out certain procedures for the control and prevention of smuggling. India and Nepal also signed a "Treaty of Transit" on 5 January 1999, resulting which India provides maritime transit and supporting services and facilities to Nepal at Kolkata and Haldia ports, which are located in the State of West Bengal, India. A Protocol attached to the Treaty of Transit specifies detailed operational modalities, including entry and exit points to and from India for the transit trade of Nepal. In addition, both countries signed a Memorandum to the Protocol that specifies the detailed procedures to be applied to imports to, and exports from, Nepal. Besides, India and Nepal entered into a Rail Services Agreement for operating and managing rail services for Nepal's transit trade as well as bilateral trade between the two countries. Specifically, it specifies transit trade between Kolkata/Haldia ports in India and Birgunj in Nepal, via Raxaul in India as well as between stations on Indian Railways and Birgunj via Raxaul, for bilateral trade.

3.1.3 Bhutan–India Agreement

India and Bhutan signed a bilateral trade agreement in 1995 that sets out the broad contour of free trade between the two countries. The Protocol to this trade agreement specifies the bilateral trade routes (including transit) and detailed trading procedures. Interestingly, there are no references to transport, although the common understanding is that the free movement of vehicles between the two countries is accommodated by the Agreement. India provides transit to Bhutan through Kolkata and Haldia ports.

3.1.4 Bangladesh–Nepal Agreement

Nepal and Bangladesh do not have a bilateral trade agreement. Instead, they have a transit agreement, signed on 2 April 1976, and a protocol attached to this transit agreement. This transit agreement and the protocol provide transit rights to Nepal in order to access overseas markets (third country markets), but they do not deal with their bilateral overland trade. In order to operate the bilateral transit trade, Bangladesh and Nepal signed an agreement entitled "Operational Modalities for an Additional Transit Route between Nepal and Bangladesh," which provides terms for the use of Banglabandha (Bangladesh)–Phulbari (India)–Khakarbitta (Nepal) as a transit corridor for bilateral trade. India provides transit to Nepal and Bangladesh exclusively for their overland bilateral trade, but not for their extraregional transit trade.

3.1.5 Bangladesh–Bhutan Agreement

Bangladesh and Bhutan signed a bilateral trade agreement on 12 May 2003 granting most favored nation (MFN) status to each other's trade. The Protocol attached to this bilateral trade agreement defines Burimari (Bangladesh)—Changrabandha (India)—Jaigaon (India)—Phuentsholing (Bhutan) as the transit route for bilateral trade between Bangladesh and Bhutan. India provides transit for the bilateral overland trade between the two countries.

3.2 Regional Understanding

SAARC has the Inter-Governmental Group (IGG) to provide advice on the facilitation of transportation in South Asia. A succession of IGG proceedings shows that harmonization of standards and mutual recognition in the transport sector has been the key issue in South Asia. In recent years, there have been some important developments in regional transportation in South Asia. As per the directives of the fourteenth SAARC Summit, held in New Delhi in April 2007, the Ministers of Transport of SAARC countries for the first time met in New Delhi on 31 August 2007. Taking note of the recommendations of the SAARC Regional Multimodal Transport Study, the SAARC Transport Ministers agreed to reach a Regional Transport and Transit Agreement as well as a Regional Motor Vehicles Agreement in 2008.[10] However, South Asia has yet to reach a regional transport and transit arrangement for cross-border movement of goods and vehicles.

3.3 Multilateral Understandings

In recognition of the fact that harmonized transport facilitation measures at the national and international levels are a prerequisite for enhancing international trade and transport along road and rail routes of international importance, United Nations (UN) offer seven international conventions, which were originally developed under the auspices of the Economic Commission for Europe (ECE)[11] set out a basic framework for the cross-border movements of goods and vehicles such as:

1. The Convention on Road Traffic, 1968.
2. The Convention on Road Signs and Signals, 1968.
3. The Customs Convention on the International Transport of Goods under Cover of TIR Carnets (TIR Convention), 1975.
4. The Customs Convention on the Temporary Importation of Commercial Road Vehicles, 1956.
5. The Customs Convention on Containers, 1972.
6. The International Convention on the Harmonization of Frontier Controls of Goods, 1982.
7. The Convention on the Contract for the International Carriage of Goods by Road (CMR), 1956.

United Nations Economic and Social Commission for Asia and the Pacific (UNESCAP) at its 48th session adopted Resolution 48/11 of 23 April 1992 on road and rail transport modes in relation to facilitation measures. It recommended that the countries in the region, if they had not already done so, consider the possibility of acceding to aforesaid seven international conventions in the field of land transport facilitation. But, there has been a less concerted effort to accede to the United Nations conventions in South Asia. The sub-regional extent of accession to these Conventions is shown in Table 6.4. Most of the South Asian countries have yet to ratify these international conventions for cross-border movements of goods and vehicles.

TABLE 6.4 International Conventions and South Asian Countries[a]

Convention	Afghanistan	Bangladesh	Bhutan	India	Maldives	Nepal	Pakistan	Sri Lanka
Convention on Road Traffic (1968)	No	Yes	No	Yes	No	No	Yes	Yes
Convention on Road Signs and Signals (1968)	No	No	No	Yes	No	No	Yes	No
Customs Convention on Temporary Importation of Commercial Road Vehicles (1956)	Yes	No	No	No	No	No	No	No
Customs Convention on Containers (1972)	No	No	No	No	No	No	No	No
Convention on International Transport of Goods under Cover of TIR Carnets (1975)	Yes	No	No	No	No	No	No	No
Convention on the Contract for the International Carriage of Goods by Road (1956)	No	No	No	No	No	No	No	No
Convention on the Harmonization of Frontier Controls of Goods (1982)	No	No	No	No	No	No	No	No

Source Compiled based on UNESCAP (2007).
Note   [a] As of December 2007.

In South Asia, Bangladesh and Sri Lanka have signed the "Convention on Road Traffic," while India and Pakistan have signed both the "Convention on Road Traffic" and "Convention on Road Signs and Signals." Bhutan, Maldives and Nepal have not signed any one these seven United Nations Conventions. Except for Afghanistan, no South Asian countries have signed the "Customs Convention on the Temporary Importation of Commercial Road Vehicles" or the "Convention on the International Transport of Goods under TIR Carnets." Accession to different versions of Conventions is likely to undermine facilitation objectives. For example, many countries are contracting parties to the Convention on Road Traffic (1949), but have not ratified the new version (1968) of the Convention. The Convention on Road Traffic (1949) is still valid in relations between the contracting parties to it.

The principles of the Customs Transit Procedures, which are covered in detail in Specific Annexure E, Chapter E.I of the Revised Kyoto Convention, provide for a safe, secure and standard transit procedure. The World Customs Organization (WCO) encourages its members to accede to international Conventions related to transit such as the TIR Convention as well as instruments provided by WCO on customs transit that facilitate transit procedures for temporary admission of goods. WCO suggests further that if members are not in a position to accede to these Conventions, when drawing up multilateral/bilateral agreements they should take into account customs transit, standards and recommended practices mentioned in the revised Kyoto Convention.

Finally, what appears is that transit in eastern South Asia (and subsequent overland transportation) is undertaken through bilateral trade agreements, with India providing overland transit to Bangladesh, Nepal, and Bhutan for their bilateral trade, and maritime transit to Nepal and Bhutan for their international trade.

4. TRANSIT AND THE WTO RULES: MULTILATERAL AND REGIONAL COMMITMENTS ON TRANSIT OF SOUTH ASIAN COUNTRIES

In November 2001, the Doha Ministerial Conference called for negotiations on trade facilitation after the 2003 WTO Ministerial Meeting, subject to agreement on the modalities of negotiation.[12] The current mandate of the Negotiating Group for Trade Facilitation (NGTF) established in 2004 is primarily to clarify and improve Articles V (Freedom of Transit), Article VIII (Fees and Formalities Connected with Importation and Exportation) and Article X (Publication and Administration of Trade Regulations) of GATT 1994. The NGTF has also focused on identifying special and differential treatment for developing and least developed countries apart from exploring areas for technical assistance and support for capacity building by the developing and the least developed country members.

GATT Article V (Freedom of Transit) sets out the basic requirement of freedom of transit through the most convenient route and further requires that no discrimination be made on the basis of flag of a vessel, place of origin, departure, entry, exit or destination. It also calls on parties not to discriminate on the basis of ownership of goods or means of transport. Further, Article V stipulates the obligation not to impose any unnecessary delays or restrictions on transit. It also requires members to impose reasonable fees and charges that would be non-discriminatory and limited to the cost of the service provided.

1. Simplification of Procedures for Transit

WTO members have made suggestions on facilitating transit through the simplification of documentary requirements and procedures required for transit. Members have suggested that transit fees, simplification of procedures for transit purposes, and so on, bear a close resemblance to provisions of Article VIII the submissions made by members to the Council on Article VIII automatically apply to transit. In this context, members have suggested that specific guidelines are needed on how unnecessary procedures can be reduced or simplified. In addition, requirements and procedures for transit should be less onerous than those for importation. Other suggestions have included the introduction of mechanisms that would institutionalize cooperation among the member countries, harmonize transit policies between members and enable the sharing of information among customs authorities, as these could further facilitate transit. Recognizing the need for simplification of transit procedures, the "Indo-Nepal Treaties of Trade, and of Transit, and the Agreement for Cooperation to Control Unauthorized Trade" was revised in 1996 allowing for new procedures to be applied in the clearance of Nepalese containerized traffic in transit to and from Nepal.

2. Exceptions to the Principle of Non-discrimination for Sensitive Items and Goods Requiring Transhipment

WTO members have pointed out that it may not always be possible to apply the principle of non-discrimination to all types of consignments. Certain goods may be subject to special provisions. However, WTO members should consider the publication of the list of such "sensitive items." Similarly, it has been pointed out that in cases where the possibility of the illegal release of transit goods exists (as in the case of landlocked countries), more sophisticated risk management techniques may be required. Also, goods in transit that require transhipment may need additional inspection (in relation to those that do not require transhipment) to prevent the smuggling of goods into the transit country.

While India allows transit facilities to Nepal, it has faced the problem of leakage of third country goods into its markets (Chaturvedi 2007). This issue has come up time and again with the Indian authorities. In fact, the issue of unauthorized trade has been addressed in the bilateral agreements between India and Nepal signed since 1961. The Indian Customs authorities maintain a list of sensitive items so that such goods are kept under closer scrutiny during transit from Indian territory. However, such a list, although circulated within customs, is not publicly available. Similarly, goods for transhipment require additional inspection to prevent smuggling. A large proportion of goods in transit from India to Nepal first arrives by sea at the Indian port of Kolkata and is then transhipped by road and rail to Nepal. India could accept the proposal that goods in transit requiring transhipment may need additional inspection.

3. Regional Transit Arrangements

The existing Article V requires WTO members to operate national transit schemes but does not recognize the issue of transit at the regional level. Members have pointed out that the solution to transit can be found through regional cooperation as can be witnessed in some of the existing international and regional transit instruments, such as the TIR Convention, the European Convention on common transit; the ASEAN Framework Agreement on the Facilitation of Goods in Transit, and United Nations instruments related to transit.

India plays a dual role in transit, both as a provider of transit facilities to Nepal and as a seeker of transit facilities from Bangladesh. It is in India's interest to enter into a bilateral transit arrangement with Bangladesh, similar to that with Nepal, so that it can access the remote areas of the north-eastern region at lower costs and time. However, Bangladesh has been reluctant to offer transit facilities to India as it fears leakage of Indian goods into Bangladesh. As the proposals on transit would address the issue of leakage of goods by allowing members to implement additional inspections of such goods and by requesting members to publish a list of sensitive items, India and Bangladesh could take into account the suggested measures in framing a bilateral treaty on transit.

4. Use of International Standards

WTO members have suggested the use of international standards for transit. Members could consider the possibility of accession to various instruments related to transit such as: *(a)* the Customs Convention on the International Transport of Goods under cover of TIR Carnets (TIR Convention), Geneva, 14 November 1975; *(b)* the Customs Convention on the ATA Carnet for the Temporary Admission of Goods (ATA Convention), Brussels, 6 December 1961; and *(c)* the Convention on Temporary Admission, Istanbul, 26 June 1990 (as per Annexure A as it relates to ATA Carnets).

As presented earlier, the TIR Carnet is a road transport document that allows containerized and, in some cases, bulk cargo to move through simplified and harmonized administrative formalities. The ATA Carnet is designed to facilitate the importation, irrespective of the means of transport, of goods that are granted temporary duty-free admission (including transit, importation for home use and temporary admission). Although they would simplify transit considerably, the use of international standards such as ATA Carnets or TIR Carnets is absent in the South Asian countries (Table 6.4). India, Bangladesh, and Nepal have not acceded to the TIR Convention or the ATA Convention. India uses ATA Carnet, for a very limited purpose, mostly for duty-free temporary admission of imports. It would be extremely difficult for countries such as India, Nepal, and Bangladesh to adhere to the requirements of the TIR Convention (in terms of specifications for vehicles and procedures). Also, at present, it is difficult to envisage the possibility of IRU recognizing an association in a member country that would accept the IRU obligations and conditions. At this stage, these countries would be unable to meet the rigorous requirements of the Convention as it would require enormous resources and a fairly large timescale. India could, however, accept these international standards on a "best endeavor basis."

4.1 Multilateral and Regional Commitments

Trade facilitation issues have received growing attention in several regional cooperation initiatives around the world. Although GATT Article V assumes greater significance in South Asia, the freedom of transit has been completely ignored in regional trade agreements in that region. Table 6.5 compares the provisions of trade facilitation measures in regional and bilateral trade agreements in South Asia. It shows that neither SAFTA nor bilateral FTAs adequately address the issue of transit. In sharp contrast, the India–Singapore CECA has several provisions on transit. For example, it provides provisions for non-discrimination, no additional fees and documentation when the goods are in transit. There is also clear provision for coordination and cooperation to safeguard the interests of exporters and importers. Evidence is given below on the application of GATT Article V in South Asian countries.

4.1.1 Bangladesh

In Bangladesh, Article V has immense relevance since it has the potential to offer transit facilities to nearby landlocked countries and a landlocked region with a country. Nepal and Bhutan have shown keenness to use two seaports in Bangladesh, that is, Chittagong and Mongla. However, it is unclear as to what specific measures have been taken by Bangladesh as part of the Article V (for example, those related to documentation, security and guarantees, seals and identifications, and charges for transit goods).

TABLE 6.5 Matters Related to Goods in Transit

Trade facilitation measures	SAFTA	India–Sri Lanka FTA	Pakistan–Sri Lanka FTA	India–Singapore CECA
Non-discrimination	No	No specific provisions	No specific provisions	Transit goods would not face discrimination
Discipline on fees and charges	No	No specific provisions	No specific provisions	No additional fees charged
Discipline on transit formalities and documentation requirements	No	No specific provisions	No specific provisions	No additional documentation required (Article 3.14)
Coordination and cooperation	Provisions regarding consignment	No specific provisions	No specific provisions	Mechanism in place

Source Chaturvedi 2007.

The private sector's role in supplementing efforts to implement Article V is also unclear. However, Bangladesh has established an extensive network of institutions for border agency coordination (Bhattacharya and Hossain 2006).

4.1.2 India

On Article V, India has extended transit to landlocked countries such as Bhutan and Nepal. Table 6.6 provides the status of trade facilitation measures on Article V in India. The Indian customs authorities require a declaration of all the transit goods as per the standard declaration form available on site as well as at the relevant offices. Customs is making an effort to enhance the level of coordination among the various border agencies. As different degrees of security concerns are present at different points in the country there is a limited use of the simplified transit declaration. Customs is also working on simplifying procedures established

TABLE 6.6   WTO Trade Facilitation Proposals and Status of Trade Facilitation Measures on Transit (Article V) in India

Groups of measures falling under those areas	Status in India
Strengthened non-discrimination	√
Disciplines on fees and charges	
Publication of fees and charges and prohibition of unpublished ones	√
Periodic review of fees and charges	√
More effective disciplines on charges for transit	√
Periodic exchanges between neighboring authorities	√
Disciplines on transit formalities and documentation requirements	
Periodic review	√
Reduction/simplification	√
Harmonization/standardization	X
Promotion of regional transit arrangements	√
Simplified and preferential clearance for certain goods	X
Limitation of inspections and controls	X
Sealing	X
Cooperation and coordination on document requirements	√
Monitoring	√
Bonded transport regime/guarantees	X
Improved coordination and cooperation	
Among authorities	√
Between authorities and the private sector	√

Source   Chaturvedi 2006, based on WTO TN/TF/W/43/Rev.4.
Note   √ represents trade facilitation measures introduced. The absence of measures is indicated by X.

for the authorized consignors involved in the transit procedures. India does not charge duty or tax on transit goods. Cash deposits are not required for goods in transit, and securities and guarantees are discharged as soon as the necessary requirements are met (Chaturvedi 2006).

4.1.3 Nepal

Transit of goods through India from or to adjacent countries is regulated in accordance with the bilateral trade and transit treaties and is subject to such restrictions as may be specified by the Directorate General of Foreign Trade in accordance with international Conventions. In order to tackle abuse of the customs transit corridors, the Government of India issues a list of sensitive commodities at periodic intervals, keeping domestic market requirements as the criteria. At present, nine such commodities are identified as sensitive items. In the recent past, the Directorate of Revenue Intelligence has caught several consignments worth millions of rupees that were being directed for domestic consumption in India. This has become a major issue, especially with Nepal.

Many features of Article V are not applicable to Nepal as it is a landlocked country. However, Nepal has launched several measures to facilitate transit trade destinations. It has signed a trade transit treaty with India for easy access to Kolkata and Haldia seaports. A standardized customs transit declaration document has also been introduced, which is in operation with India.

The foregoing discussion suggests that GATT Article V is of major significance for South Asia. First, SAFTA and bilateral FTAs could be amended in line with GATT Article V. Second, the WTO trade facilitation programs should be amended in order to strengthen the "Freedom of Transit" rights. According to Chaturvedi (2007), the current WTO trade facilitation program may have to go beyond the current mandate and take into account specific WTO commitments that may emerge during the ongoing negotiations as per GATT Articles V, VIII, and X. There are five broad concerns in Article V that are addressed by the various proposals, that is, matters related to transit goods, disciplines on fees and charges, disciplines on transit formalities, documentation requirements, and improved cooperation among authorities (WTO 2005a). However, the key obstacles to implementing Article V are related to the different standards and regulations adopted by various neighboring countries, inadequate transport infrastructure and different levels of automation

(UNESCAP 2007). The lack of common legal approaches and border-crossing formalities also hamper effective implementation. The lack of transparency in transit fees and charges that are sometimes discriminatory is another major challenge.

Among the key proposals received on Article V, the issues covered are transit regime, procedures and technical assistance. There are suggestions for developing a transit regime based on international standards as well as adherence to international instruments for dealing with goods in transit for which regional transit cooperation agreements may be put in place. The proposals emphasize reasonable, non-discriminatory and simplified procedures for cross-border movement of vehicles. It has also been suggested that the principles of simplification, standardization and transparency be followed in implementing Article V (WTO 2008). Efforts may also be made: *(a)* to minimize the burden on cargo in transit as well as the differentiation of cargo undergoing transhipment and *(b)* to review the present documentary requirements and fees for non-transhipped goods in transit as well as those for goods in transit with transhipment. Another suggestion has been to introduce risk management for authorized traders. Maximum technical assistance is possibly required for Article V as landlocked countries (for example, those in South Asia) are at different levels of development. The technical assistance and capacity-building programs need to take this factor into account. The different levels of ICT compatibility, trained manpower and security concerns are the key challenges.

5. TRANSIT AND TRADE BARRIERS AT STRATEGIC BORDER CROSSINGS: FIELD SURVEY RESULTS

In South Asia, much of the trade between India and its neighboring countries is taking place along land routes, particularly through the road corridors. However, as discussed above, there is no direct cross-border movement of road freight transportation between them, except in few cases. At the Bangladesh–India border, goods are required to be transhipped as no direct through-road transport movement across the border is allowed.[13] However, the potential for freight movement by road between the geographically adjacent countries of South Asia is tremendous, once such a through transport movement can be facilitated (ADB 2005).

In view of role of GATT Article V (Freedom of Transit) and the required facilitation, we attempt to understand the extent of transit systems in place in selected border-crossing corridors in eastern South Asia. A systematic comparative analysis is carried out of the transit arrangements and the subsequent mechanisms in place in the sub-region. This has been done through an extensive field survey, conducted in five important border-crossing corridors in Bangladesh, Bhutan, India, and Nepal (Appendix 6.1).

A non-parametric exercise is conducted to capture the performance of LCSs. The analysis is based on both secondary and primary data. Five land border-crossing corridors (and corresponding land customs stations) connecting the four countries in the sub-region are selected. Appendix 6.1 details the five border corridors that are the potential transit points falling within the Asian Highway (AH) and/or SAARC Regional Multimodal Transport corridors. The purpose of the field survey is to understand the state of affairs of the LCS in the five border-crossing corridors in the sub-region. The selection of the border corridors is based on: *(a)* their potential to provide direct connectivity by enabling through movement across the sub-region; *(b)* the ability to provide access for landlocked countries to seaports or other major transport networks; and *(c)* the potential for providing shorter routes that would allow major transportation cost savings.

Table 6.7 provides a comparison of performances of six pairs of LCSs falling in five border corridors in the sub-region. This is the first time that both sides of the border in eastern South Asia sub-region are surveyed. At a glance, these 14 LCSs have many things in common as well as several dissimilarities. While there is no mismatch in the timing of operations of customs and immigration among the LCSs, the days of operation differ between India and Bangladesh. Apart from immigration, customs and security, which are an essential part of all LCSs, the other facilities in both the physical and non-physical categories vary across the LCSs. For example, except for Birganj none of the LCSs have an exclusive container-handling yard at the border. Similarly, except for Petrapole none has effectively adopted the fast track cargo clearance system. In the case of e-governance in customs, Petrapole and Raxaul use ICEGATE software, while Benapole and Birganj use ASYCUDA. Deviating from its main usage, the field survey finds that ASYCUDA in Nepal has been used for the calculation of revenue and other administrative purposes. Customs formalities in the remaining LCSs are mostly being handled manually. The existing Electronic Data Interchange (EDI) system also suffers from certain shortcomings that add

TABLE 6.7 Status of Trade Facilitation Services at Border

	LCS Pair 1		LCS Pair 2		LCS Pair 3		LCS Pair 4		LCS Pair 5		LCS Pair 6	
Location	Petrapole	Benapole	Changrabandha	Burimari	Jaigaon	Phuentsholing	Phulbari	Banglabandh	Panitanki	Karkabitta	Raxaul	Birganj
Country	India	Bangladesh	India	Bangladesh	India	Bhutan	India	Bangladesh	India	Nepal	India	Nepal
Working time (per day)	09.00– 17.00	09.00– 17.00	09.00– 17.00	09.00– 17.00	09.00– 17.00	09.00– 17.00	09.00– 17.00	09.00– 17.00	09.00– 17.00	09.00– 17.00	09.00– 17.00	09.00– 17.00
Working days (per week) for immigration	7	7	7	7	7	7	7	7	7	7	7	7
Working days (per week) for customs	7	6	7	6	7	7	7	6	7	7	7	7
Physical												
Customs	Yes	Yes	Yes	Yes	Yes	Yes	Yes	Yes	Yes	Yes	Yes	Yes
Immigration	Yes	Yes	Yes	Yes	Yes	Yes	Yes	No	Yes	Yes	Yes	Yes
Security	Yes	Yes	Yes	Yes	Yes	Yes	Yes	No	Yes	Yes	Yes	Yes
Bank	Yes[a]	Yes[a]	Yes	Yes[b]	Yes[a]	Yes[a]	No	No	Yes[b]	Yes[b]	Yes[a]	Yes[a]
Health	Yes	Yes	No	No	Yes	Yes	No	No	No	No	Yes	Yes
Warehouse	Yes	Yes[a]	Yes	Yes	Yes[a]	Yes[a]	Yes[a]	Yes	Yes[a]	Yes[a]	Yes[a]	Yes[a]
Weight bridge	Yes	Yes	Yes	No	Yes	Yes	Yes	No	Yes	No	Yes	Yes
Container handling yard	No	No	No	No	No	No	No	No	No	No	No	Yes[b]
Currency exchange	Yes[a]	Yes[a]	Yes	No	Yes[a]	Yes[a]	No	No	No	No	Yes[a]	Yes[a]

(Table 6.7 Continued)

(Table 6.7 Continued)

Location	LCS Pair 1		LCS Pair 2		LCS Pair 3		LCS Pair 4		LCS Pair 5		LCS Pair 6	
	Petrapole	Benapole	Changrabandha	Burimari	Jaigaon	Phuentsholing	Phulbari	Banglabandh	Panitanki	Karkabitta	Raxaul	Birganj
Country	India	Bangladesh	India	Bangladesh	India	Bhutan	India	Bangladesh	India	Nepal	India	Nepal
Waiting room	Yes	Yes	No	No	No	Yes	No	No	No	No	No	No
Shops, hotels, and restaurants	Yes	Yes	Yes	Yes	Yes	Yes	Yes[a]	No	Yes	No	Yes	Yes
Non-physical												
e-commerce of Customs	Yes (ICEGATE)	Yes (ASYCUDA)	No	No	No	No	No	No	No	No	Yes (ICEGATE)[c]	Yes (ASYCUDA)[d]
Internet	Yes	No	No	No	No	No	No	No	No	No	No	No
Telecom	Yes	Yes	Yes[a]	Yes[e]	Yes[a]	Yes[a]	Yes[e]	Yes[e]	Yes[a]	Yes[e]	Yes[a]	Yes[a]
Fast Track Cargo Clearance	Yes[f]	No	No	No	No	No	No	No	No	No	No	No

Source Compiled from the field survey results.

Notes
[a] Insufficient.
[b] Located few kilometers away from the border.
[c] Only for export cargo; import from Nepal handled manually.
[d] Only for revenue calculation and not for customs operation.
[e] Insufficient and not for all.
[f] For selected goods.

to the transaction costs. For example, although the filing of declarations has been made possible online, a hard copy of the declaration is generated by the system—albeit at a later stage—and signed for a variety of legal and other requirements, both for the importer and for customs. Other supporting documents are also submitted for verification by government authorities and their agents. Thus, many shortcomings associated with documentation continue to exist under the present EDI system.

Procedural complexities very often work as deterrents to India–Bangladesh trade.[14] The customs offices in eastern South Asia still require excessive documentation, especially for imports, which must be submitted in hard copy forms.[15] An Indian exporter to Bangladesh has to obtain 330 signatures on 17 documents at several stages.[16] While most of these documents are standard for international trade, the two governments tend to add requirements that are purely local in nature. The bureaucratic response to problems and anomalies has been to introduce new procedures and documents to avoid their recurrence. This introduces a significant increase in the cost of doing business, but, in many cases, has little effect on the cause of the problems. Because of this complex, lethargic and primitive procedure, pilferage continues to rise. This often changes the composition and direction of trade in eastern South Asia.

Most of the LCSs suffer from limited warehouse capacity and the lack of banking and foreign exchange facilities. In some cases, banks are located several kilometers from the border (for example, Burimari, Panitanki and Karkabitta). Adequate foreign exchange facilities are also unavailable at these borders. Some LCSs do not even have a foreign exchange facility, such as Burimari and Banglabandh in Bangladesh, Karkabitta in Nepal, and Phulbari and Panitanki in India.

Except for Kolkata and Haldia seaports, none of the LCSs has adequate capacity (in both software and hardware terms) to deal with goods in transit. In most cases, officials are unaware of their countries' commitment under GATT Article V and the obligations therein. It appears that South Asian countries have promoted bilateral transit agreements/arrangements that are not consistent with all other commitments on trade facilitation and with the objective of reducing trade barriers. Moreover, it appears that eastern South Asian countries did not take full account of international standards and instruments when designing and applying those agreements or arrangements. Therefore, they need to cooperate and coordinate in designing and applying bilateral and regional transit agreements/arrangements.

5.1 Benchmarking the Land Customs Stations

One of the common features of the border corridors surveyed in this study is that the present trade flow is very uneven across LCSs. A regional transit arrangement in South Asia would likely enhance regional trade volume, resulting in the redistribution of trade and traffic among the corridors. Efficient corridors are thus very important in order to maximize the benefits of regional connectivity. At the same time, inefficient corridors require much attention in order to put them in the peer group and to facilitate trade along that particular corridor.

The need for seamless cross-border infrastructure, both hardware and software, is a long-standing demand in South Asia. Failure in responding to this demand has actually slowing the South Asian trade. Therefore, one of the objectives of the trade facilitation would be to eliminate the asymmetry among the corridors in anticipation of a seamless regional connectivity. An evaluation of the efficiency of the border corridors would thus help in understanding the performance level of the border corridors in South Asia.

In this paper, the relative efficiency of border corridors is measured with the help of Data Envelopment Analysis (DEA). DEA is a linear programming-based technique for measuring the relative performance of organizational units where there is a presence of multiple inputs and outputs. There is reasonable consensus among economists that the mobility of goods, services and labor across regions depends largely on the quality and quantity of various integrated facilities available, and not directly and solely on the amount of investment or capital stock. Naturally therefore, the use of DEA is likely to better reflect the input–output relationship relative to capital in such a context. In the DEA methodology, formerly developed by Charnes et al. (1978), efficiency is defined as a weighted sum of outputs to a weighted sum of inputs, where the weights structure is calculated by means of mathematical programming, and constant returns to scale (CRS) are assumed.[17]

Moreover, performance evaluation and benchmarking are a widely-used method for identifying and adopting best practices as a means of improving performance and increasing productivity, and are particularly valuable when no objective or engineered standard is available to define efficient and effective performance. Benchmarking is often used in managing service operations, because service standards (benchmarks) are more difficult to define than manufacturing standards. Difficulties are further enhanced when the relationships between the inputs and the outputs are complex and involve many unknown trade-offs. For example, DEA is a tool that can evaluate performance and benchmarking of seaport services in the context of multiple inputs and outputs.

First, we measure the TC (transaction cost) of trade at each border point through a field survey. It is calculated for each year by using equation (1)

$$TC_{ijl}^t = \sum_{k=1}^n X_k^l \, , \tag{1}$$

where Xlk represents transaction costs components observed at the border l, that is, *(a)* loading/unloading fees, *(b)* parking fees, *(c)* speed-up payments, and *(d)* clearing agent's fees, all collected through the field survey.

Second, the TT (transaction time) of trade at each border point is calculated for each year by using equation (2)

$$TC_{ijl}^t = \sum_{k=1}^n Y_k^l \, , \tag{2}$$

where Ylk represents transaction time components observed at the border l, that is, *(a)* parking time, *(b)* time taken for customs clearance, and *(c)* loading/unloading time, collected through field survey. Both TC and TT are calculated based on field survey.[18]

The DEA model considered here uses data of TC and TT for exports for 2001 to 2006 of four eastern South Asian countries and considers both sides of the border at the bilateral level. By taking TC and TT, a major portion of trade costs at the border has been covered. Table 6.8 provides the basic assumptions of DEA, while Table 6.9 lists the estimated efficiency scores of land customs stations. The following observations are worth noting.

TABLE 6.8   Basic Assumptions in the DEA Model

Particulars	*Assumptions*
Decision-making units (DMU)	Nine land customs station
Inputs	Transaction cost and transaction time, measured for each DMU (land customs station)
Output	Exports (bilateral) handled by each DMU
Time period	2001–06
Model specification	Farrell input-saving measure of technical efficiency with constant returns to scale (CRS) and strong disposability of inputs

TABLE 6.9   DEA Scores

DMU (land customs stations)	Country	2001	2002	2003	2004	2005	2006
Petrapole	India	0.510	0.490	0.500	0.570	0.550	0.620
Benapole	Bangladesh	0.040	0.020	0.030	0.030	0.040	0.050
Raxaul	India	0.330	0.170	0.400	0.590	0.690	1.000
Birganj	Nepal	0.160	0.250	0.200	0.270	0.450	0.470
Jaigaon	India	0.320	0.830	0.610	0.740	0.560	0.520
Phuentsholing (1)	Bhutan	0.170	0.170	0.240	0.380	0.390	0.410
Phuentsholing (2)	Bhutan	0.030	0.020	0.030	0.030	0.040	0.070
Burimari	Bangladesh	0.010	0.000	0.010	0.010	0.010	0.010
Kakarvitta	Nepal	0.010	0.000	0.010	0.010	0.010	0.010
Banglabandha	Bangladesh	0.000	0.010	0.010	0.010	0.010	0.000
	Average	0.158	0.196	0.204	0.264	0.275	0.316

First, the DEA scores suggest that, among the nine LCSs, Raxaul is the only efficient LCS, while the remainder is inefficient (Figure 6.2 and Table 6.10). Opposite Raxaul is Birganj (in Nepal), which is relatively inefficient but which succeeded improving its position during 2001–06. If Birganj had been as efficient as Raxaul, this India-Nepal border corridor would have made further gains to regional trade in general and in trade between India and Nepal in particular.

FIGURE 6.2   Scatter Diagram of DEA Scores, 2001–06

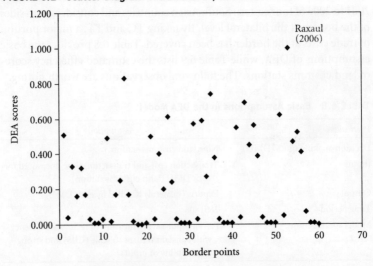

TABLE 6.10 Relative Efficiency of Land Customs Stations

Relatively efficient	Moderately inefficient	Highly inefficient
Raxaul	Birganj	Benapole
	Petrapole	Burimari
	Jaigaon	Kakarvitta
	Phuentsholing	Banglabandha

Second, Petrapole (in India), even though relatively inefficient, has improved its position. On the other side of the border, Benapole (in Bangladesh) is comparatively inefficient.

Third, the average performance of the nine border points has improved (the DEA score increased from 0.158 in 2001 to 0.316 in 2006) pointing to the fact that there has been positive development in aggregate term in border customs stations and trade facilitation.

There are indeed sizeable gains to be won by making customs points on both sides of the border efficient. The efficiency of border corridors and LCSs is an important factor in South Asia's competitiveness and its trade prospects. In order to maximize the benefits of trade liberalization in view of SAFTA and in anticipation of full regional transit arrangement, either under GATT Article V or under SAFTA, governments in South Asia should place the utmost importance on improving inefficient LCSs. If the objective is to ensure equitable growth of trade and traffic in South Asia, all the border-crossing points must improve their efficiency. Therefore, the new agenda for trade facilitation should consider measures in order to *(a)* constantly improve the performance of border corridors and LCSs and *(b)* eliminate the asymmetry between the LCSs pairs.[19]

6. CONCLUSIONS

South Asian economies are aiming to undertake trade facilitation measures that will greatly reduce current physical and non-physical barriers to trade by means of both visible infrastructure (such as multimodal corridors and terminals) and invisible infrastructure (such as reformed policies, procedures, and regulations). Due to the lack of adequate research on trade facilitation, not much information is available on the existing profile of trade facilitation measures (both at the borders and in the capital cities) in South Asia. This is an area of research that needs special attention from policy makers and researcher scholars in South Asia.

Transit is as important as trade liberalization. It is an intrinsic element of any cross-border movement of goods and vehicles, and yields significant influence on national and regional economies. The present arrangement of transit in South Asia is bilateral where India provides overland transit to Bangladesh, Nepal and Bhutan for their bilateral trade, and maritime transit to Nepal and Bhutan for their international trade. With the increasing emphasis on administrative reform, governance and security, there is an urgent need for a regional transit agreement. Among the major causes of high trade transaction costs in eastern South Asia are the cumbersome and complex cross-border trading practices, which also increase the possibility of corruption. The goods carried by road in South Asia are largely subject to transhipment at the border, which imposes serious impediments to regional and multilateral trade. The position is further compounded by lack of harmonization of technical standards. Considering the region's emergence as a free trade area from 2006 onward, a regional transit will help South Asian countries to achieve the potential benefits of moving a Customs Union in 2015 and an Economic Union in 2020.

The efficiency of border corridors is also a critical factor in a region's competitiveness and its trade prospects. Using the DEA, this paper has evaluated the efficiency of the border corridors in eastern South Asia. The average performance of the nine LCSs examined has improved over time, pointing to the fact that there has been positive development in land customs stations. However, eight of the nine LCSs surveyed were found to be still relatively inefficient (Raxaul in India being the most efficient). In order to maximize the benefits of trade liberalization, both in view of SAFTA and in anticipation of a regional transit arrangement under GATT Article V, South Asian countries should place highest priority on achieving equitable growth of trade and traffic in South Asia. It is crucial that not only all the border corridors are to be made more efficient but that an equally high level of efficiency must be achieved at all the customs stations, thereby reducing the asymmetries among the corridors.

Many of the land customs stations surveyed are inadequately equipped with information technology, and lack in coordination. "Software" aspect of trade facilitation is still important in South Asia. At the same time, to improve performance, border corridor management authorities (that is, in this case, governments) need to constantly evaluate operations or processes related to providing, marketing and selling of services to the users. Hence, it is felt that at each border a complementary and coordinated performance monitoring approach is urgently required in order to address the changing environment of global and regional trade and to achieve sustainable improvement in competitiveness. Thus, the requisite policy agenda extends broadly to stimulating the evolution of border corridor services, promulgating new performance standards, and encouraging their implementation at both the national and regional levels.

South Asian countries have promoted bilateral transit agreements/ arrangements that are not consistent with all other commitments on trade facilitation and with the objective of reducing trade barriers. Moreover, it appears that eastern South Asian countries did not take full account of international standards and instruments when designing and applying those agreements or arrangements. Therefore, they need to cooperate and coordinate in designing and applying bilateral and regional transit agreements/arrangements.

Finally, a regional transit arrangement will help South Asia to better integrate the region and also to strengthen the globalization process. The scope and issues covered under the GATT Article V, which addresses traffic in transit, have become extremely important since intraregional trade in South Asia has expanded.[20] Making transit system in South Asia, WTO offers several useful solutions.

APPENDIX 6.1

TABLE A6.1   Surveyed Border-crossing Corridors

Land corridor[a]	Countries	Border-crossing corridors	Land customs stations (LCS) surveyed
Lahore–New Delhi–Kolkata–Petrapole–Benapole–Dhaka (2,322 km)	Pakistan, India, Bangladesh	Petrapole (India)/Benapole (Bangladesh)	Wagah (Pakistan)/ Wagah Border (India), Petrapole (India)/ Benapole (Bangladesh)
Thimphu–Phuentsholing–Jaigaon–Kolkata/ Haldia (760 km)	Bhutan, India	Phuentsholing (Bhutan)/ Jaigaon (India), Changrabandha (India)/Burimari (Bangladesh)	Phuentsholing (Bhutan)/ Jaigaon (India)
Thimphu–Phuentsholing–Jaigaon–Burimari to either Dhaka–Chittagong (966 km) or Mongla (880 km)	Bhutan, India, Bangladesh		Phuentsholing (Bhutan)/ Jaigaon (India), Changrabandha (India)/ Burimari (Bangladesh)

(Table A6.1 Continued)

(Table A6.1 Continued)

Land corridor[a]	Countries	Border-crossing corridors	Land customs stations (LCS) surveyed
Kathmandu–Kakarvitta– Phulbari–Banglabandha to either Mongla (1,362 km) or Dhaka–Chittagong (1,442 km)	Nepal, India, Bangladesh	Kakarvitta (Nepal)/ Panitanki (India), Phulbari (India)/ Banglabandha (Bangladesh)	Kakarvitta (Nepal)/ Panitanki (India), Phulbari (India)/ Banglabandha (Bangladesh)
Kathmandu–Kolkata/Haldia (1,323 km)	Nepal, India	Birgunj (Nepal)/ Raxaul (India)	Birgunj (Nepal)/Raxaul (India)

Note   [a] Distances shown in this table represent the approximate lengths of the corridors.

NOTES

1. The authors acknowledge the useful comments made by Yann Duval of the United Nations Economic and Social Commission for Asia and the Pacific (UNESCAP), Bangkok on an earlier version of this paper. The authors are also grateful to Sandip Singha Roy and his team for conducting the field survey in India, Nepal and Bhutan, and to Abdul Bari for carrying out the field survey in Bangladesh. This study, which was conducted as part of the UNESCAP/ARTNeT initiative, aimed at building regional trade policy and facilitation research capacity in developing countries, was carried out with the aid of a grant from the World Trade Organization (WTO). The technical support of the UNESCAP is gratefully acknowledged. The opinions, figures, and estimates are the responsibility of the authors and should not be considered as reflecting the views or carrying the approval of the United Nations, ARTNeT, RIS and NSU. Any remaining errors are the responsibility of the authors. Usual disclaimers apply.

2. See, for example, Ray and De (2003), World Bank (2004), Asian Development Bank (2005).

3. Refer, the Declaration of the fourteenth SAARC Summit, New Delhi, 3–4 April 2007, available at www.saarc-sec.org/main.php

4. See, for example, Polak and Heertje (1993).

5. See, for example, UNESCAP (2006, 2007), WTO (2005a, 2005b).

6. See, for example, Das and Pohit (2006), Taneja (2007).

7. See, for example, Subramanian (2001), Arnold (2007), Wilson and Ostuki (2007), to mention a few.

8. This was also reported in Padeco (2005). See, also Rahmatullah (2006).

9. The India–Bhutan Agreement of 2003 states that "there shall be free trade and commerce between the two countries" and "free movement of goods flowing between the two countries." There are no references in either the Agreement or the attached Protocol, however, to road vehicles or other forms of surface transportation, or of the rules governing the use of Indian road space by Bhutanese vehicles (and vice versa). See *Agreement on Trade, Commerce and Transit between the Government of the Republic of India and the Royal Government of Bhutan*, India–Bhutan Trade Agreement, Ministry of Commerce and Industry, Government of India, New Delhi. Available at http://commerce.nic.in/trade/bhutan.pdf (accessed on 6 October 2009).

10. The routes are Gede (India)–Darsana (Bangladesh), Singhabad (India)–Rohanpur (Bangladesh), and Agartala (India)–Akhaura (Bangladesh).

11. SAARC countries have been discussing a Regional Motor Vehicles Agreement since 2007. See the note entitled "India's Chairmanship of SAARC" issued by the SAARC Division, Ministry of External Affairs, Government of India, 22 April 2008, New Delhi.

12. Currently, there are 56 transport-related international legal instruments aimed at facilitating the movement of goods, people and vehicles across international borders, initiated by the Economic Commission for Europe.

13. WTO defines trade facilitation as "the simplification and harmonization of international trade procedures," where "[i]nternational trade procedures" are defined as the "activities, practices, and formalities involved in collecting, presenting, communicating and processing data required for the movement of goods in international trade" (WTO 2009). The objective of trade facilitation is to reduce the cost of doing business for all parties concerned by eliminating unnecessary administrative burdens associated with bringing goods and services across the borders. The definition makes it clear that trade facilitation relates to a variety of activities such as import and export procedures (customs or licensing procedures), customs valuation, technical standards, health and safety standards, administrative procedures, transportation and shipping; insurance, payment and mechanisms as well as other financial requirements, and goods in transit.

14. However, the cross-border transportation of railway freight is partially permitted between India and Pakistan and India and Bangladesh on certain routes.

15. Several studies have dealt with trade facilitation issues in the context of trade between India and Bangladesh. See, for example, Chaturvedi (2006).

16. Improvements in customs procedures have definitely reduced the amount of informal payments needed for clearing cargo. Even so, under-the-table transactions to clear exports at the borders remain high. The actual amount is negotiated between the shipper and the customs agent, with both agreeing on the amount per shipment that will be reimbursed without an invoice and which will therefore be available for paying customs officials to expedite cargo clearance.

17. Refer also De and Ghosh (2008).

18. However, Banker et al. (1984) developed a model with variable returns to scale.

19. We intentionally avoided placing the large estimated values of TT and TC and their components due to space limitation. The same is freely available at http://www.unescap.org/tid/artnet/pub/wp5608.pdf (accessed on 6 October 2009). The usual caveat is that the series has been estimated based on the field survey by interviewing the selected stakeholders, which may not necessarily match the same results tabulated by any other sources. The authors of this paper have made this database available for further research on the subject.

20. There have been some developments in eliminating the barriers at borders comprehensively. For example, the Government of India's Integrated Check Post (ICP) project is a forward-looking step, which will help improve India's border infrastructure serving its South Asian neighbors. India plans about 13 ICPs, with one on the India–Pakistan border, four on the India–Nepal border, one on the India–Myanmar border and seven on the India–Bangladesh border. The cost of setting up the 13 ICPs has been estimated at Rs 7.36 billion. Of these, it is proposed to set up the four ICPs at Petrapole, Moreh, Raxaul and Wagah in Phase I at a cost of Rs 3.42 billion. In Phase II, the remaining nine ICPs are to be established at Hili and Chandrabangha (West Bengal), Sutarkhandi (Assam), Dawki (Meghalaya), Akaura, (Tripura), Kawarpuchiah (Mizoram), Jobgani (Bihar), Sunauli (Uttar Pradesh), and Rupaidiha/Nepalganj (Uttar Pradesh) at a cost of Rs 3.94 billion. Further details are available at www.mha.nic.in

REFERENCES

Arnold, J. 2007. "The Role of Trade Facilitation in Export Growth." In S. Ahmed and E. Ghani (eds), *South Asia: Growth and Regional Integration*. New Delhi: Macmillan India.

Asian Development Bank (ADB). 2005. *SAARC Regional Multimodal Transport Study (SRMTS)*. Manila: ADB.

Banker, R. D., A. Charnes, and W. W. Cooper. 1984. "Some Models for Estimating Technical and Scale Inefficiencies in Data Envelopment Analysis." *Management Sciences* 30: 1078–92.

Bhattacharya, D., and S. S. Hossain. 2006. "An Evaluation of the Need and Cost of Selected Trade Facilitation Measures in Bangladesh: Implications for the WTO Negotiations on Trade Facilitation." ARTNeT Working Paper No. 9, UNESCAP, Bangkok.

Charnes, A., W. W. Cooper, and, E. Rhodes. 1978. "Measuring the Efficiency of Decision-Making Units." *European Journal of Operational Research* 2: 429–44.

Chaturvedi, S. 2006. "An Evaluation of the Need and Cost of Selected Trade Facilitation Measures in India: Implications for the WTO Negotiations." ARTNeT Working Paper No. 4, UNESCAP, Bangkok.

———. 2007. "Trade Facilitation Measures in South Asian Ftas: an Overview of Initiatives and Policy Approaches." Discussion Paper 118, Research and Information System for Developing Countries (RIS), New Delhi.

Das, S., and, S. Pohit. 2006. "Quantifying Transport, Regulatory and Other Costs of Indian Overland Exports to Bangladesh." *The World Economy* 29(9): 1227–42.

De, P. 2008. "Realising the Gains from Full Regional Connectivity in South Asia: the Transport Costs Dimension." *Man and Development* 30(1): 27–44.

———. 2009a. "Trade Transportation Costs in South Asia: an Empirical Investigation." In D. Brooks, and D. Hummels (eds), *Infrastructure's Role in Lowering Asia's Trade Costs: Building for Trade*. Cheltenham: Edward Elgar.

———. 2009b. "Empirical Estimates of Transport Costs: Options for Enhancing Asia's Trade." In D. Brooks and D. Hummels (eds), *Infrastructure's Role in Lowering Asia's Trade Costs: Building for Trade*. Cheltenham: Edward Elgar.

De, P., and Ghosh, B. 2008. "Reassessing Transaction Costs of Trade at the India–Bangladesh Border." *Economic and Political Weekly* 43(29) 69–79.

Department of Revenue and Customs. 2007. *Bhutan Trade Statistics*. Thimpu: Ministry of Finance, Royal Government of Bhutan. Available online at at www.mof.gov.bt (accessed on 6 October 2009).

Duval, Y. 2007. "Trade Facilitation Beyond the Doha Round of Negotiations." ARTNeT Working Paper No. 50, UNESCAP, Bangkok.

International Monetary Fund (IMF). 2008. *Direction of Trade Statistics Yearbook*. CD-ROM, December 2008. Washington, DC: IMF.

Padeco. 2005. *South Asia Subregional Economic Cooperation (SASEC): Subregional Corridor Operational Efficiency Study*, Vols I to V. Manila: Asian Development Bank.

Polak, Jacob and Arnold Heertje (eds). 1993. *European Transport Economics*. Oxford: Blackwell.

Rahmatullah, M. 2006. "Promoting Transport Cooperation in South Asia." In *Regional Cooperation in South Asia: a Review of Bangladesh's Development 2004*. Dhaka: The University Press Ltd.

Ray, J. K., and P. De. 2003. *Promotion of Trade and Investment in Eastern South Asia Subregion.* New Delhi: Bookwell.

Research and Information System for Developing Countries (RIS). 2008. *South Asia Development and Cooperation Report 2008.* New Delhi: Oxford University Press.

Subramanian, U. 2001. "Transport, logistics, and trade facilitation in the South Asia subregion." In T. R. Lakshmanan, U. Subramanian, W. P. Anderson, and F. A. Leautier (eds), *Integration of Transport and Trade Facilitation: Selected Regional Case Studies.* Washington, DC: World Bank.

Subramanian, U., and J. Arnold. 2001. *Forging Subregional Links in Transportation and Logistics in South Asia.* Washington, DC: World Bank.

Taneja, N. 2007. "India's Exports to Pakistan: Transaction Cost Analysis." *Economic and Political Weekly* 42(2): 96–99.

United Nations Conference on Trade and Development (UNCTAD). 2004. Report of the Expert Meeting on the Design and Implementation of Transit Transport Arrangements, UNCTAD Trade and Development Board, TD/B/COM.3/EM.22/1, Geneva.

———. 2005. Report of the Expert Meeting on Trade Facilitation as an Engine for Development, Trade and Development Board, TD/B/COM.3/EM.24/3, Geneva.

———. 2007. *World Trade and Development Report 2007.* Geneva: UNCTAD.

United Nations Economic and Social Commission for Asia and the Pacific (UNESCAP). 2006. "An Exploration of the Need for and Cost of Selected Trade Facilitation Measures in Asia and the Pacific in the Context of the WTO Negotiations." Studies in Trade and Investment No. 57, Bangkok.

———. 2007. "Towards a Harmonized Legal Regime on Transport Facilitation in the ESCAP Region: Guidelines." Document No. ST/ESCAP/2489, Bangkok.

———. 2008. "UN to Explore Improving Market Access for Landlocked Developing Countries." Press release on the sixty-fourth Commission Session, No. N/12/2008, Bangkok, 21 April 2008.

Uprety, K. 2006. *The Transit Regime for Landlocked States: International Law and Development Perspectives.* Washington, DC: World Bank.

Wilson, J. S., and Ostuki, T. 2007. "Regional Integration in South Asia: What Role for Trade Facilitation?" Policy Research Working Paper No. 4423, World Bank, Washington D.C.

World Bank 2004. "Trade Policies in South Asia: an Overview." Report No. 29949 (Vol. 2), Washington, DC.

World Trade Organisation (WTO). 2005a. "Article V of GATT 1994: Scope and Application." Note by the Secretariat, Document No. TN/TF/W/2, Geneva.

———. 2005b. "WTO Negotiations on Trade Facilitation: Compilation of Members' Proposals (Revision)." Document No. TN/TF/M/2, Negotiating Group on Trade Facilitation, Geneva.

———. 2008. "WTO Negotiations on Trade Facilitation: Compilation of Members' Textual Proposals." TN/TF/W/43/Rev.14, Negotiating Group on Trade Facilitation, Geneva.

———. 2009. *Brief Information on Trade Facilitation.* Geneva: WTO. Available at http://www.wto.org/english/tratop_e/tradfa_e/tradfa_e.htm (accessed on 6 October 2009).

7

Transport Issues and Integration in South Asia

M. Rahmatullah[1]

1. INTRODUCTION

In a globalized economy, transport cost being a significant determinant of competitiveness; it makes an integrated and efficient transport network an essential element of the enabling environment. South Asia inherited an integrated transport system from the British, but this was fractured not only by the partition of India but by its political aftermath and now needs to be integrated again within the context of greater political harmony in South Asia, as it has entered into the second era of SAARC regional cooperation (SAFTA and Beyond). Due to lack of integration of the transport system in South Asia, the logistic costs are very high and ranges between 13–14 percent of GDP, compared to 8 percent in USA.

Integration of the transport network of South Asia is especially crucial to countries such as Nepal and Bhutan and regions such as north-east India. Such integration could serve to end their landlocked or semi-isolated status and provide shorter transport and transit links to their desired destinations including access to the sea.

Effective integration of the transport system in South Asia could also contribute greatly in enhancing access to remote areas, thereby bringing benefit of economic development to remote areas. But in order to make a real dent on poverty reduction, it is highly important to work out strategies as to how to engage the bottom half of the people to get involved in the development process. Participation of these people through a small percentage of shares in the ownership of the industry or enterprise is the way. Thus broadening of ownership is crucial for poverty reduction.

A regional overview of the South Asian economy revealed that it has been one of the fastest growing economic regions in the world (averaging around 6 percent growth per year) in the recent years. Despite such a growth, the intraregional trade among the SAARC member states has been only around US$10.48 billion in 2006, or around 5 percent of the total trade, compared to 45 percent in East Asia and 26 percent in ASEAN sub-region. This is happening despite the fact that tremendous potential exists to enhance such trade say up to US$40 billion, once the political environment becomes supportive and transport network gets further improved and integrated.

During the second half of the twentieth century, the transport system of the mainland countries of South Asia has developed only in a national context, with little consideration given to cross-border issues of compatibility, uniformity of standards in infrastructure and in acquisition of rolling stock and equipments. Similar problems however, were not observed in the island member states of SAARC.

The 12th SAARC Summit in Islamabad in 2004, called for strengthening transport, transit and communications links across South Asia. The Secretariat pursued this decision, and conducted the *SAARC Regional Multimodal Transport Study* (SRMTS) during 2005–06, with financial assistance of ADB, with the main objective of enhancing multi-modal transport connectivity among SAARC member states.

The 14th SAARC Summit held in New Delhi in 2007 decided to pursue the implementation of SRMTS recommendations, and urged their Transport Ministers to oversee the task. The SAARC Transport Ministers met in New Delhi on 31 August 2007 and decided to pursue the following sub-regional projects, proposed by only three member states.

1.1 Projects Proposed by Bhutan

1. Establishment of modern border-crossing facility including immigration, parking, and cargo handling facilities at Phuentsholing.
2. Procurement of cargo handling equipments namely, fork lifts with a capacity up to 5 mt. and cranes having carrying capacity up to 30 mt., to enhance physical facilities at the Customs Complex at Phuentsholing.

1.2 Projects Proposed by India

1. Birgunj–Katihar–Singhabad–Rohanpur–Chittagong railway corridor, with links to Jogbani, Biratnagar and Agartala.
2. Kathmandu–Birgunj–Kolkata/Haldia.
3. Agartala–Akhaura–Chittagong rail corridors.
4. Air-connectivities: Male–New Delhi and Islamabad–New Delhi.

1.3 Projects Proposed by Sri Lanka

1. Rail Corridor No. 5 between Colombo and Chennai.
2. Ferry Service between Colombo and Cochin and Colombo and Tuticorin as two pilot projects.

The Ministers' meeting decided that the Member States through mutual consultations may consider the viability/desirability of these projects. The matter could be considered again at the Third Meeting of the Inter-Governmental Group on transport, to be held in Colombo, in October/November 2008. But the trend set at the first meeting of Transport Ministers in New Delhi has not been very encouraging. As such certain dynamic initiative needs to be taken to ensure that something tangible happens within a short period.

2. MAJOR TRANSPORT PROBLEMS AND CONSEQUENCES OF NON-COOPERATION

The surface transport networks in South Asia still continue to remain fragmented due to various historical, political, and economic reasons as well as lack of cooperation among the member countries. As a result their potential as engines of economic growth at the regional level remains largely unrealized. This is happening despite the fact that the basic infrastructure and facilities to establish mutually beneficial intra- and inter-regional transport linkages already exist in many countries. The absence of such integration and continued non-cooperation in transport are having adverse impact on economic competitiveness of the countries, and they are losing on many fronts.

A container takes 35 days to move from New Delhi to Dhaka, as the maritime route is via Bombay and Singapore/Colombo to Chittagong

Port and then by rail to Dhaka. But the same container could have reached Dhaka within 5 days, if direct rail connectivity was there between New Delhi and Dhaka.

Similarly, for moving a container from Dhaka to Lahore, it is now required to travel 7,162 km by sea has instead of 2,300 km, because overland movement across India is not allowed. Transport cooperation among Bangladesh, India and Pakistan could have restored movement along shorter routes.

Since Pakistan has been denying facilities for overland trade between India and Afghanistan, New Delhi and Teheran are now jointly developing a transport corridor from India to Afghanistan and Central Asia through Iranian port of Chaubahar. This will become the key corridor to rapid expansion of economic cooperation between New Delhi, Kabul, and Central Asia.

Due to lack of adequate transport cooperation between India and Bangladesh, India and Myanmar are jointly implementing "Kaladan project" to link Sittwe port of Myanmar with Mizoram State of India, partly through Kaladan River and partly by road. This would be quite an expensive alternative for India to have access to north-east India via Sittwe port, Kaladan River and road, as an alternative to the existing route through the chicken neck. If there was transport cooperation with Bangladesh, India could have got a much shorter route across Bangladesh.

Indicated below are some of the major problems and their consequences, by different mode of transport.

2.1 Road Transport

Currently movement of trucks across the international frontier is constrained by lack of cross-border agreements between Bangladesh and India, as well as India and Pakistan. As a result, transhipment of cargo takes place at the border, which increases transport costs. Benapole/Petrapole route between India and Bangladesh carries the heaviest traffic by road, accounting for about 80 percent in terms of value. Currently, around 300 trucks are moving daily across this border point.

Between India and Nepal, Birgunj, Bhairahawa, and Biratnagar handle between them around 80–85 percent of the total international traffic of Nepal. India allows trucks from Nepal to operate on designated transit routes within India. Indian trucks are allowed anywhere into Nepal, but are given a limit of 72 hours to return to India. Nepalese trucks need permits for every trip to India with a validity of three months, but they are allowed to travel freely up to the nearest market towns and railheads in India.

India allows trucks from Bhutan to operate on designated transit routes within India, it also allows Bhutan to use Phuentsholing (Bhutan)–Changrabandha (India)–Burimari (Bangladesh) land route for their trade with Bangladesh, but this corridor is not allowed for third country trade.

India allowed a transit between Nepal and Bangladesh across the "Chicken neck," for bilateral trade only, and not for the third country trade of Nepal, which now has to pass through already congested Kolkata port. If transport cooperation was there, Nepal could have used Mongla port in Bangladesh, which has spare capacity.

The shipment of Assam tea to Europe is required to travel 1,400 km to reach Kolkata port along the "Chicken neck," since no agreement exists for India to use the traditional route through Chittagong port which would be shorter by 60 percent. The Southern border of Tripura State is only 75 km from Chittagong port, but goods from Agartala are re-quired to travel 1,645 km to reach Kolkata port through the "Chicken neck." If transport cooperation were there, goods would have traveled only around 400 km across Bangladesh to reach Kolkata.

With regard to passenger movement, there are two established routes between India and Bangladesh. The Dhaka to Kolkata and vice versa direct bus operation started in 1999 and has been doing well. The Dhaka–Agartala bus operation started in 2003, but still struggling to be a profitable route. On February 2005, two Bangladeshi private trans-port companies—"Shamoli Paribahan" and "SR Travels" jointly started the bus service between Dhaka and Siliguri (West Bengal) in cooperation with a private sector operator of Indian TATA Sumo microbuses.

Between Delhi and Lahore, cross-border bus services once a week in either direction started in 1999 but it was suspended in January 2002. These services resumed operation again from July 2003. The land-mark fortnightly bus service between India and Pakistan-administered Kashmir was launched on 7 April 2005 for the first time in nearly 60 years. Recently another two bus services between Lahore and Amritsar and Nanakana Sahib and Amritsar have commenced.

2.2 Rail Transport

Railway has great potential as a mode of surface transport for long dis-tance freight traffic. But its use is constrained by the technical problems related to different gauges, track structures and signaling, and incompatible rolling stocks. The absence of a multilateral agreement for direct intraregional movement has also been a main constraint, and as a result the full potential of railway as a mode of transport has not been fully realized.

Currently, three broad gauge (BG) rail corridors are active for export and import traffic between India and Bangladesh. On the western side, between Pakistan and India, there are two BG corridors that are currently providing connectivity, although one crossing is restricted to passenger movement only. There is limited freight movement by rail between India and Pakistan.

Indian freight trains travel only up to the border stations inside Bangladesh and Bangladesh Railway (BR) locomotives then pull the Indian wagons up to a short distance inside the country where transhipment takes place. BR wagons also do not cross the Indian border, as the rolling stock is incompatible with the air-braked stock of Indian Railways. Present load restriction over Jamuna Bridge in Bangladesh prohibits the movement of broad gauge fully loaded wagons across the bridge, although a dual gauge railway network now exists up to Dhaka. Recent investigation, however, revealed that fully loaded ISO containers on low platform flat cars of CONCOR can move over Jamuna Bridge, without any load restrictions.

Between India and Nepal, rail movements are entirely on broad gauge railway link connecting Kolkata port and other destinations in India with Birgunj ICD that started operation in July 2004. There is limited freight movement by rail between India and Pakistan.

Passenger movement by railway takes place between India and Pakistan. The Samjhauta (friendship) Express resumed its operation in January 2004, after more than 2 years suspension of services. The twice-weekly passenger train operates between Lahore and Attari (India) opposite Wagah in Pakistan. The overnight train from Delhi arrives at Attari where passengers get into Samjhauta Express for their onward journey to Lahore. Another train connection was inaugurated in February 2006 on the south-western side of India between Munabao–Khokhrapar to link Karachi with Jodhpur in India.

Passenger movement by rail between Dhaka and Kolkata started again on 14 April 2008 after 43 years, two trains operate in each direction during the weekend (Saturday–Sunday), and it is a journey of around 14 hours, which is considered very long, as the distance is only around 400 kilometers.

2.3 Inland Water Transport

Indian transit traffic and Indo-Bangladesh bilateral traffic regularly travel along two designated Inland Water Transport (IWT) Protocol routes across Bangladesh. These routes are highly underutilized, partly due to lack of adequate drafts, navigational aids, and partly due to limited number of ports of call and non-renewal of the Protocol for longer periods.

2.4 Maritime Transport

Traditionally maritime transport has been a dominant mode of transport in South Asia, in terms of carrying international trade of the SAARC member states. In this process, a number of maritime gateways flourished over the years and have been contributing a great deal in the socio-economic development of the member states.

2.5 Air Transport

Even though air transport has seen phenomenal growth over several decades, the SAARC region lags behind many other regions in terms of its usage of air travel. Connectivity between the regional centers, especially the capital cities in terms of direct flights is still very low and many capitals are not directly connected. The cost of travel is relatively high when compared to other regions. Moreover, the region has not developed strong hub operations for efficient regional transfers.

2.6 Border Crossing Problems

Considerable difficulties also exist at the land border crossings. Besides lack of bilateral agreements, other constraints include inefficient customs operations, lack of transparency in inspection procedures, informal payments and inadequate preparation of customs documentation by shippers, etc. None of the borders yet have online customs IT connectivity to facilitate clearances.

Banking, medical, communication, warehousing, security, and fire fighting facilities are deficient and wayside amenities are absent in many cases. Due to lack of adequate parking areas for trucks, vehicles are parked on the road creating acute congestion. At most of the border points, there is only one exit route for both passengers and goods.

A quick analysis of the various impacts of non-cooperation revealed that these are substantial and all the main land South Asian countries are incurring these losses. To address these impacts, and to facilitate smooth and uninterrupted movement across South Asia, it is highly important to identify certain priority corridors that could provide shorter and efficient connectivity among the countries concerned and to the outside world.

3. IDENTIFICATION OF SAARC TRANSPORT CORRIDORS/GATEWAYS

In order to address the consequences of non-cooperation in transport, along side the mobilization of political support, it was also considered necessary to identify certain SAARC corridors/gateways to provide shorter and efficient transport connectivity. An attempt was, therefore, made to identify selected corridors and gateways which could be developed further to establish an integrated transport system in South Asia for smooth and efficient movement of both goods and passengers across the sub-region.

The corridors and gateways identified under different modes are indicated below.

3.1 Regional Road Corridors

In the road sector, a total of 18 regional road corridors (both existing and potential) were identified under Phase I of SRMTS. After careful application of the criteria established earlier, the 10 road corridors of greater regional significance were identified for further detailed assessment (Table 7.1).

3.2 Regional Rail Corridor

An exercise similar to road corridors was undertaken to identify rail corridors of regional significance. Under Phase I of SRMTS, the country studies identified 15 existing and potential rail corridors for further consideration. After applying the selection criteria similar to those in road corridors, the five rail corridors of greater regional importance were identified for detailed assessment (Table 7.2).

TABLE 7.1   Selected Regional Road Corridors for Priority Attention

	Corridor	Countries	Basis of selection
SHC 1	Lahore–New Delhi–Kolkata–Petrapole/Benapole–Dhaka–Akhaura/Agartala	Pakistan, India, and Bangladesh	Potential to carry major intraregional traffic and Potential to providing shorter route leading to transport cost savings
SHC 2	Kathmandu – Birgunj/Raxaul–Kolkata/Haldia	Nepal and India	Access to landlocked Nepal to Indian ports
SHC 3	Thimphu–Phuentsholing–Jaigaon–Kolkata/Haldia	Bhutan and India	Access to landlocked Bhutan to Indian ports
SHC 4	Kathmandu–Kakarvitta–Phulbari –Banglabandha–Mongla/Chittagong	Nepal, India, and Bangladesh	Access to landlocked Nepal to Bangladeshi ports
SHC 5	Sandrop Jongkhar–Guwahati–Shillong–Sylhet–Dhaka–Kolkata	Bhutan, India, and Bangladesh	Potential to providing shorter route leading to transport cost savings
SHC 6	Agartala–Akhaura–Chittagong	India and Bangladesh	Shorter access to Chittagong port for Indian north-eastern States
SHC 7	Kathmandu–Nepalganj–New Delhi–Lahore–Karachi	Nepal, India, and Pakistan	Potential of the corridor to carry future traffic
SHC 8	Thimphu–Phuentsholing–Jaigaon–Burimari–Mongla/Chittagong	Bhutan, India, and Bangladesh	Access to landlocked Bhutan to Bangladeshi ports
SHC 9	Maldha–Shibganj–Jamuna Bridge (Bangladesh)	India and Bangladesh	Potential to provide direct connectivity to carry future traffic
SHC10	Kathmandu–Bhairahawa–Sunauli–Lucknow	Nepal and India	Potential of the corridor to carry future traffic

Source   SRMTS 2006, 25, Table 4.

3.3 Regional Inland Waterways Corridors

After careful application of the criteria established earlier, two IWT corridors of greater regional significance were selected for detailed assessment (Table 7.3).

TABLE 7.2   Selected Regional Rail Corridors for Priority Attention

	Corridor	Countries served	Basis for selection
SRC 1	Lahore (Pakistan)–Delhi/ Kolkata (India)–Dhaka (Bangladesh)– Mahishasan–Imphal (India)	Pakistan, India, and Bangladesh	Potential growth of intraregional traffic. Reduced distance and shorter transit time.
SRC 2	Karachi (Pakistan)– Hyderabad–Khokrapar– Munabao–Barmer– Jodhpur (India)	Pakistan and India	Shorter route for intra-regional traffic. Access to Karachi Port and potential third country traffic.
SRC 3	Birgunj (Nepal)– Raxaul–Haldia/ Kolkata (India)	Nepal and India	Access to the landlocked Nepal. Potential corridor for third country and bilateral traffic.
SRC 4	Birgunj (Nepal)–Raxaul– Katihar (India)– Rohanpur–Chittagong (Bangladesh) with links to Jogbani (Nepal) and Agartala (India)	Nepal, India, and Bangladesh	Access to Chittagong Port for Indian and Nepalese traffic. Shorter route for north-eastern states of India through Bangladesh.
SRC 5	Colombo (Sri Lanka)– Chennai (India)	Sri Lanka and India	Restoration of old rail ferry link to provide passenger and goods access from the island Sri Lanka to mainland South Asia.

Source SRMTS 2006, 27, Table 6.

TABLE 7.3   Selected Regional IWT Corridors for Priority Attention

	Corridors	Countries served
SIWC 1	Kolkata–Haldia–Raimongal–Mongla– Kaukhali–Barisal–Hizla–Chandpur– Narayanganj–Aricha–Sirajganj–Bahadurabad– Chilmari–Pandu	India and Bangladesh
SIWC 2	Kolkota–Haldia–Raimongal–Mongla– Kaukhali–Barisal–Hizla–Chandpur– Narayanganj–Bhairabbazar–Ajmiriganj– Markuli– Sherpur–Fenchuganj–Zakiganj– Karimganj	As above

Source SRMTS 2006, 29, Table 8.

3.4 Regional Maritime Gateways

The sea ports being the gateways of a country, these play a significant role in its socio-economic development. Even after major development of roads and rail transport in the recent decades, maritime transport continued to play a dominant role in carrying international trade.

The country reports, prepared under Phase I of SRMTS identified 19 maritime gateways that are playing significant role in carrying the international trade of SAARC countries. After careful application of the criteria established earlier, 10 Maritime Gateways were selected for further assessment (Table 7.4).

TABLE 7.4   Selected Regional Maritime Gateways for Priority Attention

SAARC state	Principal ports for SAARC trade	Basis of selection
Pakistan	Karachi	Potential to handle future traffic
	Port Bin Qasim	Potential to handle future traffic
India	J.N.P.T.	Potential to handle intra-SAARC traffic
	Kolkata/Haldia	Ability to provide access for landlocked countries to sea ports
	Cochin	Potential to handle intra-SAARC traffic
	Tuticorin	Potential to handle intra-SAARC traffic
Bangladesh	Chittagong Mongla	Ability to provide access for landlocked countries and regions to the sea ports
Sri Lanka	Colombo	Potential to handle international and intraregional container traffic as a hub port
Maldives	Male	Potential to handle future traffic

Source   SRMTS 2006, 30, Table 10.

3.5 Regional Aviation Gateways

At present there are 20 airports within the SAARC region from which there are flights to other regional destinations. In addition, five gateways were proposed for consideration, as they have the potential to develop as regional gateways in the near future.

To identify gateways of most significance for intraregional transport, after applying the criteria established earlier, 16 aviation gateways were selected for further assessment (Table 7.5).

TABLE 7.5   Selected Regional Aviation Gateways for Priority Attention

Airport	Country	Rank/feature for consideration
Dhaka	Bangladesh	Ranked 5
Paro	Bhutan	Ranked 16
Delhi		Ranked 2
Mumbai		Ranked 6
Chennai		Ranked 3
Kolkata		Ranked 10
Thiruvananthapuram		Ranked 9
Begaluru		Ranked 11
Tiruchirapalli		Ranked 15
Kochi		Ranked 12
Hyderabad	India	Ranked 14
Male	Maldives	Ranked 4
Kathmandu	Nepal	Ranked 8
Karachi		Ranked 6
Lahore	Pakistan	Ranked 12
Colombo	Sri Lanka	Ranked 1

Source SRMTS 2006, 30, Table 14.

4. PHYSICAL AND NON-PHYSICAL BARRIERS ALONG IDENTIFIED CORRIDORS / GATEWAYS

To enhance transport connectivity among SAARC member countries and to promote seamless movement across the border, an assessment was made of both physical and non-physical barriers along the identified corridors and gateways. Some of the major findings are highlighted below.

4.1 Barriers in Road Corridors

Out of a total length of 8,800 km (for 10 road corridors identified), 36 percent are four or more lanes paved road and 57 percent are two lane paved roads. The remaining roads (around 7 percent) are of poor quality, having either narrow lane (3.5 to 5.5 mm) and/or having poor surface conditions, located mostly in Bangladesh, Bhutan, India, and Nepal.

Some of the other important *physical barriers* identified included lack of parking, immigration and customs offices, baggage scanning equipments, telephone and warehousing at several border posts, as well as absence of EDI/IT, and use of cumbersome and complicated customs procedures including lack of transparency in inspection The most crucial *non-physical barrier* was found to be the lack of a bilateral transport agreement to facilitate uninterrupted movement of goods and vehicles across the borders.

4.2 Barriers in Rail Corridors

The major *physical barriers* included the lack of standardization of technologies, operation and maintenance practices, and use of different gauges, braking systems, incompatibility of rolling stock, etc. Other major physical barriers included inadequate loop lengths, missing links of shorter lengths in the borders areas, lack of physical infrastructure at interchange points, load restrictions on bridges, lack of coordination in gauge conversion programs of Indian and Bangladesh railways, and capacity constraints in certain sections of the identified corridors.

Concerning *non-physical barriers*, the most crucial one was the lack of a multilateral rail transport agreement. Other non-physical barriers included manual handling of documentation, duplication of customs checks, limited working hours, restrictions on movement of containers, open wagons and oil tankers, unidirectional traffic and the suspension of rail-cum-ferry services between Sri Lanka and India.

4.3 Barriers in Inland Waterways Corridors

It was observed that IWT corridors serve the interest of only Bangladesh and India, where levels of traffic both intra-country and transit had been reducing over the years, although during certain periods bilateral traffic has been substantial. It was, however, recognized that inland waterways transport has great potential to provide a cost-effective transport service between India and Bangladesh. To this end, one of the most crucial *non-physical barriers* identified was the renewal of the Protocol between India and Bangladesh for shorter periods. But this issue has now been addressed.

Some of the *major physical barriers* identified in the regional inland waterways included high rates of siltation, bank erosion, inadequate navigational aids and draft restriction, as well as poor condition of jetties, piers, lack of sufficient storage, poor condition of cargo handling equipments and support crafts. In addition there is no container handling facilities in inland water transport system. Cargo carrying vessels are also old, repair facilities inadequate and hinterland connectivity of the inland ports as well as cargo transfer facilities was found to be poor.

4.4 Barriers in Maritime Transport Gateways

In the context of regional maritime gateways, the major physical barriers included capacity constraints at many of the ports, together with heavy siltation at channels where depths fluctuate with tide. Channel markings were also not found to be adequate and suffered from poor maintenance. Cargo and ship handling equipment, as well as floating crafts were found to be quite old in many ports. Poor road and rail connectivity lack of ICDs and CFS were other major physical barriers, besides lack of roro ferry vessels and passenger handling facilities at Cochin and Tuticorin.

The non-physical barriers, which were found to be impacting port performances, included lack of professional management and computerization, as well as lack of EDI/IT to link up stakeholders. Customs procedures were found to be too complicated, cumbersome port documentation was still in use and labor unrest were also noted in some maritime gateways. The absence of a bilateral agreement for ferry service between Colombo and Tuticorin/Cochin was also noted as a major non-physical barrier.

4.5 Barriers in Aviation Gateways

With regard to aviation gateways, the *major physical barriers* included capacity constraints at several airports for both passengers and cargo, in terms of runways, parking areas for aircrafts, passenger handling areas, cargo processing facilities (green channel, cold storage, etc.), as well as security and baggage handling facilities. It was also observed that in Bangladesh Biman, many of the aircrafts were quite old and needed replacement. The situation has, however, changed recently, as Bangladesh Biman, has already placed order for purchasing a large number of new aircrafts.

In case of *non-physical barriers*, major constraints included the limited number of direct flights between the capitals resulting in the need for transfers and involvement of travel even outside the region, the low use of air travel compared to economic conditions, the higher air fare and airport charges compared to other regions and visa restrictions.

5. ADDRESSING THE BARRIERS

Since South Asia has now entered into the second era of SAARC regional cooperation (SAFTA and Beyond), it is crucial that a target or vision is set for integration of South Asian transport system, particularly in view of the commitments made by the South Asian leaders in the 12th SAARC Summit in Islamabad in 2006 and in the 14th SAARC Summit in New Delhi in 2007. The "Vision" should target at achieving uninterrupted movement of goods and vehicles across the countries of South Asia. The vision should call for actions to achieve the following targets to reduce transportation costs:

1. Integration of the transport system of South Asia covering all modes.
2. Improvement/rehabilitation of the weaker and unused sections and completion of missing links.
3. Improvement of cross-border facilitation measures (software), including improvement of physical facilities at the border crossing.

In order to achieve the targets set above, huge investment would be needed together with strong political commitment of South Asian leaders. According to certain estimates presented by Prabir De, to sustain 8 percent regional GDP growth, South Asia needs US$108 billion every year (about 12 percent of regional GDP) in modernizing the physical infrastructure sector. The need for a "regional infrastructure fund" is also being talked about to support the infrastructure deficit. In this context, exchange of experiences in infrastructure financing and development among countries of the region could go a long way in improving the regional infrastructure and connectivity.

To address the various physical and non-physical barriers indicated in the earlier section, an in-depth exercise was undertaken to identify measures that could be adopted, and details of these are included in the SRMTS final report, June 2006. Since the type of measures proposed were too many, an attempt was made here to prioritize the core issues that should receive immediate attention of the SAARC governments and other stakeholders to establish efficient multimodal transport connectivity together with efficient border-crossing facilitation measures. The measures, which could be taken to address the major barriers in different modes, are indicated below.

5.1 Regional Road Corridors

Improvement of Facilitation Measures at Border Crossing:

- Development of transport and transit agreements between India, Bangladesh and Pakistan to facilitate smooth movement of freight and passenger vehicles across the border.
- Adoption of facilitation measures and simplified customs procedures for efficient clearance of goods across the border points.
- Strict enforcement of restrictions on overloading of vehicles in each of the SAARC member states in order to reduce the damage of the selected corridors.
- Development of modern physical facilities at border crossings (on both sides), between India and its neighbors in order to facilitate movement of both passengers and freight.

Improvement of Transport connectivity:

- Improvements of certain stretches of the roads in Bihar, West Bengal, Bangladesh, and Bhutan, to assist Nepal, Bhutan, India, and Bangladesh in reducing transit costs;
- The last few kilometers of road corridors up to the international borders to be treated as part of National Highways in all SAARC countries, and developed accordingly.

5.2 Regional Rail Corridor

Improvement of Facilitation Measures:

- Development and adoption of a multilateral rail transport agreement by the SAARC member states to facilitate smooth movement across the region.
- Simplification and standardization of documentation, elimination of double customs checking, introduction of IT to enable data transfer, to facilitate faster clearance of goods/vehicles at border crossing.
- Bangladesh Railway to ensure quicker return of Indian rolling stocks to reduce their turn around time.

Improvement of connectivity and standardization of Technology:

- Augmentation of sectional capacity along the identified corridors namely Delhi–Mughalsarai; Sunggauli–Muzaffarpur; Mausi– Katihar;

and Tongi–Akhaura to handle the projected and potential growth of intraregional traffic.
- Provision of adequate loop lengths, efficient transhipment facilities, etc., at border crossing and interchange points.
- Construction of missing links between Jogbani–Biratnagar, Akhaura–Agartala, Jiribam–Tupul (Imphal), and re-commissioning sections such as Kulaura–Shahbazpur, and Medawachchiya–Talaimannar.
- Strengthening of bridges (Jamuna for example) and introduction of ways to enable through movement of containers across the region.
- Standardization of technologies, including track, rolling stock, and signaling. Coordination among Bangladesh and Indian railways gauge conversion programs.

5.3 Regional Inland Waterways

Improvement of Facilitation Measures:

- The existing inland waterways protocol between Bangladesh and India to be renewed, each time, for longer periods, say up to 3–5 years.
- In order to make intercountry traffic movement by IWT attractive, more ports of call in Bangladesh to be allowed.

Investment needed to revive IWT:

- Joint assessment to be made by Bangladesh and India of the future role that inland waterways could play in carrying intercountry and Indian transit traffic, and whether such role would justify investments in dredging, installation, and maintenance of navigational aids and vessels replacement.

5.4 Regional Maritime Gateways

Improvement of Maritime Infrastructure:

- Expansion of port capacity, especially to handle more container traffic, particularly at Colombo (as the regional hub), Chittagong, Haldia, and Male.

- Planning and augmentation of rail, road, and pipeline connectivity at all regional ports.
- Improved dredging and marking of channels, especially at Chittagong, Colombo, Kolkata/Haldia, and Port Qasim.

Improvement of facilitation measures and port management:

- Improvement of port and trade facilitation measures to reduce dwell times of vessels.
- Introduction of professional management capability and private sector involvement in port development and operations.
- Re-commissioning of Passenger Ferry Service between India and Sri Lanka.

5.5 Regional Aviation Gateways

Improvement of Infrastructure Facilities:

- Development and modernization of international passenger terminals, especially at Bhutanese, Indian, and Nepalese airports.
- Improvements in radar systems/ILS to increase runway capacity to international maximums.

Improvement of Facilitation Measures and airport management:

- Assessment of adequacy of layout, staffing, and IT aids for immigration, customs, and security facilities at all airports for both passengers and cargoes.
- Introduction of commercial practices in airport management and encouraging private sector in development and management of airports.
- Promotion of low-cost carrier concept by each country, wherever it is feasible.

6. CONCLUSIONS AND WAY FORWARD

In order to achieve effective integration of the transport system of South Asia, a number of important initiatives need to be pursued, as indicated below.

6.1 Mobilization of Political Support

In order to mobilize political support, it is essential to ascertain the real dimensions of the political constraints and types of reservations that are obstructing integration of the transport system in South Asia. To this end, dialogues could be organized involving the entire civil society in each of the South Asian countries, to find the real scope and depth of the political reservations, so that some solutions acceptable to the politicians could be found. Representatives of Intelligence Agencies need to be involved in the dialogues to ascertain if there is any security issue that needs to be addressed to facilitate integration.

6.2 Various Issues Need to be Addressed Together

An informal consultation with some of the SAARC member countries revealed that problems related to transport integration cannot be resolved in isolation. These need to be looked into together with other outstanding problems in trade, environment, water sharing, border disputes, etc. According to those SAARC countries, the entire range of issues, which are standing on the way to establishing a "South Asian Community" and "SAARC transport Connectivity" should be addressed together, first bilaterally and then as a South Asian group, with a view to resolve most of them together. Strong political commitments are, however, needed to address these diversified problems together.

6.3 Cost of Non-cooperation Needs to be Highlighted

A process of awareness creation through dialogues, about the mutual benefit of transport integration, or cost of non-cooperation among countries, based on a study could go a long way in persuading the political leadership about the importance of transport integration. This study could focus on a number of selected corridors/routes which could provide cost-effective connectivities *vis-à-vis* existing inefficient and long routes. Estimate of benefit should be based on potential traffic/trade that could be generated once the selected corridors/routes are available to regional traffic movement, so as to establish that it would be a win–win situation for all countries involved.

6.4 Major SAARC Countries Need to take Bold Steps

To make progress beyond what has been achieved so far, the member countries of SAARC will have to take bold decisions and make further political commitment toward integration. At the SAARC Transport Minister's meeting held on 31 August 2007 in New Delhi, only a few barriers standing on the way to regional transport integration were picked up for consideration. Unless the major countries such as Bangladesh, India, and Pakistan take the initiative to address the barriers identified, by SRMTS, it is going to take a very long time before a major breakthrough could be expected.

6.5 Integration would Need Nominal Resources

The SAARC member countries, given their physical and cultural proximity and shared history and heritage, form a natural area for integration. Most of these countries once formed part of an integrated economy, and yet they probably constitute one of the less "internally connected" sub-regions in the world today. The integration of the SAARC transport networks would, therefore, largely involve a reintegration of existing infrastructures, requiring minimum commitment of economic resources.

6.6 Need to Involve People at Large

The European Union and, to a lesser degree, ASEAN were both successful in moving their own respective regional processes forward essentially because the peoples of those countries were convinced that such cooperation was in their larger interest, and this translated to the leadership level through the domestic and regional political dynamics that gradually strengthened a sense of regional identity. But this has been greatly lacking in the South Asian region.

It is, therefore, essential that concerted efforts are made by all stakeholders, the governments, the private sector, and the civil society at large, to bring about a change in the political mind-set of the leaders, so that a long lasting solution can emerge. The Civil Society Institutions in the member countries should take the initiative to organize the dialogues referred to above. Unless this challenge of integration is addressed soon with seriousness, the countries of South Asia in general, and the land-locked countries/regions in particular, stand the risk of foregoing many of the economic opportunities that the process of globalization could have provided.

NOTE

1. This paper has heavily drawn from the "SAARC Regional Multimodal Transport Study (SRMTS)," prepared by SAARC Secretariat in June 2006. The Author was the team leader of that study.

REFERENCES

Das, Gurudas. 2001. "Trade between North Eastern Region and Bangladesh: Nature, Trends and Implications for Development Cooperation" paper presented in the seminar on *India's Northeast and Bangladesh: Problems and Opportunities*, in February 2001 at Guwahati.

De, Prabir. 2008. Comments on a paper "Transport Issues & Integration in South Asia" by M. Rahmatullah. Presented in the *1st South Asia Economic Summit*. Held on 28–30 August 2008. Colombo: Sri Lanka.

Rahmatullah, M. 2004. "Integrating Transport Systems of South Asia" in Sobhan, Rehman (ed.) (2004) *Promoting Cooperation in South Asia: An Agenda for 13th SAARC Summit*, Centre for Policy Dialogue and the University Press Ltd., Dhaka.

SAARC Regional Multimodal Transport Study (SRMTS). 2006. SAARC Regional Multimodal Transport Study Report. Kathmandu: SAARC Secretariat.

SASEC. 2005. "Subregional Corridor Operational Efficiency Study-Draft Final Report" presented in the South Asia Subregional Economic Cooperation (SESEC) Third Working Group Meeting held in 9–10 May 2005, Bangkok, Thailand.

Sobhan, Rehman. 2000. *Rediscovering the Southern Silk Route: Integrating Asia's Transport Infrastructure*, Centre for Policy Dialogue and the University Press Ltd., Dhaka.

Subramanium, Uma. 2001. "Transport, Logistics, and trade Facilitation in the South Asia Subregion" in *Integration of Transport and trade Facilitation: Selected Regional Case Studies*. The World Bank, Washington D.C.

Verghese, B.G. 1998. *India's North East Resurgent: Ethnicity, Insurgency, Governance Development*, Konark Publishers, New Delhi cited in Subramanium, 2001.

8

Harmonizing Regulatory Mechanisms

Options for Deepening Investment Integration in South Asia

Mark Andrew Dutz[1]

1. INTRODUCTION

With the gradual reduction of cross-border trade barriers, domestic enterprise regulations—for example, entry/investment, exit/disinvestment, and operational regulations, including licensing, taxation, behind-the-border trade and logistics-related rules, banking and capital market rules, legal dispute settlement mechanisms, and competition law, as well as the heavier regulation of infrastructure sectors and frameworks for public–private partnerships (PPPs)—have become an increasingly significant factor affecting the relative prices of exports, imports, and domestic production. The effects of inefficient domestic regulations transcend national borders, distorting and reducing not only trade but also investment levels. The issue has therefore become an important matter of regional economic policy. One driver of regionalization of regulatory policies is the high fixed cost of regulation and prevailing technical capacity constraints, especially in the more specialized regulatory areas and for the smaller countries. Even more important, regionalization of regulatory policies—and supporting institutional strengthening—in principle could improve the capacity of individual countries to credibly commit to more open and stable regulatory policies, and thereby facilitate increased flows of finance within and across countries. This could have a significant impact on investment levels.

This chapter presents some options for deepening investment integration in South Asia as a foundation for more substantive follow-on work in this area. As elaborated below, initial concrete steps for enhanced cooperation could include the following:

- Joint deregulation in selected areas, such as the more systematic removal of bureaucratic red tape obstacles to "doing business" and investment, the removal of key sectoral restrictions to allow 100 percent inward direct investment for all investors, the removal of double taxation, and the promotion of a regional open sky policy, starting with one such focused intervention and using it as a "quick win" demonstration pilot to create momentum for more such regional pro-competition policies.
- Financial sector integration, with relaxation of capital controls, starting with the Securities and Exchange Board of India (SEBI) entering into memorandums of understanding (MoUs) for securities markets within all South Asian Association for Regional Cooperation (SAARC) countries.
- Increased information exchange among regional infrastructure regulators, with the establishment of regional regulatory advisors to facilitate nonbinding advice on common issues.
- A regional hotline at the SAARC level (as a possible precursor to a SAARC Investment Authority) for harmonization initiatives that are focused on the areas of greatest concern to individual business people across the region, thereby fostering enhanced public–private interactions on these issues.

Although a coordinated program of regulatory reform and investment climate harmonization has advantages, such coordination takes time and effort. Because delays create the risk of providing a reason to defer individual country reforms, countries should be encouraged to proceed individually while working to agree on common reforms.

2. CONTEXT AND BENEFITS

Current low levels of extra- and intraregional investment flows could be increased through regulatory harmonization. Foreign direct investment (FDI) stock levels as a share of gross domestic product (GDP) historically have been exceedingly low in South Asia, and they remain at the lowest level for all developing country regions at 0.7 percent of GDP in 2002 (Figure 8.1). This low level of investment reflects low extraregional as well intraregional investment flows. A more disaggregated look at the number of new (greenfield) and expansion FDI projects underlying these aggregate investment stock figures present a similar picture, and highlight the low level of intraregional investment relative to total projects.[2] Of the 1,232 FDI projects in South Asia over the last 30 months (January 2002 to June 2004), only 31 or 2.5 percent are intraregional in origin—by far the largest foreign investors in the region over this period are the larger economies of the Organization for Economic Co-operation and Development (OECD), with the United States accounting for 561 projects, the United Kingdom 151 projects, Germany 64, Japan 52, and France 39. By contrast, the level of intraregional investment in Southeast Asia (including China) is more than three times higher, with 339 of the reported 4,458 projects being intraregional in origin (China alone accounts for 2,836 of these projects,

FIGURE 8.1   FDI as a Percent of GDP

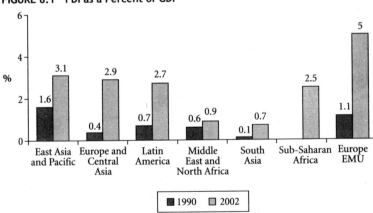

Source   World Bank 2004c.

or more than twice the number of FDI projects received by all of South Asia).[3]

In spite of the existing low levels of extra- and intraregional FDI flows, recent history suggests that these flows have the potential to increase significantly following credible regional regulatory harmonization, as evidenced by the experience of the North American Free Trade Agreement (NAFTA) and of recent new entrants to the European Union. NAFTA entered into force in January 1994 and contained 900 pages of required regulatory harmonization to which each nation was required to conform its domestic laws. In Mexico, the proportion of FDI to GDP increased from 1.1 percent in 1980–85 and 1.2 percent in 1985–93 to 3.0 percent in 1994–2001 (Lederman et al. 2003). In the Czech Republic and Poland, regulatory harmonization and integration with the European Union contributed to increases in the proportion of FDI to GDP between 1993–94 and 2000–02 from 1.7 to 10.7 percent for the Czech Republic and from 1.9 to 3.6 percent for Poland. Net benefits of similar orders of magnitude are conceivable in South Asia following credible and sustainable political rapprochement between countries underpinned by regulatory harmonization, in particular given the low starting point of investment flows.

3. CONSTRAINTS

Key obstacles to investment and growth in South Asia include regulatory obstacles to "doing business"; inadequate access to reliable, reasonable-cost infrastructure services; controls on banking and movement of capital; and the absence of facilitating harmonized frameworks on competition and infrastructure. In spite of sporadic reforms across countries within the region, a large number of regulatory obstacles continue to pose obstacles to investment and the ability to conduct business. Although the larger class of firms that typically engage in cross-border investment activities generally do not face the same problems in starting a business as smaller enterprises, regulatory obstacles across South Asian countries in registering property, enforcing contracts, hiring and firing workers, and closing a business—combined with uneven enforcement of all such rules—create a significantly more unfriendly investment climate than East Asia, and especially than higher income OECD countries, impeding entry and expansion (Figure 8.2).

FIGURE 8.2   Cost of Doing Business

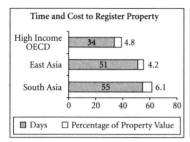

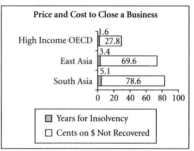

Source   World Bank 2004a.

In addition to corruption, governance, and the poor state of business regulation in South Asia, the region's most important barrier consistently highlighted in the various World Bank–sponsored Investment Climate Assessments (ICAs) is the poor quality of available infrastructure—inadequate access to power supply, followed by transportation, communication, finance, and land services (World Bank 2003a, 2003b, 2004b).[4] In India, for instance, the 2003 ICA found that, on average, manufacturers face almost 17 significant power outages per month, versus one outage in Malaysia and less than five in China. India's blended real cost of power is 74 percent higher than Malaysia's and 39 percent higher than China's. In terms of regional variance within India, the "better climate" states are much better off in the provisioning of infrastructure, including power supply, transport, and telecommunication, highlighting the importance of these indicators of the business environment in channeling investments within India. In Pakistan, the typical business estimates that it loses 5.6 percent in annual sales revenue because of power outages against a reported loss of 2 percent by its Chinese counterparts. Businesses in

Pakistan also would have to wait six to seven weeks to get a new fixed-line telephone connection, which is more than three times the wait in China. In Bangladesh, the most frequent complaint is the constraint imposed by the poor electricity system: 73 percent of large formal firms, 58 percent of urban informal firms, and 54 percent of rural enterprises assessed poor electricity as a major or very severe constraint. For rural Bangladeshi entrepreneurs, other top problems include road conditions (63 percent of respondents), access to finance (56 percent), and transportation to markets (42 percent).

In all countries, behind-the-border trade and logistics-related rules, including inefficient and differing cross-border facilities and customs procedures, and standards and certification processes written to match difficult-to-replicate features of local products rather than used as performance criteria to stimulate upgrading, further impede investment flows across the region. These results highlight the tremendous potential gains that could be achieved from increased investment in improved physical and business facilitation infrastructure services. This investment could create a virtuous circle with improved infrastructure services in turn creating an improved environment for further investment. The controls placed on banking and movement of capital into and out of South Asian countries are another key obstacle to investment and growth within the region.

Across the region, there are exhaustive controls on the movement of capital between countries. These restrictions, which extend to the repatriation and surrender of trade receipts, are a material impediment to direct and portfolio investment. Although direct investment restrictions have been extensively liberalized in India in recent years, companies seeking to invest in financial sector activities abroad must obtain approval from the regulatory authorities in India. The Indian restrictions extend to applying conditions to the sale of investments in India between nonresident investors and to the ability to open bank accounts in rupees. More generally across the region, greater licensing flexibility would be required for financial institutions; there are limits on foreign banks owning domestic banks, and limits on foreign banks entering the domestic system—typically with the minimum capital entry requirements being significantly higher for a foreign branch or subsidiary than for a domestic bank. With few exceptions, banks in one country cannot hold accounts in the currency of another (Nepali banks can hold rupee accounts, but they are not allowed to earn interest). Inward and outward direct investment is heavily restricted in a wide range of sectors (Box 8.1).

BOX 8.1   Controls on Direct Investments in South Asia: Illustrative Examples

Inward Direct Investment:

India: Restricted (less than 100 percent) in private sector banks; insurance; telecommunications; nonretail trading companies; mining for coal; diamonds and other precious stones; and airports. Restrictions also in Insurance sector and print media. Not permitted inter alia in retail trade; housing and real estate; agriculture (with exceptions); and plantations (excluding tea).

Pakistan: Permitted in services, infrastructure, social and agriculture conditions subject to the condition that the foreign equity investment be at least US$300,000 or equivalent. Not permitted in production of alcoholic beverages.

Bangladesh: All investments, except in the industrial sector, require approval.

Sri Lanka: Restricted (40 percent or less) in growing and primary processing of cocoa, coconuts, rice, rubber, spices and tea; mining and primary processing of non-renewables; timber processing using local timber; deep-sea fishing; mass communications; freight; travel; shipping agencies; education. Permitted only up to limit approval by government in: air transport; coastal shipping; alcoholic beverages; large-scale mining of gems. Not permitted in retail trading with capital of less than US$1 million; coastal fishing.

Nepal: All investments require approval. Foreign securities firms permitted for form JVs with ownership restricted to 40 percent. Not permitted in cottage and small-scale industries.

Bhutan: Controls on all direct investment transactions.

Afghanistan: All investments require approval. Only through JVs.

Outward Direct Investment:

India: Overall limit of US$100 million in one financial year through automatic route. Approval in India and abroad required in financial sector activities.

Pakistan: Prior approval under foreign exchange laws. Equity-based investments, including portfolio investments also require prior permission.

Bangladesh: All outward transfers of capital require approval (for resident-owned capita, approval only in exceptional cases).

Sri Lanka: Prior approval of MOF; priority to investments promoting domestic exports.

Nepal: No permission for Nepalese residents, except by government notice.

Bhutan: Controls on all direct investment transactions.

Source   IMF, Annual Report on Exchange Arrangements and Exchange Restrictions.

In infrastructure and the private provision of public services, there is a tremendous untapped potential for cross-country investment flows. India, for instance, has played a critical role in Bhutan's economic development by investing in hydroprojects and buying back the electricity. An ongoing proposal by the Tata Group, India's second largest conglomerate, to invest US$2 billion in Bangladesh's substantial natural gas supplies to power a complex comprising a 1,000 megawatt power station, a fertilizer plant, and a gas-fired steel finishing factory would combine Indian capital with Bangladeshi natural resources to create local production and jobs. While intercountry political tensions clearly affect the prospects of success for such deals, these types of projects would no doubt be facilitated by increased harmonization in regulatory frameworks for infrastructure and public service provision.

3.1 Policy Options

Cross-country investment flows would benefit from the increased credibility of commitments to openness and stability from regulatory harmonization, including joint deregulation of bureaucratic obstacles, financial sector integration, frameworks on competition and infrastructure, and an international best practice regional investment code. To achieve the benefits of greater cooperation in investment, progress is needed on a number of fronts. Regarding the reform or repeal of bureaucratic obstacles across the region, South Asia should set the goal of becoming the top reforming region over the next 5 years—aided by an explicit harmonization agenda. It is instructive in this regard to note that over the past year, Europe improved the most in large part because of the urgency of its own regulatory harmonization agenda: seven of the top 10 reformers that had a positive impact on "Doing Business" indicators were either new European Union members that had strong incentives to adopt best practice domestic regulations to join the club, or existing members that had to modernize to compete with the new entrants (World Bank 2004a, Table 1.1).

Regarding harmonizing financial market regulations, there are significant benefits to be reaped from transferring expertise and technology from India's relatively developed capital markets to other countries in the region. To date, Sri Lanka is the only country with which India has executed an MoU for securities markets, as recommended by the International Organization of Securities Commissions (IOSCO), although apparently discussions are under way with Nepal and Pakistan. In addition, SEBI has executed the IOSCO Multilateral Memorandum of Understanding Concerning Consultation and Cooperation and the Exchange of Information, but India is the only country in the region to have done so. As a low-cost but helpful step toward market integration, SEBI should enter systematically into these MoUs with all SAARC countries. Complementary to increased cooperation among stock exchanges through joint training and eventual cross-listings and joint issues, enhanced cooperation among all central banks in the region would help improve financial system linkages.

Regarding product market regulations, a question arises whether national efforts to update and enhance competition policy, together with possible regional harmonization efforts, should be encouraged as a priority issue. Indeed, as a direct response to the increasing role of markets in national economies, there has been a burgeoning of competition laws on a global level. India adopted a new competition law at end-2002, and a number of other SAARC countries are contemplating new policy initiatives in this area.

- At the domestic level, competition authorities—given sufficient status and ability—are well placed through their competition advocacy mandate to promote investments by helping address missing or poorly functioning rules and institutions and by removing rules and procedures that suppress entry and rivalry. In principle, competition authorities could be the natural advocates throughout the rest of government at central and local levels to improve the investment climate and remove bureaucratic obstacles to doing business, helping spur the entrepreneurial dynamism of national and international firms for the benefit of national consumers.
- At the international level, in response to an increasing level of cross-border trade and investment, there also has been an increasing level of competition policy activity. While the practice of competition policy at the level of international markets to date has been principally concerned with cross-border mergers and the operation of international cartels, arguably larger competition issues arise from the range of government-imposed regulations as well as private conduct that limits foreign access to national markets. As part of the enforcement of any new or updated regulation, it will of course be important to ensure that national competition law enforcement does not undermine cross-border trade and investment. This would benefit from a degree of harmonization

in national laws and approaches, including ensuring that national competition authorities treat cross-border trade and investment in the same way they treat trade and investment activities within their own national borders.

Regarding harmonization of policy frameworks on infrastructure and public service provision, without doubt, a significant number of international business opportunities are being inhibited by the existing state of regulatory policies in the infrastructure sectors across countries. In addition, the market areas for electricity, transportation, and communications infrastructure, which operate more efficiently when their networks are organized according to the patterns of their transactions, often transcend national borders. In the energy sector, cross-border cooperation would allow India and Bangladesh to use their coal and gas reserves more efficiently, while allowing Bhutan and Nepal to further develop their large untapped hydropower potential, and electricity and gas grids should efficiently link supply and demand irrespective of national borders. Similar cross-border opportunities exist in transport, logistics and customs facilitation, and communications and information technology infrastructure (for specific examples of cross-border infrastructure investment opportunities, see Sobhan 2004).

The following areas of the legal and regulatory framework for infrastructure and public service provision should be aligned with the expectations of international and local sponsors, lenders, and investors:

- Clarity and commitment regarding the scope of central and local government levels to award projects, including sectors, types of infrastructure, and financing mechanisms for which PPPs may be granted.
- A one-stop permitting arrangement to facilitate administrative coordination and rapid issuance of required approvals, permits, licenses, and consents.
- Clarity regarding project site, assets, and easements.
- Adequate finance, security, and insolvency provisions.
- Clear regulatory authority with separation between economic regulator and providers, and transparent regulatory decisions.
- Rights for the provider where necessary to collect cost-recovery or sufficient subsidy-augmented tariffs or user fees.
- Efficient appeal and dispute resolution procedures.

One area in which immediate benefits may be realized from regional harmonization is the development and effective implementation of appeal and dispute resolution procedures for projects that require such assistance. Finally, significant gains could be achieved from cross-country sharing of information regarding potential PPP deals and ongoing experimentation with the required policy, legal, and regulatory frameworks to ensure that these deals are both affordable and bankable.

Regarding harmonization of national investment laws through a regional best practice investment code, it may be desirable to strike a better balance between private interests (investor rights) and public goods (investor obligations), particularly given that traditionally investors have suffered from too many obligations and arbitrary interventions and not enough enforceable rights. A number of approaches may be taken toward establishing regional investment agreements (FIAS 2000; von Moltke 2000; World Bank 2003c). The approach advocated in the SAARC regional investment code proposal (SAARC 1997) appears, in spirit, to be close to the NAFTA approach of developing a set of specific rules for investment inspired by national investment laws. The proposed draft agreement appears largely in line with best practice recommendations on FDI legislation, containing an article on most of the following six core topics:

- Definitions of FDI and foreign investors, although it may be desirable to restrict the law to direct investment, because portfolio investment is normally regulated under another legislation.
- Guarantees of national treatment and Most Favored Nation treatment, ensuring that every foreign investment and investor will be treated at least as well as investors from any other foreign country or from the host country.
- Guarantees against expropriation except for clear public purpose and with due process of law, with "prompt, adequate, and effective" compensation.
- Repatriation and the right to convert and transfer funds.
- Freedom to invest in all sectors of the economy, with as few sectoral restrictions as possible; such an agreement would provide a context for agreement between countries of the region on a list of sectors to be included on a common negative list (and would apply only to sectors, not size of project, technology used, or foreign ownership limitation), with any list appearing in accompanying regulations rather than in the law itself.

- Agreement among countries of the region on the fact that investor entry will be through a minimal registration system, which should be simple, short, inexpensive, accessible, and not through any screening or ex ante approval process.
- Dispute settlement, including the right to international arbitration and guarantees that foreign arbitral awards will be recognized by the host country's courts and executed by the host country's government.

Consideration may be given to a regional SAARC Investment Authority to help at the regional level to carry out the activities aimed at attracting and facilitating intraregional and extraregional FDI, including investment generation, investor servicing, and image-building activities, with an emphasis on information sharing and capacity building in all these areas across participating governments.

Depending on the level of political consensus surrounding the adoption of a SAARC-level investment code, the countries of the region may wish to consider a more gradual approach as typified by the adoption of the 12 Nonbinding Investment Principles (NBIPs) by the Asia-Pacific Economic Co-operation forum in 1994.

The 12 NBIPs are as follows:

- Transparency—all laws, regulations, and administrative guidelines pertaining to investment to be made publicly available in a prompt, readily accessible manner.
- Nondiscrimination between source economies.
- National treatment.
- Investment incentives—members will not relax health, safety, and environmental regulations as incentives to encourage investment.
- Performance requirements—members will reduce the use of requirements that distort or limit trade and investment.
- Expropriation and compensation.
- Repatriation and convertibility.
- Settlement of disputes.
- Entry and sojourn of personnel.
- Avoidance of double taxation.
- Investor behavior—foreign and domestic investors must abide by host laws, regulations, and administrative guidelines.
- Removal of barriers to capital exports.

Transparency, for instance, could be adopted as the initial focus, since its implementation does not require changes in policies other than their clarification and public articulation, beginning with an agreement to provide a regional Investment Authority with comprehensive, liberal, and transparent national investment policy statements. This policy could be pursued toward the eventual goal of fully harmonized national investment codes.

It has been argued that the main underlying cause of the 1997 Asian financial crisis was the poor quality of the afflicted countries' economic institutions (Huang and Yeung 2004). The crisis did not happen because the region lacked trade and FDI opportunities, but rather because poor governance and corruption led to inefficient allocation of capital. Strong market-supporting institutions can absorb the shocks that come from increased integration into the global economy. As South Asian leaders consider the promotion of increased trade and FDI liberalization, they also should have the vision to ensure that market expansion measures are accompanied by appropriate regulatory harmonization and supporting institutional strengthening—in product, infrastructure, and financial markets. It is important for leaders to have a balanced awareness of benefits and risks of cross-country harmonization, however. A coordinated program of regulatory reform has some advantages, but coordination takes time, negotiation, and effort, and thus could provide countries with a reason to defer individual reforms. Countries should be encouraged to proceed individually while working to agree on common reforms.

NOTES

1. The author thanks Xavier Forneris and Andrew Stone for helpful feedback and suggestions, and Juan Costain for significant inputs on financial sector integration issues and priorities. The findings, interpretations, and conclusions expressed herein are those of the author and do not necessarily reflect the views of the Board of Executive Directors of the World Bank or the governments they represent.
2. The following data are based on the LOCO monitor global corporate FDI project database, an FDI tracking and analysis tool developed by OCO Consulting (a spinoff of Price water house Coopers), covering more than 21,000 announced and opened greenfield and expansion FDI projects worldwide with source-destination information (mergers and acquisitions, privatization, and alliances are not included; joint ventures are included when they lead to a new physical operation).

3. China in fact became the largest recipient of FDI inflows in 2003 (not counting "transhipped" investment through Luxembourg) with US$54 billion, slightly more than 2002, while flows to the United States halved to US$30 billion (UNCTAD 2003).
4. The ICAs did not especially highlight labor regulation as disproportionately constraining in the region, because they did not examine this issue empirically.

REFERENCES

Foreign Investment Advisory Service (FIAS). 2000. *A Review of Investment Policy Harmonization Initiatives: Implications for the East African Community*. Washington, DC: World Bank.

Huang, Y., and B. Yeung. 2004. "ASEAN's Institutions Are Still In Poor Shape." *Financial Times*, 5 September 2004.

International Monetary Fund (IMF). *Annual Report on Exchange Arrangements and Exchange Restrictions*. Washington, DC: IMF.

Lederman, D., W. Maloney, and L. Serven. 2003. *Lessons from NAFTA for LAC Countries: A Summary of Research Findings*. Washington, DC: World Bank.

Sobhan, F. 2004. "Promoting and facilitating investment in South Asia." In Rehman Sobhan (ed.), *Promoting Cooperation in South Asia*. Dhaka: University Press Limited.

South Asian Association for Regional Cooperation (SAARC). 1997. "Draft agreement between the Governments of Bangladesh, Bhutan, India, Maldives, Nepal, Pakistan and Sri Lanka for the promotion and protection of investment." Prepared by delegation of India during the First SAARC Meeting on promotion and protection of investment, New Delhi, 29–30 September.

United Nations Conference on Trade and Development (UNCTAD). 2003. *World Investment Report 2004*. Geneva: UNCTAD.

von Moltke, K. 2000. "An International Investment Regime? Issues of Sustainability." Winnipeg, Canada: International Institute for Sustainable Development.

World Bank. 2003a. *Bangladesh Investment Climate Assessment*. Washington, DC: World Bank.

———. 2003b. *Improving the Investment Climate in Pakistan: An Investment Climate Assessment*. Washington, DC: World Bank.

———. 2003c. "International Agreements to Improve Investment and Competition for Development." Chapter 4 in *Global Economic Prospects and the Developing Countries*. Washington, DC: World Bank.

———. 2004a. *Doing Business in 2005: Removing Obstacles to Growth*. Washington, DC: World Bank.

———. 2004b. *The Investment Climate in India: Why Is Industry Doing So Much Better in Some Cities and States Than in Others?* Washington, DC: World Bank.

———. 2004c. *World Development Indicators*. Washington, DC: World Bank.

9

Managing the Food Price Crisis in South Asia[1]

Richard Vokes and Savindi Jayakody

1. INTRODUCTION

After a sustained period in which a relatively benign global environment has contributed to strong growth in poverty reduction in many developing countries, the situation changed dramatically in 2008. Through the first half of the year, the oil and food price crisis hit developing countries and the world's poor hard. Adding to this crisis are the direct and indirect impacts of the global financial crisis and the resultant global economic recession in major industrial economies. Both oil and food prices have now come down from the peaks seen in the first half of the year. As of October 2008, oil prices in particular were less than half the peak reached in July 2008, when the price hit US$147 per barrel, although the market remains highly volatile. In the case of food prices, despite the recent easing, the expectation is that prices will remain high over the medium to long term.

Although all three crises are linked, this chapter focuses on the food crisis in South Asia and its impact and long-term implications for the countries and the region. The chapter includes a review of the main causes of the recent food price increases, which while now relatively well documented, still need to be understood properly if countries are to determine the appropriate response or set of responses to the crisis. It also reviews the role and scope for regional cooperation in dealing with the crisis, particularly in light of the Colombo Statement on Food Security, which was agreed on at the 15th South Asian Association for Regional Cooperation (SAARC) Summit held in Colombo in August 2008.

2. BACKGROUND AND NATURE OF THE CRISIS

According to the United Nations Food and Agriculture Organization, "during the first three months of 2008, international nominal prices of all major food commodities reached their highest levels in nearly 50 years [Figure 9.1], while prices in real terms were the highest in nearly 30 years" (FAO 2008a, 2). Before the latest increase, the real price of food had been on a downward trend since 1950, although the trend started to reverse in 2000.[2] A sharp upturn began in mid-2007 and continued through the early part of 2008. Prices of rice and wheat in the international markets rose by 165 percent and 89 percent, respectively, between April 2007 and April 2008. Prices of cereals and some other food commodities like oils, fats, and sugar have eased since April–May 2008. Production prospects for grains in 2008 are good and could reach record levels, in part because

FIGURE 9.1   Long-run Movements in Real Prices of World Grains (US$ per metric ton)

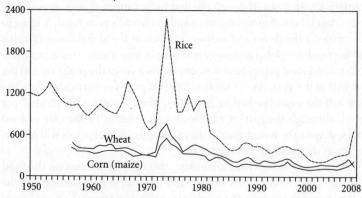

Source   Extracted from Timmer 2008, 2.
Note   2008 represents data for the first five months. Prices were deflated by the U.S. consumer price index, with 2007 prices as the base.

of the supply response to high prices. However, it is generally accepted that food prices are likely to remain high over the medium to long term, albeit below their recent peaks, reflecting the fact that structural as well as more short-term cyclical factors have played a significant part in the current crisis.

2.1 Cyclical Factors

A number of cyclical, short-term factors contributed to the food price crisis. Natural calamities in parts of South Asia (twin floods and cyclone in Bangladesh, drought in Afghanistan, and floods in Pakistan and Sri Lanka) reduced harvests, particularly for rice. According to an Asian Development Bank (ADB) paper, "These declines in rice production took place against a backdrop of declining global rice stocks [Figure 9.2] ... ironically a response to sharply declining prices in the early 1990s" (Timmer 2008, 5). Given that only about 6 to 7 percent of total world rice production enters world trade, the impact of even relatively small changes in production on world prices is magnified. In addition, stockpiles of other major cereals had been falling (FAO 2008a, 5). The ADB also reported that "[d]eclining stocks, along with the instability of the global financial markets, helped to trigger the initial round of speculative demand in recent years as part of the wider commodity boom" (ADB 2008g, 6). The steep decline of the US dollar against all major currencies in 2007–08, also contributed to

FIGURE 9.2   Global Rice Closing Stocks and Stock-to-use Ratio

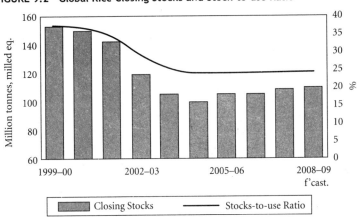

Source   http://www.fao.org/docrep/o11/ai474e/ai474e05.htm(accessed in August 2008).

an increase in the prices of commodities, most of which are denominated in US dollars.

Once prices began to rise, a number of factors added to pressure on supplies and prices. Hoarding by farmers, households, and traders is an inevitable response to rapidly rising prices and shortages. As prices began to rise through 2007, efforts by public food grain agencies to replenish stocks were another significant factor in what has been termed an explosion of "precautionary" demand. These efforts further contributed to upward price pressures in the global markets, especially in the case of rice, given the limited quantities traded on world markets (Timmer 2008, 17). Export restrictions, price controls, and subsequently outright export bans imposed by some key countries (for example, People's Republic of China (PRC), India, Pakistan, Thailand, and Vietnam) also reduced supplies in the world rice markets and increased uncertainty about future rice supplies, contributing significantly to the surge in rice prices, especially from the end of 2007.[3] Finally, "a lack of efficient logistics systems and infrastructure for food grain marketing and distribution in several countries tightened the market further as experienced by Afghanistan, Bangladesh, Nepal, Philippines, and Tajikistan" (ADB 2008g, 7).

2.2 Structural Factors

Apart from the cyclical factors noted above, a number of longer term structural factors contributed significantly to the recent crisis. Given the growing energy intensity of agriculture, including smallholder agriculture, rapidly rising oil prices through 2007–08 soon fed through to production costs, with sharp rises in domestic energy, fertilizer, irrigation, and transport costs, despite the continuation of large subsidies in many countries. This highlights the close links between the twin crises of high oil and food prices (ADB 2008g).

Even before the recent large increases, concerns over rising oil prices, energy security, and climate change had prompted governments to take a more proactive stance toward encouraging production and the use of biofuels, with both the United States and European Union mandating targets for the increased use of biofuels. This led to increased demand for biofuel raw materials, particularly soy, maize, and palm oil. As an example, "almost all of the increase in global maize production from 2004 to 2007 (the period when grain prices rose sharply) went for biofuels production in the U.S., while existing stocks were depleted by an increase in global consumption for other uses" (World Bank 2008b, 1). With some authoritative sources estimating that it accounted for as much as 30 percent of the price increases through 2007–08, the diversion of food crops and substitution of food cropland to biofuel feedstocks remains one of the more controversial and hotly debated elements in the food price crisis (Rosegrant 2008).

The rapid rates of urbanization and industrialization have both led to the conversion of land from agriculture. With this conversion has come a growing competition for water. "An ADB study shows that the water available for agriculture has declined sharply over the past several decades, particularly in Asia. Water scarcity will be increasingly challenging for PRC and India, where irrigation water consumption as a share of total consumption is projected to decrease by 5–10% by 2050 compared with 2000" (ADB and IFPRI 2008, 8).

Rising incomes, linked to growing urbanization and industrialization, as well as rising rural incomes in countries such as PRC and India have been a significant factor driving increased food demand. The demand for food grain consumption of poor and low-income quintiles of the population increases more than the growth of incomes. Food grain demand also has increased dramatically because of the high-income elasticity of demand for meat and animal-based products in Asia. Meat prices have doubled since 2000 and butter and milk prices have tripled. India consumed 20 percent more meat, fish, and eggs in 2007 than in 1990 (ADB 2008g, 9). This trend is projected to continue once the global economy comes through its current turmoil and downturn.

While demand has been rising sharply, productivity levels, especially for rice, have stagnated. The growth in demand for rice in Asia has been well below the rate of population growth since the 1990s. An important factor accounting for the slowdown in yield growth and the poor agriculture sector performance is reduced public investment in agriculture. In Asia, agriculture spending as a share of total spending almost halved between 1980 and 2002 (OPM 2008, 1). Productivity growth in agriculture has been constrained by the pace of development of high-yielding and pest-resistant varieties. National, regional, and international agricultural research institutions have lacked the resources needed to carry out basic research for varietal development, follow-up adaptive research, and technology dissemination under diverse agro-ecological conditions.

Policy inadequacies and weak institutions have undermined the incentives for agricultural production. Interventions such as food grain support prices, input subsidies, and involvement of public agencies in food grain imports, marketing, and distribution lead to distortions and tend to be ineffective over the medium term and inhibit supply increases. Subsidies on food crops in 2008 amounted to US$1 billion in Bangladesh and US$16 billion in India (ADB 2008g, 8). Such subsidies have contributed to the wasteful use of water resources, degradation of land, and imbalances in fertilizer use. As an example, the Indian states of Punjab, Haryana, and western Uttar Pradesh, the main success "stories" of the Green Revolution in India, are now suffering from severe soil degradation, groundwater depletion and contamination, and declining yields (ADB 2008g, 8–9).

Finally, with agriculture especially vulnerable to weather events and natural disasters, climate change and the resultant increase in storms, floods, changes in rainfall patterns, and rise in sea level all increase both the short- and long-term risks to agricultural output.

3. IMPACT OF THE CRISIS IN SOUTH ASIA

3.1 Poverty Impact

The food price crisis has serious macroeconomic implications for South Asia, but it is the human dimension of the crisis that has been at the forefront of recent concerns.

Recent World Bank studies suggest that total world poverty has already increased by between 73 and 105 million people because of rising food and energy prices (Heads of Multilateral Development Banks Meeting Discussion Paper-MDBs Meeting 2008, 1). Given the large number of near poor in South Asia, we can assume that a significant proportion of these people are to be found in the region. Despite the fact that the number of people living in extreme poverty (an income of less than US$1.25/day) in South Asia fell from 59.0 percent in 1981 to 40.0 percent in 2005 (World Bank 2008d), the region is still home to 500 million people, more than half of Asia's poor. The human cost of the crisis thus has been particularly severe in South Asia.

Food price inflation is highly regressive. Food expenditure as a proportion of total household expenditure of the poor is as high as 75 percent in Afghanistan and India and 63 percent in Sri Lanka. In Bangladesh, rice comprises 71 percent of the calorie intake per person in rural areas and 60 percent in urban areas. Higher food prices led poor people to limit their food consumption and shift to less balanced diets, causing nutritional deprivation in Bangladesh" (SARD 2008, 2).

Although the sharp rise in food prices severely affects those who are already living below the poverty line, the fact that a large share of households in South Asia are concentrated at an income level only slightly above the poverty line, with as many as 1 billion South Asians living on less than US$2 per day, means that many households have been pushed back into poverty by the food and energy price crisis. For example, "a 10% increase in food prices is estimated to increase the urban poor in India by 8 million. Other countries experiencing an increase in urban poverty of a million or more due to the impact of higher food prices include Bangladesh, Indonesia, and Pakistan" (ADB 2008d, 41). A simulation study carried out by the ADB using household data and national poverty lines suggest a "10% increase in food prices pushes an additional 7.05 million people into poverty in Pakistan, while a 20% rise doubles that figure" (ADB 2008c, 15).

The erosion in the poor's purchasing power not only increases the severity of food deprivation and malnutrition but also squeezes out other expenditures, such as for clothing, schooling, and health care. The combined impact of the food and energy price crisis thus put at risk the chances of achieving the Millennium Development Goals (MDGs) by 2015. As a recent UN note on the food crisis stated, "Higher food prices have not only set back progress towards the reduction of poverty and hunger (MDG1), but will also make it more difficult to achieve the targets for education (MDG2), child and maternal mortality reduction (MDGs 4 and 5), and the spread of major diseases (MDG6)" (United Nations 2008c, 2).

That said that the impact of the food crisis on the poor is clearly not uniform. Poor households in urban areas, as well as small farmers and landless laborers who are net food purchasers, are the ones most seriously affected. Net producers in the rural areas can benefit from higher prices, although higher prices of inputs, including fuel and fertilizer, have certainly offset some of this benefit. The evidence of a strong supply response to higher prices also points to positive terms of trade effects to many rural inhabitants. Even so, available evidence suggests that more households have lost as a result of the food price increase than have gained (Young and Mittal 2008, 11).

All South Asian countries have been affected by the crisis, but it is the major net food and grain importing countries, namely Afghanistan, Bangladesh, and Nepal, that have been most seriously affected. In Afghanistan, the crisis hit when the country was already facing difficulties owing to a prolonged period of drought and the growth of poppy cultivation at the expense of food crops. Because Afghanistan's wheat imports come almost entirely from Pakistan, it was also hard hit by the imposition of Pakistan's export ban in May 2007. In January 2008, the government and the United Nations launched the Afghanistan Joint Emergency Appeal to provide a safety net for 425,000 vulnerable households (2.6 million people) who were placed at risk of food insecurity during the winter and during the first half of 2008. This appeal succeeded in bringing in 87,100 metric tons of food (81,200 metric tons of wheat, 3,100 metric tons of pulses, 2,500 metric tons of vegetable oil and 300 metric tons of iodized salt) to be distributed by the end of August 2008 (United Nations 2008a, 5). The government took several other steps to reduce the impact of food prices, including the removal of the import tax on both wheat and wheat flour and tax deductions for other staple items. The very high food prices have encouraged some farmers to move to legal crops, a process supported by the United Kingdom's Department for International Development (DfID 2008). Even with these supports, Afghanistan continues to face a fragile food situation as it moves into winter, and further extensive food aid will be needed.

In Bangladesh, too, the crisis hit against a backdrop of natural calamity, with the country losing about 2 million metric tons of rice (7.3 percent of domestic production) to the twin floods of July–August and the cyclone of November 2007 (World Bank 2008a). To offset the shortfall, Bangladesh imported rice from India until this avenue was closed with the imposition of India's ban on rice exports (except basmati rice) in February 2008, which aggravated the rice shortages in Bangladesh and increased inflationary pressure on rice prices.

Bangladesh has benefited from considerable emergency assistance, including from the ADB, World Bank, and U.S. Agency for International Development, mainly aimed at providing relief and strengthening social safety nets with support targeted at the poor through food for work and school feeding programs. As an example, the ADB's emergency loan, amounting to US$170 million, approved in July 2008, provided "short-term transitional support to help the government meet increased expenditures for its safety net programmes to enable it to restore the purchasing power of the poor and vulnerable who are at a greater risk of hunger and malnutrition by enhancing their access to food, livelihood support and employment)" (ADB 2008f, iv). In Bangladesh, where 25 percent of the population is extremely poor, roughly 7 percent of the population has access to social protection or safety net programs.

In Nepal, where 80 percent of all households are net food purchasers, some 3.9 million people are estimated to be at risk of food insecurity.

According to the United Nations World Food Programme (WFP), "While India's export ban did have some impact on Nepal, the existence of a large informal trade between India and Nepal along its porous border limited the upward pressure on prices" (WFP and NDRI 2008, 12). In October 2008, the World Bank approved a US$36 million Nepal Food Price Crisis Response Program, which financed activities to mitigate both the short-term and medium- to long-term impact of rising food prices in Nepal. The program included support for *(a)* the implementation of social safety net measures to maintain access to basic needs (mainly food) among vulnerable households in food insecure districts and *(b)* agricultural productivity activities to expedite a supply response through the implementation of measures to raise the yields and consequently the production of staples.

India and Pakistan, as grain exporters, were better placed to face the food price crisis and resorted to export bans to alleviate pressure on domestic prices. They introduced measures to reduce pressure on prices, including the reduction in import duties, and took measures to strengthen social safety nets and social protections to help the most vulnerable members of their populations.

3.2 Macroeconomic Impact

The food price crisis, coinciding with and in part linked to the oil price crisis, has had significant macroeconomic impacts, most notably on inflation, public finances, and balance of payments. This crisis presented a major challenge to short-term macroeconomic management even before the more recent turmoil in the global economy.

3.2.1 Inflation

Given the large weight of food prices in the consumer price index basket,[4] the pass-through effects of food price inflation are high, with food price inflation becoming a significant driver of inflation (Table 9.1). The upward trend in inflation has continued since the first quarter of 2008. Inflation in India was more than 11 percent by the end of September, while in Pakistan it rose sharply to reach 23.9 percent in the same month. In Sri Lanka, the inflation rate reached 26.2 percent in July, although it decelerated to 24.3 percent by the end of September 2008.

The risks of an oil, food, and wage price spiral have lessened somewhat with the recent sharp downturn in oil and food prices. However, in countries like Sri Lanka—where wages in the public sector are indexed to

TABLE 9.1 Inflation Rate versus Food Price Inflation, March 2008

South Asian country	Inflation rate (%)	Food price inflation (%)
Afghanistan	13.0	32.0
Bangladesh	10.1	11.8
Bhutan	6.0	9.0
India	7.7	6.1
Maldives	13.0	26.0
Nepal	7.2	13.0
Pakistan	12.0	32.0
Sri Lanka	23.8	34.0
Average for South Asia	**11.6**	**20.5**

Source ADB unpublished country reports.

the Consumer Price Index and private sector wage board salaries increased by 15 to 35 percent in July 2008 (Employees Federation Committee, Sri Lanka) in part due to political pressure—the pass-through effects have been particularly strong. In such countries, it will take longer to rein in inflation.

To contain inflationary pressures, most countries in the region had correctly been tightening monetary policy. India and Pakistan lifted policy rates and cash-reserve ratios, and Sri Lanka raised the yield on government securities. For example, the Reserve Bank of India raised its repo rate by 50 basis points to a 7-year high of 9 percent in July 2008. Bangladesh was something of an exception, keeping an accommodative policy to facilitate economic recovery from natural disasters in 2007.[5] The adoption of counter-inflationary policies has been complicated, at least in the short term, by the global credit crisis, its impact on the banking sector in at least some South Asian countries, and the prospects of recession in industrialized economies, which remain vital export markets for the region.

3.2.2 Fiscal Impact

The fiscal impacts of the crisis have come from the rising cost of relief and social protection, increases in the cost of fuel and fertilizer subsidies, and increases in the cost of grain procurement.[6] Short-term measures to ease prices rise, such as duty and tariff waivers or reductions, added to the fiscal pressures. While Bangladesh, India, Nepal, and Sri Lanka provided general relief by lowering domestic trade tax on petrol and removing customs duty on crude oil, in Bangladesh, this relief was combined with

increased spending through targeted subsidies on food grains for the poor
and fertilizers for farmers. In Bangladesh, food subsidies are expected
to double in its current fiscal year to well over US$1.5 billion (Kuroda
2008, 2). To keep food prices under control, India increased procurement
and raised its minimum support prices for both rice and wheat. According
to a simulation study done by the International Food Policy Research
Institute (IFPRI), 10 percent, 20 percent, and 30 percent increases in the
procurement prices of rice and wheat would increase budgetary costs
by 4 percent, 9 percent, and 13 percent, respectively, in India. Thus, the
crisis has added to fiscal deficits at a time when a number of countries,
notably India, Pakistan, and Sri Lanka, already faced large fiscal deficits
(Table 9.2).

TABLE 9.2   Macroeconomic Performance in South Asia, 2007

Country	Percent of GDP			External reserves (months of imports cover)
	Fiscal surplus/ deficit	Current account balance	Debt	
Afghanistan	−2.9	−1.4	n.a.	4.9
Bangladesh	−3.2	1.4	44.9	3.3
Bhutan	−3.4	10.5	n.a.	n.a.
India	−5.5	−1.9	16.4	12.4
Maldives	−7.9	−45.0	n.a.	3.0[a]
Nepal	−2.0	0.5	43.4	10.3
Pakistan	−5.8	−4.8	56.1[a]	n.a.
Sri Lanka	−7.7	−4.3	85.8	3.7

Source   ADB unpublished country reports.
Notes   n.a. = not available.
    [a] Estimated.

According to the South Asian Regional Department (SARD), "The
tightening of fiscal space has brought with it the risk of crowding out
other public investment. The failure to pass on the increased fuel prices
to the consumers posed a financial risk, forcing cutbacks on development spending thereby eroding growth prospects in the future" (SARD
2008, 2).

3.2.3 The Impact on the Balance of Payments

For most countries in the region, the main impact on the balance of payments has come through increases in the cost of oil rather than food,
although for the main grain importers, Afghanistan and Bangladesh, the
increase in the cost of food imports was also significant. India imports

about 73 percent of its oil requirements, while Afghanistan and Sri Lanka are 100 percent dependent on oil imports. Sri Lanka saw its crude oil import bill increasing from US$75.52 million in August 2007 to US$253.39 million in August 2008, an increase of 235.5 percent, before the recent sharp decline in oil prices brought relief. The adverse impact of the increased cost of both oil and food imports on the current account balance was partly offset by the strong inflow of foreign remittances, particularly in Bangladesh, Nepal, and Sri Lanka. Even so, the International Monetary Fund (IMF) provided US$218 million in emergency assistance to Bangladesh in April 2008 for balance-of-payments support to reduce pressure on foreign exchange reserves. By contrast, India, with more than 12 months of import cover, was in a relatively strong position to handle pressures on the external account (Table 9.2). Pakistan's ban on wheat exports from May 2007 and the export ban on non-basmati rice by India in February 2007 resulted in forgone export revenues. Because food prices are expected to remain high over the medium to long term, both countries stand to benefit once normal trading patterns are established.[7]

3.2.4 Macroeconomic Policy Priorities in Managing the Crisis

The current turmoil in global financial markets and the severe economic recession in industrialized economies add to the challenges of macro-economic management at least in the short to medium term. The growth rate in South Asia declined in 2008 and it is expected to decline further in 2009 (ADB 2008a, 4). Inflation is expected to remain high at least in the short term, however, highlighting the need to continue corrective policy measures to rein in inflation and reduce fiscal imbalances, while at the same time providing targeted support to more vulnerable groups.

4. THE LONG-TERM RESPONSE TO THE CRISIS: REVITALIZING AGRICULTURE AND THE RURAL SECTOR

While governments continue to struggle with the immediate effects of the food crisis, it is widely accepted that a key element in the long-term solution to high food prices lies in the revitalization of agriculture and the rural sector, thereby addressing many of the structural issues that have contributed to the food crisis. To transform the crisis into an opportunity for farmers and build resilience to future food crises, a transition to viable long-term investments in support of sustained agricultural growth is urgently needed. As the Indian Prime Minister, Manmohan Singh, has stated, what is needed is a second Green Revolution that boosts production by raising productivity (Singh 2008).

Unlike the first Green Revolution of the 1960s and 1970s, which apart from high-yielding hybrid seeds and inorganic fertilizer, also relied heavily on irrigation, a second Green Revolution will require new elements, because inorganic fertilizers that use oil as a feedstock are increasingly costly and water resources are becoming scarce or difficult to develop.[8] Biotechnology or genetically modified crops are likely to play an important role, thus raising the need to share research and new technologies.

Productivity growth in agriculture will require a significant increase in investment in adaptive research and dissemination. The capacity of public sector institutions engaged in agriculture research and technology dissemination in most Asian countries has weakened over the years, in line with the general neglect of the agriculture sector. While rebuilding their capacity is important, policies to attract private investment and participation of civil society institutions will be important as well.

Investments for sustained agricultural growth include expanded public spending for rural infrastructure, agro services, agricultural research, and science and technology. Improvements in connectivity to the markets will help lower production and marketing costs, reduce waste of inputs and produce, and improve returns to agriculture. Therefore, investments in rehabilitation, maintenance, and development of existing and new farm-to-market roads need to be a priority area for public sector intervention. Improvement in postharvest handling and processing capacity would enhance food security by limiting waste, and would increase income, supply, and employment. New and innovative crop insurance mechanisms should be introduced and tested at a larger scale. Information technology, improved weather data, and the expected high returns to insurance make innovation in this field much more feasible. Furthermore, the role of telecommunications and information communication technology in improving market connectivity can make an important contribution, as the Grameen Phone Program has shown in rural Bangladesh.

Stronger links between smallholder agriculture and agribusiness companies should be further developed to enable farmers to benefit from changing patterns of consumption and retailing. Access to credit is another critical requirement, especially for small farmers; financial institutions, including microfinance institutions, need to expand operations rapidly to improve access of farmers and the rural poor to credit (United Nations 2008b, 29).

Investments in agriculture still may not generate the envisaged returns unless reforms, pricing, trade reforms, and other policies accompany these investments. Since the mid- to late 1990s, most Asian countries have initiated reforms aimed at removing distortions arising from interventionist price and trade policies; however, progress has been mixed and most countries have faltered on the reforms. As a result, farmers in most Asian countries still make their production decisions based on distorted prices and are unable to benefit from the higher prices in international markets. The distortions need to be corrected and divergence between economic and financial returns narrowed. Otherwise, farmers will continue to operate suboptimally and return on investment will continue to be low in the sector (ADB 2008c, 13).

Because increased agriculture production is heavily dependent on the availability of rich soils, water resources, and catchment areas such as forests, an environmentally sustainable approach must be taken to avoid yet another food crisis resulting from the depletion of water sources, salination of soils and water tables, and permanent loss of biodiversity and ecosystem services. Removing distortions in input pricing, such as electricity for farmers and fertilizers, will help to ensure that environmentally sustainable practices are adopted. For example, conservation agriculture, as well as water and soil conservation, will be critical.

Considerable scope exists to redirect public expenditure from subsidies to more productive investment (for example, India), but the negative impacts of the food and energy crisis, coupled with weakening economic prospects, present formidable political constraints (Chand and Kumar 2004). While every effort needs to be made to rationalize public expenditure in agriculture, external assistance will have to play an important role in helping to revitalize agriculture.

As the following examples show, this revitalization is already happening. In Afghanistan, the World Bank recently approved an additional US$28 million (to the original US$65 million) for the Emergency Irrigation Rehabilitation Project in July 2008, while under the Global Food Crisis Response Program, an additional US$8 million was approved for the National Solidarity Program to rehabilitate small-scale irrigation infrastructure in vulnerable communities.

In India, the ADB approved an initial loan of US$75 million to enhance rural economic growth and reduce poverty in the existing irrigation systems within four northern river basins and along part of the Mahanadi

River Delta in Orissa. Additionally, the loan will be used to institution-alize effective mechanisms to implement agricultural growth based on participatory irrigation management. The outcome will be enhanced productivity, efficient water use, sustainability of irrigated agriculture, and improved performance of irrigation service delivery and water resources management (ADB 2008e). In Pakistan, the ADB also approved a loan worth US$75 million (ADB 2008b) in March 2008 for a water resource project to *(a)* increase the sustainable water storage capacity; *(b)* develop sustainable rural water supplies and small-town domestic water entitlement; *(c)* develop efficient irrigation schemes with community-based management; *(d)* enhance dam planning, management, and implementation capacity; and *(e)* improve farmers' access to production support and market services.

5. REGIONAL COOPERATION AS A RESPONSE TO THE FOOD CRISIS

Donor assistance will have to play a key role in supporting the long-term response to the food crisis, but the crisis has highlighted both the need and scope for greater regional cooperation, not least within the frame-work of SAARC of which all eight South Asian nations are now members. Low agricultural productivity and poor infrastructure connectivity are common problems. Many of these countries have similar agro-ecological zones, which in some cases cut across national boundaries. These countries face many of the same challenges in ensuring food security, especially for the urban poor, and can benefit from sharing experience and knowledge (FAO 2008b, 27).

The food price crisis was one of the key issues addressed at the 15th SAARC Summit held in Colombo in August 2008. In the Colombo State-ment on Food Security (Ministry of Foreign Affairs, Sri Lanka 2008), SAARC members agreed "to ensure region-wide food security and make South Asia, once again the granary of the world ... to evolve and implement a people-centered short to medium regional strategy and collaborative projects that would lead to:

- Increase food production.
- Investment in agriculture and agro-based industries.
- Agriculture research and prevention of soil degradation.

- Development and sharing of agricultural technologies.
- Sharing of best practices in procurement and distribution.
- Management of climatic and disease related risks in agriculture.

The members agreed to draw up a SAARC Agriculture Perspective Plan for 2020 and to pursue greater cooperation with the international community to ensure food availability and nutrition security in South Asia. Finally, they agreed to make the SAARC Food Bank operational.

With the exception of the Food Bank, these efforts address the long-term structural issues and the need to revitalize agriculture. The fact that the management of climatic risks is mentioned is especially important because this is an area where transboundary cooperation will be critical, although to be effective, this cooperation will need to encompass the sensitive issue of water resource management. The Extraordinary Meeting of Agriculture Ministers of the SAARC that took place in early November 2008 in New Delhi adopted the SAARC Declaration on Food Security. This Meeting also covered areas such as climate change, integrated nutrient management, biotechnology and bio resource management, and development of a harmonized network for safe movement of agriculture commodities. (South Asia Watch on Trade, Economics and Environment 2009, 38). While food security is a central issue, it will also be important to examine carefully the costs and benefits of different approaches to food security. As experience during the first Green Revolution showed, achieving 100 percent self-sufficiency in basic grains can be extremely costly. In addition, while recent prices rises have made food crops attractive to farmers, the low income elasticity of demand for basic staples means that, in time, these prices will again decline relative to those of other agricultural commodities. Forcing farmers to grow basic stables to meet national food security objectives may run counter to efforts to boost incomes and reduce poverty and thus meet resistance.

In contrast to the other actions listed in the Colombo Statement, the SAARC Food Bank is a short-term response measure designed to help countries weather periods of food shortage. Originally proposed at the 14th SAARC Summit held in New Delhi, the Food Bank would provide supplies in addition to country strategic reserves (SACEPS 2008). The Secretariat for the Food Bank will be housed in Bangladesh, although stocks would be held around the region, with contributions from each country according to the size of its population. The Food Bank will commence with an initial reserve of around 240,000 tons of food grains. The first meeting of the

Board of the Food Bank was held in Colombo in October 2008, at which time guidelines for the determination of prices, terms, and conditions of payment were discussed. As with all buffer stocks, determining the "right" size and balancing the costs and benefits will be challenging. Given the importance of maintaining the quality of seeds and encouraging farmers to use new varieties, a SAARC Seed Bank would be a useful complement to the proposed Food Bank.

Although not specifically mentioned in the Colombo Declaration, continued progress toward the implementation of the South Asian Free Trade Agreement (SAFTA) and closer trade and market integration could mitigate such crises in the future. In this regard, avoiding the imposition of export bans and price controls is clearly desirable.

6. ROLE OF INTERNATIONAL COOPERATION

Development partners have responded to the food crisis by providing emergency assistance to the countries most affected, including those in South Asia. Much of this assistance has been aimed at strengthening social safety nets to protect the poor. The IMF has indicated that it stands ready to provide rapid financial support to address the balance-of-payments needs of countries hit by food and other commodity shocks. In addition, development partners have begun to provide assistance to support agriculture and rural development, and this can be expected to expand significantly because of the renewed attention and priority accorded to agriculture and the rural sector. Ensuring that small farmers, landless laborers, and lagging regions benefit from such assistance will be essential to ensuring that targets for poverty reduction get back on track, even if at times this may conflict with efforts to maximize production gains.

International assistance to global public goods, especially agricultural research and development, will be necessary to complement and support efforts at the country level. Again, this assistance will need to pay particular attention to the needs of poorer groups and regions by focusing on the following:

- "Orphaned" crops relatively neglected by the research and extension efforts that fostered the Green Revolution (for example, sweet sorghum is a food, feed, and fuel source important for parts of Africa that could benefit from genetic improvement).

- Crop varieties suited to harsh growing conditions and adapted to the changing conditions being experienced or expected in countries affected by climate change (for example, tolerance of water stress, temperature stress, excessive rainfall and flooding, and so on).
- Improved crop varieties that require fewer chemical inputs (for example, pest-resistant varieties, varieties requiring limited fossil-fuel-based fertilizers).
- Agricultural techniques that achieve sustainably high yields with minimal adverse or even positive environmental impacts.
- Second-generation biofuels, obtained from plant residues and animal wastes, that can reduce land-use change and avoid some of the emissions associated with certain current biofuel programs (United Nations 2008c).

More generally, research on biofuels versus food trade-offs and climate change is needed so that policies to promote biofuels are consistent with the goals of agricultural development, food security, and environmental sustainability.

Climate change is another area in which international cooperation will be needed to address its underlying causes and to help countries and regions reduce carbon emissions and cope with the consequences of climate change and the costs of risk mitigation. Although uncertainties remain, there is a growing consensus that agricultural production globally is likely to be reduced by climate change, with developing countries experiencing the greatest production losses and increased food insecurity (Braun 2008, 3; Lobell and Field 2007, 6; Rosenzweig et al. 2001, 102).

The issue of climate change is particularly important to South Asia. Himalayan glaciers are among the fastest retreating glaciers globally as a result of global warming. The Himalayan glaciers feed into seven of Asia's greatest rivers (the Ganges, Indus, Brahmaputra, Salween, Mekong, Yangtze, and Huange He), ensuring a year-round water supply to hundreds of millions of people in the Indian subcontinent and PRC. As glacier water flows dwindle, not only is irrigation and agricultural production reduced, but the potential economic and environmental benefits from hydropower are also threatened (WWF 2005).

As Braun (2008) has stressed, the viable mitigation strategies for dealing with climate change in the agricultural sector in the developing world face a range of constraints. Such strategies cannot be expected to make a significant difference in the short to medium term. Thus, climate change adaptation has become an imperative (Braun 2008). As Braun has noted, many adaptation strategies are extensions of good development policy, including *(a)* promoting growth and diversification; *(b)* investing in research and development, education, and health; *(c)* creating markets in water and environmental services; *(d)* improving the international trade system; *(e)* enhancing resilience to disasters and improving disaster management; and *(f)* promoting risk-sharing, including social safety nets and weather insurance (Braun 2008). As he further stresses, however, effective adaptation strategies must go beyond good development policy to explicitly target the impacts of climate change, particularly on the poor (Braun 2008).

Finally, Braun notes that improvements in the international trade system and efforts to reduce trade distortions, especially in agricultural commodities, are needed to help developing countries and their farmers benefit from international trade. Despite the recent setbacks in the Doha Round and the many sensitivities that surround trade liberalization, this is an area in which greater international and regional cooperation is required.

7. CONCLUSION

A unique combination of both cyclical and structural factors led to the recent dramatic increase in food prices and particularly to the peaks experienced in the early part of 2008. Prices have now been easing for some months. Because of the supply response to higher prices and efforts by governments to rebuild stocks (to minimize the risk and social, economic, and political costs of a similar shock in the future), a combination of bumper crops should help bring greater stability to global food markets. Given a number of structural factors involved in the upward trend in food prices, however, real food prices are expected to remain above their pre-2007 levels at least until 2015.

Although more definitive research is needed, it is undeniable that the food price crisis, along with the oil price crisis, has imposed major hardship on poor and vulnerable groups in South Asia (and other developing countries and regions). Measures taken by governments, both on their own and with extensive emergency help from development partners, have gone a long way to alleviate the adverse impact of the crisis on the most vulnerable groups. That said, the food situation in Afghanistan remains fragile and further emergency assistance should be a priority.

On the macroeconomic side, the adoption of policies to rein in infla-tion, coupled with the easing of global prices, especially of oil, are reducing the macroeconomic risks. The effects of the food and oil price crisis is now being overshadowed by the effect of the turmoil in global financial markets and the resultant global economic recession in industrialized economies, thereby presenting the governments in the region with new macroeconomic challenges.

This new crisis should not, however, be allowed to divert attention from the need for an effective long-term response to the food price crisis. A key component of this response should include efforts to revitalize development of the agricultural and rural sector. This development calls for a reprioritization and rationalization of government investment in the sector as well as expanded support from development partners. In providing renewed support to agriculture and rural development, the focus should be not only on efforts to boost food production, but also on the most effective means to increase incomes and build secure livelihoods for farmers and the nonfarm rural population.

Regional cooperation could play an important role in the long-term response to the crisis and in helping to mitigate future shocks. The elements included in the Colombo Statement on Food Security represent a good beginning. If the region is to come up with a truly effective long-term response to the crisis, however, regional cooperation must go beyond the Colombo Statement to encompass more directly trade, water management, and climate change issues.

Finally, a long-term solution to the food crisis calls for enhanced international cooperation. Enhanced external assistance, especially to support development in the agriculture and rural sectors, is one priority. Cooperation on climate change and its impact also will be essential, and should include the development and implementation of adaption strategies, as well as efforts to reduce international trade distortions, not least in agricultural commodities.

NOTES

1. The views expressed in this chapter are those of the authors and do not necessarily reflect the views and policies of the Asian Development Bank or its Board of Governors or the Governments they represent.
2. The main exception to this downward trend was the period 1973–74, the time of the previous world food crisis, when prices in real terms rose well above even the peaks recorded in 2008 (Timmer 2008, 1).

3. Policy options, such as export restrictions and minimum export prices, intended to protect domestic consumers reduce incentives to producers and increase uncertainty thereby weakening the supply response.
4. Weight of food in the consumer price index basket: Bangladesh, 58.8 percent, Bhutan, 32 percent, India, 15.4 percent, Nepal, 53 percent, and Sri Lanka, 46.7 percent (SARD 2008).
5. Countries with currency pegs, including Bhutan, Maldives, and Nepal, however, have less room for active use of monetary policy to address increasing inflation pressures (ADB 2008a, 125).
6. Sri Lanka removed fuel subsidies in 2007.
7. There is some expectation in the market that India will lift its ban soon.
8. Some farmers in Tamil Nadu, southern state of India, are using less water and fewer seeds to grow more rice (World Bank Web site, October 2008).

REFERENCES

Asian Development Bank (ADB). 2008a. *Asian Development Outlook 2008 Update*. Manila: ADB.
———. 2008b. *Barani Integrated Water Resources Sector Project: Pakistan*. Manila: ADB.
———. 2008c. *Food Prices and Inflation in Developing Asia*. Manila: ADB.
———. 2008d. *Key Indicators for Asia and Pacific 2008*. 39th ed. Manila: ADB
———. 2008e. *MFF—ORISSA Integrated Irrigated Agriculture & Water Management Investment Program (Facility Concept): India*. Manila: ADB.
———. 2008f. *Proposed Loan and Technical Assistance Grant Emergency Assistance for Food Security Project (Bangladesh)*. July. Manila: ADB.
———. 2008g. *Soaring Food Prices: Response to the Crisis*. Manila: ADB.
Asian Development Bank and International Food Policy Research Institute (ADB and IFPRI). 2008. *Reducing Poverty and Hunger in Asia: The Role of Agriculture and Rural Development*. Manila: ADB.
Braun, J. V. 2008. "Supply and Demand of Agricultural Products and Inflation How to Address the Acute and Long Run Problem." Prepared for the China Development Forum, Beijing. March.
Chand, Ramesh, and Pramod Kumar. 2004. "Determinants of Capital Formation and Agriculture Growth." *Economic and Political Weekly* 39(52): 5611–16.
Department for International Development (DfID). 2007. *Poverty Fact Sheet*, November. London: DfID.
———. 2008. "Afghan Farmers Stamp on Poppies to Beat Food Crisis." World Food Programme. 15 September. Available at http://www.dfid.gov.uk/news/files/afghan-farmers.asp (accessed on 6 October 2009).
Food and Agriculture Organization (FAO). 2008a. "Soaring Food Prices: Facts, Perspectives, Impacts and Actions Required." High Level Conference on World Food Security: The Challenges of Climate Change and Bioenergy, Rome, 3–5 June.
———. 2008b. "Regional Strategies and Programme for Food Security in the SAARC Member States." Final Draft Report, June.
Kuroda, H. 2008. "Statement by President of the Asian Development Bank at the 78th Meeting of the Development Committee." ADB, 12 October.

Lobell, D., and C. Field. 2007. "Global Scale Climate-Crop Yield Relationships and the Impact of Recent Warming." *Environmental Research Letters* 2: 6.

Multilateral Development Bank (MDB). 2008. "Discussion Paper on the Food Price Crisis." Heads of MDBs Meeting, Washington, DC, 13 October.

Oxford Policy Management (OPM) Briefing Notes. 2008. "The Decline in Public Spending to Agriculture: Does It Matter?" OPM, October.

Rosegrant, Mark. 2008. "Biofuels and Grain Prices: Impacts and Policy Responses." International Food Policy Research Institute (IFPRI), May.

Rosenzweig, C., Ana Iglesias, X. B. Yang, Paul R. Epstein, and Eric Chivian. 2001. "Climate Change and Extreme Weather Events." *Global Change and Human Health* 2 (2): 90–104.

Singh, Man Mohan. 2008. Speech at Global Agro Industrial Forum, New Delhi, 10 August 2008.

South Asia Centre for Policy Studies (SACEPS). 2008. "Recommendations to the Fifteenth SAARC Summit." Kathmandu: SACEPS.

South Asia Watch on Trade, Economics and Environment. 2009. "SAARC Declaration on Food Security." *Trade Insight* 5 (1).

South Asian Regional Department (SARD). 2008. "Regional Summary of Inflation in South Asia 2008." Unpublished. Manila: ADB.

Timmer, C. Peter. 2008. "Causes of High Food Prices." ADB Economics Working Paper Series, No. 128, ADB, October.

United Nations. 2008a. "Afghanistan Joint Emergency Appeal July 2008, High Food Prices and Drought Crisis." New York: United Nations.

———. 2008b. "High Level Task Force on the Global Food Crisis: Comprehensive Framework for Action." New York: United Nations.

———. 2008c. "Issues Note for Special Meeting of the Economic and Social Council on Global Food Crisis." New York: United Nations.

World Bank. 2008a. "End Poverty in South Asia. Beggar Thy Neighbour?" 9 March Available at http://endpovertyinsouthasia.worldbank.org/beggar-thy-neighbor (accessed on 6 October 2009).

———. 2008b. "Rising Food Prices: Policy Options and World Bank Response." Unpublished Paper, World Bank, Washington, DC.

———. 2008c. "A New Way of Cultivating Rice." Washington, DC: World Bank. Available at http://web.worldbank.org (accessed on 6 October 2009).

———. 2008d. *World Development Indicators Poverty Data-A Supplement to World Development Indicators.* Washington, DC: World Bank.

———. 2008e. *World Development Indicators 2008.* Washington, DC: World Bank.

World Food Programme and Nepal Development Research Institute (WFP and NDRI). 2008. "Market and Price Impact Assessment Nepal." Final Report, July, United Nations.

World Wide Fund for Nature (WWF). 2005. "Water Crisis Looms as Himalayan Glaciers Retreat." Available at http://www.panda.org/news (accessed on 6 October 2009).

Young, S., and A. Mittal. 2008. "Food Price Crisis." Policy Brief. Oakland, CA: The Oakland Institute.

10

Labor Migration, Employment, and Poverty Alleviation in South Asia

Sridhar K. Khatri

L abor migration presents both challenges and opportunities in today's global world. As the scale, scope, and complexity of the phenomenon have grown, states and other stakeholders have become aware of these challenges and opportunities with the growing realization that economic, social, and cultural benefits can be realized and negative consequences can be minimized.

According to the World Bank's *Migration and Remittances Factbook, 2008,* the global remittance flow has increased phenomenally over the past three and a half decades. From US$2 billion in 1970, it increased to US$131.5 billion by 2000 and had reached US$317.7 billion in 2007, of which US$239.7 billion went to the developing countries. These figures do not reflect the unrecorded flow through unofficial channels at the global level that may account for an additional 50 percent (World Bank 2008, 17).

Studies have compared the importance of remittances to the economy of the receiving countries with foreign aid, private capital flow, and foreign direct investment (FDI). The findings discovered that remittances by migrants to developing economies (estimated at US$150 billion per year) are three times the amount provided through official development assistance (ODA) and that migrants contribute to development and poverty reduction through remittances and investment of their skills. When compared with FDI to these countries, remittances account for more than half of the total flow. In addition, remittances were found to be more stable than private capital flows and less subject to changing economic cycles, and because they are unilateral transfers, they do not create liabilities for the receivers.

Recognizing international migration as *the top global policy agenda*, on December 2003 the secretary general of the United Nations encouraged a Core Group of States to establish the Global Commission on International Migration with the objective of providing a framework for the formulation of a *coherent, comprehensive* and *global response* to the issue of global migration. In 2005 the Commission presented its report, which recognized that while globalization provides millions of women, men, and children with better opportunities in life, it has also brought about disparities in the standard of living and level of human security available to people in different parts of the world. On the whole, the Commission concluded that *the international community has failed to capitalize on opportunities and meet the challenges associated with international migration.*

Some of the observations made by the Commission are as follows:

- There is a lack of capacity in the less prosperous regions of the world, particularly at the official level, to formulate and implement effective migration polices. There is a need for more professional training, better knowledge of migration issues, institutions, and laws, for a better understanding of the way in which migration and other issues affect each other.
- Countries often face difficulties in formulating a coherent migration policy because important decisions taken in development matters, trade, and the labor market are not linked to their impact on labor migration.
- Interstate cooperation and consultation in formulating migration policies are lacking, even though migration is a transnational issue that requires cooperation among states at the global, regional, and sub-regional level.
- Multilateral international organization working in the field of migration usually work in a disconnected manner and there is therefore a strong need for them to cooperate and coordinate their policies with each other (Global Commission on International Migration 2005, 2–3).

1. SOUTH ASIAN LABOR MIGRATION

According to the World Bank's *Migration and Remittances Factbook, 2008*, in 2007, South Asia received US$43.8 *billion* in remittances from its migrant workers working throughout the world. When unofficial remittances (estimated) are combined, the total is believed to be double that amount. In Pakistan, remittances increased six fold from just over US$1 billion in 2000 to US$6.1 billion in 2007; in Bangladesh, it increased from US$1.9 to US$6.4 billion; in India, it increased from US$12.89 to US$27 billion; in Nepal, it increased phenomenally from US$111 million to US$1.6 billion; and in Sri Lanka, it increased from US$1.16 billion to 2.7 billion (Maimbo et al. 2005; World Bank 2008).

India is the largest remittance-receiving country in the world, with Pakistan (fifth) and Bangladesh (seventh) not far behind. Remittances alone represent 3.10 percent of India's gross domestic product (GDP), which is a sharp increase from 0.7 percent in 1990–91. Remittances were higher than revenues from India's software export (US$23.6 billion in 2005–06), more than the country's expenditure on education, and more than double the combined state and federal government's expenditures on health care (Chishti 2007, 2–3). In comparison to the total foreign exchange earnings from garment exports, a major foreign exchange earner for Sri Lanka, remittance income rose from 42 percent in 2000 to 69 percent in 2005 (Ranasinghe 2007).

In addition to financial benefits to the sending countries, migration provides opportunities to build their human, capital, and social assets. Returning migrants usually gain new skills during employment abroad through what is today recognized as beneficial transfer of know-how and competencies called "brain gain." Other contributions can be less tangible than remittances but not necessarily less relevant. Migrants can play an important role in their home country by strengthening political debate, strengthening the role of civil society, encouraging education for non-migrants, and emancipating women and minority groups (de Hass 2006).

2. DESTINATION OF SOUTH ASIAN LABOR MIGRATIONS AND SOME KEY ISSUES

The three types of migration from and within South Asia are *(a)* permanent migration to Europe, Australia, and North America; *(b)* contract labor migration to the Gulf States and Southeast Asia; and *(c)* cross-border and seasonal migration within the region. South Asian countries have not been alert in addressing the complex issues involving individuals, household, community, private sector, and the state. A burgeoning labor recruitment industry in the region charges high emigration rates and has been criticized for taking advantage of innocent laborers who take huge loans or use their life's savings to go abroad. Moreover, there is a paucity of reliable data in the region; many movements of people go unrecorded and the available data may not be disaggregated by gender and skills. The method of data collection varies across countries, and the actual number of laborers going abroad far exceeds the official estimates.

2.1 Remittances: Official versus Unofficial Figures

Official figures on migration are gross underestimations, as a significant proportion of intraregional migration occurs through informal or unauthorized channels and thus is not recorded. High remittance returns (Siddqui 2007a) are difficult to record properly because a significant portion is sent through informal channels. Informal channels are known by such various names as "alternative remittance systems," "ethnic banking," *feich'ien* (China), *hundi* (Pakistan and Bangladesh), *hawala* (India and the Middle East), *padala* (Philippines), and *hui kuan* (Hong Kong, China).

Of the US$39.8 billion in remittances received by South Asia in 2006, a study by the Refugee and Migratory Movement Research Unit study suggests that 40 percent came through the formal channel, with the *hundi* accounting for another 40 percent. This is followed by hand-carrying of remittance by the workers themselves, which comes to 8 percent, and remittances brought over by friends and relatives accounting for another 4 percent. The use of informal channels to send monies by Nepali workers in India is much higher than the regional average. Out of the Rs 12 billion that come to Nepal from India, 99 percent come through the unofficial channel (Pyakurel 2007).

2.2 Destination of South Asian Migrant Workers

The Gulf States remain the primary destination of South Asian migrant laborers, followed by the Southeast Asian countries. This is true even for India, which has substantial advantage in sending people with technical skills and professional expertise to the United States and other industrialized nations. The outflow of migrant labor from India to the

Middle East increased at a phenomenal rate in the late 1970s and reached a peak in 1981. From 1979 to 1982, on average, nearly 234,064 Indians migrated annually as laborers to the area, but during 1983 to 1990, there was a significant decline to an average migration of 155,401 per year, largely because of the oil glut of the early 1980s. The first Gulf War of 1990 forced nearly 160,000 Indians to return home abruptly. But between 1992 and 2001, migration to the region was nearly 360,000 per year, thus surpassing the "Gulf boom" of the late 1970s and early 1980s. Similarly, migration from India to industrialized countries grew steadily between 1950 and 2000. The flow was particularly impressive during 1990s, especially that of information technology (IT) professionals to original destinations like Canada and the United States, and newer destinations such as Australia, Germany, Japan, and Malaysia. The average inflows of Indian immigrants to these destinations increased from around 10,300 persons per year in the 1950s to around 60,000 per year during the 1990s (Srivastava and Sasikumar 2003, 16).

2.3 Level of Skills and Age-group of Migrant Workers

India's focus is on skilled migration, whereas Sri Lanka's female laborers constitute the bulk of those going abroad for work. Migrant laborers from Pakistan and Bangladesh are essentially unskilled workers, as are workers from Nepal, which was a relatively late entrant into this labor market. The average age of migrants is between 20 and 35 years, which represents the most productive age-group of workers.

A major challenge facing the region is the demographic change in which one-third of the people are below the age of 20 years. The next 15 to 20 years will be critical due to the "youth bulge" (ages 15 to 24) that are becoming evident in the region. World history shows that when a country's population of youth goes up by 17 percent, political instability of one kind or the other always emerges (Subedi 2007).

2.4 Role of Women Migrant Workers

Globally, women account for about half of the total migrant workers. The contribution of women to the migrant labor force is an issue that has been largely overlooked or neglected in the region. Poverty is usually the main, although not the sole, cause for migration of women. Recent trends suggests that more women workers will go abroad in the future, despite the ban on women laborers going abroad from Nepal (until recently) and

Bangladesh. Women migrants who go to work abroad from countries where restrictions exist usually face "double jeopardy" in terms of violation of their labor rights in both the sending and receiving countries. Sending countries usually treat these women as irregular migrants and therefore they are unrecognized as a labor force and remain unprotected; in the receiving countries, these women are denied their labor rights in the absence of multilateral and bilateral labor agreements. As irregular migrants, women end up paying more than men to go abroad, because they need to rely more on unlicensed brokers and pay excesses to other unscrupulous elements to circumvent official regulations in the sending and transit countries (Bhadra 2007).

Studies suggest that women are better managers of their resources than men. They save more money then men from their earnings and use it more effectively in areas that have a direct bearing on poverty reduction (Bhadra 2007; Joshi 2007).

2.5 Changing Nature of the Labor Market

The labor market is not static and indigenization takes place on a regular basis. Given the fluid nature of the labor market, sending countries need to monitor developments and take appropriate measure if they are to gain from labor migration. In 2001–02, Nepali laborers were accepted by Malaysia and the Republic of Korea only after Bangladeshi laborers were rejected.

There is also a trend in some of the Middle Eastern states toward "nativization" and "Arabization" of the labor market. The United Arab Emirates (UAE) has adopted policies that would favor integrating more nationals into the labor market, which is now occupied by foreigners.

2.6 Generational Shift in the Use of Remittances

The shift in the use of remittances can have significant policy implications for the sending countries. Nepal's case shows that the first generation of migrant laborers used the remittance to buy land and invest money in their place of origin, while the second generation was more prone to invest their money in towns and urban areas close to their homes. The third generation moved outward and invested their income in big cities and the capital. In the future, remittances coming to Nepal might get transferred into mortgage economy in the West, with the home country missing out on the potential benefits (Dixit 2007), especially in case of British Gurkhas who have been offered permanent residency in the United Kingdom.

There is, however, a caveat to this projection of the generational shift in migration if we consider it as cyclical rather than transitional. In 2001, the largest source of remittance coming to India was from the United States, which suggests that instead of remittance converting perpetually into the mortgage economy; it may revert to the home country of the migrants. The outcome would depend on a number of factors, including what the economy in the home country holds for these migrants (Dubey 2007a).

3. PROBLEMS FACED BY MIGRANT WORKERS

Migrant workers are often subjected to neglect, harassment, and violation of rights in both the sending and receiving countries, because sending states are reluctant to address the issue seriously for fear of labor market losses. These states make inadequate investments to develop institutional structures to look after the welfare of migrant workers and establish an effective regulatory framework to check for corruption and exploitation. These states often freeload, benefiting at the cost of the migrant workers who invest their resources to bring financial benefits and their newly acquired skills to their country of origin. In the receiving countries, embassies of the South Asian countries are not proactive in dealing with complaints or are ill-equipped to handle them because of a lack of adequate staff and resources.[1] The real issue is the transparency and accountability in the sending country itself.

3.1 Violations of the Rights of the Migrant Workers

Violations of the rights of migrant laborers start at home by agents and recruitment agencies in the sending countries and continue in the receiving countries. The question of migrant workers' access to justice systems is a matter of serious concern. A United Nations Development Fund for Women (UNIFEM) study on Nepal found that the rights-based approach was missing and women, in particular, were viewed as sexual symbols. This may be the common scenario in the South Asian justice system as well (Joshi 2007).

Migrant workers do not have the mechanisms to protect their interest in the receiving countries because there is no scope for bargaining between employer and employee, including the right to form unions, particularly in the Middle East. Hardly any of the South Asian states have prepared for the rehabilitation of workers, although governments are beginning to think along these lines.

3.2 Limited Role of Trade Unions in South Asia

In most of the countries in South Asia, there is less and less concern over labor rights as trade unions[2] are usually viewed as trouble shooters and receive negligible attention of the concerned authorities. Trade unions often are close to political parties, have a narrow membership base, function with obsolete strategies influenced by over-age leaders on the basis of personal power-oriented leadership, and hold confrontationist attitudes. Moreover, in many South Asian countries, laws do not cover those unable to prove their status as workers. For example, India has about 200 laws to cover workers, but 90 percent of workers are in the informal sector and are not protected because they lack documentation that could prove their status as workers or employees. Therefore, the informal migrants remain legally unprotected. Government policies regarding worker-related programs and activities are directed at workers in the organized sector. At the regional level, trade unions have failed to make collective efforts to see that labor issues are included in the South Asian Association for Regional Cooperation (SAARC) agenda and other regional activities. The South Asia Regional Trade Union Congress (SARTUC), the only trade union at the regional level, exists more on paper than in practice (Sharma 2007; Sinha 2007).

The mind-set of governments in both the sending and receiving countries is an additional problem source. Sending governments usually see migration as "manpower export," thus treating the issue like any other commodity to be exported. Migration is driven by "pull" and "push" factors, in which the "pull" factor is determined by the needs of the marketplace. Another misused concept is "illegal migrants." Human beings cannot be "exported" as commodities or considered "illegal."

4. CONTRIBUTION OF REMITTANCES IN POVERTY ALLEVIATION AND EMPLOYMENT

In 2006 the United Nations Population Fund (UNFPA) looked at 74 low- and middle-income developing countries and found that there is statistically significant correlation between remittances and decline in poverty. It noted that a 10 percent increase in the share of remittance in a country's GDP can lead to a 1.2 percent reduction in poverty. Although the methodology used to reach the findings in the study is somewhat controversial, the positive impact of remittance on employment and poverty alleviation is widely accepted (World Bank 2005).

4.1 Remittances and Poverty Alleviation

Comparable data on the relationship between migrant remittance and poverty alleviation for South Asia are not available, but the World Bank *Global Economic Perspective Report* (2006) notes that remittance inflow has made it possible for Bangladesh to cut poverty by 6 percent. In Nepal, a study done by the Nepal Living Standard Survey found that the contribution of remittances in reducing poverty between 1996 and 2003 was 11 percent. Other contributors included the increase in agricultural wages, an increase in nonfarm activities, and some reduction in the dependency ratio. Remittances not only help to reduce poverty, but also reduce the depth and severity of poverty in Nepal and other countries.

One study on Pakistan found that remittances have a positive and significant effect on the accumulation of two assets in rural Pakistan: irrigated and rain-fed land. It was found that, as a rule, Pakistani migrants avoid investing in areas that they do not know (such as business) in favor of committing their resources to what they know best (namely, land) (Adams 1998). Other empirical studies on Pakistan indicate that incomes of migrant workers were five to eight times higher than what they would have earned in their home country, and they remitted on average 78 percent of their earnings (Burney 1998; Kazi 1998; Siddiqui and Kemal 2007).

4.2 Migration and Inequality

The general theory of migration holds that the poorest of the poor do not migrate. It is only those who have access to resources and information who migrate. First-generation migrants are therefore always from a relatively well-to-do background. Only when they go through their social network do some poorer people migrate. The new generation theory of migration based on social network focuses on information. This theory suggests that whoever has information will migrate, while money becomes secondary (Black 2003; Siddqui 2007a).

> It is generally accepted that "inequality is clearly a major driver of migration." International migration is a powerful symbol of inequality through which

millions of workers and their families move each year across borders and continents seeking to lessen the gap between their own position and those perceived to be economically better off. The real debate is not about the effect of inequality on migration, but the effect of migration on inequality. Examples can be found of migration both increasing and decreasing inequality in various parts of the world. The final conclusion usually depends on the criteria that are used to evaluate the impact of migration on inequality. These criteria could depend on the *scale of analysis* because circumstances that affect equality within the household may be different within a village or between and within regions or countries. *Location* is another important factor because in destination countries migrants may not have equal access to rights compared with local workers. In places of origin, the selectivity of migrants, the sending of remittances, and the social change that is brought about also might affect socioeconomic inequality. The *time period* is another significant factor because inequality is likely to change over time, because of the effect of networks that reduce the costs of migration and thus extend the opportunity to migrate to a wide group of people. And finally, the *type of inequality* could be significant because, other than economic inequality (income and wealth levels), other types of inequality are involved, including inequality between men and women, between generations, or between different ethnic and caste groups (DRCMGP 2006, 2).

Analysis of the impact of migration at the village level in Bangladesh indicates that there is a multidimensional aspect to migration and inequality. A study of the movement of laborers from Talukpur, a village in Sylhet district, to the United Kingdom found that international migration can increase inequalities within villages of origin. Well-to-do individuals and villages that have better access to long-distance migration are able to improve their position in relation to the poor. Migration becomes the pole around which inequalities are clustered because it brings not only economic inequalities, but also broader social and cultural cleavages. Conversely, the study also shows that although inequality has increased between well-to-do households and the very poor, it has decreased between the traditionally rich people in the village and the many poorer households who now have opportunities to earn money abroad. In Talukpur, migration has not only brought money to the community but also brought considerable changes in landownership and has altered the political, social, and economic power base of the area (Gardner 1995, quoted in DRCMGP 2006, 2).

When examining the relationship between migration and inequality, the key words to remember are *access* and *opportunity*. Where poor people have greater choice in terms of migration, the net effect on inequality is likely to be positive. Similarly, the more opportunities there are for migrants, the more beneficial the results. In fact, restrictions on migration can increase inequality, as has been the case of the unskilled female migrants from Bangladesh who have been forced to use "illegal" methods to migrate and thus become vulnerable to exploitation and subject to gender income inequality (Gardner 1995).

4.3 Multiplier Effects of Remittances

When looking at remittances, one must remember that poverty reduction cannot be linked only to individual household cases, because poverty reduction takes place through the uses of remittances by states and individuals. Remittances come in foreign exchange, and states use that foreign exchange in different ways that lead to poverty reduction. Individuals use their remittances, which creates a multiplier effect that may lead to income generation within the society, leading to poverty alleviation in some corners, but not particularly for the family that has migrated. What individuals receive is in local currency and what the state keeps is in foreign exchange. Thus, among other things, a poverty reduction scenario takes place through (a) debt servicing and import substitution, which comes through the availability of foreign exchange—provided that it is through official sources—and results in the accretion in the country's foreign exchange reserve and (b) the way the country uses the money for development (Siddqui 2007b).

The notion that remittances do not result in reducing poverty if they are spent on affluent consumption has been belied by recent development theory, particularly by Amartya Sen. Sen has defined development not in terms of creating goods that will produce goods, but in terms of widening individual opportunities and multiplying freedoms that individuals will enjoy. One can enjoy no greater freedom than being able to eat today, especially when one was not able to do so yesterday. Development happens when a family is able to spend more on food, because it widens opportunity and prevents deprivation. If a family is in a position to spend 40 percent of its income on food, then it leads to a reduction in poverty because it has a direct impact on calorie intake. Similarly, expenditure on education has instrumental value in laying the foundation for growth (Dubey 2007b).

The belief that remittances are transitory and windfall income is not accurate. Remittances are becoming more stable than FDIs and ODAs. The global economic structure has changed substantially, and the assumption behind the Keynesian theory is wrong (Dubey 2007b). Globalization is a two-way process in which immigration and emigration are part and parcel of the same thing. When a sending nation expects receiving nations to open their door to laborers, it also must be willing to open its own door to others. The notion of a global village with greater interdependence is real, especially where migration is concerned (Rana 2007).

Migration has a multiplier affect on the economies of the countries of origin. In the public sector, a lot of employment has been generated to better manage migration. This includes generation of new jobs to promote government awareness campaigns, including pre-departure briefings. In addition, new ministries have been created or the existing ones have been expanded, thus employing more human resources to manage activities linked with migration. Such expansion can be seen in civil aviation, customs, immigration, and in all other agencies that are linked to managing and governing migration. In the nongovernmental sectors, private recruiting agencies, their agents and subagents, travel agencies, banks, and medical centers have made money processing migration, as jobs have been created in nongovernmental organizations and the media to deal with these issues.[3]

4.4 Impact of Remittances Is Not Always Automatic

The impact of remittances on poverty reduction and employment is neither straightforward nor automatic. Roger Ballard's study of two areas of divided Kashmir, one in Pakistan (Mirpur) and the other in India (Jullandur Doab), illustrates that for remittances to have a positive impact on the people, the proper macro-level policies must exist with the right type of development infrastructure to alleviate poverty in any given area. Migration management will be difficult when there are deficiencies in policy and institutional infrastructure to maximize benefits from remittances. Remittance is one of the faultier fields of development economics. Associated with it are sociological, political, cultural, and other factors. To be successful, it requires long-term planning, in which the countries need to give it a priority in their policies (Koirala 2007). Moreover, foreign employment is but one of the means by which countries can reduce poverty. It is only a stopgap measure, a means to an end. It does not absolve governments from their responsibility for job creation and establishing provisions for welfare nets for those truly in need. It is not the panacea for poverty alleviation (Sainju 2007).

5. STATUS OF LEGAL FRAMEWORK ON LABOR MIGRATION

5.1 International Conventions

There are general and specific international legal provisions for the protection of the rights of migrant workers. They include the Universal Declaration of Human Rights, the International Covenant on Civil and Political Rights, International Covenant on Economic, Social and Cultural Rights, Convention Against Torture and Other Cruel, Inhuman or Degrading Treatment or Punishment, and Convention on Elimination of All Forms of Discrimination against Women (CEDAW). The issue of protection of migrant workers has also been highlighted in various International Labour Organization (ILO) documents, standards, and activities.

By far the most comprehensive legal document is the United Nations Convention on the Protection of the Rights of all Migrant Workers and Members of the Families. It recognizes the rights of all migrants, including irregular migrant workers, to a minimum degree of protection irrespective of their situation. While the Convention seeks to discourage illegal labor migration, it provides additional rights for migrant workers, including their family members. It is the only document of its kind, as it protects migrants through the whole migration process. These phases include decision making, pre-departure, migration preparation, transit and employment at destination country, and return and reintegration (Haque 2007). Sri Lanka is the only South Asian country that has ratified the Convention.

States have been reluctant to become a party to the Convention for the following reasons:

- The recommendatory nature of the Convention, which calls on the contracting parties to accept binding obligations in the future.
- The lack of political will on the part of the states.
- The lack of awareness of the value of the Convention.
- Reluctance to take measures to reconcile incompatible national legislations with the requirements of the Convention.
- Unwillingness to make administrative changes involving a wide range of state agencies that might incur additional costs on national resources (Haque 2007).

5.2 SAARC Social Charter and Citizen's Social Charter

In South Asia, the legal framework has yet to develop fully to protect the rights and interest of migrant workers. The SAARC Social Charter was adopted by the 12th SAARC Summit in Islamabad (January 2004), with the objective of establishing a people-centered framework for social development and guiding their work to build a culture of cooperation and partnership. The SAARC Charter does not recognize migrant labor as a distinctive group and therefore does not mention laborers or workers. Unlike the European Social Charter, the Southern African Development Community Social Charter, or the Association of Southeast Asian Nations Social Charter, SAARC member states make no commitments to respect the ILO core labor standards.[4]

A parallel initiative taken by the South Asia Centre for Policy Studies (SACEPS) led to the formulation of a Citizen's Social Charter and national social charters in six of the SAARC countries. Unlike in the formulation of the SARC Social Charter, SACEPS was able to mobilize and sustain a constituency in the civil society, which could be used to promote the concept behind the Charter and monitor its implementation. The Citizen's Social Charter does not contain an independent section on labor, but it does mention that, while its scope shall not be limited by the Universal Declaration of Human Rights, it will be guided by, among others, the ILO Convention on the Right of Workers and CEDAW. The Citizen's Social Charter recognizes that human resource development for a productive workforce must include the well-being of the workforce through promotion and protection of their rights (Art. 116 and 118). It proposes action plans to implement labor legislation, establish appropriate institutions, and provide the conditions necessary to ensure the rights of workers (Art. 119) (SACEPS 2005, 6–16).

5.3 National Regulations

Among the five major sending countries of the region, only Bangladesh has a comprehensive overseas employment policy, which was only adopted in 2006 after its earlier Emigration Ordinance 1982 and three of its rules were found to be inadequate in protecting migrant workers from fraudulent practices. Three Bangladeshi government agencies manage the welfare of migrants: the Ministry of Expatriates' Welfare and Overseas Employment; its Bureau of Manpower, Employment and Training (BMET); and Bangladesh Overseas Employment and Service, Ltd. (BOESL). Whereas

BOESL functions as a consultant and recruitment agency for Bangladeshis looking for foreign employment, BMET protects the interests of the emigrants and provides vocational guidance and counseling. Bangladesh has set up a Wage Earners' Welfare Fund to expand the scope of coverage for migrant workers (Maimbo et al. 2005, 16–18).

The Indian Emigration Act of 1983 focuses on the welfare of migrants and promotion of overseas employment. In an attempt to make the system more responsive to the interests of migrant workers, the Indian government has made some changes and adjustments. The Office of Protectorate General was transferred to the Ministry of Labor from the Ministry of External Affairs, and system of public hearings was introduced to redress workers' grievances. Eight offices of the Protector of Emigrants are located in various parts of the country. Currently, a proposal to establish a National Manpower Export Promotion Council is seeking to make both government functionaries and recruitment industry more accountable (Maimbo et al. 2005, 18–19).

Nepal's Foreign Employment Act 1985 aims to regulate the provision of recruiting agency licenses and the procedure of selecting workers. The Foreign Employment Bill 2007 passed by the interim government is an improvement on the Employment Act and takes a rights-based approach. It envisions the creation of a board to manage foreign employment and includes provisions to create a new government department that will be dedicated to this issue. Additional provisions are included to establish tribunals to adjudicate complaints by migrant workers, to set up a Welfare Fund, to protect the right of women to seek jobs abroad, to provide compulsory insurance on contracts, and to expand the rights of recruitment agencies to operate outside Kathmandu.[5]

Pakistan has a comprehensive emigration system that operates under the Ministry of Labour, Manpower, and Overseas Pakistanis. Under the Emigration Ordinance of 1979, the Bureau of Emigration and Overseas Employment, which is under the Labour Ministry, regulates migration in the private sector, while the Overseas Employment Corporation regulates public sector migration. Migration for purposes other than foreign employment is controlled by the Ministry of Interior through its various departments (Maimbo et al. 2005, 20).

In Sri Lanka, migration and remittances are looked after by the Ministry of Employment and Labour, along with its implementing machinery, the Sri Lanka Bureau of Foreign Employment (SLBFE). Although the Ministry is responsible for formulating policies and monitoring the administration of foreign employment, the SLBFE implements a wide range of workers' welfare programs, both at home and in the host country (Maimbo et al. 2005, 21).

All five South Asian countries have labor attachés posted to their missions in countries that receive significant numbers of their workers. Pre-departure trainings in one form or the other are usually provided by the sending countries, with some provisions in those missions to receive complaints from their workers. These complaints are usually related to nonpayment or underpayment of wages, lack of medical facilities, and poor food and living conditions.

The receiving countries in the Gulf Cooperation Council (GCC) have come to realize the need for a common strategy to address the socioeconomic impact of foreign workers. On 1 May 2007, the Doha Declaration on Foreign Workers in the GCC was issued at the conclusion of a regional symposium of high government officials, academics, and decision makers from the sending and receiving countries, including experts in the areas of population, labor, and migration. The Declaration recognized the importance of strengthening cooperation among the GCC states and called for further integration of their policies through exchange of relevant information among member states, including through international agencies such as the ILO and other UN bodies (Sinha 2007). A similar declaration for the sending countries from South Asia has yet to emerge.

6. DESIRED GOALS[6]

The idea of decent work that the ILO has been promoting underlines the theme of productive work that generates adequate income, in which rights are protected and in which there is adequate social protection. The objective is to promote opportunities for men and women to obtain decent work under conditions of freedom, equality, security, and human dignity. If these are the generally accepted international principles, then sending countries need to take up the main issues of the Four Pillars of Decent Work: *right to work, right at work, social protection, and social dialogue*. This ILO model focuses on a rights-based approach that has been subscribed to by all states in the world.

6.1 Making the Recruitment Industry Accountable

An urgently needed area of focus is to hold the recruitment industry accountable. The private sector plays a major role in the recruitment of migrant workers and presently accounts for more than 90 percent of the recruitment in Bangladesh, India, Pakistan, and Sri Lanka (Haque 2007). While the recruitment industry is essential in promoting migration, migrants are cheated by harmful practices of some of these agencies, as the regulatory mechanisms that do exist do not operate properly. Making the intermediary or subagents accountable through licensing is essential, as is seeing that they operate properly in countries where such provisions already exist. Many potential migrants lose their investments because this aspect has not been looked into adequately, and many households have become paupers as a result of the activities of unscrupulous agents and subagents. The recruitment industry is burgeoning: there are around 800 agencies in Bangladesh, 760 in Nepal, and 1,182 in Pakistan (Azam 2005). The renewal of their licenses, however, is not tied to their performance. The performance criteria need to be linked not only to the number of workers they send abroad, but also to the terms under which they are sending these workers and how they respond when workers have problems. Some form of point system has to be introduced to assess agency performance.

6.2 A More Proactive Migration Policy by the Sending States

In terms of interministry and interagency cooperation, there is major institutional confusion. Each of the ministries of the government operates on the basis of its own turf and without adequate mechanisms. South Asian countries can learn from the experience of the Philippines in this regard. The Migrant Workers and Overseas Filipinos Act of 1995 includes specific provision that requires the government to establish a Migrant Workers and Other Overseas Filipinos Resource Centre within the jurisdiction of the Philippine Embassy. The Centre functions as a joint undertaking of various government agencies and operates 24 hours a day, including holidays. In addition to providing information and advisory programs to arriving migrant workers, it offers counseling and legal services, and welfare assistance. Some of its other functions include assisting women through gender-sensitive programs, providing training and upgrading skills, hosting orientation programs for returning workers, and regularly monitoring situations that might affect migrant workers. To ensure better coordination at home, an interagency committee of various branches of government is established to allow free exchanges of database files so that information on migration is shared by the authorities (Government of Philippines 1995).

When negotiating Memorandums of Understanding (MoUs) and bilateral agreements, the rights of the migrant workers are essential. Industrial actions are illegal in most of the traditional societies in the Middle East; therefore, it becomes incumbent on the governments in the region to protect worker rights through formal agreements with the receiving countries.

6.3 Pre-departure Training

Pre-departure training, including rudimentary language training, can make a lot of difference in how well migrant workers, especially women, adjust to the new environment in the receiving countries. Studies on women laborers working in the Middle East have found that with better pre-departure training they have been able to work more easily with their employers. As a result of this training, verbal and physical abuses also have dropped significantly (Siddqui 2007c).

6.4 Enhancing Worker Skills

As demands for skilled workers is rising internationally, India and other South Asian states need to reorient their workforce to this lucrative market. A study of unskilled Nepali migrants going to Malaysia in 2006 showed that unless they stay in dirty conditions or with friends, workers hardly save any money after deducting the cost of migrating to the receiving countries, commission, living expenses, and so on. Skill development is important, especially since demand for skilled workers (particularly for nurses in Europe and North America) are rising, while the demand for unskilled workers will grow at a decelerated rate. Studies show that Nepal could send another 40,000 workers abroad in the skilled sector, if only it had the human resources available (Bal Kumar 2008; Sharma 2007).

6.5 Promoting Safe Migration

Facilitating safe migration can lead to a win–win situation that will meet the labor market needs of destination countries and provide economic benefits, knowledge, and skills to the migrant workers. Recommendations for such policies in the region include *(a)* developing awareness campaigns both in the countries of origin and destination; *(b)* establishing bilateral labor agreements and MoUs to ensure rights through formalizing wages, obligations, and privileges; and *(c)* expanding the role of consular service in the destination countries to protect the rights of migrants.

Safe migration should include dealing with the threat of HIV/AIDS, because the disease ignores national boundaries and spreads from nation to nation. Initiatives to ensure safe migration should address specific problems by reducing vulnerability of migrant workers through proper orientation; providing access to prevention, treatment, and care in both sources and destination countries; and developing a favorable regional policy to address the problem (Adhikari 2007).

Another critical issue is the question of trafficking of women and children. Trafficking is the dark 'underside of globalization and migration. It is a global phenomenon that is sustained by demand and fueled by poverty and unemployment. After Southeast Asia, South Asia is the home to largest number of internationally trafficked persons, which is estimated to be around 150,000 annually. India and Pakistan are major countries of destination for trafficked women and girls, and are also the main transit points into the Middle East. Trafficking of children is of particular concern because it is an extension of serious child labor problems (UNFPA 2006).

Historically, trafficking has been associated with the effort to combat prostitution, but today it has a broader meaning and includes initiatives to check forced labor, forced marriage, sale of organs, and other deceptive and coercive criminal practices. As the former UN Special Rapporteur Radhika Coomaraswamy noted on violence against women that *traffickers fish in the stream of migration.* Migrant workers, in particular, are vulnerable to trafficking and other abuses, especially if they are undocumented, because they cannot complain about their working conditions for fear of being arrested and deported (Baruah 2006; McGill 2002).

6.6 Learning from Best Practices

Many good practices already exist in the region. The Bangladesh Government's Overseas Employment Policies is a step forward. In India, the requirement for public hearing is another good example. In Sri Lanka, the training and preparation of workers is a practice that other countries in the region can build into their laws.

A number of countries in the region provide incentives to migrant laborers and services to assist in the reintegration of returning migrants. Bangladesh has its own bank representatives in the receiving countries, provisions for investments in privatized Bangladeshi industries, a special savings incentive in the form of a Wage Earner Bond, and housing opportunities on government land developments. To encourage Pakistanis abroad to remit their funds to their home country, the Pakistani government in June 2001 announced separate privileges for nationals remitting US$2,500 per year and for nonresident Pakistanis (NRPs) remitting a minimum of US$10,000 through the banking channels. Those belonging to the former category are entitled to duty-free imports up to US$700 during any year, while NRPs are entitled to duty-free convenience of a value up to US$1,200. NRPs are entitled to the merit-based quota system assigned in all public professional colleges and universities, participation in a lottery for choice plots in public housing schemes at attractive prices if paid in foreign currency, and expedited allocation of shares in privatizations. In addition, bona fide remittances are not subject to tax.

Sri Lanka has gone further than other countries in South Asia to promote labor migration. Migrants are provided pre-departure loans to cover departure expenses, including travel costs. Eligible migrants and their families are provided with free life insurance and, once abroad, they can maintain nonresident foreign-currency accounts, which they fund through their remittances. The only catch is that they must open an account with a state bank.

In India, some state governments, like Kerala, have set up Human Resources Corporation to promote labor exports. No specific national programs and service assist in the reintegration of returning migrants, although there are various forms of incentives to the nonresident Indians. These incentives include options for dual citizenship and the ability to move capital freely between their two homes without undue bureaucratic interference. For instance, on 10 January 2004, the government announced that anyone could buy dollars up to US$25,000 a year to remit abroad, while Indian companies were allowed to invest up to 100 percent of their net worth overseas (Maimbo et al. 2005, 16–23).

Lessons can be learned from the best practices of other countries that have substantial experience in this area. The Philippines can offer a number of successful examples. Over the past 20 years, the Philippines has built up laws designed to attract resources of its sizeable diaspora. These laws include incentives and privileges for migrant workers to invest, donate, purchase real estate property, or open local enterprises in areas that are normally reserved for Filipino citizens. Additional attractions include new laws allowing overseas Filipinos to participate in Philippine elections and to hold dual citizenship.

6.7 Reducing the Cost of Migration

South Asian countries also need to reduce the cost of migration through recruiting agencies and institutions, and to reduce the cost of remitting money to the home country. For instance, the cost for migrating from Sri Lanka is one of the lowest in the region (US$689), while the cost for Pakistan (US$1,300), Nepal (US$1,500), and Bangladesh (US$1,700) is considerably higher. Sri Lanka has been able to bring down the emigration cost by adopting two strategies. It raised the annual license fee for recruiters from Rs 100 to Rs 10,000 because the initial low fee provided incentives for corruption in under-the-table transactions by bureaucrats. Second, the SLBFE has made arrangements with airlines for block bookings to key destinations, which has enabled it to pass discounts on to workers. In addition, because the migration process is always under the "unremitting scrutiny" of civil society organizations to ensure accountability, they have become an effective medium for reducing emigration transaction costs (Rodrigo 1992, quoted in Waddington 2003, 9).

6.8 Remittance Management

Innovative experiences of countries in remittance management also can be shared with and learned from other countries. A workshop organized by RMMRU with World Bank officials on remittance transfer highlighted the fact that the pace at which remittances were increasing in South Asia was not matched by the level of offers of investment products for the remitters. Central banks usually meet the needs of long-term migrants and relatively better-off short-term migrants, but other migrants do not have many choices. The bankers at that workshop felt that diversified products were needed to match the demands of different age-groups and small remitters. Other methods that could be used to better manage remittance include the following:

- *Creating better investment opportunities* by catering to the local needs of the migrant workers by encouraging them to invest in high-profile projects such as bridges, flyovers, and airports dedicated to migrants.
- *Making better use of modern technology* by improving services so that transfer of remittances to the country of origin is achieved quickly and more effectively at lower costs.
- *Locating bank representatives in receiving countries* to provide easy access and better services to the migrant workers.

- *Reexamining the role of the unofficial remittance channels* so that the effective role played by the *hundi* system in transferring resources to the country of origin may not become ineffectual in the name of checking unofficial financial flows to finance terrorism.

6.9 Engaging Diasporas

The need for donor agencies and countries to engage migrants and diaspora organizations in development cooperation is increasing. Because migrants may already be mobilized for development on their own initiative, it is the development actors that should be "mobilized" to establish a two-way working relationship. Developing a successful alliance calls for giving the diaspora organizations a real say in policy formulation and access to substantial funding. Any development policy that seeks to utilize the support of the diaspora should avoid setting a double agenda, because diaspora organizations are unlikely to cooperate with initiatives that have the hidden agenda of curbing migration in the guise of development efforts.

Diaspora organizations might be involved in development policies in a number of ways, including the following:

- Active involvement of migrants and migrant organizations in policy formulation.
- Supporting capacity building and network formation among migrant organizations to enhance their interest in development activities.
- Providing financial or organizational support to sustain development initiatives of migrants.
- Involving migrants and diaspora organizations as experts or consultants in projects designed by development agencies.
- Involving migrants and diaspora organizations in programs of permanent or temporary return (de Hass 2006, 94–96).

7. PROMOTING MIGRATION: A REGIONAL APPROACH THROUGH SAARC

Collaboration of South Asian countries is essential in creating a more uniform policy for sending, receiving, and transit countries. Currently, competition is negative among countries in South Asia. Collective efforts are needed to deal with the problems of missing and irregular migrants, as well as the increasing securitization of labor migration issue that threatens to make the position of the laborers more insecure in the receiving countries. More action research is needed on labor migration from South Asia, because the problems of migration are different in each country (Adhikari 2007). Some of the issues for which more work needs to be done through a collective effort are discussed below.

7.1 Treating Migration as a Major Human and Economic Issue

The Citizen's Social Charter could serve as a guiding document to further sharpen the SAARC Social Charter. For too long, labor flows across borders have been treated, whether at the World Trade Organization (WTO) or in South Asia, as illegal migration by ministries in charge of international security, rather than as trade and economic affairs. Migration needs to be treated as a major human and economic concern. Major research is needed to understand the underlying economics, the social implications in the receiving and sending countries, and the political fallout of the labor flows within and outside the region. The output of such research could be instrumental in developing a realistic and humanitarian policy to formalize the process of labor flows and to integrate them into the broader process of economic cooperation in South Asia (Sobhan 2004, 12–13).

7.2 Developing the Necessary Information and Data

Return migration is an inevitable aspect of temporary or contract migration, but there is a paucity of information to evaluate the number of those who return to their country of origin. There is also a lack of information on aspects such as occupational structure, skills acquired, resource position, investment capabilities, and investment plans of return migrants. The lack of data has impaired the formulation of any meaningful reintegration plans for those returning to their country of origin. This underscores the need for further research in this area, which can be implemented only through a collective effort (Srivastava and Sasikumar 2003, 16).

7.3 Examining the Issue of Consumption versus Investment of Remittances

The impact of remittance on the national economy of South Asian countries is not fully understood. Surveys from a range of countries have found that remittances, up to 80 percent in some regions, are spent on consumption and welfare, whereas only a small amount is invested in land and housing and new productive investments. The specific implication of consumption and investments needs to be examined to clarify the impact of remittances on poverty and economic development in South Asia.

7.4 Establishing a SAARC Task Force on Migration

SAARC should establish a task force to look at the complex phenomenon of migration from the point of view of its influence on growth prospects of the South Asian countries and to derive relevant conclusions out of that effort. The task force could begin by examining existing laws and policy documents in the region, which could produce recommendations on the kinds of actions to be taken. The task force should be based on a technical-level study on the pattern of migration, the evolution of policies, and demographic trends, both regionally and internationally. It should look at the adequacy or inadequacy of the data, as well as their conformity with international standards and whether regional standards of collecting such data could be established (Dubey 2007b).

SAARC countries should subscribe to the UN Convention on the Protection of the Rights of all Migrant Workers and Members of the Families as well as to the many other ILO protocols. South Asian countries could take the lead in including the movement of natural persons on the WTO agenda, which excluded it earlier. The benefit of the WTO is that once member nations agree on the norms, they become enforceable through sanctions.

NOTES

1. In the case of Nepalese migrant workers, see Gurung 2000.
2. Trade unions operate in all the South Asian countries, except Bhutan and Maldives.
3. Aside from the possibility that remittances may increase inequality and cause dependency, they make significant contributions to reducing poverty or vulnerability in the majority of household and communities. The impact of remittances on poverty reductions is usually examined at four different levels. First, at the local level, remittances contribute directly to raising household incomes as well as broadening opportunities to increase incomes. They allow households to increase their consumption of goods and services. At this level, remittances may be an unreliable source of future incomes, however, because they can only make specific contributions at a particular moment in time and, in the long term, they can stop altogether if the migrants return to the home country

or if they are integrated and become permanent residents in the host country. Second, at the community level, remittances generate multiplier effects on the local economy by creating new jobs, especially when new economic and social infrastructures and services are put in place. Remittances can especially make a difference in remote rural areas where state resources have not been effective. Third, at the national level, remittances provide states foreign currency and contribute to the GDP. However, in countries with low GDP, remittances can distort the function of the capital market and destabilize exchange rate regimes through the creation of parallel currency markets. And fourth, at the international level, they can transfer resources from the industrial to the developing countries and thus reduce inequality (see Chimhowu et al. 2003).

4. The eight core labor standards include (a) Con. 97: Freedom of Association and Protection of the Right to Organize; (b) Con. 98: Right to Organize and Collective Bargaining; (c) Con. 105: Abolition of Forced Labor; (d) Con. 138: Minimum Age for Employment; (e) Con. 182: Worst Forms of Child Labor Convention; (f) Con. 100: Equal Remuneration for Work of Equal Value; (g) Con. 29: Forced Labor; and (h) Con. 111: Discrimination in Employment and Occupation.

5. Information provided by Sharu Joshi to the author after the seminar (2007).

6. Unless otherwise indicated, the summary in this section is based on a presentation made by Abrar 2007.

REFERENCES

Abrar, Chowdhury. 2007. "Patterns of Migration of South Asians to the Gulf Region: Their Main Problems and Issues." Seminar presentation on *Labour Migration, Employment and Poverty Alleviation in South Asia*, Kathmandu, August 9–10.

Adams, Richard, Jr. 1998. "Remittances, Investment and Rural Asset Accumulation in Pakistan." *Economic Development and Cultural Change* 47 (1): 155–73.

Adhikari, Jagannath. 2007a. Comments from the floor on Athula Ranasinghe's paper, "Remittance Economy and Its Contribution to Poverty Alleviation in South Asia: A Case Study of Sri Lanka." Seminar presentation on *Labour Migration, Employment and Poverty Alleviation in South Asia*, Kathmandu, August 9–10.

Adhikari, Madhav. 2007b. Comments on Ganesh Gurung's paper on "Remittance Economy and Its Contribution to Poverty Alleviation in South Asia: A Case Study of Nepal," Seminar presentation on *Labour Migration, Employment and Poverty Alleviation in South Asia*, Kathmandu, August 9–10.

Azam, Farooq. 2005. "Public Policies to Support International Migration in Pakistan and the Philippines." Draft working paper produced for the World Bank conference on *New Frontiers of Social Policy: Development in a Globalizing World*, Arusha Conference, December 12–15.

Bal Kumar, K. C. 2007. "Remittance Economy and Its Contribution to Poverty Alleviation in South Asia: A Case of Pakistan," discussant on presentation at the Regional Seminar on *Labor Migration, Employment and Poverty Alleviation in South Asia*, Kathmandu, August 9–10.

Baruah, Nandita. 2006. "Trafficking in Women and Children in South Asia: A Regional Perspective." Available at http://www.Empowerpoor.org/downloads/Trafficking%20in%20South%20Asia.pdf (accessed on 6 October 2009).

Bhadra, Chandra. 2007. "Women's International Labour Migration and Impact of their Remittance on Poverty Reduction: Case of Nepal." Seminar presentation on *Labour Migration, Employment and Poverty Alleviation in South Asia*, Kathmandu, August 9–10.

Black, Richard. 2003. "Migration, Globalization and Poverty: The New DFID-Funded Development Research Centre on Migration." Department for International Development ASREP-SLSO Lunchtime Seminar, London, February 24. Available at www.livelihoods.org/hot_topics/docs/Migr_240203.doc (accessed 6 October 2009).

———. 2006. "Migration and Inequality: Policy Implications." Briefing Paper No. 7, Development Research Centre on Migration, Globalization and Poverty, October. Available at www.migrationdrc.org/publications/annual_reports/Migration_DRC_Annual_Rep_2006-07.pdf (accessed on 6 October 2009).

Burney, Nadeem. 1998. *A Macro-Economic Analysis of the Impact of Workers' Remittances from the Middle East on Pakistan's Economy.* Working Paper No. 8, ILO-UN Project.

Chimhowu, Admos, Jenifer Piesse, and Caroline Pinder. 2003. "The Socio-economic Impact of Remittances on Poverty Reduction." Paper presented at *The International Conference on Migrant Remittances: Development Impact, Opportunities for the Financial Sector and Future Prospects,* London, October. Available at www.worldbank.org/WBSITE/EXTERNAL/TOPICS/EXTFINANCIALSECTOR/EXTTOPCONF3/0,,contentMDK:20987992~menuPK:2739101~pagePK:64168445~piPK:64168309~theSitePK:15878 50,00.html

Chishti, Muzaffar A. 2007. "The Phenomenal Rise in Remitttances to India: A Closer Look." *Migration Policy Institute Policy Brief,* May.

de Hass, Hein. 2006. "Engaging Diasporas: How Governments and Development Agencies Can Support Diaspora Involvement in the Development of Origin Countries." Oxford: International Migration Institute, Oxford University. Available at http://portal.unesco.org/shs/en/files/9758/11509951971engaging_diasporas_heindehaas.pdf/engaging_diasporas_heindehaas.pdf (accessed on 6 October 2009).

Development Research Centre on Migration, Globalization and Poverty (DRCMGP). 2006. "Migration and Inequality: Policy Implications," Briefing Paper No. 7, October. Available at http://www.migrationdrc.org/publications/briefing_papers/BP7.pdf (accessed on 6 October 2009).

Dixit, Kanak Mani. 2007. Comments from the Chair on Ganesh Gurung's paper "Remittance Economy and Its Contribution to Poverty Alleviation in South Asia: A Case Study of Nepal." Seminar presentation on *Labour Migration, Employment and Poverty Alleviation in South Asia*, Kathmandu, August 9–10.

Dubey, Muchkund. 2007a. "Looking Back and Moving Ahead: Concluding Observations on the Key Points Raised by the Conference." Seminar presentation on *Labour Migration, Employment and Poverty Alleviation in South Asia*, Kathmandu, August 9–10.

———. 2007b. Comment from the floor on Athula Ranasinghe's paper on "Remittance Economy and Its Contribution to Poverty Alleviation in South Asia: A Case Study of Sri Lanka." Seminar presentation on *Labour Migration, Employment and Poverty Alleviation in South Asia*, Kathmandu, August 9–10.

Gardner, Katy. 1995. *Global Migrants, Local Lives: Travel and Transformation in Rural Bangladesh.* Oxford University Press: New York.

Global Commission on International Migration (GCIM). 2005. *Migration in an Interconnected World: New Direction for Action.* Available at http://www.gcim.org/attachements/gcim-complete-report-2005.pdf (accessed on 6 October 2009).

Government of Philippines. 1995. *Republic Act No. 8042: Migrant Workers and Overseas Filipinos Act of 1995.* Available at www.nrco.dole.gov.ph/pdf/Republic%20Act%20 No.%208042.pdf (accessed on 6 October 2009).

Gurung, Ganesh. 2000. "Patterns in Foreign Employment and Vulnerability of Migrant Workers." Kathmandu: Nepal Institute of Development Studies. Available at http:// www.childtrafficking.com/Docs/gurung_nids_2000__vulnerabi.pdf (accessed on 6 October 2009).

———. 2007 "Remittance Economy and Its Contribution to Poverty Alleviation in South Asia: A Case Study of Nepal." Seminar presentation on *Labour Migration, Employment and Poverty Alleviation in South Asia*, Kathmandu, August 9–10.

Haque, Syed Saiful. 2007. "Global Rules and the Welfare Provisions for Migrant Workers." Seminar presentation on *Labour Migration, Employment and Poverty Alleviation in South Asia*, Kathmandu, August 9–10.

Joshi, Sharu. 2007. Discussant on Chowdhury R. Abrar's paper on "Patterns of Migration of South Asian to the Gulf Region: Their Main Problems and Issues." Seminar presentation on *Labour Migration, Employment and Poverty Alleviation in South Asia*, Kathmandu, August 9–10.

Kazi, Shahnaz. 1998. *Domestic Impact of Remittances and Overseas Immigration: Pakistan.* Working Paper No. 7, ILO-UN Project.

Koirala, Bimal. 2007. Comments from the Chair on Tasneem Siddqui's paper on "Contribution of Remittance in Poverty Alleviation in South Asia." Seminar presentation on *Labour Migration, Employment and Poverty Alleviation in South Asia*, Kathmandu, August 9–10.

Maimbo, Samuel Munzele, Richard Adams, Reena Aggarwal, and Nikos Passas. 2005. "Migrant Labour Remittance in the South Asia Region." World Bank, Report No. 31577, Washington, DC, February.

McGill, Eugenia. 2002. *Asian Development Bank Regional Technical Assistance No. 5948: Combating Trafficking of Women and Children in South Asia: Supplemental Study on Legal Frameworks Relevant to Human Trafficking in South Asia,* July. Available at www. adb.org/documents/events/2002/reta5948/study_human_trafficking.pdf (accessed on 6 October 2009).

Pyakurel, Bishwombar. 2007. Discussant on "Contribution of Remittance in Poverty Alleviation in South." Seminar presentation on *Labour Migration, Employment and Poverty Alleviation in South Asia*, Kathmandu, August 9–10.

Rana, Madhukar. 2007. Comments from the floor on Athula Ranasinghe's paper "Remittance Economy and Its Contribution to Poverty Alleviation in South Asia: A Case Study of Sri Lanka." Seminar presentation on *Labour Migration, Employment and Poverty Alleviation in South Asia*, Kathmandu, August 9–10.

Ranasinghe, Athula. 2007. "Remittance Economy and Its Contribution to Poverty Alleviation in South Asia: A Case Study of Sri Lanka." Seminar presentation on *Labour Migration, Employment and Poverty Alleviation in South Asia,* Kathmandu, August 9–10.

Rodrigo, C. 1992. "Overseas Migration from Sri Lanka: Magnitude, Patterns and Trends." *Asian Exchange* 8 (3/4): 41–74.

Sainju, Man. 2007. Comments from the floor on Ganesh Gurung's paper on "Remittance Economy and Its Contribution to Poverty Alleviation in South Asia: A Case Study of Nepal." Seminar presentation on *Labour Migration, Employment and Poverty Alleviation in South Asia*, Kathmandu, August 9–10.

Sharma, Shiva. 2007. Comments from the floor on Chowdhury Abrar's presentation on "Patterns of Migration of South Asians to the Gulf Region." Seminar presentation on *Labour Migration, Employment and Poverty Alleviation in South Asia*, Kathmandu, August 9–10.

Siddiqui, Rizwana, and A. R. Kemal. 2007. "Remittances, Trade Liberalization, and Poverty in Pakistan: The Role of Excluded Variables in Poverty Change Analysis." Paper No. 4228. *Munich Personal RePEe Archive*. Available at http://mpra.ub.uni-muenchen. de/4228/ (accessed on 6 October 2009).

Siddqui, Tasneem 2007a. "Contribution of Remittance in Poverty Alleviation in South." Seminar paper. Seminar presentation on *Labour Migration, Employment and Poverty Alleviation in South Asia*, Kathmandu, August 9–10.

———. 2007b. Comments from the floor on Chandra Bhadra's paper on "Women's International Labour Migration and Impact of their Remittance on Poverty Reduction: Case of Nepal." Seminar presentation on *Labour Migration, Employment and Poverty Alleviation in South Asia*, Kathmandu, August 9–10.

———. 2007c. Comments on Athula Ranasinghe's paper on "Remittance Economy and Its Contribution to Poverty Alleviation in South Asia: A Case Study of Sri Lanka." Seminar presentation on *Labour Migration, Employment and Poverty Alleviation in South Asia*, Kathmandu, August 9–10.

Sinha, Pravin. 2007. "Security 'Decent' Conditions for Migrant Workers: Should It Be Part of the SAARC Social Charter?" Seminar presentation on *Labour Migration, Employment and Poverty Alleviation in South Asia*, Kathmandu, August 9–10.

Sobhan, Rehman. 2004. "The 12th SAARC Summit: Charting a Road Map for South Asian Cooperation." In Rehman Sobhan (ed.), *Promoting Cooperation in south Asia: An Agenda for the 13th SAARC Summit*. Dhaka: The University Press Ltd.

South Asia Centre for Policy Studies (SACEPS). 2005. *A Citizen's Social Charter for South Asia: An Agenda for Civic Action*. Dhaka: The University Press Ltd.

Srivastava, Ravi, and S. K. Sasikumar. 2003. "An Overview of Migration in India, Its Impacts and Key Issues." Paper presented at a *Regional Conference on Migration, Development and Pro-Poor Policy Choices in Asia*, Dhaka, June 22–24.

Subedi, Bhim. 2007. Discussant on Ganesh Gurung's paper on "Remittance Economy and Its Contribution to Poverty Alleviation in South Asia: A Case Study of Nepal." Seminar presentation on *Labour Migration, Employment and Poverty Alleviation in South Asia*. Kathmandu.

United Nations Population Fund (UNFPA). 2006. *A State of World Population 2006: A Passage to Hope, Women and International Migration*. Available at http://www.unfpa. org/upload/lib_pub_file/650_filename_sowp06-en.pdf (accessed on 6 October 2009).

Waddington, Clare. 2003. "International Migration Policies in Asia: A Synthesis of ILO and Other Literature on Policies Seeking to Manage the Recruitment and Protection of Migrants, and Facilitate Remittances and Their Investment." *Migration Development and Pro-poor Policy Choices in Asia* International Labour Organization. Geneva: (ILO).

World Bank. 2005. "Two Current Issues Facing Developing Countries: Workers' Remittances and Economic Development." Chapter 2 in *World Economic Outlook 2005: Globalization and External Imbalances*, pp. 69–78. Available at http://www.imf.org/external/pubs/ft/ weo/2005/01/pdf/chapter2.pdf (accessed on 6 October 2009).

———. 2006. *Global Economic Perspective Report 2006: Economic Implications of Remittance and Migration*. Washington, DC: World Bank.

———. 2008. *Migration and Remittances Factbook, 2008*. Available at http://www-wds. worldbank.org/external/default/WDSContentServer/IW3P/IB/2008/03/14/000333038_ 20080314060040/Rendered/PDF/429130PUB0Migr101OFFICIAL0USE0ONLY1.pdf (accessed on 6 October 2009).

Promoting Tourism in South Asia

Renton de Alwis

1. INTRODUCTION

South Asia is home to a solid one-third of the world's population. Some of the best brains that run the world have South Asian roots or lineage. The region is home to the highest and the second highest mountain peaks of the world (Everest and K2). Most of the world's quality water resources are in the region with the river systems originating from the Himalayas. Some of world's best ocean resources (coral reefs of Maldives), beaches (Coxes Bazaar), and mangrove areas (Sunderbans) are located in the region. Its biodiversity is unmatched (Sinharaja, Chitwan). Home to marvels such as the Taj Mahal, Ajanta, Sigiriya, Timpu, and Taxila, the heritage and cultures of the region date back thousands of years. For centuries, the region has been a hotspot for seafaring nations looking for spices and other riches. It was the playground of several colonial powers, and is now home to almost all of the world's religions. The cuisine of the region is exquisite, and its people are friendly and warm. The South Asian region has the key ingredients to delight its visitors.

Yet, with some 400 million people remaining below the poverty line and 71 million people affected by violence or its threat, most of South Asia remains conflict ridden. Poverty, health, child, and gender-related issues are pulling down the region's image.[1]

In 2007, the South Asian region received less than 1.1 percent (9.7 million) of the 898 million visitors from around the world (UN World Tourism Organization 2008). In comparison, Europe received 53.5 percent of the global arrivals, and the Asian region, including East and Southeast Asia, received 19.3 percent. The volume of arrivals to the Asia Pacific region more than doubled between 2000 and 2007, from 85 million to 198 million (UNESCAP 2008). Within this growth scenario, regrettably, most of South Asia saw only marginal growth, with the exceptions of some significant growth to India and Maldives.

For several decades now, the region has promoted tourism. As far back as the early 1980s, the World Tourism Organization (now UNWTO) set up a Secretariat in Colombo for South Asian Tourism Promotion and attempted to promote the region. This initiative failed because of inadequate support and interest from the individual nations' state tourism organizations. In the 1990s, the SAARC Chambers of Commerce and Industry (SCCI) began a Nepal-based initiative to promote tourism to the region.[2] A special tourism committee was formed and several rounds of meetings were held. A promotional tagline "Magic That Is South Asia" was coined, and talk of a regional tourism year was initiated. It was thought that tourism would improve if private sector business and tourism stakeholders took the lead in moving regional tourism initiatives forward. Several South Asian tourism business and trade marts[3] have been held since the 1990s.

On the formal intergovernmental sphere, tourism occupies an important position. The official Web site of the SAARC Secretariat[4] presents tourism as follows:

The SAARC Leaders have always recognized the importance of tourism and emphasized the need to take measures for promoting tourism in the region. During the Second Summit, the Leaders underscored that concrete steps should be taken to facilitate tourism in the region. Tourism has been an important dimension of most of the subsequent Summits. At the Twelfth Summit held in Islamabad in January 2004, the Leaders were of the view that development of tourism within South Asia could bring economic, social and cultural dividends. There is a need for increasing cooperation to jointly promote tourism with South Asia as well as to promote South Asia as a tourism destination, *inter alia*, by improved air links, they stated in the Declaration. To achieve this and to commemorate the twentieth year of the establishment of SAARC, the year 2005 was designated by the Leaders as "South Asia Tourism Year." Member States were required to individually and jointly organize special events to celebrate it.

On the formal action front, the site reports the following:

The Working Group on Tourism was established by the Council of Ministers during its Twenty-fourth Session held in Islamabad in January 2004. This was done after a comprehensive review of the SAARC Integrated Programme of Action by the Standing Committee at its Fourth Special Session held in Kathmandu in August 2003. This intergovernmental process will compliment the endeavors by SAARC Chambers of Commerce and Industry (SCCI) Tourism Council, thus ensuring public–private partnership for the promotion of tourism.

The First Meeting of the Working Group on Tourism was held in Colombo on 16–17 August 2004. In addition to the SAARC Member States and representatives of the SAARC Secretariat, representatives of the SCCI Tourism Council and the ASEAN Secretariat also attended the Meeting.

Besides reviewing the implementation of program of activities relevant to its mandate, the Working Group made a number of recommendations for promotion of tourism in the SAARC region, for example, printing of a SAARC Travel Guide, production of a documentary movie on tourism in SAARC, promotion of sustainable development of Eco-Tourism, Cultural Tourism and Nature Tourism, collaboration in HRD in tourism sector by having programmes for exchange of teachers, students, teaching modules and materials, Promoting Cooperation in the field of tourism with other relevant regional and international tourism organizations. It also proposed a number of activities to celebrate the South Asia Tourism Year–2005 in a befitting manner.

When comparing the progress made on the ground and by other regional tourism initiatives that began much later than SAARC—such as the Association of Southeast Asian Nations (ASEAN), Pacific Tourism Commission, European Union (EU) Tourism, and the Mekong Tourism Initiative—progress must be classified, at best, as wanting.

With the backdrop of the frustration of SAARC's underperformance, in 1997, a separate initiative was undertaken by several governments of the South Asian region, titled the South Asian Growth Quadrangle, consisting of Bangladesh; Bhutan; 13 of the north, east, and north-east states of India; and Nepal. The Asian Development Bank (ADB) supported the initiative under the South Asian Subregional Economic Cooperation (SASEC) program, which includes a tourism component.[5] This is an ongoing program within the South Asian development framework of the ADB.

In addition, also in 1997, another initiative was created to link some of SAARC's countries with Myanmar and Thailand, as the Bay of Bengal Initiative for Multi-Sectoral Technical and Economic Cooperation

(BIMSTEC), to take advantage of the historical link and turning them into economic opportunities. Named BIMSTEC to represent Bangladesh, India, Myanmar, Sri Lanka, and Thailand Economic Cooperation, it set up a Tourism Working Group and has conducted several rounds of meetings, but to date, it has not achieved much progress. Since 2005, the ADB has supported this initiative as well.

2. THE DICHOTOMY THAT IS SOUTH ASIA

South Asia can indeed be described as a dichotomy. Although it has not lived up to expectations as a regional grouping, at the individual country level, tourism development in SAARC presents several unique models, containing some successful best practices.

Bhutan has presented a model of tourism development,[6] in which its operations are based on the model of a kinked demand curve (Sen 2004) to create a premium value for the destination. Bhutan limits access to a few tens of thousands of tourists each year at a premium charge, placing the per capita yield from one tourist at a high level. Bhutan has a business model aimed at conserving its heritage, culture, and natural resources. This model is in keeping with its unique development indicator of "Gross National Happiness," in contrast to the conventional development measurement of gross national product.

Maldives, known today as one of the most successful island destinations in the world, works on a business model of establishing strong partnerships with foreign investors and tour operators. Beginning with investments from Sri Lankan conglomerates in the early 1980s (still accounting for about 20 percent of all hotel rooms), Maldives Tourism, offering the "sunny side of life" as its positioning platform,[7] is driven by some of the best international and regional brand names in the island tourism business.

Nepal is an example of a pioneering brand of unique community-based tourism initiative. With its early model of the Annapurna Tourism Development Project[8] and the Bhakthipur Conservation Project[9] of the 1980s, Nepal introduced a good tourism operational model, offering its unique nature and heritage conservation, community benefit, and sustainable funding features.

Sri Lanka is addressing the challenge of global warming and climate change faced by all nations of the world. It has extended its conventional position as a tourist destination of a treasured island with a warm people offering nature, culture, and adventure[10] to include an extensive green cover. Through its Tourism Earth Lung initiative it is working toward being a carbon-neutral destination by 2018.[11]

Table 11.1 illustrates the country-wise spread of visitor arrivals to the South Asian region (the newest member country, Afghanistan, is not included).

TABLE 11.1 Country-wise Spread of Visitor Arrivals to the South Asia Region

South Asia	Year					% Change 06/07	CAGR % 2003–07
	2003	2004	2005	2006	2007		
Bangladesh	244,509	271,270	207,662				
Bhutan	6,261	9,249	13,626	17,342	21,093	21.6	35.5
India	2,726,214	3,457,477	3,918,610	4,447,167	4,977,193	11.9	16.2
Pakistan	500,918	647,993	798,260	898,389	839,500	−6.6	13.8
Nepal (Air)	275,438	297,335	277,346	283,819	360,350	27.0	6.9
Maldives	563,593	616,716	395,320	601,923	675,889	12.3	4.6
Sri Lanka	500,642	566,202	549,308	559,609	494,008	−11.7	−0.3

Sources UN World Tourism Organization 2006 and Pacific Asia Travel Association statistical reports, various years.

The figures illustrate the powerful position of India in driving arrivals to the region with close to 5 million visitor arrivals in 2007, with Pakistan and Maldives also showing their prowess. What is also significant is that, except for Sri Lanka, where a war against terrorism and the tsunami (December 2004) affected growth, all other countries in the region performed well in light of the new regional dynamism. In the case of Sri Lanka, in spite of the lack of growth in recent times, public–private sector partnerships have been established for the tourism industry to take off on a sustainable development path.

The largest intraregional tourism-generating market is India, and with better connectivity and thawing of political tensions, the potential growth of Indians traveling within the region will become even more significant. Also offering potential are Pakistan and Bangladesh. Between Nepal, India, and Sri Lanka, Buddhist pilgrimage travel is currently a strong phenomenon (Table 11.2). The low bases of visitation seen in the statistics between countries of South Asia are no indication of their potential. If access (air, sea, and road transport) is efficient, better border formalities are established, and restrictions are eased, these numbers have the potential to grow exponentially. In each of the countries, the growing middle class is offering new opportunities for travel (Singh 2005).

TABLE 11.2 Intraregional Travel between SAARC Countries, 2007

To	India	Pakistan	Maldives	Nepal	Bhutan	Sri Lanka	Bangladesh	Afghanistan
India		106,283	45,787	83,037	6,729	204,084	480,240	23,045
Pakistan	48,242		341	1,655	90	4,312	6,352	80,459
Maldives	17,327	1,013		333	31	9,654	1,284	25
Nepal	96,275	2,566	181[a]		2,135[a]	1,303	7,892	n.a.
Bhutan	n.a.	n.a.	n.a	n.a.		n.a.	n.a.	n.a.
Bangladesh	86,232	5,671	220	3,378	1,187	2,322		104
Afghanistan	n.a.	n.a.	n.a.	n.a.	n.a.	n.a.	n.a.	
Sri Lanka	106,067	10,204	29,539	885	n.a.		1,665	n.a.

Sources UN World Tourism Organization 2007 and Pacific Asia Travel Association statistical reports 2007.

Notes n.a. = not available.

[a] Data are for 2006.

To make things more dynamic for South Asia and South Asia tourism, action must be taken. No amount of patting each other on the back or being politically or diplomatically correct will move the region forward.

The following three problems have prevented South Asian tourism from taking off:

- Lack of a pragmatic approach of political and bureaucratic leadership toward identifying and exploiting sociopolitical and economic opportunities, and the environment of mistrust between India and Pakistan.
- Self-imposed limitation of access to and within the region as a result of an introvert attitude.
- Resultant political instability, the absence of rapid economic growth, and failure to distribute the growth achieved to reduce poverty.

3. THE OUTLOOK FOR THE FUTURE

3.1 Powered by India's Growth and Recent Pragmatism

India presents the region's largest economy as well as the largest tourism operation. India has been the principal trendsetter in determining the region's future, whether it was negative or positive. With an economy growing at 9.2 percent in 2007 and 9.6 percent in 2006, it is cited as one of the most promising prospects of the world for the future. Growth is supported by market reforms, huge inflows of foreign direct investment, rising foreign exchange reserves, both an information technology (IT) and a real estate boom, and a flourishing capital market. India has reduced poverty levels by 10 percent and achieved growth in the services sector of more than 11 percent, with the sector accounting for about 53 percent of the economy.

The concept of "Chindia," in which the growth dynamics of both China and India will complement Asia's newest prospects for economic superpower status, augers well in positioning India as a modern growth economy with a proud heritage and culture, rather than as a poverty-stricken country.

As a result, India's tourism industry is experiencing a strong period of growth, driven by the burgeoning Indian middle class (for domestic and outbound travel) and growth in high-spending foreign tourists. The tourism industry in India is substantial and vibrant, and the country is fast becoming a major global destination as well as an outbound visitor-generating market. India's travel and tourism industry is one of the most profitable industries in the country and is credited with contributing a substantial amount of foreign exchange. This contribution is illustrated by the fact that, during 2006, 4 million tourists visited India and spent US$8.9 billion.

Several reasons are cited for the growth and prosperity of India's travel and tourism industry. Economic growth has added millions annually to the ranks of India's middle class, a group that is driving domestic tourism growth. Disposable income in India has grown by 10.11 percent annually from 2001–06, and much of that is being spent on travel.

Thanks in part to its vibrant IT and outsourcing industry, foreigners are making a growing number of business trips to India, often adding a weekend break or longer holiday to their trip. Foreign tourists spend more days in India than in almost any other country worldwide. Tourist arrivals are also projected to increase by more than 22 percent per year through 2010, with a 33 percent increase in foreign exchange earnings recorded in 2004.

The tourism authorities at the central and state levels have played an important role in the development of the industry, with promotional campaigns such as "Incredible India,"[12] which promoted India's culture and tourist attractions in a fresh and memorable way. The campaign created a new image of India in the minds of consumers around the world and has led directly to an increase in interest among tourists. Similarly, campaigns such as, "God's Own Country" for Kerala,[13] Goa Tourism's

"Go Goa,"[14] and Uttar Pradesh Tourism's "Amazing Heritage—Grand Experiences"[15] made significant impacts on regional tourism development in India. In the earlier part of this decade, it was the success of Kerala's regional campaign that led to the "Incredible India" campaign.

The tourism industry has helped growth in other sectors as diverse as horticulture, handicrafts, agriculture, construction, and even poultry. Recent increased growth in tourism in India has created jobs in a variety of related sectors: almost 20 million people are now working in India's tourism industry.[16]

Recent trends of terrorism, threats to food security, poverty still at undesirable levels, increasing fuel costs, and looming security issues will continue to pose challenges to unleashing the full potential of India as well as the region. An evident breakthrough in thinking of the middle class elite and youth in India and an equally strong desire to break through protectionist and introverted attitudes of other individual nations and the collective psyche of the leadership of the region provide a potential silver lining for tourism. Success is the best driver of change. Within the region, tourism success stories of private sector–driven initiatives, including Bangladesh, India, Maldives, Pakistan, and Sri Lanka amidst many external challenges, demonstrate what is possible in terms of solid achievement.

3.2 The Changing Face of Tourism in Pakistan

Pakistan's tourism assets are described on its official Web site as follows:

> Stretching from the mighty Karakorams in the North to the vast alluvial delta of the Indus River in the South, Pakistan remains a land of high adventure and nature. Trekking, mountaineering, white water rafting, wild boar hunting, mountain and desert jeep safaris, camel and yak safaris, trout fishing and bird watching are a few activities, which entice the adventure and nature lovers to Pakistan.
>
> Pakistan is endowed with a rich and varied flora and fauna. High Himalayas, Karakoram and the Hindu Kush ranges with their alpine meadows and permanent snow line, coniferous forests down the sub-mountain scrub, the vast Indus plain merging into the great desert, the coast line and wetlands, all offer a remarkably rich variety of vegetation and associated wildlife including avifauna, both endemic and migratory. Ten of 18 mammalian orders are represented in Pakistan with species ranging from the world's smallest surviving mammals, the Mediterranean Pigmy Shrew, to the largest mammal ever known; the blue whale.[17]

With the economy of Pakistan growing, visitor arrivals to Pakistan more than doubled in the 1996–2007 period, increasing from 369,000 to 839,500. A significant sharp increase in 2004 and 2005 was the result of the relaxation of boarder restrictions and the new influx of tourists from India, a most desirable trend that lacked consistency in operation.

The number of visitors to Pakistan has increased significantly, but it has not translated into a corresponding growth in foreign exchange receipts. Earnings from tourism increased from US$146 million in 1996 to US$185 million in 2005. Earnings per tourist were equal to less than one-third of the global average. Of the four provinces in the country, Punjab has been the most active in developing tourism. Pakistan today remains a small player in global tourism.

The number of visitors traveling the country in 2005 was less than 1 percent of the world total. Pakistan's earning from tourism was only 0.03 percent of the global average. These proportions are less than Pakistan's share in global population (2.75 percent) or in global output (0.4 percent). The share of revenues and number of tourists traveling is much greater for the countries of East Asia, as well as for China and India. It is obvious from these numbers that Pakistan is not fully realizing its potential. This could change if a different approach to the development of tourism were developed that builds on developing an interest on the part of the citizenry to travel for pleasure within the country and then begins attracting people from the other nations. Such an approach is better done by the provinces and districts. In other words, what is required is a local touch.

3.3 Maldivian Island Magnetism, "Lazing off" of Bangladesh and Looking beyond Conflicts in Nepal and Sri Lanka

The Maldives Web site succinctly describes this atoll island nation's charm as follows:

> Sun, sand and sea, a thousand "Robinson Crusoe" islands, massive lagoons with different depths and infinite shades of blue and turquoise, dazzling underwater coral gardens; a perfect natural combination for the ideal tropical holiday destination. However there is more to the Maldives than just the 1,190 coral islands, forming an archipelago of 26 major atolls. Stretches 820 kilometers, north to south and 120 kilometers east to west. 202 are inhabited, 87 are exclusive resort islands.[18]

Maldives will continue to attract visitors to the region, with its magnet-like pull, and will hold a high-end position among the region's other tourist destinations.

Bangladesh's tourism assets are presented as follows in its official Web site:[19]

> As a holiday making land, Bangladesh exposes many flamboyant facets. Its tourist attractions are many folded, which include archaeological sites, historical mosques and monuments, resorts, beaches, picnic spots, forests and tribal people, wildlife of various species. Bangladesh offers ample opportunities to tourists for angling, water skiing, river cruising, hiking, rowing, yachting, sea bathing as well as bringing one in close touch with pristine nature.

However, visitor arrival levels to Bangladesh have remained around 250,000 a year for several years now, showing only marginal growth. Political instability, access limitations, inconsistency in promotional efforts, and frequent changes in the leadership positions of the industry seem to keep Bangladesh tourism from realizing its full potential. Although Bangladesh has the potential to become a major destination for visitors, both intraregional and globally, it needs a major overhaul of its governance and industry organizational structures to realize its full potential.

For Nepal and Sri Lanka's tourism industries to realize their full potential, they need to be free from political instability and conflict. Both exotic destinations can be called "destinations waiting to happen." Sri Lanka, which has the potential in the short and the medium term to attract a few million visitors a year, has been limited for several decades to a half million arrivals. Nepal, which also has the potential to generate a million visitors in the medium term, has at best generated 380,000 visitors. The rapid growth it showed in 2007 of 27.1 percent upon the signing of the peace accord in 2006 is testimony to its ability to "unleash itself"[20] quickly once the political issues are resolved.

Sri Lanka is no different. Upon signing its Peace Accord in 2002, visitor arrivals rapidly increased by 27 percent in 2004, and in spite of the impact of the devastating tsunami in 2004, it continued to record an increase in arrivals. The correlation between conflicts and tourist arrivals is stark, and optimal performance of the tourism sector in South Asia will be possible only if the nations within the SAARC framework resolve to take a pragmatic approach to resolving internal conflicts and see the benefits of working in unison.

Although this chapter does not cover the affairs and contributions of the newest SAARC member country, Afghanistan,[21] it is imperative that the same yardsticks be applied to progress to be made in that country.

Tourism is a movement for generating peace.[22] The understanding among people that travel and tourism bring about is the best recipe for ensuring that conflicts are resolved through discussion and compromise, rather than through violent means. Poverty alleviation and removing the root causes that drive terrorism are both possible through the generation of understanding that can be gained through tourism. Ease of access, therefore, becomes a key determinant in creating such an environment.

4. THE AVIATION REVOLUTION

Until early 2000, the aviation industry in South Asia (with the exception of Maldives) operated under heavy protection. While Sri Lanka liberalized its skies somewhat, it was still dominated by its national carrier (Sri Lankan Airlines), and determining traffic rights and freedoms was not entirely liberalized. Earlier in this decade, the Indian aviation industry began to take a strong look at liberalizing its skies. Several new private airlines came into operation around 2003. India's first low-cost carrier (LCC), Air Deccan, set off the LCC boom in India. Air Deccan later sold 26 percent of its stake to Kingfisher Airlines.

In 2007, the two Indian government-owned airline companies, Air India and Indian Airlines, were merged to form the National Indian Aviation Company Limited (NIACL). This was considered a major breakthrough in conventional thinking in India's aviation history.

In April of the same year, India's largest private carrier, Jet Airways, bought rival Air Sahara for US$340 million. Jet Airways has ordered 20 Boeing 737-800 aircraft to add to its fleet of 60. Although most of the other 16 scheduled airlines registered with India's Director General of Civil Aviation are undertaking austerity measures in response to rising fuel prices, India's aviation industry has never been so robust, with companies such as SpiceKet, Kingfisher, Air India Express, Yamuna Airways, Magic Air, Paramount Airways, Air One, Indus Air, and Go Air, among those in the offing.

Several private airlines are now flying between India and Sri Lanka and India and Maldives. Other destinations need to open up to private airlines. The most recent operation of Bangladesh's Best Air to Colombo and Male and Sri Lanka's Deccan Air's proposed flights connecting Male with Anuradhpura, an ancient city in the interior of Sri Lanka, are excellent best practices.

The airports pose another area of constraint. With the Indian government succeeding in privatizing the Delhi and Mumbai airports, several other Indian state governments began to look at expansion of airports based on a business model different than that adopted under complete state control. The European Union's South Asia Civil Aviation Programme[23] and the U.S. Trade and Development Agency's (USTDA) US–India Aviation Cooperation Programme[24] are geared toward supporting the airport development and facilitation initiatives of the region. Male and Colombo airports have followed similar business models with liberalized management structures, which have proven successful. These examples will serve as a pull factor for most other state-run airports in the region to shift gears, which should augur well for the future ease of access within the region. Yet there is much to be done for the region's aviation facilities to be on par with rest of Asia and in particular with those in most of ASEAN and China.

5. SEA AND WATERWAYS TRANSPORT

The South Asian region is endowed with ocean-based transport potential that needs to be explored fully. The ports at Colombo, Chennai, Mumbai, and Chittagong offer ocean-liner connections, although it has not been a popular mode of transport for visitors. Cruise liners traveling between Europe, Singapore, and Australian ports have been using ports such as Colombo and Mumbai as stopovers. None of South Asia's ports has developed as dedicated cruise destinations, but they have the potential to do so. Fast ferry transport services are possible between several destinations in the region. Bangladesh, India, Maldives, and Sri Lanka ports offer excellent opportunities.

A comprehensive report on South Asian transport was prepared by the USTDA in 2005 and serves as a guide to all transport sector opportunities in the region (Domus 2005).

The internal waters of most of the countries of the region offer immense possibilities. With the exceptions of Bangladesh, Maldives, Kashmir, and Kerala and other parts of India, use of internal waters for tourism-related activity is limited. Sri Lanka, with its Dutch canal systems and man-made network of ancient irrigation tanks offers numerous opportunities for water-based tourism activities. Nepal, Sri Lanka, and parts of India, Pakistan, and Bangladesh also use their waters for white-water rafting and other adventure pursuits. Possibilities for regional joint venture operations in these areas exist between private sector entities, through which experiences can be shared and the region can be better positioned.

6. ACCESS WITH ROADS AND HIGHWAYS

The Asian Highway network is the largest highway that connects Southeast Asia with South Asia and then on to Europe. A network of 141,000 kilometers of standardized roadways criss-crossing 32 Asian countries,[25] the Asian Highway is the single most potent infrastructure project undertaken by the nations of ASEAN and SAARC.

This project was initiated in 1959 to promote the development of international road transport in the region. During the first phase of the project (1960–70), considerable progress was achieved; however, progress slowed down when financial assistance was suspended in 1975.

Entering into the 1980s and 1990s, regional political and economic changes spurred new momentum for the Asian Highway Project. It became one of the three pillars of the Asian Land Transport Infrastructure Development project, endorsed by the United Nations Economic and Social Commission for Asia and the Pacific (UNESCAP) Commission at its 48th session in 1992, comprising Asian Highway, Trans-Asian Railway, and land transport projects.

UNESCAP and ADB are undertaking a number of joint activities to promote international road transport along the Asian Highway under a regional project. This project aims to assist in providing a transport infrastructure linking Asia to Europe, to promote regional and international cooperation for the economic and social development of the region, and to open new potential for trade and tourism.

Countries linked by the Asian Highway share a wealth of historical and cultural heritage and unspoiled natural beauty. These countries could join together in promoting tourism under a common tourism banner. Promotion of tourism would provide excellent opportunities to strengthen not only intraregional cooperation within South Asia, but with Southeast Asia, China, the Middle East, and Europe.

Accordingly, UNESCAP at its 52nd session suggested that member countries initiate activities to promote tourism along the Asian Highway. A questionnaire survey to identify major tourism attractions was subsequently conducted by the Secretariat. The results of the survey identified tourism attractions and suggested various national and regional levels to promote tourism.[26]

The Intergovernmental Agreement on the Asian Highway Network was adopted on November 2003 by an intergovernmental meeting held in Bangkok, was open for signature in April 2004 in Shanghai, and entered into force in July 2005.

A total of US$26 billion has been invested in the improvement and upgrading of the Asian Highway network. However, there is still a shortfall of US$18 billion. The UNESCAP Secretariat is working with its member countries to identify financial sources for the development of the network to improve their road transport capacity and efficiency, which in turn will facilitate tourism development in the region, providing adequate return on the investment.

7. REMOVING BARRIERS FOR ENTRY

It is critical that air, sea, and road access be expanded and enhanced if regional tourism development is to take off, but it is equally critical to ensure that most artificial barriers in terms of visa facilitation are made as easy as possible for visitors to the region and for each of the countries in the SAARC alliance.

Currently, except for Maldives, Nepal, and Sri Lanka, visa formalities are cumbersome for the rest of the countries of SAARC. Almost all countries in the ASEAN region[27] allow visa free or visa-upon-entry facilitation for intraregional travel. The ASEAN group goes one step further to offer an ASEAN Air Pass,[28] whereby traveling to one ASEAN country qualifies a traveler to visit other countries at a concessionary airfare. An ASEAN Hotel Pass (Hip-Hop Pass)[29] with similar incentives is also in effect. In the European Union, most member countries may be visited with a common EU visa, obtained from one of the member countries. ASEAN is aiming to have a common ASEAN visa by 2009. The South Asian region is far from achieving such levels of freeing formalities among the SAARC member countries and for visitors to the region.

In 1998, the SAAEC Expert Group on the Visa Exception Scheme recommended that there was a need to expand the Scheme by nearly doubling the number of categories entitled to be included for visa exemption. At present, some 21 categories of persons are exempted from requiring visas for travel within the SAARC region.[30] The Expert Group deliberated on improving the existing guidelines and procedures of the Scheme. The simplification of visa procedures across the board should help accelerate trade and tourism in the region through the facilitation of increased people-to-people contact. A 2007 review of the decisions on trade and access facilitation[31] indicated that a gap existed between the decisions taken at the various stages to ease visa facilitation and its implementation. To achieve results, the region's officials need to shift from a control mind-set to one that is customer oriented and pragmatic.

8. PROMOTING SOUTH ASIAN TOURISM IS NOT ABOUT PROMOTION

To develop a tourism promotion plan for South Asia, the following elements are needed: a conducive environment for attracting international visitors, an effective potential demand on which the region can rely, and a program of promotion to deliver the region from the shackles it has been bound by in the past. The reality on the ground is far from meeting those needs (Adeney and Wyatt 2004; Lal 2006).

The South Asian region possesses all the ingredients needed to be a prime international tourism destination. Given the successes achieved by India and Maldives, individual countries have the opportunity to get it right. However, as a regional entity, South Asia needs to be repositioned in the minds of the international visiting public by erasing a negative perception that is currently associated with the region's poverty, chaos, and disorganization.

Getting this perception right requires deciding what must come first. To deliver on the promise of successful tourism, the region needs to get its collective act right, or create a desired promotional platform as a pull factor for the region's stakeholders to get the act right eventually.

Intraregional tourism promotion is a precursor to promoting the region for international visitors. Taking that route will strengthen the capacity within the region to develop better structures and institutions to correct some of the problems that are endemic in the region's polity.

The following process-based actions are proposed to achieve the objective discussed in this chapter:

- Further liberalize air access between countries of SAARC, facilitating any SAARC airline to operate to other SAARC countries without restriction.
- Facilitate ocean and other water-based, road and highway, and railway transportation of people of SAARC (to serve tourism as well) through the liberal operation of fast ferry services, shipping services, and cruising operations, and by exploring road and rail transport options.
- Undertake joint programs at both regional and bilateral levels to jointly develop the infrastructure and institutions[32, 33, 34] needed to establish tourism operations and investments, which should be driven by the private sector[35] or as public–private partnership ventures.
- Commence joint initiatives at both governmental and private sector operator levels to enhance the current Buddhist circuit,[36] the Ramayana Trail,[37] and other regional and bilateral thematic tour circuits.
- Undertake the publication of an annual South Asian Tourism Events Directory (to be published a year in advance to enable tour sales for those events).
- Commence a twinning of cities program within the SAARC region.
- Establish a SAARC joint Climate Change Response using Sri Lanka's pioneering Tourism Earth Lung[38] initiative as the platform.

9. CONCLUSION

Tourism promotion can be compared to dream selling. To sell dreams to people, the dreams sold must be beautiful and believable. In promoting and branding South Asia as a tourist destination area, the challenge faced by the marketer is to ensure that the three key characteristics of brand identity are met: quality, consistency, and integrity. To ensure that these characteristics are maintained, an intense and continuous effort is needed at both the destination and the regional levels.

This challenge stretches beyond the capacity of the marketer, to the level of the policy and strategic leadership in each of the South Asian countries, engulfing the collective conscience of the region. The need to position and promote the South Asian region has been identified, and the will exists, at least as demonstrated through the many resolutions that are made at the various fora. What is lacking, however, is consistent commitment, in terms of action on the ground, to transform the need and will into solid action.

When looking at the relative success stories of regional cooperation in ASEAN and the European Union, the key success factors have been the pragmatism with which the leadership of these alliances has looked at the issues in seeking solutions. For South Asia and for South Asia tourism, it should be no different.

NOTES

1. World Bank, South Asia Poverty Web reference, http://web.worldbank.org/WBSITE/EXTERNAL/COUNTRIES/SOUTHASIAEXT/0, ,contentMDK:20969099~pagePK:146736~piPK:146830~theSitePK:223547,00.html.
2. See http://www.saarcchamber.com/.
3. See http://www.saarctradefairsl.com/ and http://www.satte.org/.
4. See http://www.saarc-sec.org/main.php?t=2.10.
5. Asian Development Bank, Web document, http://www.adb.org/Documents/Reports/SASEC/Tourism-Development/; South Asia Sub-regional Economic Cooperation: Tourism Development Plan, 2004; and http://www.adb.org/documents/events/2001/reta5936/tourism/tour_proceedings.pdf.
6. See www.tourism.gov.bt/.
7. See http://www.visitmaldives.com/.
8. See http://www.visitnepal.com/acap/.
9. See http://www.nepaltourism.info/aroundkathmandu/bhaktapur_history.html.
10. See www.srilankatourism.org.
11. See www.earthlung.travel.
12. See www.incredibleindia.org.
13. See www.keralatourism.org.
14. See www.goatourism.org.
15. See www.up-tourism.com.
16. See www.economywatch.com.
17. See http://www.tourism.gov.pk/tourisminpakistan.html.
18. See http://www.visitmaldives.com/Maldives/.
19. See http://www.bangladeshtourism.gov.bd/overview_country_profile.php.
20. "Unleash Yourself – Naturally Nepal, Once is not Enough" is Nepal's promotional tagline as presented at http://www.welcomenepal.com/nepal/index.asp.
21. See http://www.kabulonline.com/ for more destination information.
22. See http://www.tourismforpeace.org/.
23. See http://ec.europa.eu/europeaid/where/asia/regional-cooperation/support-regional-integration/saarc_en.htm.
24. See http://www.ustda.gov/program/regions/southasia/.
25. See http://www.unescap.org/ttdw/index.asp?MenuName=AsianHighway.
26. See http://www.unescap.org/ttdw/common/tis/ah/tourism%20attractions.asp.
27. See http://www.aseanvisa.com/.

28. See http://www.visitasean.travel/AirPass.aspx?MCID=78.
29. See http://www.aseansec.org/hiphop.htm.
30. See http://www.south-asia.com/saarc/dec98.htm.
31. See http://www.ipcs.org/ConferenceReport-SAARC.pdf.
32. See http://www.southasianmedia.net/.
33. See http://www.isasnus.org/.
34. See http://www.anderson.ucla.edu/zone/clubs/saba/index.html.
35. See http://www.doingbusiness.org/southasia.
36. See http://ebudhaindia.com.
37. See http://www.tourslanka.com/ramayana-sri-lanka/tours/ramayana-site-tours-excur sions.php.
38. See http://www.earthlung.travel/.

REFERENCES

Adeney, Katharine and Andrew Wyatt. 2004. "Democracy in South Asia: Getting beyond the Structure-Agency Dichotomy." *Political Studies* 52 (1): 1–18.
Asian Development Bank (ADB). 2004. *South Asia Sub-regional Economic Cooperation; Tourism Development Plan*. Manila: ADB.
Bezhbaruha, M. P. 2007. *The Guest is God; Reflections on Tourism*. Delhi: Gayan Books.
Breckenridge, Carol A. 1995. *Consuming Modernity: Public Culture in a South Asian World*. Minnesota: University of Minnesota Press.
Chandana, Jayawardena, ed. 2006. "International Trends & Challenges in Tourism & Hospitality Business." HCIMA Sri Lanka International Group. Colombo: Vijitha Yapa Publications.
Domus A. C. 2005. *LLC for US Trade and Development Agency, South Asia Transport and Trade Facilitation Conference Briefing Book 2005*. Washington, DC. Available at http://mba.tuck.dartmouth.edu/digital/Research/AcademicPublications/Asia TransportAnalysis.pdf (accessed on 6 October 2009).
Engardio, Peter (ed.) 2006. *Chindia*. New York: McGraw Hill.
Lal, C. K. 2006. "The Complexities of Border Conflicts in South Asia." *South Asian Survey* 13 (2): 253–63.
Mustaghis-ur-Rahman. 2005. "Public Private Sector Partnership (PPP) for Social Development." *International Journal of Applied Public-Private Partnerships* 1 (2).
Panda, Tapan K. and Sitikantha Mishra. 2008. *Tourism Marketing*. Delhi: ICFAI Books.
Sen, Debapriya. 2004. "Kinked Demand Curve Revisited." *Economics Letters* 84 (July).
Siddiqui, Anjum. 2007. *India and South Asia: Economic Developments in the Age of Globalization*. New York: M. E. Sharpe.
Singh, Nirvikar. 2005. "The Idea of South Asia and the Role of the Middle Class." Santa Cruz Center for International Economics, Paper 05–08 (April 29). Available at http://repositories.cdlib.org/sccie/05-08 (accessed on 6 October 2009).
UN Economic and Social Commission for Asia and Pacific (UNESCAP). 2008. *Statistical Year Book for Asia and the Pacific 2007*. Bangkok: UNESCAP.
World Tourism Organization. 2006. *Year Book of Tourism Statistics 2002–2006*. Madrid: World Tourism Organization.

Part III

Private Sector
Perspectives on
Cooperation

Regional Cooperation in South Asia

Bangladesh Perspective[1]

Yussuf A. Harun

1. INTRODUCTION

South Asia covers 3 percent of the world's land surface, contains 22 percent of the world's population, and shares 1 percent of the world's trade. The region is characterized by poverty, representing half of the world's poor, and frequently suffers from devastating natural calamities, border conflicts, and ethnic and religious disturbances.

South Asian countries have not been major players in the world trade. The inability of the member countries to diversify their exports structure in favor of more modern products has resulted in slower export growth and lower value realization. However, because of the quota system in the readymade garments (RMG) sector, and preferential market access resulting from bilateral treaties, the least developed countries (LDCs) have been able to maintain moderate growth.

The irreversible process of globalization has confronted the developing countries with many daunting challenges. The flow of development assistance is stagnating and is increasingly being linked to the promotion of the donor countries' trade objectives. This has triggered an intense competition for foreign direct investment (FDI) among developing countries. Under the Uruguay Round, rules governing intellectual property rights, subsidies, countervailing duties, trade-related investment, environment, and health issues would eventually be the same for industrial and developing countries. Therefore, the basic challenge facing South Asian Countries in this new regime is raising their economies' efficiency and international competitiveness and implementing a "pro-poor" growth strategy to tackle pervasive poverty. One of the ways to meet this challenge is to overcome regional apprehensions and constraints and move toward regional trade liberalization, cooperation in investment, and economic integration, which will pave the way for the most efficient use of the region's resources through additional economies of scale, value addition, employment, and diffusion of technology.

Although it is widely believed that any increase in intraregional trade as a direct result of liberalization will be limited in South Asia, the indirect effects of intraregional trade liberalization are likely to be significant. The economies of South Asia are likely to be substantially impacted by lower intraregional transport and transaction costs; more favorable terms of trade; economies of scale in investment, production, and distribution; higher efficiency and technical competence from increased intraregional competition and cooperation; more active investment from outside the region because of an expanded market; and liberalization of capital and human resource movement. Sustained regional integration can transform South Asia into a major economic growth zone of the world by the mid-twenty-first century, as the region has the largest population concentration in the world with huge opportunities for economic growth because of the unsatisfied needs of the large number of poor people in the region.

2. OPPORTUNITIES FOR ENHANCED REGIONAL INTEGRATION

Economists and business leaders have divergent opinions about the benefits of the economic integration of South Asian countries. Many believe that most preconditions needed to enhance the probability of a successful free trade area (FTA) are not present and South Asian countries would be better off liberalizing unilaterally and trying to tie up with established blocs such as the North American Free Trade Agreement (NAFTA) or the

European Union. Another argument put forward in favor of moving to an FTA is about the cost of non-cooperation, which is, lost opportunities. Opinions vary widely regarding the distribution of gains among member countries. Most experts believe that although unilateral liberalization offers greater benefit, regional cooperation is likely to prove beneficial in a wide range of areas. Regional Integration will create exciting opportunities for exploiting synergies based on comparative advantages, investment in cross-border infrastructure projects, and coordinated programs to address challenges in governance, environment, social development, and other fields that spill over national boundaries.

A most recent example of cross-border investment is the US$255 million Lafarge Surma Cement plant sponsored by the Lafarge Group of France. The plant, which is due to be commissioned in 2005, is located at Chatak, Sylhet, in Bangladesh; the main source of raw material is a limestone quarry in Meghalaya, north-east of India, connected by a 17 km cross-border long-belt conveyer. The project is expected to create about 400 jobs in Sylhet and about 70 jobs in Meghalaya.

The region is locked into a set of common problems that can be resolved only through regional cooperation. For example, most of Nepal's rivers flow into Uttar Pradesh and Bihar in India. Indeed the tributaries in Nepal that feed the Ganges join up in Uttar Pradesh and Bihar before entering West Bengal and Bangladesh. Therefore, in harnessing the waters of the Ganges, India needs Nepal's active participation. Similarly, any program of water management by Bangladesh, whether for flood control or irrigation, will not be feasible without the ultimate collaboration of the upper riparian states of India and Nepal. With proper planning and investment, the water resources of the region could well be used for the generation of electricity, which could meet the energy needs of the entire South Asia region.

Another important potential resource in the region comes from the huge reserve of coal in Assam, Bihar, Orissa, and West Bengal. A large reserve of natural gas is found in Bangladesh and the north-eastern part of India.

Fifty years ago, the transport networks of South Asia were one of the most integrated in the developing world, but these were disrupted following the partition of the region into seven independent states. At present, highways, waterways, and rail links that traverse each country stop at national borders and thus are unable to service the region. The rebuilding of this physical infrastructure has been constrained by security-driven apprehensions, which the countries found impelling enough to sacrifice mutual economic benefits.

In this process of rebuilding the transport infrastructure of the eastern region of South Asia, Bangladesh emerges as the hub around which reconstruction of land links could take place. Bangladesh once had a major highway linking mainland India with both north Bengal and north-east India. The development of land alignments, which would provide north-east India access to the sea through the Bay of Bengal and integrate its market with Bangladesh, could establish this undeveloped region as a staging post for economic links within South Asia and with landlocked south-west China. The Chittagong port could be built up as the nodal point for handling the region's trade.

There are several sectors in which Bangladesh and India can move from a competitive relationship toward a rediscovery of lost complementarity. Jute is one example, and RMG of Bangladesh and the textile industry of India is another. The phasing out of the textile quota system in 2005 will leave South Asian exports more vulnerable to competition from other developing countries. The European Union has allowed Bangladesh special market access, if its raw material is sourced regionally under a regional accumulation system. In the case of Bangladesh, only 65 percent of total exports to the European Union can access the Generalized System of Preferences (GSP) because of noncompliance with rules of origin. With regional accumulation, it can increase to 90 percent. If Bangladesh accepts regional accumulation, there could be a significant increase in intraregional trade. Unfortunately, as of early 2009, the powerful textile manufacturing lobby in Bangladesh has prevailed on the government not to accept regional accumulation.

The Rakhine state of western Myanmar bordering Bangladesh has a single patch of bamboo forest stretching over 7,000 square kilometers and producing 2.2 million tons of a single species of bamboo equivalent to 800,000 metric tons of pulp, which could support the paper industry in Bangladesh. Marine resources on the Myanmar side of the border could be collectively developed and processed on the Bangladesh side of the border where facilities exist for fish processing. The vast limestone deposit in the Rakhine state can provide raw materials for the joint venture cement clinkers factory in Myanmar with a ready market in Bangladesh.

Tourism has remained untapped in the region, attracting less than 1 percent of the international tourist arrivals, although the cultural and natural riches of the region are beyond dispute. Whether it is ecotourism, religious tourism, or adventure tourism, the region has a spectacular variety of tourism to offer.

3. OBSTACLES TO REGIONAL INTEGRATION

Despite the opportunities, progress in achieving regional cooperation in South Asia has been at best modest because of a host of economic and political factors. Although there is substantial informal trading, official trade among South Asian countries accounts for only 5 percent of the total trade volume, and intraregional investment is only 1 percent of the total investment. In comparison, intratrade in NAFTA is 54.6 percent, in the European Union it is 63.4 percent, and in the Association of Southeast Asian Nations (ASEAN) it is 22.2 percent. In terms of trade openness, South Asian countries are not as open as their counterparts in other regions of the world such as ASEAN. On average, trade (both exports and imports) equals less than 30 percent of the gross domestic product (GDP) in the South Asian region compared with more than 75 percent for ASEAN.

On the economic side, the main inhibiting factor has been the competitive rather than complementary nature of products. The exports of South Asian countries, with the exception of India, are highly concentrated. The countries mainly export labor-intensive products, such as textiles and agricultural produce, and import petroleum and capital-intensive goods. Regional trade has not taken off perhaps because, until the late 1980s, all the countries in the region had been pursuing import substitution policies aimed at promoting domestic industries that bred privilege and rent seeking, and fostered rampant corruption and the growth of unofficial cross-border trade. In addition, low growth and demand within the region, reliance on industrial countries for capital finance and purchase credits, and inherited mutual suspicion have resulted in an extraregional pattern of trade. Efforts for integration are further impeded by the poor state of infrastructure; a low savings rate; endemic balance-of-payments problems; a rapidly growing labor force; inefficient state-owned enterprises; shallow financial markets; poor governance; low labor productivity; a poor network of complementary industries and services; complex and opaque regulatory, fiscal and legal conditions; paratariff and nontariff barriers; regulated investment regimes; the slow implementation of trade and economic reforms; a lack of information and business contacts; and technological backwardness. Other reasons for low intraregional trade and investment include widely varying FDI policies, the absence of any cross-border investment moves from within the region, the absence of any bilateral and multilateral investment guarantees for intra-SAARC (South Asian Association for Regional Cooperation) investment, the limitation in foreign ownership, the absence of support from financial institutions for intra-SAARC investment, and transit problems to the landlocked areas of the region.

The lack of political will is considered to be the major hindrance to the success of regional integration. The tension between India and Pakistan, distorted perception of national interest and dictations of so-called security, and to a lesser degree, distrust of India by her smaller neighbors, and the chronic and huge trade imbalance with India have created an atmosphere that is not conducive to regional cooperation. Bias against regional partners is perhaps inborn in the government machineries of the region that have thus far monopolized the decision-making process and literally kept the public sector alienated from mainstream economic participation. Another important missing ingredient is a shared perception of common benefit—all the members must feel they are sharing the costs and benefits of the cooperation equally. India's economic preponderance and comparative advantage in a wide range of products has resulted in asymmetric trade relations with her neighbors, further hindering regional integration. India accounts for more than 80 percent of South Asia's combined GDP, population, and trade. Therefore, as the predominant economic force, India must respond through proactive leadership and demonstrate early harvest and goodwill to encourage the smaller partners and dispel historic suspicions. If, for example, we examine the Indo-Bangladesh relationship, we can readily identify several economic issues that are hindering cooperation.

India accounts for almost half of Bangladesh's trade deficit. Yet Bangladeshi exports have often faced various types of nontariff and paratariff barriers in India. In the famous case of lead battery exports, Bangladesh has gone to the Dispute Settlement Board of the World Trade Organization (WTO) to argue against India's imposition of antidumping measures. India allowed nonreciprocal duty-free access to goods manufactured in Nepal and Bhutan, but it has pursued restrictive trade policy relations with Bangladesh with various barriers to trade.

North-east India shares 84 percent of its common border with Bangladesh. Bangladesh is the natural hinterland. Yet Bangladeshi products, particularly agro processed items are subject to about 60 percent customs duty, an additional customs duty, and a surcharge. In addition, there are many nontariff barriers and limited letter of credit-opening facilities in the north-east. This has frustrated Bangladeshi exporters who argue that, if India is allowed transit facilities, this market may be lost completely by Bangladesh. Bangladesh, on the other hand, has imposed restrictions on certain importable items from India in terms of specified entry points.

India's recent proposed project to link 37 major rivers, including the Ganges and the Brahmaputra, and divert their flow from north-east India to its water-deficit southeast area has caused great concern in Bangladesh. If implemented, this scheme will deprive Bangladesh of its fair share of water. Bangladesh depends on the Ganges and Brahmaputra for 85 percent of its dry-season surface water. If the flow of these rivers stops because of the river-linking project, seawater will gradually fill southern rivers, increasing salinity and reducing fertility.

India has been inflexible thus far in relaxing the value-addition criteria of its rules of origin. It fears that in a free trade regime, Chinese and Thai products will enter Bangladesh, Nepal, and Bhutan and be re-exported to India at zero tariff.

4. PROGRESS OF REGIONAL COOPERATION

The global trend toward free trade and the formation of intraregional blocs spurred South Asia into action and, in 1985, SAARC was formed by seven South Asian countries—Bangladesh, Bhutan, India, Maldives, Nepal, Pakistan, and Sri Lanka—as a forum for the discussion of intraregional issues, particularly the improvement of relations between the very large India and her smaller neighbors. In 1995, the SAARC Preferential Trading Agreement (SAPTA) was inaugurated for bilateral reductions in tariffs and nontariff barriers on specified commodities on a reciprocal basis, but with special treatment given to the LDCs. The eventual objective was for SAPTA to become, by 2001, a South Asian Free Trade Agreement (SAFTA) based on multilateral tariff reductions. But SAARC had been brought to a standstill because of worsening relations between India and Pakistan, caused by the nuclear tests conducted in 1998 and the Kashmir dispute in 1999. In the meantime, SAPTA failed to yield the desired benefits to its members, particularly the LDCs, for the following reasons:

- The tariff cuts were not deep enough.
- The actively traded goods were not given the tariff preferences.
- Modalities of the removal of nontariff and paratariff barriers were not well articulated in the agreements.
- The rules of origin criteria acted as an impediment.

The slow progress of the SAARC forum prompted the members to pursue bilateral and other regional and sub-regional groupings centered primarily on India. India concluded a bilateral FTA with Nepal, Bhutan, and Sri Lanka. Discussions are in progress for similar agreements with Maldives and Bangladesh. At the same time, Bangladesh is also discussing a bilateral FTA with Sri Lanka and Pakistan. In 1997, the Bay of Bengal Initiative for Multi-Sectoral Technical and Economic Cooperation (BIMSTEC) was formed to foster socioeconomic cooperation among Bangladesh, India, Sri Lanka, and Thailand. The principles are contained in the "Bangkok Declaration." In 1997, Myanmar was admitted into BIMSTEC and earlier this year Nepal and Bhutan also joined the bloc. There were two other initiatives known as the South Asian Growth Quadrangle (SAGQ), comprising Bangladesh, Nepal, Bhutan, and parts of India, and the Kunming Initiative. In 2000, the Asian Development Bank (ADB) under a technical assistance program established the South Asia Business Forum under the South Asia Sub-Regional Economic Cooperation (SASEC) at the request of the participating countries to support the official-level SAGQ initiative in light of the successful Greater Mekong Sub-region (GMS) cooperation. The Kunming Initiative envisages integrating resource-rich areas of the Yunan province of China, northern Myanmar, north-east India, Bangladesh, Nepal, and Bhutan into an Asian communication network. The areas would be interlinked with the networks of west and Central Asia as well as Europe, with the potential for Bangladesh to emerge as a hub.

Two recent developments have rekindled hopes for the acceleration of regional cooperation. Following improvement in the relationship between India and Pakistan, the seven member countries of SAARC signed an FTA at the Islamabad Summit in January 2004 to go into effect from 1 January 2006. The second development was the signing of an FTA by the seven BIMSTEC members.

The Islamabad summit had achieved consensus on the following:

- Framework agreement on SAFTA.
- Social charter on poverty reduction.
- A common pact against terrorism.
- Communality in other areas like environment, energy, and telecommunications.

The SAFTA agreement will be implemented on the basis of the following principles and mechanisms:

- Modalities of tariff reduction.
- Rules of origin.
- Negative list.
- Elimination of nontariff and paratariff barriers on the movement of goods.
- Safeguards.
- Dispute settlement mechanism.
- Revenue loss.
- Special measures for LDCs.

5. STEPS FOR ENHANCED REGIONAL INTEGRATION

To move toward successful integration, the sequencing of actions is crucially important. The South Asian region should develop its own short-, medium-, and long-term strategies for economic integration. Each stage should be implemented effectively before moving on to the next in order to build a sound foundation for progress. In this context, the development of the European Union may be studied, which is considered to be the most advanced model for regional grouping. European integration evolved over four stages:

1. First, a preferential free trade regime was developed in which member countries reduced or eliminated tariff and nontariff barriers among them.
2. Second, a Customs Union created a common external tariff so that import duties were the same for each member country.
3. Third, the Economic Union was formed, which further integrated the market, eventually leading to a single market.
4. Fourth, a monetary union was established in which the national currencies of the member countries were replaced by a single currency.

South Asian countries need to address the following key issues, however, to move toward successful cooperation.

5.1 Political Environment

The political environment needs to be improved by the regional governments and political leaders. Political fragility makes it difficult for governments to take initiative, which opposition parties can exploit. The governments, private sector, academia, professionals, and social sector organizations have to work in unison.

5.2 Complementarities

A careful identification of areas in which South Asian countries have comparative advantage and greater potential for growth based on sound economic ground is required, along with a strategy for cooperation focusing on intra-SAARC trade, joint ventures, and third country exports. A comprehensive investment survey with a view toward identifying the production capabilities and export-promoting investment projects must be given priority for any integrated approach to the investment regime in South Asia. Such a survey should examine the capacities, production and supply constraints, price competitiveness, problems of specification, and design and level of technology in the selected areas. Thus, the creation of a single market in the region through cooperation in investment and trade liberalization would function as the driving forces for sectoral and structural adjustments in agriculture and industry and between the public and private sector through a reallocation of resources, which would pave the way for greater integration of the region into the global economy.

5.3 Trade Reform and Facilitations

Trade reform and facilitations require complementary policies such as a regulatory framework, improved governance, stable law and order, reduced corruption, upgraded infrastructure, and an improved overall investment climate. To achieve these reforms, the South Asian government and the private sectors have to work together. According to a Canadian government research tariff, reductions from the WTO Uruguay Round of trade negotiations are likely to be worth around 2 percent of world trade. By comparison, the potential gains from trade facilitation reform are likely to be worth some 0.66 percent of world trade. In South Asia, the potential gains are expected to be much greater, as the system is shackled by excessive paperwork, discretionary powers of the bureaucrats, and various bottlenecks. The burden of such inefficiencies falls more heavily on smaller businesses, often 30 percent to 40 percent higher than larger firms. As tariff and nontariff barriers come down, efficiency in trade facilitation will become one of the key factors for determining competitiveness.

The following areas of reform and facilitation are necessary for the integration of the economies:

- Standardize basic customs nomenclature regulations, documentation, and clearing procedures. Implement the progressive harmonization of product safety and technical standards, reciprocal recognition to tests and accreditation of testing laboratories of member countries, and certifications of products. Divergent national or regional standards can create technical barriers to trade even when there is political agreement to do away with trade restrictions. Therefore, international standards can create a level playing field for all competitors.

- Create customs cooperation to resolve disputes at customs entry points, simplification of import licensing, and banking procedures for import financing.

- Prevent the sizeable amount of unofficial trade flows from taking place across national boundaries of South Asian countries despite the liberalization of their respective trade regimes. To bring the un-official trade into the official channel, policy interventions are required both in terms of bringing down tariff and nontariff barriers, removing policy distortions, and creating a positive and facilitating environment for the promotion of trade.

- Discourage countries from monopolizing trade through state-owned trading organizations. Instead, greater participation by the private sector should be encouraged. However, state trading companies may be employed usefully for promoting intraregional trading in specific areas.

- Create transit facilities to promote trade with landlocked members.

- Set up food-testing facilities at borders and create more entry points for quarantine checks.

- Pursue agreement on rail links to operate inland container depots.

- Develop infrastructure at load crossing stations (checkpoints) through which trade takes place, such as approach, roads, bridges, telegram facilities, electricity connections, weighbridges, customs offices, and warehouses.

- Simplify the preshipment inspection system.

- Obtain agreement to facilitate the movement of vehicles up to transhipment points at land ports.

- Facilitate the movement of business professionals for a long duration, with the creation of at least a 1-year multiple visa.

- Exchange information on products and services, market practices, and intelligence.

5.4 Transport

For South Asia, the crucial transport links to be industrial would be along the alignment of Asia Highway (AH). The AH network is a component of the Asian Land Transportation Infrastructure Development (ALTID) project developed by the United Nations Economic and Social Commission for Asia and the Pacific (UNESCAP), which also includes the Trans-Asian Railway (TAR) project, including measures for the facilitation of land transportation. The route criteria for ALTID projects include capital-to-capital links, connection to main industrial and agricultural centers and growth zones, connection to major sea and river ports, and connection to major inland container terminals and depots.

In recent years, China has upgraded the old Burma road between Kunming and Myanmar as part of its association with the AH. The link between Kunming and the Bay of Bengal is 5,800 kms shorter than Yunan's link with the nearest Chinese port at Shanghai or China's pacific coast. The Jamuna bridge in Bangladesh would make it possible for the AH to provide uninterrupted travel between Bangladesh and Calais routed through India, Pakistan, and either into Central Asia or through West Asia into Europe. At the same time, the bridge could establish a link between Nepal and Bhutan through an unbroken land route to the port of Chittagong, which may emerge as a far cheaper alternate route to Kolkata–Haldia in India for Nepal and Bhutan. For a long time, India has denied transit facilities to Nepal and Bhutan for sending their goods overseas through Bangladesh, and Bangladesh has denied India transit for the movement of its goods to and from north-east India. If these barriers are removed, it would enable India to send goods to its north-eastern region at a fraction of the present costs, while Bangladesh exports could penetrate deeper into the Nepalese and Indian north-eastern areas as well as to the mainland markets. Bangladesh could benefit from substantial freight and port charges from Chittagong and Mongla ports providing access to Indian and Nepalese exports. India and Nepal may participate in the capacity and infrastructure development of Chittagong and Mongla ports. It is estimated that this integration of the transport network alone would increase intra-SAARC trade by three times.

Western Myanmar, bordering Bangladesh, is separated from the rest of Myanmar by the Arakan Mountain range. The hinterland of the Chittagong port, therefore, could well be stretched up to the foot of the Arakan Yoma. The road that once linked Chittagong and Akyab is now called Arakan road. The rehabilitation of this road will help reestablish the old surface link between Ghumdhum on the Bangladesh side and Tumbro on the Myanmar side, the traditional trade route that could eventually be connected with the AH that links up with Southeast Asia. The proposal to build a bridge over the Palk Strait stretching 27 kms between Talaimenhar in Sri Lanka and Dhanuskodi, Tamil Nadu, in India, will complete the connection of the BIMSTEC region.

To ensure productive and sustainable cooperation in the transport sector, the member countries have to ensure appropriate institutional arrangement for customs clearance, border crossing, documentation, payment mechanism, financial services, cost-sharing arrangements, pricing, traffic discipline, and safety and dispute settlement procedures.

5.5 Port

Because of the lack of investment and modernization, and unhealthy trade unionism, the Chittagong port has become costly, inefficient, and technologically outdated. For example, a containership turnaround time in Chittagong is five to six days against only one to two days in Bangkok and Singapore, and the container charges are double the charges in other neighboring countries. The port now requires massive infrastructure development, including deepwater facilities and an enhanced capacity to handle growing containerized traffic and complete automation of its services. As the region integrates, the throughput at Chittagong port is estimated to increase at least four times over the next two decades.

5.6 Energy

Initiatives need to be taken for the formulation of plans to develop hydro, gas, and coal-based power generation, and to establish a regional power grid. Although tremendous potential exists for power generation, most of the countries are faced with power shortages and rising demand. In Bangladesh, only 20 percent of the population has access to electricity and about 10 percent to natural gas. Laws and regulations relating to cross-border energy trade, pricing, and contracts needs to be harmonized. This would enable member countries to meet rising demands for energy for both consumer and industrial use in a more cost-effective manner. Technology is integrating the energy sector around the world. Therefore, the South Asia region should develop its own strategy and capability to deal with multinational energy corporations from a position of strength.

5.7 Water Resources

An intergovernmental task force should formulate plans for the comprehensive development of water resources in the Ganges–Brahmaputra–Meghna river basin for flood management, irrigation, water transport, and electricity generation.

5.8 Telecommunication

The telecommunication technology of the member countries could be harmonized for the socioeconomic advancement of the region through the establishment of infrastructure and human resource development, and the reduction of intraregional telecom tariffs, cellular roaming, and mutual recognition arrangements. Production and consumption areas of the region should be connected by telecom network. For the rapid development of the telecom sector, a level playing field has to be created between basic infrastructure and service companies, and between wholesale and retail Internet providers. A regional Internet exchange should be created to facilitate more efficient traffic flows in the region and provide faster access to Web sites. Establishing a gateway within the South Asian region will save the internal traffic of the region from being routed through Singapore or other countries outside the region. The region's e-commerce will develop the skills, expertise, logistics, and solutions that would open access to the goods and services of the region in the global market.

5.9 Investment

Despite a potentially large market, cheap labor, huge resources, and considerable progress in the liberalization of the economies, the SAARC countries have not been able to attract significant foreign investment. The SAARC members' share of total inward FDI into developing countries in 2000 was only 1.5 percent, most of which went to India.

According to balance-of-payment accounts, the FDI-to-GDP ratio of Bangladesh was around 0.5 percent in the fiscal year (FY) 1999, the highest FDI receiving year. Bangladesh has poor political ratings and ranked 34th in Asian countries in term of country risk profile. The level of intra-SAARC investment is also dismal.

Investment cooperation is an essential companion to the liberalization of trade because it is with the intraregional investment that the economies of South Asia can achieve true industrial and market integration. The following steps may be taken to promote FDI into South Asia and to encourage intra-SAARC investment:

- Set up a center to gather information and analytical work, and to monitor investment activities and potential.
- Monitor and evaluate the present status of FDI and its impact on the region's economy and sociopolitical development.
- Identify different categories of investment, including infrastructure, labor, and capital-intensive sectors, state-owned enterprises, and agro-based industries, and at the same time, examine factors underpinning the mismatch between potential and revealed performance of member countries in the area of FDI relating to these sectors.
- Pool experience across member countries and its comparison with other regions to reach a consensus on the best policy practices.
- Analyze multilateral agreements on foreign investment and competition policy and its impact on the member countries to evolve a regional position.
- Synchronize an economic reforms program of the member countries to ensure policy predictability and consistency of their investment policies.
- Harmonize investment policy practices and incentives to stop a "race to the bottom" when competing for incentives.
- Finalize regional investment and protection agreements as well as avoid a double taxation agreement.
- Enhance effectiveness of FDI institutions, such as Investment Promotion Boards, with coordination between regional and international institutions.
- Identify mechanisms and best practices to enhance efforts for strategic partnerships between the government and private sector.
- Strengthen local technology acquisition capability.
- Adopt a legally binding code of conduct for a regional joint venture to ensure rights of the host country and investors, as well as to establish a standard of accepted practice to generate confidence in regional cooperation in investment, including a dispute settlement mechanism.
- Simplify entry and exit for investment, which will act as an important incentive, especially for portfolio investors financing regional projects.
- Grant fast track approval for regional projects.

- Form a Regional Development Bank that could draw on the resources of the regions' existing development finance institutions to promote regional joint ventures.
- Abolish, in the long term, all barriers to intraregional investment by allowing free flow of capital throughout the region, including the repatriation of profits; this will greatly facilitate regional investment.

5.10 Capital Market

Without a strong and supportive capital market in the region, the industrial and trading development cannot be sustained. To this end, the South Asian Federation of Exchanges has been formed. Coordinated steps are required to be taken in following areas:

- Facilitate cross-border security trading; a harmonized network is required for trading, clearing, and a settlement system.
- Mobilize and diversify SAARC investors and the market base.
- Attract increased foreign institutional investors.
- Harmonize listing rules and best business practices in capital markets to allow free investment among stock members in the region and to set up a common stock exchange within the region.
- Coordinate accounting bodies and harmonize accounting standards in line with international standards, including financial disclosures and statements.
- Establish a South Asian Security Exchange Commission and codification of securities laws.
- Ensure that banking systems in member countries are interconnected and exchange rates are harmonized.
- Harmonize corporate governance practices, ethics, concern for the environment, and commitment to regional and social responsibilities.
- Move toward unified currency systems and establish a regional apex bank.

Urgent reforms are necessary to facilitate the deepening of capital markets in the member countries so that they can play a role in financing private sector participation in infrastructure projects on a build–own–operate (BOO) or build–operate–transfer (BOT) basis. The Bangladesh financial market is small and dominated by the banking system. The capital market is underdeveloped. The combined market capitalization of the two stock exchanges in Dhaka and Chittagong is only about 2.4 percent of GDP. The setting up of a regional financial center at an appropriate location in the region will facilitate banking and insurance, other financial services, and shipping for intraregional investment as well as identification of lucrative investment opportunities for both FDI and portfolio investment.

5.11 Tourism

The development of tourism can yield substantial benefit through a multiplier effect. To promote South Asia as a common tourist destination, joint efforts are required in areas such as upgrading infrastructure, improving air linkages, simplifying and harmonizing administrative procedures, and developing human resources and joint marketing. To promote intra-SAARC tourism, the following steps may be taken:

- Open dedicated immigration counters for SAARC nationals at all airports in the region.
- Rationalize airport tax for SAARC nationals.
- Establish uniformity in the visa regime among SAARC countries, including the reduction of visa fees to a reasonable rate.
- Create special airfares and hotel rates for SAARC nationals.

5.12 Human Resource Development

South Asia is characterized by high population growth, which is dependent upon mainly agriculture for their income and employment. A significant effect of rapid population growth is the subsequent explosion in labor force, leading to lower private savings and lower domestic resource mobilization. Poorly developed human resources in the region have led to the scarcity of managerial, entrepreneurial, and technical skills, and the ability to conduct adaptive research is severely constrained.

Therefore, improvement in the quality of human resources through education and vocational training is the key to move toward a knowledge-based economy. It is clear that South Asian economies need to improve their competitiveness by moving away from traditional low-value exports to high-tech products. To achieve this, the region will need to make concerted effort to improve investment in human capital, research, and development. At the same time, they need to enact legislation and set up institutions to promote innovation and protect intellectual property rights (IPR).

5.13 Environment

Environmentally sound technologies are keys to the long-term sustainability of economic growth. The environmental problems in South Asia are enormous and interrelated. Effective cooperation among the countries is urgently needed to address issues of deforestation and biodiversity loss, cleaner production, waste, and pollution management; to preserve rare species of wildlife and plants; and to avoid fragmentation of the ecosystem that spans national borders. Cooperation can be strengthened by improving the environmental information systems and management capacities.

5.14 Private Sector

The role of the private sector is crucial for the successful economic integration of the region. Through close government and private sector partnerships, the intergovernmental policy framework for the expansion of trade and investment can be implemented. Trade reform and facilitation, market development, infrastructure development, the enforcement of IPR, and conservation of the environment, all require the direct support and participation of the private sector. The private sector has a critical role to play under SAFTA in several areas:

- Certification and management of rules of origin.
- Identification of nontariff and paratariff barriers.
- Preparation of a negative list.
- Monitoring of the FTA.
- Imposition of antidumping, safeguarding, and countervailing duties.
- Dispute settlement procedures.

The national chambers of South Asian countries have already formed the SAARC Chamber of Commerce and Industry (SCCI). It has drawn up a regional framework for arbitration and prepared a draft agreement on the movement of goods and people. It has been trying to bring the South Asian states together on WTO issues through regular programs and has been working on the harmonization of standards and promotion of investments. Through the Tourism Council, Women Entrepreneurs Council, Construction Council, Tea Council, and ICT Council, SCCI has been trying to bring the South Asian private sector together and enhance cooperation in these important areas. Given the extremely low negotiating powers of the individual member states (except India), it is clear there is a strong case for collective strategy.

In many cases, the advantages given to LDCs of preferential market access are eroded by complicated rules of origin and burdensome sanitary and phytosanitary requirements in the importing countries. National chambers can initiate studies to identify major nontariff measures on regional exports to various global markets and make an assessment of their impact for the national government's consideration. Above all, the private sector in the member countries can mobilize public opinion by removing apprehensions and misgivings with a view of empowering the governments toward accelerating the process of regional integration.

5.15 Multilateral Organizations

The role of multilateral organizations in South Asian regional cooperation has been limited and tentative. One of the reasons could be the unstable relationship between India and Pakistan, which has been hindering and threatening the process. The ADB has taken an initiative for sub-regional cooperation under SASEC.

The signing of SAFTA, however, has now opened up a whole new horizon for multilateral organizations like the World Bank to play an important role in stimulating and promoting regional cooperation over a wide area, including small and medium enterprise (SME) development, regional infrastructure development, skill upgrading, and human resources development.

The region's knowledge and understanding of trade issues are limited. South Asia needs to build capacity and specialization on trade policy, multilateral trade issues, and laws both in the government and private sector. At present, the mechanism for consultation in trade policy among governments and stakeholders in most member countries is weak. The region lacks the capacity to implement the WTO agreement, to understand the texts of agreements and their implications, to negotiate effectively in the increasingly loaded agenda items of WTO, to understand the preferences available and conditions attached thereto, to conduct trade negotiations, to formulate trade policy and strategy, and to monitor and assess the impact of policies and agreements. At the industrial and agricultural level, almost 90 percent of the entrepreneurs in the region fall into the category of SME. Today, they require new support and new institutions. For example, farmers want soil tests for field-specific fertilizer. Agro processors want advice on packaging, longer shelf life, international product standards, cold chain support, and vitamin fortification.

In the case of Bangladesh, the road network linking Dhaka with the countryside failed to have the multiplier effect on the rural economy. The region needs to develop regional market-based growth centers. All these needs call for innovative alliances between the government, private sector, and nongovernmental organizations. Multilateral organizations can select their own programs in this vast arena to support national and regional efforts for building capacity.

6. CONCLUSION

The SAARC process has so far been "Summit based." For it to gain momentum and continuity, the implementation process should be diffused among the various stakeholders in the member countries and supporting institutions should be set up urgently. At the same time, it is important that the current rapprochement between India and Pakistan continues to improve in order to sustain the integration process. On the other hand, the proliferation of a regional trade agreement, if not coordinated, may result in the "spaghetti bowl" phenomenon, hindering regional integration. The BIMSTEC FTA, India–Sri Lanka FTA, India–Nepal FTA, India–Bhutan FTA, Bangladesh–Pakistan FTA, and India–Bangladesh FTA can potentially create a chaotic situation if not properly coordinated by the member countries. Following its accession to WTO, China has been liberalizing fast and is expected to capture 10 percent of global trade by 2020, second only to the United States with 12 percent. Already 400 of the fortune 500 companies have a presence in China. It is expected that China's share of FDI to developing countries will continue to rise, posing significant challenges to other developing economies. This would definitely have a profound impact on the South Asia region if it fails to bring about a significant structural transformation in terms of both production capacity and competitive strength through regional integration at an accelerated pace. As for Bangladesh, regional integration, sub-regional cooperation, or a bilateral FTA provide no panacea for its problems; they can only create opportunities. For South Asia to take advantage of global trade, it must press ahead with its own agenda of unilateral trade liberalization, institution building, economic reforms, and improved governance.

NOTE

1. All rights reserved. The findings, interpretations, and conclusions expressed herein are those of the author(s) and do not necessarily reflect the views of the Board of Executive Directors of the World Bank or the governments they represent. Copying and/or transmitting portions of all of this work without prior permission may be violation of applicable law. The World Bank encourages dissemination of its work and will normally grant permission promptly. Any queries in this regard should be addressed to the Office of the Publisher, World Bank, 1818 H Street NW, Washington DC 20433, USA, fax 202-522-2422, email: pubrights@worldbank.org.

13

Regional Cooperation in South Asia

India Perspectives

Sonu Jain

1. INTRODUCTION[1]

The South Asian region comprising eight countries (Afghanistan, Bangladesh, Bhutan, India, Maldives, Nepal, Pakistan, and Sri Lanka) is one of the most densely populated and poorest regions in the world. It has 23 percent of the world's population and accounts for a mere 2 percent of world output. The region has 40 percent of the poorest people in the world, and its relatively young population is one of the least literate and the most malnourished in the world (Figure 13.1; Table 13.1). Of these eight countries (excluding Afghanistan), seven are members of the South Asian Association for Regional Cooperation (SAARC), which was established in 1985.

2. RATIONALE FOR REGIONAL INTEGRATION

Regional cooperation and its more advanced form of regional economic integration would enable SAARC countries to integrate more efficiently with the rest of the world and take fuller advantage of global flows of investment, technology, and trade opportunities. Regional integration permits diversification of individual economies and promotes development in their peripheral regions.

FIGURE 13.1   GNI Per Capita–Population Density

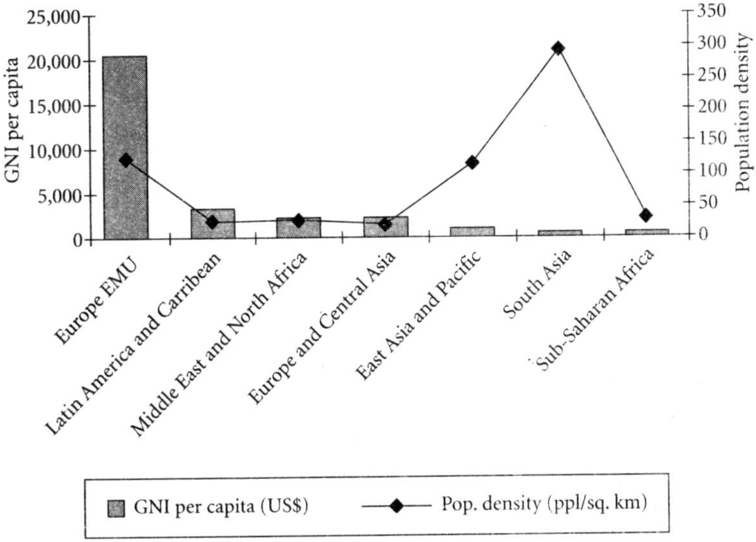

Legend: ▩ GNI per capita (US$)   ◆ Pop. density (ppl/sq. km)

Source   World Development Indicators, 2004 (World Bank 2004).

TABLE 13.1   Indicators of Poverty and Mortality

	Share of people living on less than US$1 a day (2001)	Child mortality rate per 1,000 live births (2002)	Maternal mortality ratio per 100,000 live births (2000)
East Asia and Pacific	15.6%	42	115
Europe and Central Asia	3.7%	37	58
Latin America	9.5%	34	193
Middle East and North Africa	2.4%	54	165
South Asia	**31.1%**	**95**	**566**
Sub-Saharan Africa	46.5%	174	917
Europe (EMU)	—	6	10

Source   World Bank 2004.
Note   EMU = European Monetary Union.

Regional economic cooperation permits countries to overcome constraints posed by the relatively small size of their individual markets and the low purchasing power in their economies. Integrating smaller economies into larger regional economic space expands the size of the market and facilitates cost reductions through economies of scale and scope. Regional cooperation and economic integration result in the threshold scales necessary to attract larger volumes of foreign direct investment (FDI). Figure 13.2 shows that FDI as a percent of gross domestic product (GDP) in South Asia is among the lowest in all regions, and regional integration will help to improve South Asia's performance in attracting FDI.

FIGURE 13.2   FDI as a Percent of GDP

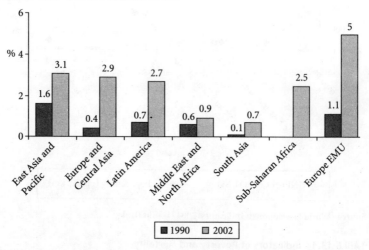

Source   World Bank 2004.

Regional cooperation in South Asia will also help to increase the level of intraregional trade among South Asian economies. At present, this is at a low level of 4.2 percent and actually has been declining over the years, having been 4.8 percent in 1980 (World Bank 2004). Freer trade and lowering of trade barriers will help these countries take full advantage of their mutual comparative advantage.

Apart from the strong economic rationale for regional cooperation and integration, such cooperation enables the member countries to reduce negative externalities and conflicts. Transboundary challenges like trafficking of women and children, drug smuggling, wildlife trade, and cross-border terrorism can be overcome only through regional initiatives. Successful economic cooperation would yield a substantial peace dividend with direct welfare raising impact for the entire region.

2.1 Initiatives for South Asian Regional Cooperation

2.1.1 Regional Level

The initiative of South Asian regional cooperation was launched in 1985 with the establishment of SAARC. Initially, the focus was essentially on noneconomic areas, but economic cooperation formally entered the SAARC agenda in 1995 with the operationalization of SAARC Preferential Trading Agreement (SAPTA). So far, four rounds of trade negotiations have been concluded under SAPTA, covering more than 5,500 commodities. Even though each round has contributed to an incremental trend in the product coverage and the deepening of tariff concessions over previous rounds, intraregional trade continues to remain almost stagnant, at a mere 4 percent. This stagnation is due to the tariff concessions offered under SAPTA, which were too insignificant, or to the commodities covered under SAPTA, which do not form a significant part of the existing or potential trade basket of the SAARC countries.

Figure 13.3 illustrates that, at present, intraregional trade (as a percentage of total region export) among SAARC countries is less than 5 percent, whereas it is 73 percent for member countries in Asia-Pacific Economic Cooperation (APEC), 61 percent in the European Union, 57 percent in the North American Free Trade Agreement (NAFTA), and 23 percent in the Association of Southeast Asian Nations (ASEAN).

So far the progress in this region has been modest. But a major breakthrough has been made early this year, with the signing of the South Asia Free Trade Agreement (SAFTA), which came into force on 1 January 2006.

Figure 13.3   Intraregional Trade as a Percentage of Total Regional Exports

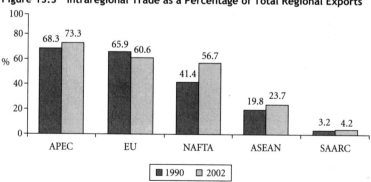

Source World Bank 2004.

Note APEC = Asia-Pacific Economic Cooperation; ASEAN = Association of Southeast Asian Nations; EU = European Union; NAFTA = North American Free Trade Agreement; SAARC = South Asian Association for Regional Cooperation.

The focus of SAFTA is primarily on tariff reduction and the trade of goods. Vital areas like the trade of services are left untouched. Many items that are critical for the success of SAFTA—such as the formulation of rules of origin, preparation of the negative list, creation of a fund to compensate least developed countries (LDCs) for the loss of revenue from eliminating customs duties, and the identification of areas for providing technical assistance to the relatively weaker countries—are left untouched. Moreover, no datelines have been fixed for concluding the negotiations on these items, except for the compensation fund that must be in place before the commencement of the SAFTA. The agreement does not subscribe to phasing out a negative list, but rather provides for the list to be reviewed after every 4 years. The agreement provides for the elimination of quantity restrictions (QRs) as soon as a 0 to 5 percent tariff level is achieved; however, it does not prescribe the elimination of other nontariff and paratariff restrictions. Some of the important measures missing from the agreement are the finalization of the pending draft investment agreement; the creation of a SAARC Investment Area, South Asian Development Fund, South Asian Development Bank, and South Asian Energy Grid; vertical industrial integration; and the harmonization of fiscal and monetary policies. These significant omissions point to the weak politics in pursuing regional cooperation.

2.1.2 Bilateral Level

With regional cooperation making only modest progress, bilateral free trade agreements are gaining momentum in this region. Although some bilateral initiatives are in place, including those between India and Sri Lanka, India and Nepal, and India and Bhutan, others are under negotiation, such as those between Pakistan and Sri Lanka and India and Bangladesh. Some sub-regional economic cooperation programs have been launched to bring together the four countries in the eastern part of South Asia. These four countries have joined together under the Growth Quadrangle (India, Nepal, Bangladesh, and Bhutan) and another possible sub-regional initiative is being considered between South India, Sri Lanka, and Maldives.

The *Indo–Sri Lanka Free Trade Agreement (FTA)*, which came into effect in 2000, has boosted bilateral trade between the two countries. Sri Lanka's export to India increased from US$71 million in 2001 to US$168 million in 2002, while India's export to Sri Lanka went up from US$604 million in 2001 to US$831 million in 2002 (UNCTAD 2003). Additionally,

FTA has made Sri Lanka a hot destination for FDI, because many foreign investors consider it to be the window into the vast Indian market. The Indo-Sri Lanka bilateral FTA has been advanced to an Indo-Sri Lanka Comprehensive Economic Partnership Agreement (CEPA) in which the liberalization of services (in addition to investment) has been included. The Indo-Sri Lanka case ought to be a model for similar agreements in South Asia.

Under the Indo-Bhutan relationship, Bhutan has built hydroelectricity ventures by collaborating with India for a buyback facility. Hydroelectricity exports from Bhutan to India provided more than 45 percent of the government's revenues and accounted for 30 percent of GDP in 2003.

Long-existing *Indo-Nepal treaties* were formalized as the Indo-Nepal Trade and Transit Treaty in 1996. The duty-free provision of the agreement induced Indian joint ventures to operate from Nepal. The volume of exports from Nepal has consequently increased considerably; specifically, few items were exported to India in bulk quantity. The need for value addition norms was introduced in 2002 to protect the Indian domestic industries and producers. As a consequence, rules of origin procedures were introduced in the renewed Treaty of Trade in 2002. The renewed treaty introduced specific modifications, including value addition requirements of 30 percent; quantitative restrictions on the export of vegetable ghee, acrylic yarn, copper, and zinc oxide; and the existence of a negative list. These developments have not only seen a degree of retrogression in Indo-Nepal bilateral trade but have also affected attempts at economic diversification in Nepal.

The South Asian Growth Quadrangle was launched in 1997 involving four countries of the region, namely Bhutan, Bangladesh, India, and Nepal, primarily aimed at creating an enabling environment for rapid economic development through the identification and implementation of specific projects. At the request of these four nations, the Asian Development Bank (ADB) launched assistance for sub-regional cooperation under the South Asia Sub-Regional Economic Cooperation (SASEC) Program in 2001. Technical assistance was provided to identify and prioritize sub-regional projects in five major sectors: transport and communication; energy and power; environment; tourism; and trade, investment, and private sector cooperation. The SASEC program is one of the most successful among all of the initiatives taken in the past. Last year, the ADB approved a US$450,000 technical assistance grant to develop a tourism plan for the four countries belonging to SASEC, with ecotourism and Buddhist circuits as the common themes.

In addition to the activities under the SASEC program, the ADB has provided support for several standalone investment projects having significant sub-regional implications. These projects include the West Bengal Corridor Development Project[2] and the Road Network Development Project.[3] In addition, the ADB's Private Sector Group has invested in Lafarge Surma Cement, the first sub-regional private sector project, which will transport limestone from Meghalaya, India, to a cement plant in Bangladesh through a cross-border conveyor system.

The World Bank has been actively involved in various poverty alleviation, health, infrastructure, social, and environmental projects in this region. Following Sub-Saharan Africa, South Asia is the largest regional recipient of concessional lending from the International Development Association (IDA), the World Bank affiliate that provides interest-free loans to the world's poorest countries. In FY03, new World Bank lending commitments to South Asian countries was US$2.9 billion for 31 projects.

3. PROSPECTS AND PROBLEMS FOR SOUTH ASIAN REGIONAL COOPERATION: A PRIVATE SECTOR PERSPECTIVE

The private sector looked seriously at SAARC sometime in 1994 with the establishment of the SAARC Chamber of Commerce and Industry (SCCI). The objective of SCCI was to represent the private sector and promote regional trade and investment in this region. It has played a significant role in bringing together the national chambers of commerce and industry of the seven SAARC countries under one umbrella. The Federation of Indian Chambers of Commerce and Industry (FICCI) is a nodal point and Indian representative of SCCI. SCCI has undertaken a number of positive initiatives since its inception by commissioning studies and reports and publishing books, convening seminars, workshops, and trade fairs, and fostering a closer dialogue with the governments on trade and economic matters. SCCI has done outstanding work in forging a consensus in the private sector to facilitate regional cooperation.

The Confederation of Indian Industry has also taken some initiatives in the past for regional cooperation in South Asia. It is working actively with the Chambers of Commerce of Bangladesh, Nepal, and Sri Lanka through Joint Economic Councils to resolve bilateral issues since growth at the regional level was modest. At the regional level, it has brought together the private sector through forums for chief executive officers, audio–video conferencing, trade fairs, missions, publications, and so on.

3.1 Prospective Areas of Regional Cooperation in South Asia

Questionnaires sent out by the Confederation of Indian Industry (CII) to a select group of members active in the region, reveal that a significant chunk (95 percent) of respondents would benefit substantially from greater regional cooperation in South Asia. The potential areas highlighted below are taken from the responses of the questionnaire and interviews conducted for the study (except for "Harmonizing Standards," "Nontariff Barriers," and "Common Currency for the Region," which do not emerge from the survey of private sector but represent CII's views on promoting regional economic cooperation in South Asia).

3.1.1 Harmonizing Standards

There is a need to accelerate adoption of best practices and international voluntary standards to have a stronger voice for the region in debates at the World Trade Organization (WTO) and other international standard-setting bodies. The lack of standardization in South Asia wastes efforts to export local products, because they do not meet regulations in other markets. In addition to this, harmonization of standards has played a critical role in the development of regional blocks and global marketplace. Eighty percent of world merchandise trade is affected by standards and regulations that embody standards. They are a means to ensure satisfactory compliance with health, safety, and environmental requirements. Standards were the principal element of EU's Single Market Program as they provide a common language and framework for commerce and economic development worldwide. Movement toward SAFTA and standardization must be coordinated.

3.1.2 Nontariff Barriers

In the current scenario, as tariffs continue to decline, there has been emergence of nontariff barriers as a measure of protection. Given the extremely low negotiating power of the individual member states at WTO, there is a strong need for a collective strategy to this issue. The European Union, United States, and Japan are the principal export destinations for the four

South Asian countries, Bangladesh, India, Pakistan, and Sri Lanka, with the share of exports in these markets to the total exports reaching more than 50 percent. In 1998, up to 94 percent of the South Asian exports to these countries were facing nontariff measures (NTMs).

SAARC exports are severely impacted by NTMs in major markets. Also, for successful regional integration within SAARC, it is crucial to reduce technical and regulatory barriers to trade by countries within the region.

3.1.3 Enhancing Trade through the Negative List Approach

For successful regional cooperation, it is important to change the current approach, which involves lengthy negotiations for each sector and product. Instead, a negative list approach can be adopted, by which products not identified on this list can be subjected immediately to a tariff reduction. This is a more transparent approach and an appropriate step toward trade liberalization. *However*, it is important that negative list should be limited in scope and should be reviewed after every 2 years with a view toward reducing the number of items on these lists.

3.1.4 Trade Facilitation

According to a study by Pohit and Taneja (2000), the main sources of transaction costs in Indo-Nepal and Indo-Bangladesh trade are delays caused by complex customs and transit procedures. Delays in custom clearances happen on account of verification of Harmonized Commodity Description and Coding System (HCDCS) classification, chemical tests, customs valuation, and labeling requirements for carrying description (to enjoy tariff preferences). Because of these delays, informal trade has surged and the government is losing revenue. It is thus essential to work out harmonization arrangements in areas such as customs procedures, arbitration, double taxation, proper channels to access market information and legal systems, and electronic data exchange leading to paperless trade. These arrangements would help reduce transaction costs and make intra-SAARC trade more efficient and prosperous for business.

3.1.5 Transport Infrastructure

The availability of transport infrastructure is crucial in providing an impetus for economic activities, especially international trade. The transport infrastructure has immensely helped the European Union to grow fast. Over the years, a number of initiatives have been taken by South Asian countries at the bilateral, sub-regional, and regional level, but trade is yet to grow at the expected rate. There is a need to strengthen trade instruments, such as transport linkages, among the members. The current level of trade can be doubled if appropriate regional agreements on roads, rail, shipping, and air are put in place, enabling seamless movement. To attain competitiveness, countries have to cooperate with each other in building and operating infrastructure facilities. The region is strategically situated at the crossroads of Asia between the oil-rich countries in West and Central Asia and the dynamic economies of Southeast Asia. The region should make full use of its geographic advantage.

3.1.6 Common Currency for the Region

A common currency is a characteristic of strong regional economic integration. Currency unification promotes intercountry trade and investment by reducing transaction costs arising from currency conversions and by eliminating exchange risk and uncertainty. However, the objective of common currency can be achieved only in a phased manner. The first and immediate step in this regard should be the introduction of a parallel currency. The region can create a reserve fund that can provide funding to regional public goods like transport, energy, information technology (IT), and so on to promote trade and investment. The provision of regional public goods and concessional assistance for the lagging regions will help build mutual trust and confidence in the region.

3.1.7 Development of Financial Sector

There is an acute need of adequate financial infrastructure, including banking, insurance, clearance mechanism, and capital market to facilitate trade and investment. This sector is not fully developed in this region and the existing network is both insufficient and fragile. The banking sector is saddled with huge non-performing assets, indicating the serious need for banking sector reforms. A well-developed banking sector will help simplify procedures for import financing as well. The state of development of the capital market is yet another area of concern. Most of the member states have a long way to go for appropriate development and modernization of capital market institutions. Because India has a relatively well-developed capital market, it may help smaller economies to develop stock exchanges and to train stockbrokers and other intermediaries. To date, Sri Lanka is the only country with which India has executed a Memorandum of Understanding (MoU) for securities markets, although discussions are also under way with Pakistan, in addition to Nepal.[4] In as much as this is a low-cost step toward market integration, it would be a straightforward recommendation that the Securities and Exchange Board of India (SEBI) enter into an MoU with all the SAARC countries.

3.1.8 Vertical Integration within the Region and Increasing Value Addition in Traditional Exports

Trade complementarities did not develop within the region because of the lack of vertical specialization through a production-sharing arrangement. Vertical specialization allows the countries to reap economies of scale by concentrating on a specific production process in the value addition chain. For example, trade can take place if one country specialized in yarn and fabrics, while another specializes in finished garment products. In the case of primary commodity exports, regional cooperation will allow greater value addition because South Asia is exporting these commodities in bulk, and value addition takes place in importing countries, thereby resulting in lower value realization. A good example of such cooperation and joint venture was the jute industry in which Bangladesh produced the jute and West Bengal had the processing mills. Joint ventures are an effective way to expand and diversify the production base and trade structure of the economy.

3.1.9 Electricity

Electricity demand in most of South Asia is currently outstripping supply. Despite having diversity of energy resources among South Asian countries, there is little energy and electricity trade in the region. The potential of cooperation in improving energy supply in South Asia is enormous. Hence, the development of regional energy resources by exploiting complementarities will result in greater welfare of the region as a whole.

Hydroelectricity

Nepal and Bhutan have substantial untapped hydroelectricity potential, estimated at 43,000 megawatts and 30,000 megawatts respectively, which could be developed both for domestic consumption as well as for exports. The beneficial outcome for both India and Bhutan arising from cooperation between these two countries on the Chukha hydro-electricity project is an eye opener. In October 2002, Australia's Snowy Mountains Engineering Corporation (SMEC) signed an agreement with the Nepal government for the development of the 750-megawatt West Seti hydroelectric dam in one of the poorest provinces in Nepal. This plant will primarily export power to India. Presently, however, only a very small proportion (11 percent) of this plant's potential has been exploited.

Natural Gas Exploitation

There is likely to be a sizeable shortfall of gas in and around this region unless some major exploration happens or the shortfall is met through imports either via pipelines or liquid natural gas (LNG). Bangladesh is endowed with natural gas reserves, but the gas trade is constrained by the region's inadequate domestic infrastructure. Pakistan and Afghanistan also have an important role to play as transit states, as they provide the best route for access to Central Asia's energy. According to one study, Pakistan alone stands to benefit by at least US$1.5 billion a year if trade in this sector is galvanized.

Nonconventional Energy

India has proven its capability in the field of wind energy, with its in-stalled capacity of 900 megawatts, second only to the United States. This capability needs to be shared with other countries in the region where there is potential for tapping wind energy. For instance, Sindh province (in Pakistan) could make use of the wind power by cooperating with India.

Thermal Power

Thermal power is the dominant source of energy in this region and accounts for about 92 percent of the installed capacity in Bangladesh, 73 percent in India, and 69 percent in Pakistan. India has a large reserve of coal (206 billion tons), accounting for about 7 percent of world reserves. Because energy demand in these countries is likely to record higher growth in the years to come, there is scope for cooperation among countries for their mutual benefit. For example, Bangladesh could import coal from Raniganj (West Bengal, India) and reap the benefit of proximity because coal can be transported at minimum cost by rail. There is also potential for cooperation between India and Pakistan in electricity generation using coal.

3.1.10 Water Resources

Economic cooperation initiatives can help the region's countries better harness and utilize the available natural resources. For example, South Asia, while being endowed by ample water resources, continues to suffer annually by both floods and droughts and faces an increasing shortage of potable and irrigation water. Greater regional cooperation in the utilization and harnessing of transboundary rivers (the Ganges, the Brahmaputra, and the Meghna) and a cooperative approach toward river basin development is needed to effectively address the water problems and other issues that cannot be addressed satisfactorily by countries acting independently.

3.1.11 Trade in Services

A free trade area in services in South Asia will complement the achievement of SAFTA, which is currently a free trade agreement in goods. One of the objectives of SAFTA is to increase the competitiveness of South Asian industries, thereby promoting growth in the region. A more liberal trading regime in services will increase the degree of competition among service suppliers in the region and make them more cost efficient, thereby benefiting people of this region. Numerous business opportunities are available in the services sector, which has been untouched so far. These sectors include health services, education services, rural banking services, environmental services, entertainment, and so on. The region has 40 percent of the poorest people in the world, and its relatively young population is one of the least literate in the world. Liberalization of education and health services will surely improve the life of people in this region. For rural development, the Grameen Bank model[5] of Bangladesh should be replicated in other countries of South Asia.

3.1.12 Tourism

South Asia's diversity in its offerings of tourism products is well known. The main tourism activities in this region involve pleasure and sight seeing, trekking, mountaineering, rafting, wildlife, and cultural tourism. However, according to one study about 75 percent of tourists coming to this region are conventional tourists coming for pleasure and sightseeing, and hence its large potential remains untapped. This sector has wide-ranging multiplier effects, as tourism cuts across several other sectors and generates new employment opportunities. If it is well managed, tourism development can contribute to the preservation of the culture and conservation of the ecology of the region. To exploit this sector's potential, tourism development is one of the priority areas under ADB's SASEC program. Since 2002, for the South Asia region, ADB has provided US$3 million in Technical Assistance grants and about US$20 million in concessional loans annually for regional and sub-regional cooperation projects for the tourism sector.

3.1.13 Information and Communication Technology

Across the globe there has been continued growth of information and communication technology (ICT). At this juncture, South Asian countries are at a crossroads: either these countries could ride the surging information wave or be swamped by it to be further marginalized in the global economy. South Asian regional cooperation for ICT is necessary because their combined resources, and shared gateways, will allow for more traffic to flow to the region and from the region. The electronic commerce within the region will help develop the skills, expertise, essential institutions (banking, arbitrage, logistics), and unique solutions that will allow merchants of South Asia to access the world market for their goods and services. It will help simplify complex documentation procedures. Furthermore, it is desirable that all South Asian countries develop roaming facilities. Such an agreement can be the driving force in increasing intra- and interregional trade. ICT is being used to promote people-to-people contact among SAARC member countries through the audio-visual exchange of culture and ideas to promote awareness on literacy, health, participatory governance, and other socioeconomic issues.

3.1.14 Traditional Medicine and Pharmaceuticals

South Asian countries possess a competitive advantage in the field of traditional systems. Since ancient times, it has been a supplier of herbal, Ayurvedic, and Unani medicines throughout the world. The production and exports of pharmaceuticals have become more and more knowledge based around the world. According to one study, medicinal plants-related trade is estimated at US$60 billion per year, and growing at about 7 percent annually. There is considerable potential to further expand the market as well as the market share of South Asia in the future. Among the South Asian countries, India has emerged as a leading producer of pharmaceutical products. Because of the lower manufacturing costs and the research and development (R&D) expertise, Indian companies are able to produce and export drugs at extremely competitive prices. The progress of the Indian pharmaceutical sector is a positive reflection on South Asia as a whole and other countries can gain substantially by this.

3.1.15 Agro Food Processing

Agro food processing is one of the priorities of most of the South Asian countries. However, food processing as a business concept is yet to gain ground in the region. India has made considerable progress in this regard compared with its neighbors. But only 7 percent of the food produced in India is being value added, despite the fact that it is the second largest producer of food in the world. India should exploit its IT knowledge to enhance the productivity of the food-processing sector and to create more knowledge-based food-processing activities. In Sri Lanka, most of the food processing comes under the small and medium enterprise (SME) category, especially those making ready-to-serve beverages, squash, jam, chutney, pickles, and sauce. The industry by and large is into processing fruits and vegetables, cereals, milk, confectionery, oilseeds (coconut), and spices. Pakistan is doing well in fresh and dry fruits trade and made considerable advances in food processing. It is suggested to set up modern food machinery design and development centers in India and Pakistan with facilities for design R&D, pilot plant, fabrication workshops, and consultancy facilities. Thus, as a whole, South Asia has immense untapped business potential in this sector.

3.2 Issues in Regional Cooperation in South Asia

3.2.1 Hydroelectricity

Although Nepal has huge hydroelectric potential, investments are not happening. This is primarily due to the lack of political will and inconducive investment climate. Such projects require huge investments, the gestation period is long, and it involves high risks. There are other policy issues, such as sharing of cost and benefits of the projects, determination of power tariff, cost of transmission line and its sharing mechanism, environmental issues, and funding arrangements. The Chukha model of power trading between India and Bhutan has worked well, however, and any power trading arrangement in the region should work on similar lines.

3.2.2 Natural Gas Exploitation

Projects with cross-border implications are more often treated along political lines rather than on commercial considerations. Because of the lack of political will of the Bangladesh government and strained relation between India and Pakistan, potential in this area has not been tapped till now.

3.2.3 Tourism

Because of indifferent policy initiatives, the real potential is not realized in the tourism sector. Each country is trying to carve out a niche without really taking advantage of synergies that may arise. Infrastructure connectivity, internal conflicts, and other bottlenecks continue to prevent this region from attracting high-profile tourists.

3.2.4 ICT

Many countries are unable to take full advantage of technologies to enhance the use of ICT because of high costs. Wider application of technology and rural penetration will reduce costs significantly as economies of scale are high and marginal costs are minimized. The private sector should take the lead in setting up the required infrastructure in the region.

3.2.5 Water Management

Water management between India and Bangladesh is on high priority, but progress has been held back because of mistrust.

3.3 Common Issues

3.3.1 Lack of Connectivity

No SAARC country has a common border other than India and intraregional transportation and communication links remain weak.

Improvements in these sectors are critical to derive the full benefits of geographic proximity. In the absence of road connectivity between Nepal–India–Bangladesh, Nepal cannot access ports in Bangladesh. Likewise, India cannot use Bangladeshi roads to access its north-eastern states, thereby resulting in increased transportation costs. No container trains are running between India and Pakistan and similarly between India and Bangladesh, although passenger trains are running among these countries. The infrastructure needs to be upgraded and developed.

3.3.2 Geopolitical Issues

The Indo-Pakistan conflict over Kashmir, conflicts between Sri Lankan government and Liberation Tigers of Tamil Eelam (LTTE), Maoist rebels in Nepal, the rise of global terrorism in Afghanistan (where Osama bin Laden and other terrorists have refuge) have threatened peace in this region and have made this region a less preferred option for the investor abroad. Presently, South Asian countries are spending a high proportion of their GDP (2.7 percent) on military expenditures and on handling local uprisings (World Bank 2004).

Trade relations between these countries will play a crucial role in subsiding tensions as countries realize the economic benefits from trade and cooperation. According to the India-Pakistan Chamber of Commerce and Industry, bilateral trade between India and Pakistan through formal channels is worth US$230 million annually, but trade through illegal channels has flourished and is now estimated at about US$1.5 billion annually. Experts believe that official trade between the two neighbors could go up to US$4 billion in 2 to 3 years, if trade relations are normalized.

3.3.3 Asymmetry between Countries

There is a fear that India being a large nation accounting for 70 percent of the region's GDP will eat up the share of other countries. However, many experiences within the region demonstrate that advantages outweigh initial misgivings. Since India and Sri Lanka entered into bilateral agreement (in 1998), the trade gap between these two countries has reduced by two-third. Hydroelectricity export from Bhutan to India provided more than 45 percent of the government's revenues and accounted for 30 percent of GDP in 2003.

3.3.4 Free Movement of People

Visa regulations and inability of businessmen to visit freely within the region has hindered trade, investment, and tourism in the region. To facilitate trade, visas for business purposes should allow multiple entries, be for a minimum duration of 5 years, and should not contain any city-wise permission. For tourism promotion, a one-time visa can be given without delays. Work permits should be given to professionals, especially in some key sectors like IT and health care.

3.3.5 Lack of Information

Lack of knowledge about a country's trade and economic policies has hindered trade in this region. For instance, there is a strong feeling in Pakistan that Indian agriculture is highly subsidized at the production and export stages. However, estimates of the aggregate measure of support (AMS) put the AMS at between 5 and 7 percent (much lower than the 10 percent that is allowed under the WTO). Other estimates have even gone to the extent of saying that Indian agriculture is negatively subsidized and therefore can never be protected. Another example of the lack of information is that custom officials are not always aware of FTAs, resulting in delayed clearances.

4. PRIORITY SECTORS FOR COOPERATION: STEPS FORWARD

The prospects of the regional cooperation and related issues are discussed in the previous section. This section will shed some light on how to address the roadblocks in some of the priority sectors.

4.1 Tourism

The appropriate approach to the tourism sector will be to create a tourism product that makes traveling to the region a pleasant experience through an environment of peace, stability, and security and an integrated physical infrastructure that does not fail. Effective coordination of public and private efforts will achieve synergy in development of this sector.

A common marketing strategy and fund, human resource development through cross intraregional investments in hotel management, and a common policy related to fleet and charter flights will help achieve the desired results.

4.2 Trade Facilitation

Although a technical committee on transport was established in 1983, and 17 meetings have been held to date, the policies are yet to be implemented. The region needs a regional transportation and transit system that offers efficient transport options and low transaction costs. To ensure the seamless movement of goods, the region should identify additional routes by road and rail, augment shipping links, and increase flights and air cargo facilities. An open sky policy in South Asia would foster people-to-people contact in the region. There should be harmonization of procedures and green channel treatment of imports within the region. Harmonization of technical standards should include truck size, weight regulations, railway gauge, and rolling stocks across South Asia. Recommended modernization of land customs stations should include warehousing, parking facilities, and simplification of clearance procedures on a priority basis. A common transport policy for South Asia would result in free movement of goods vehicles in South Asian countries.

4.3 Hydroelectricity

Regional energy grids have to become a reality for growth in this region. This would entail setting up of power projects and then linking the transmission grids of all the countries of the region. A SAARC grid is one way to ensure quality power at low cost, as well as ensure mutual support during contingencies. Cooperation among South Asian countries should steer toward setting up a data bank to prevent duplication of R&D in the field of renewable energy. Countries like Nepal and Bhutan should invite the World Bank or ADB and thus initiate regional cooperation for the exploitation of its water resources.

4.4 Natural Gas Exploitation

Arrangements should be made on multilateral basis to enable and facilitate exchanges in natural gas. A trans-SAARC gas pipeline should be constructed across this region. By sharing pipelines, countries would be able to share the operating costs of the projects and be able to reap benefits of economies of scale. It is crucial to promote cooperation within SAARC and between SAARC and the Economic Cooperation Organization (Afghanistan, Pakistan, and the Central Asian Republics).

4.5 Health Care

In India the public health care system is at a low level, and in other SAARC countries it is even worse. India, however, has seen a growing competence level in science and health and has developed various centers of excellence without any grand plan by individual efforts. SAARC countries can benefit from India's experience. Indian hospitals are training doctors and building state-of-the-art hospitals in other SAARC countries. Although some progress has been witnessed in the area of cardiology, much needs to be done in other fields as well. Since people residing in South Asia have a common gene pool, countries can benefit from collaborative research. Developing health care systems by building hospitals through joint ventures will lower the cost of medication and will provide better health care facilities to all individuals.

5. CONCLUSION

Despite trade barriers, informal trade has flourished across the South Asian frontiers. In 2002, this region's share in world output was merely 2 percent, and its share in FDI inflow in developing countries was just 2.8 percent. South Asia faces the danger of marginalization in the global economy. Regional cooperation is an effective modality that can put South Asia firmly on the global map and improve its access to financial and technology flows. Lots of theoretical work has been done so far on prospective areas in which countries in this region will gain and impediments have been identified, but no action has been taken to address these issues. The countries of Southeast Asia have achieved commendable success in development with regional cooperation, with ASEAN playing a key role in this process. Both NAFTA and the European Union are success stories for regional grouping. South Asia needs to speed up its arrangements for trade facilitation, and meaningful initiatives need to be taken by SAARC in this direction. The private sector's interest is directly and substantially involved in the creation of a regional economic space. To achieve this, the sector expects the governments to take a long-term view of benefits arising from regional cooperation. Governments must ensure that economic progress takes precedence over political issues. Doing so will build confidence and trust.

NOTES

1. Draft incorporates inputs from SAARC Chamber of Commerce, RIS, CII, responses from questionnaire and interviews with industry people.
2. A north–south road corridor from Raiganj, near Siliguri, to Barasat, the north of Kolkata in West Bengal, India with links to border points in Bangladesh.
3. Nepal's east–west Highway, which links to India and Bangladesh through Kakarbita.
4. In the last fiscal year, the World Bank sponsored an exploratory mission of staff from SEBI to Nepal to review the capital markets and meet with Securities Board of Nepal (SEBON) officials with a view toward executing an MoU between the two regulatory bodies and extending cooperation and training in the field of securities market regulation (particularly relating to supervision, surveillance, and enforcement).
5. It helped in alleviating poverty and generating employment in Bangladesh.

REFERENCE

Pohit, Sanjib and Nisha Taneja. 2000. "India's Informal Trade with Bangladesh and Nepal: A Qualitative Assessment." ICRIER Working Paper Number 58, ICRIER, New Delhi.

14

Regional Cooperation in South Asia

Pakistan Perspective

Khalid Amin

The one premise on which there is universal consensus among economists is that international trade is good for the socioeconomic development of all countries. South Asian countries will benefit significantly from greater economic integration and trade liberalization by taking advantage of the benefits of regionalism and globalization. The optimum economic benefits of regionalism and globalization can be reaped through the dynamic vehicle of the private business sector.

Despite its potential benefits, socioeconomic integration has been miserably slow in the South Asian region. It is the least integrated economic region of the world, despite having enormous physical resources and 22 percent of the global population. The regional trade of South Asia remains dismally low at 4 percent as compared with the regional trade of the European Union at.67 percent, the North American Free Trade Agreement (NAFTA) at 62 percent, the Association of Southeast Asian Nations (ASEAN) at 26 percent, the Common Market for Eastern and Southern Africa (COMESA) at 22 percent, the Gulf Cooperation Council (GCC) at 8 percent, and the Economic Cooperation Organization (ECO) at 6 percent. Regional trade among the seven South Asian Association for Regional Cooperation (SAARC) countries in 2002 was US$5 billion out of which India's share was 76 percent (US$3.8 billion) and Pakistan's share was 8 percent (US$0.4 billion). The regional trade among the remaining five countries is limited to around 16 percent (US$0.8 billion) of the total regional trade. Although SAARC was formed in 1985, it has never taken off as a useful economic vehicle.

1. OPPORTUNITIES FOR GREATER REGIONAL INTEGRATION

1.1 Potential for Regional Integration in South Asia

If positive regional economic development policies are implemented, duly supported by efficient operating systems, the optimum potential of regional integration can be achieved within 5 years. If Trade, Traffic, and Transport (3Ts) are allowed free operation, South Asian regional trade, which has stagnated around US$5 billion per year, can surpass US$15 billion within 5 years. The private business sector is convinced that if the 3Ts are facilitated, the optimum potential of socioeconomic integration can be realized within a short time. This realization is based on the conviction that regional integration will provide a large market for exportable surplus, while considerable imports from around the world, when shifted to regional countries, will save considerable cost and delivery time. To realize this goal, strategic, policy, and institutional initiatives are required at the highest political level, which should be implemented through an effective public–private mechanism with a clearly defined implementation schedule.

The private sector is convinced that great bilateral and multilateral trade prospects exist if regional countries separate politics from trade and focus on each other's economic potential. Major economic and social factors favoring regional trade include proximity (leading to lower freight cost, short delivery time, and low inventory cost) and a common language. Free trade would allow businesses to take advantage of an enormous market of more than 1.34 billion people. The private business sector believes that the implementation of free trade in the region would facilitate regional socioeconomic integration and a solution for long-outstanding political problems.

1.2 Private Sector Opportunities for Regional Economic Integration

Because of the size of their economies, India and Pakistan, with a combined population of 1.15 billion people, have the greatest potential for economic integration in the South Asia region.

Because of restrictions on bilateral trade between Pakistan and India, official bilateral trade accounts for around US$250 million. Unofficial trade through third countries is estimated at US$2.5 billion per year. According to estimates of the Federation of Pakistan Chambers of Commerce and Industry (FPCCI), if free trade is allowed between India and Pakistan, bilateral trade can cross US$5 billion per year within 3 years. If the existing unofficial trade is regularized, the government can earn additional customs revenue of US$450 million per year, which can pass US$750 million per year in 3 years.

Several items are manufactured in Pakistan and India that can be traded profitably between these two counties (Box 14.1).

BOX 14.1   Potential Items of Export between India and Pakistan

Potential items of export from Pakistan to India	Potential items of export from India to Pakistan
• Cotton, yarn, and fabrics • Rock salt • Dry dates • Fresh and dried fruits • Finished leather and leather goods • Natural gas, electricity • Vegetables • Fish (fresh and frozen) • Sugar and molasses • Limestone • Fertilizer • Marbles (including Onyx) • Precious and semiprecious stones • Articles of textiles and clothing • Accessories • Knotted carpets • Scientific instruments	• Iron and steel • Auto components and spares • Pharmaceuticals and raw materials • Castings and forgings • Tea • Nonmetallic mineral products • By-products of refinery • Plastic materials • Intermediaries for chemicals • Agro-based raw materials (for example, oilseeds) • Cement • IT-related software

Source Author's estimates.

1.2.1 Textiles

The textile sector, which contributes more than 67 percent to Pakistan's exports, is expected to do well even in the free trade regime. In the last 4 years, the Pakistani textile sector has invested US$4 billion to bring its production on par with world quality. More value added items—namely, bed wear, knitwear, and readymade garments—have allowed Pakistan to join the elite club of major exporters of textile goods during 2002–03. Pakistani bed wear products are considered superior to those of Indians. In fact, Pakistani home textile products are considered world leaders in terms of quality and cost. A similar situation prevails in knitwear and certain cotton fabrics. Indians have an edge in Georgette and some other silk products, but as far as cotton textiles are concerned, Pakistan is much more developed. India has an advantage, however, in the case of blended textile products that are made from a combination of manmade and natural fibers, which are preferred in clothing worldwide. Presently, Pakistan's blended cloth has a ratio of 27:73 against an international ratio of 52 percent synthetic yarn in blended textiles, whereas in India and China, the standard manmade fiber content is 35 percent in blended textiles. Some varieties of cotton produced in Pakistan are of better quality than those of India. Pakistan imports cotton from the Arab Republic of Egypt, the United States, and the central Asian states for production of fine-count yarn. Pakistan's cotton is suitable for producing low-to medium-count yarn (used for towels and home textile products) because of its staple length and moisture absorption properties.

1.2.2 Machinery, Equipment, and Components

Although Pakistan is a major producer and exporter of textile products, it meets its requirements of textile machinery and spares through imports from Europe and the Far East. Pakistan's industry can consider imports of textile and other machinery from India, which is of reasonable quality and comparatively cheaper in price. In India a large portion of the needs of textile mills are met by indigenous machinery, which is a major advantage for the Indian textile industry when compared with Pakistan where textile machinery and spares are imported from East Asia and Europe. Most of the textile manufacturers of India have collaborated with leading textile machinery manufacturers, such as Reiter (Swiss) and Shubert and Sulzer (German) and have demonstrated their ability to absorb and adapt new technology. A few of these manufacturers are successfully exporting machinery and accessories. Some of the textile machinery imported by Pakistan from Switzerland and Germany is reportedly made under license in India at a much lower cost. The opening up of trade with India will help Pakistan acquire textile machinery directly at much lower prices. Seed-crushing machines are cheap in India and are being imported into Pakistan via Dubai. Machines from India are on Pakistan's negative list and therefore have to be ordered from Dubai. According to the All Pakistan Textile Mills Association (APTMA), Pakistani companies import approximately US$3.5 million worth of spare parts and light machinery (for example, needles for weaving and knitting machines, and so on) annually from India via Dubai and Hong Kong, China.

A vast scope for import of certain components from India would facilitate the emergence of technology-intensive industries in Pakistan, such as auto components, bicycle components, components for machine tools industry, components of textile machinery, and components of electrical and electronic machinery.

1.2.3 Automotive Components and Spares

The automobile industry of India has developed immensely in the last 15 years because of deregulation of the Indian economy. Because of a good engineering base and a huge population whose purchasing power has considerably increased over the last decade, India is able to produce a wide range of passenger and commercial vehicles and their spares at 35 percent less cost than Pakistan. Annually, Pakistan imports around US$775 million worth of automobile components and spare parts, 95 percent of which are from Japan. If India could be used as an additional source of supply, Pakistan could save around US$155 per year on cost of imported auto parts. Pakistan could benefit considerably from importing cheaper automotive components from India and thereby reduce its cost of locally produced vehicles and their spares. Simultaneously, India would earn substantial incremental export earnings.

1.2.4 Pharmaceuticals

Because of the Indian government's effective policies, the price of pharmaceutical products produced by local as well as multinational corporations (MNCs) are three to seven times cheaper in India than those in Pakistan. Prices are also low because of a large market and huge consumption of pharmaceutical products without any requirement for prescriptions from a licensed medical practitioner. India also has a substantial production of local herbal medicines and health products that have a good demand in Pakistan. Presently, many such products are entering the Pakistani market through illegal or third country sources.

1.2.5 Petroleum

Pakistan imports petroleum products of US$1.72 billion annually, including 4,014,439 metric tons of diesel worth US$919 million in cost and freight value, mostly from Kuwait and Saudi Arabia, but disallows imports from India. India exports diesel of more than 5 million tons (annually), including to far off countries in Latin America. Because of proximity and associated economics, diesel imports from India to Pakistan could be a win–win situation for the two countries. Indian companies, like Reliance Petroleum and the state-owned Indian Oil Corporation, are well poised to meet this demand. India is the only country in the South Asian region that has naphtha cracking facilities. Pakistan exports naphtha and can put up a naphtha cracker plant in collaboration with the Indians, and thus, after meeting its own requirements of the end product, can export the surplus to other countries in the region. Pakistan is keen on the Iran–India gas pipeline, which can be laid via Pakistan. This will enable India to import gas from Iran through an offshore pipeline across Pakistan. If the 2,700-km pipeline plan translates into a reality, it could provide immense economic benefits to both countries.

1.2.6 Tea

Although Pakistan does not produce tea, it is one of the largest consumers and importers of tea in the world, importing around US$183 million worth of tea annually. Sixty percent of the tea is imported from Kenya (US$116 million) and only 12 percent is imported from neighboring South Asian countries. There is great scope for promoting tea imports from Bangladesh, India, and Sir Lanka into Pakistan for mutual benefit of the regional countries.

1.2.7 Cement

Indian surplus cement production can meet considerable cement demand in Pakistan and Afghanistan at a much cheaper rate. The current prices of cement in Pakistan are around Pakistani rupees (PRs) 220 a bag. In India, prices are approximately Indian rupees (Rs) 135 a bag. The Pakistani rupee today stands at roughly PRs 58 to US$1 and the Indian rupee stands at Rs 46 to US$1. Thus, Pakistan would be able to buy Indian cement at about PRs 167 a bag, thereby achieving a cost saving of Rs 53 per bag.

Cement units in Gujarat and Rajasthan can supply the market in southern Pakistan. India exported about 6.5 million tons of cement during 2002–03, mainly to Bangladesh, Nepal, South Africa, Sri Lanka, and West Asia besides exporting small volumes to North Africa. Present demand in Pakistan for imported cement is not large, but it could increase substantially if major construction projects get under way. It would not be feasible if it were through the Wagah border, because Punjab does not have the capacity to transport cement from Rajasthan, and it would be expensive to transport cement from Gujarat. The road link into Sindh from Rajasthan would be ideal for cement exports from India to Pakistan. About 75 to 85 percent of cement exports from India are from coastal units. These units might not be able to feed more export demand because they have long-term interest in the domestic market. Exports from other states would not be feasible because the inland freight differential would be higher than the difference in international prices. The alternative available would be coastal shipping into the Karachi port. Cement would need to be listed in a trade agreement if the two countries decided to accord each other Most Favored Nation (MFN) status.

1.2.8 Tourism

There is great scope for promoting tourism in the region because of historic, social, and cultural links. Tourism is a potential area of interest for international donors who think it can promote integration in the region. Recently, the Asian Development Bank (ADB) provided assistance for the development of tourism for the South Asia Sub-Regional Economic Cooperation (SASEC), which includes Bangladesh, Bhutan, India, and Nepal. The ADB sees great advantages for India and Pakistan in the tourism industry. As a result of the partition of India in 1947, a large number of families were divided and continue to remain apart. Besides meeting family and friends, people of India and Pakistan are keen to visit these countries for sightseeing and vacation. Both countries have a lot to offer tourists in terms of social, cultural, and historical interests. The present meager tourism trade of around US$15 million per year can be easily expanded to more than US$155 million per year after the liberalization of visas and the improved provision of intercountry transportation facilities.

1.2.9 Infrastructure Projects

The ADB plans to finance sub-regional infrastructure projects to promote trade between India and Pakistan, including electricity and gas sales. The World Bank is planning to pursue sub-regional cooperation between India and Pakistan by financing infrastructure projects to enhance linkages between the two countries. The ADB has identified road projects, border facilitation, electricity exports, gas pipelines, tourism, and the trade of goods as some of the areas for which the Bank would provide financing. The ADB is considering a plan for a political risk guarantee to India to pave the way for the Afghanistan, Pakistan, and Turkmenistan gas pipeline project. The ADB believes that Pakistan can export electricity to India, and it is ready to finance the development of the required infrastructure.

1.2.10 Banking and Capital Markets

To facilitate payments for bilateral trade and commerce, banks of both countries should be allowed to open branches in major cities. Similarly the stock exchanges of the two countries should permit the listing and trading of stocks of both countries, which would provide financial depth and diversification to the investors and stockbrokers.

1.2.11 Financial and Corporate Regulations

As privatization of businesses and economic activities is promoted, the need for the government to have an effective regulatory role increases. Individual countries in the South Asia region are making efforts to develop and institute a financial and corporate regulatory framework, but due to limitations in indigenous expertise and experience, achievements are limited. Considerable developments in India and modest developments in Pakistan have taken place in implementing a regulatory framework for financial institutions, stock and commodity exchanges, telecommunication operators, media operators, trade bodies, and trade dispute resolution.

Efforts have also been made in India and Pakistan to promote a professional framework for corporate governance. Collaboration among the regulators of South Asian countries could be useful in the cost-effective and timely development and implementation of a regulatory framework in the relevant financial and corporate sectors.

1.2.12 WTO Issues

Trade is being rapidly globalized under rules and regulations formulated by the WTO. South Asian countries need to intelligently comprehend the requirements and implications of WTO rules and regulations. In the compliance areas where the countries have no serious reservations, the government and related businesses of the South Asia region could jointly formulate and implement a closely monitored implementation schedule for actions required under the WTO regime. In areas and economic sectors where modifications or deferment in implementation of WTO requirements are critical, a joint stand and strategy by the South Asian countries could be effective in safeguarding the economic interest of the respective countries and regions.

1.2.13 Joint Ventures

Profitable business collaboration and joint ventures could be considered between entrepreneurs of India and Pakistan, including call centers, process outsourcing in sectors such as auto parts, pharmaceuticals, cosmetics, applied R&D, technical training, entertainment, hospitality, and organized tourism.

1.2.14 Trade through MNCs

India and Pakistan have a number of common MNCs operating in their respective countries. These multinationals can act as meaningful conduits for trade if they source raw materials from each other. MNCs operating in the South Asian region can greatly influence regional economic integration by building a supply chain for their requirements of raw materials and finished goods in the regional countries.[1] Vast opportunities exist in the area of consumer goods. This potential needs to be explored through sector-wise studies and research.

1.2.15 Technical Cooperation

India and Pakistan have considerable interest in collaboration, the transfer of technology, and the sharing of knowledge in the following sectors:

- R&D for crop productivity.
- Seed development and processing.
- Food processing, preservation, canning, and so on.
- Storage and warehousing.
- Auto components production.
- Mercantile laws.
- Automation in government and private sectors.
- Harmonization of systems (trade, customs, and taxation).

The interest of these two countries is also observed in cooperation for technical services and networking among the institutions to build indigenous capacities in the following fields:

- Quality and productivity management.
- Energy conservation.
- Environment management.
- Technical education and training.
- Entrepreneurship development.

1.3 Economic Integration with Other Countries of South Asia

Besides India, Pakistan can also benefit from greater socioeconomic integration with other countries of the South Asia region. The private sector feels that free trade agreements (FTAs) with all countries of the region would be economically beneficial for all countries in the long run. Some of the sectors in which South Asian countries could profitably trade with each other include textiles, tea, leather products, fruits and vegetables, automobiles and auto parts, steel, household appliances, software development, education and technical training, R&D, tourism, and entertainment. A liberal policy to grant visas will give an enormous boost to regional trade and tourism and will greatly facilitate socioeconomic Integration. (Specific studies would be required to identify complementarities and comparative advantages between other countries of South Asia.)

2. WHY ECONOMIC INTEGRATION HAS NOT FLOURISHED IN THE SOUTH ASIAN REGION

Despite the apparent possibilities, economic integration has not flourished in the South Asian region. Following are some of the major factors that have retarded the region's economic integration.

2.1 Lack of Political Commitment

India and Pakistan, which are the major countries of the South Asian region, continue to nurture their long-standing hostility over the Kashmir dispute. Serious political differences also exist between India and Sri Lanka (prolonged civil war between Indian-backed Tamil Tigers and the Lankan government). The politicians and military leaders of these countries maintain rigid positions on these political issues, claiming their solutions, as per their points of view, to be prerequisites for consideration of socioeconomic integration. In particular, the military leaders, to perpetuate their leadership role and vested interests, maintain a hostile posture toward their neighboring countries.[2] Hence, political issues are perpetuated and not allowed to be resolved.

2.2 Limited Role of the Private Sector in Influencing Economic Policy

The private sector is in favor of greater regional economic integration because of the realization of the existence of economic complementarities and comparative advantages in a large number of economic sectors. Socioeconomic insulation is considered unnatural and economically detrimental for the private business sector. The private business sector feels that if free trade is allowed in the region, it will be able to sell the surplus produce to a larger market, while imports of deficit products and services will be available from nearby countries that are presently imported from around the world. This will increase economic profitability because of a reduction in time and cost of transportation. In the South Asian countries, however, the private business sector has a limited role in the formulation and implementation of economic policy. Excessive authority and control over financial resources with the armed forces and bureaucracy have given them excessive power and involvement in socioeconomic affairs at the cost of the private and business sectors. The federal budget, trade policy, taxation policy, monetary policy, and other socioeconomic policies are formulated by the bureaucracy quite independent of the proposals of the private business sector. Consequently, the private sector has to spend a lot of time and money revising the unfavorable policies and procedures announced. Similarly, legislation on important issues is formulated by the bureaucracy and tabled in the Parliament without due consultation with and consideration of the private sector.

2.3 Fear of Indian Dominance

India is, by far, the largest country in the South Asian region, accounting for 80 percent of the aggregate regional gross domestic product (GDP). Because of its comparative size and historically dominating economic orientation in the region, other countries in the region are hesitant to allow a free bilateral trading arrangement. All regional countries consider trading with India as a last resort. Regional countries feel that if greater regional integration were allowed, India would soon dominate and control their economies.

2.4 Inefficient Local Business Environment

Any business has to first excel in its country of origin before it can succeed in doing business abroad. The countries of South Asia suffer from an unfriendly and inefficient business environment. As a result, the risk and cost associated with establishing and operating a business is comparatively less attractive.

2.5 Limited Economic Complementarity

The basis of bilateral and multilateral trade is economic comparative advantage in the production and trading of goods and services. Most of the countries of South Asia produce and export similar goods and services that comprise basic food and textile items (for major items of trade by South Asian countries, see Appendix 14.1). Of late, India has expanded into the production of a considerable volume of machinery, software and IT services, vehicles, and jewelry with comparative advantage and marketability in the South Asia region.

2.6 Meager Economic Surplus

The countries of South Asia have a large human population of 1.34 billion, which continues to grow at an alarming rate of more than 2 percent per year. The huge population exerts tremendous pressure on demand for local consumption of most of the basic items of production, leaving little surplus for export. The situation is not improving, as the annual increase in population is excessive while the increase in production is unsatisfactory.

2.7 Restricted Awareness of Possibilities of Regional Integration

Because of the limited exchange of goods, services, people, and information, there is little awareness of the potential for and possibilities of bilateral and multilateral trade among the countries of South Asia. Lack of adequate and relevant information and exposure breeds undue fears, apprehensions, and misunderstanding.

3. MEASURES TO PROMOTE GREATER REGIONAL INTEGRATION IN SOUTH ASIA

The South Asia region has shown poor progress in the last three decades in terms of regional integration and trade. The countries involved have wasted a lot of time and resources without any positive action and material socioeconomic achievement. The 25th meeting of the Council of Ministers ended on 21 July 2004, at Islamabad, after making decisions that seek to enlarge and strengthen cooperation among the members in several socioeconomic areas. These decisions are laudable; however, unless a serious effort is made by the leaders of South Asian countries to professionalize and institutionalize an effective Strategic Plan for Economic Integration (SPEI), which is implemented with utmost seriousness and sincerity, these recent SAARC deliberations and decisions, like those of the last two decades, will effect no significant change in the status quo of the South Asian region. It is high time that the leaders of the South Asian countries progress beyond meetings, signing protocols, and economic studies and get down to real action on achieving specific economic targets.

Following are some of the proposals for promoting rapid economic integration in the South Asian region.

3.1 Strategic Initiatives

3.1.1 Separation of Economic Integration and Free Trade from Politics

To sustain their vested interests, decision makers in the armed forces, bureaucracy, and politics in the South Asian countries (particularly Pakistan and India) insist on a complete and absolute solution to the political disputes according to their respective traditional and inflexible positions. Pakistani military leadership continues to insist that Kashmir is the "core" issue, and without its solution to the full satisfaction of these leaders, socioeconomic relations with India cannot be normalized. The solution of Kashmir has been made an essential prerequisite for economic integration between the two countries. The two countries have fought three wars over the Kashmir issue and annually waste around 22 percent of their federal budget on the armed forces. Against this position, the general public, and particularly the private business sector in both countries, feels that politics should be kept separate from bilateral trade and socioeconomic integration. The civilians and the business community are convinced that the Kashmir issue has nothing to do with the socioeconomic welfare of their countries. In fact, the general feeling of the private business sector is that a huge amount of financial resources have been wasted over the last 57 years on the pretext of the "Kashmir Issue" without any positive outcome to date. Business professionals feel that if political problems are separated from socioeconomic integration and free trade promotion, a substantial amount of financial resources could be diverted to socioeconomic development. Socioeconomic integration would also ease political rigidity and undue apprehensions and facilitate the solution of pending political problems. Moreover, to resolve political issues, political leadership should be convinced to give up its "positioned approach" to solving these issues and, instead, should adopt the most effective negotiating and problem-solving technique of "best alternative through negotiated approach" (BATNA). Under BATNA, the concerned parties do not take any preconceived "position," but instead evaluate several alternate solutions and choose from among them the best alternate solution that meets their respective objectives. By using the BATNA technique to solve problems, neither party loses, but instead each party achieves a satisfying and lasting best solution.

3.1.2 Creating Awareness that Economic Advantage is Key to Socioeconomic Prosperity

International organizations, such as the World Bank, and private business institutions with economic clout, such as the FPCCI, can reorient the thoughts of political leadership in countries of South Asia through meetings, presentations, and seminars with leaders in politics, the armed forces, and bureaucracy toward the reality that, in modern times, nations prosper on the basis of superior economic performance rather than the possession of a large territory or physical resources. The European Union, Japan, and the United States possess only 10 percent of the land and physical resources but own more than 78 percent of the financial wealth of the world because of their economic superiority.

If South Asian countries genuinely desire to prosper as sovereign states, their leaders must be refrained from wasting human and financial resources on unproductive and futile pursuits, such as securing more physical territory or expanding military might. Instead, they should re-channel their resources and focus on the socioeconomic development of their countries. Sensible nations now seek economic power, not territorial enlargement. China is a good example. It refuses to be provoked or distracted by Taiwan, China, from its focused economic pursuit. South Asian countries, too, can become strong economic powers if they earnestly dedicate their optimum resources to the development of their economic strengths. Limiting nondevelopment and defense expenditure to a bare minimum should be a prerequisite for foreign assistance and cooperation.

3.1.3 Strategic Plan for Economic Integration

A South Asian SPEI should be formulated, which specifies the areas of economic integration, regional trade, and socioeconomic development that will be pursued within a period of 3 years. This plan should be formulated around a number of parameters (Table 14.1), with a statement of existing status and quantified targets for achievement within a specified time frame.

The SPEI should have quantified targets for achievement in the specified areas with a predetermined time schedule for achievement and should note who has responsibility for the achievement of each target. The South Asian SPEI should be prepared by a committee, including the following from each of the South Asian countries.

TABLE 14.1   Data Format for Measuring Progress with Economic Integration

Areas of economic integration	Current (US$ value p.a.)	Target (US$ value p.a.)	Achievement schedule
Bilateral Trade (US$ value)			
Regional Trade (US$ value)			
Socioeconomic Development (specific areas):			
Free Trade Agreement			
Joint Ventures (Trade and Industrial)			
Promotion of Monetary Union			
Banking, Insurance Cooperation			
Education Cooperation			
Research and Development Cooperation			
Agricultural Development			
Health and Population Control			
Tourism			
Media, Entertainment, and Information			
Facilitation Factors:			
Harmonized tariff, subsidies, and restrictive trade practices			
Transportation (air, rail, water, and road)			
Communications (air, rail, road, sea, and telecommunication)			
Trade Delegations and Exhibitions (Number and sectors)			
Trade Exhibitions (Number and sectors)			
Development of infrastructure			
Visa liberalization (number of visas issued)			

Source Author.
Note   p.a. = Per annum.

- Chairman, Planning Commission.
- Secretary, Ministry of Commerce.
- Secretary, Ministry of Finance.
- Secretary General, Federation of Chambers of Commerce and Industry.
- Development Economist from the World Bank.

The SPEI and its implementation schedule should be endorsed by the heads of states of the South Asian countries in a summit meeting. Thereafter, quarterly meetings should be held to review implementation of the plan and its actual achievements should be compared against agreed-on quantified targets. In the case of negative deviations, urgent corrective action should be decided and implemented.

3.1.4 Enhancing the Role of the Private Business Sector for Regional Economic Integration

The private business sector is the vehicle for national economic development and regional socioeconomic integration. The private sector in South Asian countries should be allowed a much greater role in economic policy formulation and implementation. Despite propagation of an FTA with all South Asian countries by the FPCCI, the government has not made any progress in this direction. Despite the FPCCI's strong representation, to have even a single product included on the government's list of importable items from regional countries is a tedious and drawn-out process. This is primarily due to inadequate information and the noncommercial orientation of government functionaries. The concerned government departments take months to grant permission for allowing trade delegations or trade exhibitions from the regional countries. Despite being a major producer of textile products, Pakistan does not produce textile machinery or spares, which have to be imported. India produces a reasonable quality of textile machinery at competitive prices. The APTMA has been persistently demanding, for the last 8 years, that the government should allow the import of textile machinery and spares from India but to date, textile machinery and spares have not been included on the list of items importable from India.

On the recommendation of the FPCCI, the government should immediately allow additions to the list of importable items, permission for trade delegations to visit, and clearance for trade fairs and business visits.

The enormous economic benefit achieved from the active participation of the private business sector is evident from the formulation and implementation of Textile Vision 2005. This 5 year strategic plan called for the Textile Industry of Pakistan and it exports to be upgraded. Initiated by Mr Abdul Razak Dawood, the commerce minister of Pakistan from 1999–2002, the plan broke the 5 year stagnation of total exports at US$7.5 billion.

Thanks to this strategic plan, which was successfully implemented through the private textile sector, Pakistan's exports crossed US$12 billion in 2004. Shaukat Aziz, who holds a master's degree in business administration and has a successful track record in the private commercial sector, was appointed as the finance minister of Pakistan and successfully transformed the bankrupt national economy into a sound and vibrant economy. Similarly, the Pakistan International Airline (PIA), which had become an almost bankrupt state enterprise, was turned around after the appointment of a chief executive from the private business sector. The role of the private sector can be enhanced by the following measures:

- Except a few strategic enterprises, all state enterprises should be privatized as early as possible. Seaports and airports should be privatized to reduce distribution time and the cost of foreign trade. The privatization of railways, the Water and Power Development Authority (WAPDA), the Karachi Electric Supply Corporation (KESC), Pakistan Steel, municipal corporations, and so on will greatly reduce their cost of operations and enhance their efficiency and quality of service.
- Federal budget, trade policy, and all other financial, monetary, fiscal, and industrial development policies should be formulated on the basis of the recommendations of the FPCCI.
- The FPCCI, supported by its member trade bodies, should strongly propagate the immediate signing of an FTA with all South Asian countries as soon as possible.
- A representative of the FPCCI should be a director on the board of all government policy-making organizations and committees.
- The president of the FPCCI should be granted official status equivalent to the minister of state for official protocol.
- Trade offices and bank branches should be allowed to be opened in all regional countries.
- Greater interaction and coordination should be promoted between the FPCCI and various government departments.
- Heads of the Export Promotion Bureau and all state enterprises (until these are privatized) should be business professionals from the private business sector.
- Leading business professionals (based on annual exports, imports, and investments) should be recognized through awards on the country's national day.
- Business professionals should take greater and active part in politics so that a larger number of these professionals are elected as parliamentarians, whereby they can influence legislation of business policy promoting local and regional trade and commerce.
- An FCCI of South Asian countries should form and actively use business councils for bilateral trade promotion between regional countries.

3.2 Institutional Changes

3.2.1 Making the Regional Trade Organization Effective

The SAARC has been around since 1985 without achieving any economic benefit for its member countries. Presently, the SAARC is headed and manned by government servants representing the seven member states. The few subsidiary organizations of the SAARC managed by the private sector, such as the SCCI, are constrained in their operations as they can only operate within the limited parameters permitted by the SAARC Secretariat. The SAARC should be transformed into a vigorous instrument of regional integration and free trade through an effective plan for re-organization. The following steps should be taken to make the SAARC effective and efficient in promoting regional socioeconomic integration:

- **Professionalize the SAARC organization and operations.** The SAARC should be headed by a professional secretary general who should be qualified in business administration with a successful track record of developing and operating large business organizations. The secretary general should reorganize the SAARC organization by having professionally qualified personnel supported by efficient operating systems. The secretary general should be given quantified annual operating targets for achievement.
- **Reconstitute a SAARC board of directors.** The SAARC board should be reconstituted to include proactive, dynamic, and results-oriented professionals. A SAARC board of directors should include the finance ministers and representatives of the private business sector of the respective countries. The board should meet regularly every quarter to discuss and decide on a specific agenda. Decisions on the agenda items should specify target areas for achievement, a schedule for achievement, and responsibility for achievement. Each subsequent meeting of the SAARC board of directors should start with a review of achievements against of the targets set in the last meeting.
- **Formulate a strategic operating plan.** A 5 year plan and an annual strategic plan for the SAARC should be formulated, and after approval by the board of directors, it should be implemented seriously and strictly by the SAARC secretary general. The strategic plan should specify the areas of economic integration and trade with quantified action targets, along with time targets for achieving those targets. Progress on the achievement of targets should be

monitored by the board of directors through monthly, quarterly, and annual reports.
- **Revise the SAARC Web site.** The existing SAARC Web site provides little useful information for the promotion of regional trade and economic integration. A meaningful Web site should be launched, which should become a ready reference mechanism for all pertinent aspects of trade, industry, regulatory procedures, trade and investment queries, travel facilitation, and so on.

3.2.2 Promotion and Activation of FPCCI Business Councils

In recent years, the FPCCI has formed business councils for the promotion of trade and commerce between Pakistan and important trading partner countries. The members of these business councils of various countries are from the existing private business sector or potential trade partners of entrepreneurs in those countries. The business councils have proven to be an effective platform for the promotion of bilateral trade. This concept needs to be implemented and strengthened in all countries of South Asia.

3.2.3 Trade Delegations and Exhibitions

The frequent exchange of trade delegations promotes understanding and goodwill and removes misgivings and apprehensions. These delegations provide opportunities to materialize contracts for trade and business joint ventures. During 2008, the FPCCI organized five trade delegations to and from India, and as a result of personal meetings of business professionals from the two countries, the trade of several products has been promoted. Two single-country exhibitions organized by the FPCCI in India successfully introduced Pakistani products to the prospective individual and corporate customers. Similarly, as a result of the Indian tea delegation's visit to Pakistan last year, export of Indian tea to Pakistan has increased by 20 percent.

3.2.4 Ambassadors from the Private Business Sector

The present ambassadors in South Asian countries are from the foreign service or the armed forces and are mostly appointed on recommendations rather than merit. These ambassadors have no economic, commercial, or managerial orientation or expertise. The ambassadors and their staff hardly spend any time on the promotion of bilateral or regional trade or the promotion of regional economic integration. Except for the few countries that are politically sensitive, all other country ambassadors should be appointed from private business sectors that have successful track records of economic and commercial achievements. These ambassadors should be given quantified annual targets for the promotion of trade and economic integration, and their performance should be evaluated accordingly.

3.3 Policy Changes

3.3.1 Improving the Local Business Environment

Before any business can effectively enter the South Asian export market, it needs to be viable and competitive locally. This requires that the local business environment and cost of doing business be made viable and attractive. The governments of South Asian countries need to improve the local conditions of business risk, the cost and time of setting up and operating business, infrastructure, and communications. These improvements require the allocation of greater resources to these sectors from the federal budget, which should be diverted from a large allocation to unproductive expenditures.

3.3.2 Harmonization of Tariff Structure

Marked differences in the tariff structure of South Asian countries are a major obstacle in the implementation of regional FTAs. India and Bangladesh have the highest tariffs in the South Asian region, which is coupled with a subsidy policy for certain sectors. If a uniform tariff structure is agreed upon and is simultaneously implemented equitably in all South Asian countries, in consultation with the private sector, a level playing field will be provided and no country will feel disadvantaged due to tariff disparities that can adversely affect the cost competitiveness of traded goods and services.

3.3.3 FTA and MFN Status Should Be Signed and Implemented

All countries of South Asia should immediately sign an FTA and grant MFN status to the member countries. In the short run, there could be some economic distortions, but within 3 years, all countries in the region would improve economically. After an initial adjustment, all countries would find a new economic equilibrium in which they would be producing and trading goods and services in which they have a comparative and competitive advantage.

3.3.4 Open All Modes of Transportation

The availability of an efficient means of transportation is essential for the efficient movement of goods and services. Presently, all modes of transport, including air, rail, road, and sea, are not available among the countries of South Asia. All possible modes of direct transportation between South Asian countries should be opened to facilitate the efficient movement of goods and people. The availability of efficient and cost-effective modes of transport will reduce the time and cost of travel and transport within the South Asian region for goods and people.

3.3.5 Liberalization of Visas

A restrictive visa policy and an inefficient visa-processing staff and system greatly retard the movement of people among South Asian countries. A liberal visa policy should be implemented, through efficient visa staff and assistants, that allows a 5 year multiple entry visa with no restriction on movement throughout each South Asian country and without a requirement to report to the police. Business professionals recommended by their representative chambers and associations, students, and tourist groups organized by authorized tour operators should be granted a visa within 24 hours. Greater personal interaction among the people of South Asian countries, particularly the private business sector, will promote positive understanding and goodwill, which is the basis for economic integration. Business visitors and recreational tourists will generate significant revenue from tourism and provide opportunities for accelerated socioeconomic integration and regional trade.

3.3.6 Avoidance of Double Taxation

Presently, an agreement avoiding double taxation is limited to Bangladesh, India, Pakistan, and Sri Lanka. An extension of this facility to the entire South Asian region will promote regional trade.

3.3.7 ATA Carnet Facility

ATA Carnet (Admission Temporaries/Temporary Admission) is an international customs arrangement that permits the temporary duty-free and tax-free import of goods into countries that are members of this chain. This arrangement greatly facilitates duty-free entry (and exit) of goods in member countries, which are intended for trade fairs, transit trade, samples, and professional activities. In South Asia, only India is a member of the ATA Carnet chain. Through the endeavors of the FPCCI, Pakistan will soon complete the membership formalities. To facilitate regional trade, all South Asian countries should become members of ATA Carnet.

3.3.8 Greater Investment in Education and Human Resource Development

In the twenty-first century, the essential condition for the survival and growth of nations and corporate entities is possession of internationally superior technical knowledge and human resources. Unfortunately, in South Asian countries, the level and standard of education, especially technical and professional education, and expertise of human resources is dismally low. As a result, these countries are unable to produce and trade high-tech and high-value products and services. As a consequence, the total value of products produced and traded remains low. South Asian countries need to prioritize technical education and the development of human resources by allocating at least 5 percent of their federal budget to this sector. The governments in South Asian countries have failed to provide universal education or improve the standard of education offered. The private sector should be encouraged to take a significant role in the field of education. Basic, higher-level as well as professional and technical education should be provided by privately managed institutions for efficiency and effectiveness. Governments should provide and control only the essential operating parameters of the private education and training institutions and should leave operations to the private sector. Associations, CCIs, and large business groups should be required by the government to establish technical training institutions in their respective business sectors.

4. CONCLUSION

In spite of enormous physical and human resources, the South Asian region has economically suffered too much for too long because of the negative orientation, ignorance, and follies of the political leaders. During the last three decades, while other economic regional blocks have made tremendous progress in their socioeconomic development, the South Asian countries have miserably lagged behind.

The political and trade leadership of South Asia urgently need to realize that war or confrontation is not an option and that the only way to progress and prosper is through peaceful coexistence. If the United States could allow MFN status to China (its archenemy for five decades), and if Russia and the United States (with their long-standing conflicts in social, political, and economic fields) could become allies, what is restraining the countries of South Asia from economic integration? If the European nations, having a past full of tensions and conflicts, can emerge as the most powerful economic block in the world, South Asia , too, could form a vibrant and useful economic arrangement. For the South Asian region to become economically integrated, India and Pakistan (being the larger countries and nuclear powers) have a responsibility to take the lead for transforming the region into an economic block worthy of its physical and human potential. Given the required political will and active support of the private sector, this expectation can soon be realized.

NOTES

1. Globalization is rapidly encompassing the entire world. Corporate entities, production, distribution, and procurement systems are being globalized to take advantage of economic volumes and comparative and competitive advantage. Small and stand-alone business units will find it extremely difficult to survive and prosper against the gigantic economic strength of the multinational corporate conglomerates. From a global perspective, the private business enterprises in the South Asian Countries are of small and medium size. Long-term survival and growth of such enterprises lies in becoming a link in the supply chain of multinational organizations. To qualify for the global value chain linkage, these private business units will have to fulfill the WTO requirements for quantity, environment, human relations, and ethics.
2. Key socioeconomic decisions in South Asia region countries are made by the top officials of the bureaucracy and the armed forces, which are based on considerations of self-preservation and promotion rather than the considerations of national or regional economic development. For example, in Pakistan, less than 6 percent of the annual federal budget is allocated to factors that contribute to economic development, such as education, maintenance of law, order and security, research and development, communications, and health. Moreover, 90 percent of this meager budgetary allocation is spent on administrative costs. On the other hand, more than 22 percent is spent on the armed forces and 30 percent on debt servicing against 10 percent and 15 percent, respectively, by Malaysia, resulting in marked economic development differences of the two countries.

APPENDIX 14.1

TABLE A14.1 Major Items of Exports and Imports of SAARC Countries, 2002
(items comprising 75% of trade value)

Country	Major export items	Major import item
Bangladesh	Jute and Jute Products, Tea, Ready-made Garments, Frozen Fish, and Shrimps, Seafood (US$5 billion or 75%) Leather and Leather Goods, Fertilizer, Spices, Vegetables, Manpower.	Petroleum (Crude), Official Equipments, Plant, and Machinery, Automobile, Construction Materials, Dyestuffs Chemicals, Ferrous and Nonferrous Metals, Minerals, Iron and Steel (US$6 billion or 75%) Textile, Edible Oil, Milk Products, Raw Cotton, Cement, etc.
Bhutan	Timber, Dolomite, Spices, Calcium Carbide, Gypsum, Electricity, Cement, Fresh and Canned Fruits and Juices, Alcoholic Beverage (US$80 million or 75%) Cardamom, Timber Products, Minerals.	Petroleum Products, Machinery, Iron and Steel, Automobile, Textiles, Agriculture equipments. Consumer Goods (US$120 million or 75%), Sugar, Edible Oil, Rubber, Tires, Wheat.
India	Software, Pearls, Jewelry and precious stones, Pharmaceuticals, Machinery, Vehicles, Metal Products, Tea Mate, Clothing, Iron Ore and Steel, Films (US$42 billion or 75%) Cotton Products, Petroleum, Handicrafts, Leather and Products.	Crude Petroleum Products, Machinery, Pearls, Precious and Semi-precious Stones, Chemical Products, Edible Oils, Vegetables and Fruits, Food Stuff (US$43.5 billion, 75%) Vehicles, Fertilizers, Rock Salt, Cotton, Sugar, Ceramics and Melamine.
Maldives	Dried Skipjack, Canned Fish, Frozen Skipjack, Shark Liver Oil, Salted Dried Skipjack and Reef Fish, Apparel and Clothing Accessories (US$67 million or 75%), Red Coral, Cowries Shells and Mica.	Consumer Goods, Petroleum and Food Items, Manufactured Goods, Machinery, Vehicles, Chemicals, Steel, Rice, Cement (US$292 million or 75%) Wheat, Sugar, Tobacco, Beverages, Paper.
Nepal	Cotton Garments, Woolen Goods and Carpets, Oil Seeds, Pulses, Hides and Skin, Niger Seeds, Jute and Jute Products, Handicrafts, Tea, Leather Goods, Paper and Paper Products (US$440 million or 75%), Silverware and Jewelry, Tooth Paste, Polyester Yarn, Toilet Soap, Pashmina Pro-ducts, Vegetable Ghee.	Food and Live Animals, Chemicals and Drugs, Manufactured Articles, Construction Materials, Petroleum, Oil and Lubricants, Raw Wool, Automobiles and Transport Equipments, Machinery, Fertilizer, Textiles, Edible Oil (US$1.07 billion or 75%) Cement, Electrical Goods, Industrial Raw Material.

(Table A14.1 Continued)

(Table A14.1 Continued)

Country	Major export items	Major import item
Pakistan	Raw Cotton, Textiles, Cotton Cloth, Cotton Yarn, Synthetic Textiles, Garments, Hosiery Rice (US$7.1 billion 75%) Carpets and Rugs, Leather, Leather Products including Leather Garments and Footwear, Ceramic, and Fish and Fish Products.	Petroleum and its Products, Chemicals, Nonelectrical Equipments, Machinery, Transport Equipments, Iron and Steel Products (US$7.6 billion or 75%) Edible Oils, Electrical Goods, Fertilizers, Tea.
Sri Lanka	Tea, Rubber, Gems, Marine Foods, Semi Precious Stones, Coconut Oil and Coconut Products (US$3.6 billion or 75%), Readymade Garments.	Machinery, Petroleum, Chemicals, Pharmaceuticals, Iron and Steel, Vehicles, Textiles, Dairy Products, Fertilizers (US$4.7 billion or 75%), Pulp and Paper Products, Sugar.

Source   Compiled by author.

FIGURE A14.1   South Asian Trade Integration Framework Benchmarked to the European Union

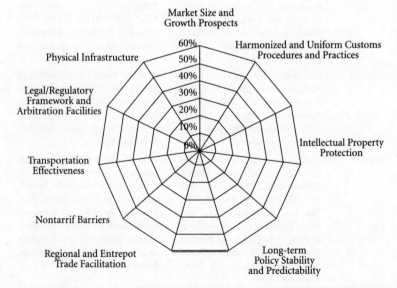

Source   Author.

FIGURE A14.2   **South Asian Investments Integration Framework Benchmarked to the European Union**

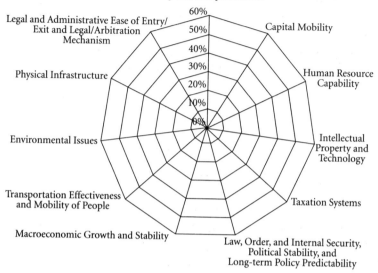

Source Author.

FIGURE A14.3   **South Asian Regional Governance Framework Benchmarked to the European Union**

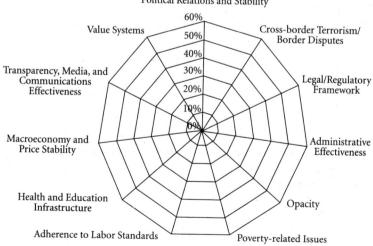

Source Author.

15

Regional Cooperation in South Asia

Sri Lanka Perspective

Chandra Jayaratne

1. BACKGROUND

For the past decade, South Asia has been the second fastest-growing region in the world, after East Asia, with an average annual growth rate of 5.3 percent. Yet it remains one of the poorest regions. Forty-five percent of the population lives below the international poverty line of US$1 a day, comprising about 40 percent of the world's poor. South Asia's extremely poor reduced by only 14 million between 1990 and 2002 and in the best case and worst case scenarios the extremely poor in South Asia in 2015 is estimated to reach 140 million and 327 million, respectively, compared with 434 million in 2002 (ADB 2004).

Countries in the South Asian region have emphasized the need for greater regional integration in areas related to trade and investment. The private sectors of all South Asian nations, at the level of chambers of commerce, appear to have a consensus that a greater flow of goods and services and investment resources between countries in the region will accelerate growth, reduce poverty, and enhance competitiveness.

However, individual member groups of the private sector and product associations express significantly different views.

The regional integration initiatives commenced with the formation of the South Asian Association of Regional Cooperation (SAARC). The most recent 12th Summit of the leaders of SAARC held in Islamabad led to a commitment for further regional integration initiatives. However, regional integration has been slow. South Asia has lagged behind other regions in enacting essential investment climate reforms. India was among the 10 top reformers in 2003, yet it remains in the bottom quartile in rank among 145 countries. In South Asian countries, it takes nine procedures, 45 percent of income per capita, and 47 days to start a business, whereas in the industrial nations the comparatives are six procedures, 8 percent, and 27 days, respectively (World Bank 2005). Intraregional trade has remained stagnant at less than 2 percent of total trade in the last 25 years. Slow integration is not only true of trade but also in other areas of co-operation. For example, the South Asia Co-operative Environment Programme (SACEP) established in 1982 has been largely ineffective in promoting environmental protection and management.

The private sectors of all South Asian nations recognize that political, economic, and implementation capacity; social, cultural, and other similar factors; business environment, including country risk ratings for trade and investments; and global perceptions have a significant impact on regional integration-led trade, investments, and growth.

2. PRIVATE SECTOR EXPECTATIONS FROM REGIONAL INTEGRATION

The private sector believes that the right political, economic, and social policy framework, and accompanying governance framework, can lead to political stability, peace and harmony, networking for economic growth, poverty alleviation, and improved living standards. This, in turn, will enhance regional integration, including cross-border trade and investment opportunities, yielding growth options for the private sectors of the region. In light of the above, the Sri Lankan private sector has set the following expectations as the outcome of regional integration initiatives:

- From low intraregional trading and investments to a set of nations that optimize intraregional cooperation.

- From a set of nations that do not effectively cooperate and network, seeking to improve global competitiveness in trade (goods and services) to a region that effectively integrates and cooperates in penetrating global trading market opportunities.
- From business entities domestically competing at the firm level supported by fragmented chambers of commerce, to regional resource allocation optimization focused on global competitiveness and seeking a regional integration strategy that leverages chambers of commerce, *think(s) beyond boundaries*, and drives production and services initiatives toward the value added export of goods and services.
- From low-quality, low-productivity, low-technology leveraging production systems, with low costs as the only competitive advantage, to a set of nations that benchmark China for productivity, quality, and technology.
- From a set of nations with high unemployment and low human development indexes to a high people-engaged, high human development-oriented region.
- From shortages of food supplies and resources and at times a famine-affected region, to a self-sufficient resource-rich, food security assured region.
- From weak macro economies to sustainable surplus-yielding economies, continuously accelerating the pace of transformation and structural reforms.
- From a set of nations with low indexation in achievement of millennium development goals, to full realization of such goals.
- From a low level of per capita income and large disparity in incomes and wealth among citizens, to a prosperous region with all citizens enjoying an acceptable standard of living, education, and health, registering more than US$3,000 per capita by the year 2020 with a low Gini coefficient, where less than 10 percent of the population is below the poverty line and thus the most admired, advanced, and fastest-developing region of the world.

The private sector in Sri Lanka sees definite benefits of regional integration in enhancing cross-border trade and investments and recognizes value enhancement for the private sector and growth for the nation. Integration has been in the forefront of making submissions, leading the way with action strategies and pressurizing the Sri Lankan government and officials to seek greater integration and achieve the stated expectations.

The Sri Lankan chambers of commerce have linked up with local embassies of regional nations, visiting officials, and business delegations from these countries, and have networked with regional chambers of commerce and trade (for example, Indian and Pakistan Chambers of Commerce, especially the Confederation of Indian Industry [CII] and the Federation of Indian Chambers of Commerce and Industry [FICCI]). The Sri Lankan private sector has canvassed publicly and actively worked toward regional integration and, pending such integration, has actively promoted cross-border trade and investments among its membership. The SCII has failed to realize the leadership role expected to support network development and promote trade and investments.

3. ISSUES AFFECTING EFFECTIVE REGIONAL INTEGRATION AND REGIONAL INTEGRATION-LED GROWTH AND DEVELOPMENT

A variety of issues have prevented effective regional integration and have prevented South Asian nations from more rapid development and benefitting from cross-border and global trade and investments.

3.1 Political Disputes, Mistrust, and Tension

Disputes, mistrust, and tension have affected development in the following ways:

- Despite many agreements and conventions executed at the leadership level, regional leaders have low commitment and political will, and lack a common binding value system.
- The disparity in size (that is, area) among nations of South Asia has led to mistrust and tension, with India a towering neighbor seen as a constant hegemonic threat.
- Private sector business leaders share a common belief that the Indian bureaucracy will not permit any integration, unless their own dominance in decision making is preserved.
- Some of the nations being established are separated by wars.
- Cross-border terrorism, internal conflict, and strife are compounded by perceptions of support for troublesome elements coming from neighboring countries.

- Diversity and divisiveness exists among and within countries in ethnicity, caste systems, religious, social, and cultural dimensions.
- Leaders leverage the above issues to win votes and elections and in the process create prejudices and hatred among ethnic, religious, and other groups.

3.2 Economic Conditions

The following economic conditions have affected development:

- Disparity in the state of economic development.
- Macroeconomic instability.
- A low level of infrastructure development, poor transportation, and transhipment facilities.
- Competing economies for the same resource pools and markets and the consequential rivalry.
- Failures in economic integration initiatives among South Asian nations, including ineffective implementation of SAARC and South Asian Free Trade Agreement (SAFTA) commitments.
- Competition with other regional economic groupings like Indian Ocean Rim Countries, the Bay of Bengal Initiative for Multi-Sectoral Technical and Economic Cooperation (BIMSTEC), and bilateral trade and investment agreements diluting SAARC implementation.

3.3 Policy and Regulatory Deficiencies

The following policy and regulatory deficiencies have affected development:

- Short-term and unpredictable policies and regulatory frameworks resulting partly from unstable political structures; South Asian nations need clear, consistent, long-term applicable policies on trade and investments.
- Protective barriers (established by politically powerful network business groups) affecting cross-border trade and investments (that is, both tariff and nontariff barriers); protectionist-based inflexible tariff regimes and nontariff barriers prevailing among member nations, despite SAFTA initiatives and other bilateral trade agreements.

- Weak and ineffective regulatory and enforcement mechanisms.
- A lack of many elements of the essential framework for attracting investment (for example, intellectual property protection and arbitration mechanisms).
- A shortage of investment capital with regulatory, legal, and administrative issues negatively affecting capital mobility and the ease of entry and exit.

3.4 Lack of a Common Position, and Uniform Rules and Practices

The following disparities among position, rules, and practices have affected development:

- The lack of an agreed regional position in international forums (for example, World Trade Organization [WTO], World Intellectual Property Organization [WIPO]), leading to an ineffective bargaining capacity in these forums.
- Conflicting focus of nations, with some preferring individually negotiated bilateral trade and investment regimes in preference to regional initiatives.
- Nonuniform taxation systems, customs rules and practices, administrative inefficiencies, and ineffective application of incentive regimes.
- Complex and nontransparent rules and regulations, standards, procedures, and documentation.

3.5 Low Implementation Capability

Low implementation capability has affected development in the following ways:

- Low efficiency and effectiveness of policy implementation and project management.
- Low capability of the public sector.

3.6 Other Factors

The following other factors have affected development:

- A lack of recognition in the United States and Europe of the SAARC as a region for trade and investment opportunities.
- Difficulties of regional travel, transportation and human resource mobility, and travel-related barriers.
- Law, order, and internal security concerns.
- The lack of a binding value system to build pillars of integration, in the wake of diversity and the lack of nationalistic feeling and a commitment to regionalism with some elements openly opposing regionalism.
- Ineffective media and communications.
- A lack of initiatives to optimize on regional natural resources and capability, including unique social, religious, cultural, environmental, and eco treasures.
- Low effectiveness of multilateral agencies in getting individual nations to achieve commitments and address macroeconomic, social, poverty alleviation, and development goals, and a lack of focused support for regional integration within programs and initiatives of these institutions.

4. THE WAY FORWARD

4.1 Political Leadership Initiatives

The following leadership initiatives should be taken:

- Following a Summit, leaders of all nations in the grouping (especially India and Pakistan) should agree to a way forward for implementation with commitment to address the bilateral political issues, border disputes, cross-border terrorism and trade in arms, drugs, and human trafficking issues. These issues should be negotiated and resolved with commitment under an internationally mediated support framework that is facilitated through a special joint initiative of the SAARC Secretariat and the Commonwealth Secretariat, symbolically given leadership by Nelson Mandela and Lee Kuan Yew, with the Secretary General of the Common Wealth Secretariat acting as the Convenor.
- The leaders of the SAARC should recognize that the previous commitment to establish a South Asian Economic Union by 2010 will not be a reality. Leaders should then agree that regional integration

could be achieved by 2020, to match the political, economic, social, and other integration benchmarks of the European Union. The benchmark assessments should target the respective drivers of integration embedded in the European Union, and for this purpose, current benchmark webs of the region as a whole and each member country in the areas of governance, trade, and investments should be mapped and reassessed twice a year and placed before the meetings of the heads of state and prime ministers.[1]

- The SAARC Secretariat should arrange separate annual meetings, alternating in each member nation, in which the heads of state, deputy heads of state/prime ministers, and leaders of opposition; foreign ministers, finance ministers, trade, commerce, industry, and science and technology ministers; health, education, employment, and environment ministers; and respective shadow ministers compulsorily devote some time for a retreat, where network relationships are developed, progress on previously agreed action programs is assessed, and additional commitments required are determined.

4.2 Strategic Analysis and Review

The following analyses and reviews should be made:

- The SAARC Secretariat, supported by Consultants with expertise, should conduct an audit review and strategic analysis of all issues that have affected the effective implementation of SAFTA, especially nontariff barriers and inefficient and ineffective national facilitation initiatives. This review should lead to an agreed-upon strategy to be implemented in stages, with a regular half-yearly post-audit process to support the implementation framework.[2] This initiative may be broadened in scope to include an agreed-upon time frame for the liberalization of services, including personal and professional services as well.

- The SCCI, facilitated by the SAARC Secretariat, should develop a set of proposals for a reform agenda and regional action program to make the region an attractive investment destination globally. This should build on a review of the Global Competitiveness Report, comparative regional competitiveness, and business studies.

- Retired and senior public officials (ministry secretaries, service commanders, Central Bank governors, and research scientists) should establish a think tank under the Regional Strategic Review Council framework to develop policy papers and act as consultants and advisors for the implementation of regional initiatives of the SAARC Secretariat.

4.3 Harmonization of Policies, Standards, and Procedures

The following action should be taken to harmonize policies, standards, and procedures:

- Ensure that a group of experts agrees on the global conventions and practices that should be adopted regionally for achievement of the objectives of SAARC, and also on the harmonization of national policies, treaties, and agreements that optimize regional integration-led value enhancement (for example, anti-money laundering, intellectual property protection, investment protection, and so on) and to the harmonization of commercial, arbitration, and regulatory structures.
- Ensure standardization, simplification, and streamlining of trade, investment, registration, customs, and other impacting administrative procedures across the region, to reduce service delivery time and transaction costs and to encourage trade and investments; establish a Union Integration Customs group, tasked with the responsibility of facilitation, removal of barriers, harmonization, standardization, and administration of the rules of origin.
- Pursue trade facilitation initiatives, expediting border crossings and quick customs clearances.
- Encouraging intraregional trade through the maintenance of regional customs bonds, efficient port facilities, and improved transport links.
- Implement the commitments to establish a SAARC Regional Standards Board.

4.4 Education, Training, and Skills Development

Recognizing that one of the most important resources in the region is its people, all countries together and individually should pursue the following education, training, and skills development:

- Network with the private sector and agree to a strategy for the region to have required skills by 2010 to be globally competitive and attract investments and outsourcing opportunities (special emphasis on English, IT, science, and technology).
- Provide training and development needs to citizens to leverage overseas skilled job opportunities and meet the skill development needs of returning overseas employed, unskilled laborers.

4.5 Banking and Finance

The following banking and finance initiatives should be taken:

- Establish a closer network among the Central Banks of the region to expedite structural reforms, gradually remove capital controls, and ensure price stability (exchange rates, interest rates, and inflation).
- Negotiate a line of support from the International Monetary Fund (IMF) for South Asian nations to drawdown in defending currency under agreed-upon contingencies, and each member country should contribute 10 percent of the expatriate worker remittances (estimated at US$20 billion) to this foreign exchange reserve fund and invest such funds in bonds tracking returns linked to petroleum prices.
- Remove present restrictions on intraregional capital market transactions as a first step toward establishing a regional stock exchange for capital mobilization and enhanced foreign direct investments in the region.
- Enhance the efficiency and effectiveness of the Asian Clearing Union processes, eliminating the long delays experienced at present, and terminate failing arrangements; abandon South Asian common currency (SAEURO) initiatives for the present.
- Facilitate early adoption by all South Asian countries of the International Accounting Standards, improving the integration of financial information and facilitation of regional stock market transactions and a common listing process (leveraging the South Asian Federation of Accountants).

4.6 Development Funds

The following actions should be taken to improve development funds:

- Establish a regional fund for price support and technology transfer support during the period of adjustment (related to trade liberalization) to help small farmers and small and medium enterprises (SMEs) improve competitiveness (this fund may be established with the help of the multilateral agencies).
- Obtain a commitment among the nations of South Asia to contribute annually to a South Asian Resource Development Fund (operated as a Regional Development Bank under the aegis of the World Bank and supported by all multilateral agencies), an agreed-upon percentage of the gross domestic product (GDP) of the prior year, based on the principle of capacity to pay, with the Fund objectives being to support the South Asian nations' regional integration-led growth and development.

4.7 Transportation and Communication Linkages

The following actions should be taken to enhance transportation and communication linkages:

- Research and develop the most cost-effective regional transport and transhipment options (including rail, ferry, and road) and strategies, benchmarked with the best advantaged global hub centers.
- Apply open skies and competitive shipping liberalization policies across the region.

4.8 Information Technology

The following action should be taken to ensure connectivity across the region:

- Significantly leverage ICT on a regional basis, leveraging the high strides achieved by India in e-governance, e-education and training, e-driven back offices and call centers, and the associated capabilities and skills development of human resources.
- Establish a regional intranet for all government and private sector trade and contract opportunities in all South Asian nations and post all cross-border employment resource opportunities (both available and wanted).
- Support the regional integration-led growth and development by extending the World Bank-supported Global Information Gateway

project in Sri Lanka to become a single gateway link for information, technology and best practice transfers and knowledge sharing, and trade and investment facilitation and networking with the diaspora around the world.

- Encourage the International Trade Centre (ITC) to make available specific South Asian market analysis tools, including Trade Map and Product Map facilities, and encourage the SCCI to facilitate regional chambers to leverage access via a centralized server.

4.9 Research, Development, and Innovation

The following research, development, and innovation initiatives should be taken:

- Develop a structure for technology and intellectual property-related value options to be acquired by a central source and made available to business entities on rental terms, thus optimizing the collective resource acquisition advantages, as practiced in China.
- Establish a center for research, commercial exploitation, sustainable growth, extraction, and promotion of medicinal and herbal plants, spices, and allied plants of value in western markets, including traditional and herbal teas.
- Develop Ayurveda through research, education, and training to become the foremost natural medicinal practice recognized in the world and leverage global competitive advantages.

4.10 Energy, Natural Resources, and Environment

The following energy, natural resources, and environment initiatives should be pursued:

- Develop regional joint initiatives to exploit the region's resources of the sea, natural gas, and oil both on shore and off shore on a sustainable basis with care for the environment.
- Make South Asian Energy Cooperation initiatives a priority of regional integration, as energy availability and costs are a key impacting factor of competitiveness, and optimize all options of least cost production of electricity using the hydropower potential of some nations, the alternate energy potential of the region (solar, dendro, wind, and sea waves), and integrated coal and nuclear plants.

- Actively pursue the SAARC Energy Grid proposal with regional buyback arrangements; closely network with the U.S.-funded South Asian Regional Initiative for Energy Cooperation and development.
- Encourage the SAARC and SACEP to agree on a common action program to be implemented with commitment in ensuring regional environmental protection and effective management, and implement this program with commitment (special attention to be focused on water management).

4.11 Judicial Reforms and Governance

The following measures should be taken to encourage judicial reforms and improve governance:

- Establish a Regional Judicial and Good Governance framework linked to the International Court of Justice and Transparency International, whereby:
  - mediation and settlement of disputes and complaints arising from SAARC trade, investment, and political integration initiatives are resolved by the nations collectively;
  - a judicial system reviews regional constitutional issues affecting the regional integration effectiveness, serious internal conflict, and related national legal issues;
  - a regional bribery and corruption control initiative is pursued;
  - a regional audit and control system guides and arbitrates on national audit and governance effectiveness; and
  - a regional commercial arbitration and dispute settlement system is in place.

- Establish a regional Institute of Directors affiliated with the SCCI to facilitate the management of talent development, effective networking, and commitment to the enforcement of good governance codes of practice.
- Promote a regional university to become a center of excellence for regional development and integration relations studies, public administration, management and good governance education, training, and research with a specific emphasis on capacity building in the public sector.

- Encourage Transparency International to set up a regional center and focus attention on promoting good governance and control of bribery and corruption.
- Establish a regional media complaints and media freedom assurance council.
- Establish the monitoring of regional elections and a control support system.

4.12 Liberalization of Travel-related Regulations

The following travel-related regulations should be liberalized:

- Support regional integration initiatives and cross-border movement of people by withdrawing visa requirements for travel among South Asian countries by their respective citizens.
- Extend to all visitors to the region the benefit of applying for a South Asian Union visa via any visa-issuing South Asian embassy over-seas; as a first step, negotiate and remove the strict controls now applied to travel between India and Pakistan for their respective citizens.
- Allow settlement of hotel, entertainment, and hospital bills by residents of South Asian countries using local currency credit cards.

4.13 Tourism

The following action should be taken to encourage tourism in the region:

- Promote the South Asian region as a unique high-value experience option, offering ecotourism destinations; for this purpose, levy an additional tax from every tourist, and channel the receipts via the Regional Development Fund for tourism promotion.
- Exploit the potential of care services-related business options targeting the rich, elderly, and aged citizens from the Western Hemisphere.
- Network regional airlines and the travel/tourism trade to encourage intraregional tourism, form alliances among national carriers, and create SAARC hotel pass systems and incentive programs; target the region as an attractive destination for conventions and meetings.

- Establish links among regional nations, historical, cultural, and leisure/sports bodies; develop a value option for the world and tourists of a unique presentation of the region's history, culture, leisure, and sporting activities; and develop a SAARC cultural troupe in each nation.

4.15 Cultural and Social Aspects

The following cultural and social initiatives should be taken:

- Establish a South Asian regional television channel to promote regional integration, positive and value adding news, competitiveness enhancing skills and knowledge dissemination, education, and preventive health care promotion; seek the promotion of a "South Asian Value System."
- Establish in each nation a peace, conflict resolution, interracial-interreligious dialogue, compassion, and mindfulness development centers, with a network coordination center, to become the global leader in extending research and promoting the spread of Buddhism, Hinduism, Muslim, and allied faiths.
- Initiate a high-level composite task force to implement the SAARC Social Charter with specific reference to children, women, and gender issues.
- Convene a group of experts to determine the best strategy for sustainable population control measures that will not be rejected regionally if implemented, because of religious or cultural value systems, while ensuring a productive workforce for regional competitiveness.
- Encourage, communicate, and build on the value system of voluntary giving to the poor and deserving, in a spirit of caring and sharing, with the deep affiliation to religious values in the people of South Asia, acknowledging that each of the major religions encourage these values (*Dana* in Buddhism, *Sadhana* in Hinduism, *Sakath* in Islam, and Charity in Christianity).
- Target a regional integration strategy for supportive value system development, especially focusing on the young and on women, and initiate regional contests of talent, sports, culture, and art.
- Prioritize poverty alleviation as the regional Millennium Development Goal commitment through a regional task force initiated by

the SAARC Secretariat, with representation by the prime ministers and a key minister alternate, key officials, the SCII, and nongovernmental organizations (NGOs), along with multilateral and other donor agencies, coordinating the adoption and implementation of pro-poor growth strategies and policy interventions and resource pooling; optimize cost benefits from initiatives across the region, with specific reference to the implementation of the suggestions made in the Independent South Asian Commission on Poverty Alleviation's report *Our Future Our Responsibility*.

4.16 Global Competitiveness

Global competitiveness should be enhanced as follows:

- Establish a Regional Competitiveness Council that will track and facilitate the removal of barriers to competitiveness and also lead the initiative in *(a)* determining the global competitiveness by enhancing best resource allocation among the nations of the region in export trade; *(b)* developing market access information databases and promotional strategies; and *(c)* determining the nations and the states with the optimum competitiveness in resource sourcing, processing, value addition, packaging, and transhipment so that countries can plug into relevant parts of the global supply chain.
- Develop competitiveness-related quality and productivity benchmarks to match China (by 2010).
- Attract foreign investments and encourage trade by developing and publicizing long-term sustainable and predictable macroeconomic, employment, investment, and trade policies and associated incentive packages for the region and each nation, and embody such policies within legislative and regulatory structures.
- Focus special attention on shared services for the region as a whole as a part of the competitiveness initiative.
- Benchmark Japanese skilled workers and work practices with the facilitation of multi-lateral agencies established in each nation, centers that transfer best practices, and values that enhance skills, productivity, and quality.
- Agree to minimum benchmarks for environmental health and safety standards complying with international labor standards.

4.17 Other Initiatives

Other initiatives to pursue are as follows:

- Promote and regionally commit to the concept of a "South Asian Inc.," as a way of life, regional integration, leadership focus, international investment and trade, tourism promotion, and vertical and horizontal coordination of initiatives, to enhance productivity and minimize resource waste.
- Position South Asia as a market with a middle class the size of the population of the United States, rich in historical, cultural, and spiritual values and ecofriendly, as well as rich in diversity experiences, where the mobilized capability of people match the best in the world.
- Better focus, coordinate, and enrich the experiences and capabilities of regional community-based development entities and microfinance initiatives by a collective network of regional initiatives for value chain enhancement.
- Arrange a well-coordinated economic and social research network with other NGOs and multilateral agencies.

5. AREAS OF CAUTION WITH REGIONAL INTEGRATION INITIATIVES

It is important that regional leaders and officials are accountable for integration initiatives. Several areas of caution must be effectively managed in order to ensure optimum benefits and to meet these integration goals. These areas include the following:

- Recognize that multilateral trade initiatives as opposed to regional trade initiatives have yielded higher sustainable economic growth rates. The importance of western markets to a majority of South Asian nations underscores the fact that more liberal trade practices as a whole must be given due priority, even if a drive for regionalism is adopted as the focus strategy. Therefore leaders must ensure that regional integration initiatives are not a stumbling block but rather a building block toward effective rule-based multilateral trading systems.

- Encourage the SAARC Secretariat to set up panels of experts to regularly meet and review the risks associated with the regional initiatives, with specific reference to those areas that have greater national and other sensitivities, balancing the rights and privileges of the bigger nations with those of the smaller and economically weaker nations.
- Encourage fair and quick dispute resolution by independent panels, which will be necessary to ensure top priority to the principles of the SAARC, encompassing Sovereign Equality, Territorial Integrity, Political Independence, and Noninterference in Internal Affairs of other states and to the mutual benefit of the region.
- Recognize that for a free trade area to be *trade creating and welfare improving*, members of such a union must be least cost producers of exportables.
- Consider the impact of presently concluded bilateral trade agreements and Most Favored Nation status concessions available to some countries from the key western investment and trade partners.
- Ensure that the landlocked and least developed member nations of South Asia are dealt with on an inclusive basis in all union integration negotiations and are seen by all to have received an equitable sharing of resources with due care and concern.
- Ensure that regional shared manufacturing and services initiatives do not result in a loss of competitiveness out of economies of scale, and support production in the least cost-producing quality-assuring set of nations, as referred to by Michael Porter in his theory of comparative advantages of nations.
- Acknowledge that most South Asian economies have traditionally been agrarian based, with states adopting protectionist policies on agricultural produce. The dominance of agricultural products in regional economic output, competing at most times, reduces the comparative advantages of exportables for each state.
- Understand that the majority of the population and voters living in rural areas are engaged in agriculture and small and microindustries; that these populations comprise the majority of those affected by poverty, lack of education, low skills, access to technology and markets, and poor health and other infrastructure; and that they may find regional integration-led reforms with long-term economic and social benefits not to be acceptable options.
- Prepare for the fact that regional integration-led reforms may lead to the emergence of new groups of extremists focusing on nationalism,

religious, and other discrimination complaints and they may hold
back the strategy for implementation.

- Address the negative impact on rural poor, small farmers and SMEs
  to prevent the integration process itself from being rejected.
- Recognize that improved human resource mobility and cross-border
  movements may increase the dangers of the spread of AIDS and
  other communicable diseases.
- Acknowledge that the market economy model with taxation as the
  means to ensure equitable distribution of wealth in the region may
  be unacceptable within a time frame expected by the poor.
- Select the leadership of the SAARC Secretariat, SCCI, and other regional bodies and task forces only on meritocracy criteria to ensure
  that only the best suited persons fill the positions.
- Manage the risk of the regional integration strategies being rejected
  by small peer groups by carefully positioning institutionally well-
  planned and timely national referendum processes.

5.1 Role of the Private Sector in Regional Integration-led Growth and Development

The private sector must be a key committed partner in the process of regional integration-led growth and development initiatives, recognizing
that political and bureaucratic stumbling blocks need to be overcome to
reach the established goals. The following initiatives should be taken by
the private sector:

- Establish a binding network commitment facilitated by national
  chambers of commerce and industry, effectively linking up, benefiting from, and discharging obligations via facilities integrated
  through the SCCI.
- Establish well-represented task forces to commit and agree to strategies and implementation follow-up, toward SCCI becoming the
  voice of business of the region, nationally, regionally, and globally,
  and encouraging economic cooperation, investments, and trade
  based on regional value enhancement (with a special emphasis on
  global market opportunities to promote regional capability).
- Set up a regional initiative as a networked task force for the em-
  powered promotion and removal of roadblocks to optimize regional
  trade and investment (intraregional as well as global) and develop
  strategies to promote trade and investments. The long-term value-
  realizing strategy should optimize global and intraregional trade

via free trade agreements, with regional trade agreements to be determined in the context of current country commitments and WTO implementations.

• Set up a regional initiative of employee relations via a special task force, which will handle all social charter issues relevant to employment and compliance with International Labour Organization (ILO) standards.

• Set up three task forces to support the achievement of the Millennium Development Goals and the promotion of good Corporate Governance and Corporate Social Responsibility across the region.

• Set up a chief executive officer round table, consisting of the top 20 companies of India, the top 10 of Pakistan, the top five of Sri Lanka and Bangladesh, and the top two companies of all other member nations, tasked with the responsibility of acting as an independent review and strategy development support group for the above initiatives, with the objective of realizing the vision of the South Asian business becoming the newly emerging, low-cost, quality-optimized, manufacturing and outsourcing partner hub of the advanced economies.

5.2 Role of the Multilateral Agencies in Regional Integration-led Growth and Development

Multilateral agencies have a significant influence over macroeconomic, social, and political structures, and good governance in individual nations of South Asia. A commitment toward regional integration and networking among the multilateral agencies with a focus toward achieving this key objective is a necessary prerequisite for growth and development. Multilateral agencies may be able to support this initiative by having a regional coordinating center led by a regional director. This director would provide leadership to the focus of regional integration in the respective country programs and ensure effective networking to achieve objectives.

5.3 Role of the Civil Society in Regional Integration-led Growth and Development

Civil society groups and NGOs must be encouraged and given incentives by the nations and multilaterals and other funding donors to work in tandem with regional programs. These organizations should coordinate and network to ensure that the focus of regional integration objectives is met. Through mass media, the charismatic leaders of South Asian nations must instill in the people of the region a regional commitment to growth and development, and at all times should leverage the agreed-upon value system as the core binding agent. Civil society must, through its effective voice and collective action, be the watchdog and independent assessor of progress in pursuing the reform and other processes in the respective nations.

6. CONCLUSION

The private sector's hopes for regional integration-led growth and development lie in farsighted visionary leadership of the region's nations. By effectively networking with all stakeholders, a united initiative can be pursued to achieve these goals with commitment. Toward reaching these goals, in addition to leadership commitment, there is an urgent need for the following:

- An implementation action plan for the agreed SAARC initiatives, with time targets and accountability to be developed.
- Networks and alliances strengthened between bureaucrats and chambers and the private sector.
- The enhancement of effective communication, positioning South Asia as the next wave of global trade investment and a travel option after China and Vietnam.

NOTES

1. Refer to the specimen spider-web assessment criteria for each area as shown in Appendix 14.1.
2. As a first step toward implementing this initiative of trade liberalization, remove by the end of 2004 (well before the next phase change of SAFTA trade liberalization-led tariff reductions became effective in 2006) the significantly high-impact quantitative restrictions on trade enforced by SAARC countries, and deepen the concessionary framework interim both in terms of trade coverage and level of concessions, giving priority to the respective producer country competitive advantages and complementary product ranges from the perspective of the exporting nations of the region.

Recognizing the current SAARC commitment to an Economic Union by 2010, review and revise with accountability, the phase 1 and phase 2 liberalizations presently aimed at reducing the tariff by 0 to 5 percent by January 2016 for the least developed countries.

REFERENCES

Asian Development Bank (ADB). 2004. *Poverty in Asia: Measurements, Estimates, and Prospects*. Manila: ADB.

DeRosa, D. A. 2007. "The Trade Effects and Preferential Agreements: New Evidence from the Australia Productivity Commission." Working Paper No. 07-01, Peterson Institute for International Economics, Washington, DC.

Independent South Asian Commission on Poverty Alleviation (ISACPA). 2002. *Our Future Our Responsibility*. Kathmandu: SAARC.

United Nations Conference on Trade and Development (UNCTAD). 2003. *Handbook of Statistics 2003*. Geneva: UNCTAD.

World Bank. 2004. *World Development Indicators 2004*. Washington, DC: World Bank.

———. 2005. *Doing Business in 2005*. Washington, DC: World Bank.

Part IV

The Political Economy
of Cooperation

16

Weaker Economies in SAFTA
Issues and Concerns

Mohammad A. Razzaque[1]

1. INTRODUCTION

The trade and welfare effects of regional trade arrangements (RTAs) are ambiguous. These effects depend on a number of factors, including inherent member characteristics, intraregional trade patterns before the formation of the trading bloc, member trade with the rest of the world, member trade regimes, and the design and implementation of RTA policies. Therefore, it is not true that preferential trading arrangements will always be trade creating or welfare enhancing on the whole. Furthermore, even when positive gains are achieved, their distribution among the members is unlikely to be equal, and the possibility of some members actually experiencing net adverse consequences cannot be ruled out *a priori*. In North–South RTAs, involving rich and poor countries, the latter tend to do well. However, when preferential trading blocs include low-income countries only, the poorest members tend to lose, resulting in greater divergence between the relatively advanced developing countries and weaker members.

In fact, countries that form an RTA are usually heterogeneous, as reflected in their *(a)* size in terms of geographic area and population as well as gross national output, *(b)* economic structure as manifested in the composition of goods and services produced and traded, and *(c)* policy intervention mechanisms in place by way of fiscal, financial, and trade-related measures, which influence domestic production and trading activities. These varied characteristics of the members greatly influence their gains from an RTA. Under the South Asian Free Trade Agreement (SAFTA), the member countries vividly portray their inherent dissimilarities and also point toward a somewhat uncomfortable scenario of unequal distribution of potential gains from the regional cooperation scheme. Although all the SAFTA members are low-income developing countries, four of them (that is, Bhutan, Bangladesh, Maldives, and Nepal) are among the least developed countries (LDCs) because of a number of overriding problems that constrain their economic growth and development.[2] Consequently, to what extent these relatively weaker economies can benefit from SAFTA constitutes an important question, which is the principal objective of this chapter.

This chapter is organized as follows: after this introduction, Section 2 briefly provides the theoretical perspectives on the situation of weaker members in an RTA involving low-income countries only; Section 3 provides some empirical evidence on the concerns of the poorest countries in SAFTA; Section 4 discusses a number of potential scopes of regional cooperation that can help weaker members gain and benefit; and Section 5 provides some concluding remarks.

2. POOREST MEMBERS IN SOUTH–SOUTH RTA: THEORETICAL INSIGHTS

The relative gains to individual member countries have attracted research and analyses, the results of which may be interpreted as providing worrying evidence of unequal distributional and adverse consequences for the weaker economies in an RTA. That is, in a regional integration scheme involving only the low-income countries (that is, South–South cooperation), the poorest member countries will lose.[3] This outcome is ingrained in comparative advantage of member countries relative to each other within the RTA and to the rest of the world as a whole.[4] Based on the theoretical premise, one example from South Asia will help explain this point. Consider the relative comparative advantages of Bangladesh and India in manufacturing production. Most people would think that India has a comparative advantage relative to Bangladesh, but not relative to the world. Under SAFTA, given this comparative advantage, India will export manufactured goods to Bangladesh, and, as such, tariff preferences exchanged within the trading bloc are likely to result in trade diversion for Bangladesh, because some of the previously manufactured goods imported from the world will be replaced by supplies from India. For India, however, gains are achieved from being able to supply goods and services to the Bangladesh market, protected from competition with the rest of the world.

Bangladesh, as an unskilled labor-abundant country, has a comparative advantage in such labor-intensive items as readymade garments (RMG), as reflected in its exports to the rest of the world. Many Bangladeshi exporters believe that Bangladesh also has comparative advantage in garment making relative to India. Therefore, the situation becomes such that India has a comparative advantage in manufacturing, in general, relative to Bangladesh and not to the rest of the world, whereas Bangladesh enjoys comparative advantage in RMG relative to both India and the rest of the world. Under a free trade area, Bangladesh's garment exports to India will be trade creating as the latter actually imports from the least cost supplier. For Bangladesh, however, trade diversion would be the outcome when Indian suppliers replace imports from the rest of the world.

The analysis of gains from trade under the multilateral liberalization is quite different from that under an RTA. In the case of multilateral trade negotiations, the primary source of gains from trade liberalization is the reduction of home tariffs. When it comes to RTAs, gains for a country primarily arise from a reduction in the partner countries' tariffs.[5] That is, the preferences to be received from partner countries become important under a regional arrangement, which is what mercantilists would want. This preference results from the tariff concessions offered to partner countries, which are like transfers of income (in terms of foregone tariff revenues). It is likely that an advanced developing SAFTA member country, such as India, would increase its exports to weaker economies once the regional preferences have been exchanged. The increase in the imports from partners amounts to trade diversion. In this example, while supplying countries within SAFTA gain by receiving a better price in their weaker partners' countries, the latter lose more than what the supplying countries gain. This loss can be attributed to the fact that the additional transfers from supplying countries (that is, the relatively advanced developing countries) are received by increasing exports, but the increased exports are more expensive compared with the imports they replace from the rest of the world.[6]

Two important factors determine the extent of trade diversions. Considering an extreme case, if all imports before the formation of the bloc are sourced from members within the RTA, there cannot be any trade diversion. However, when only a portion of imports is sourced from the relatively advanced RTA members, the scope of trade diversion can be quite substantial. This is particularly so if the union members have large supply-side capacities, thereby having the potential of replacing the rest of the world supplies in the aftermath of the formation of the trading bloc. Related to this, a fundamental determinant of making partners' exports more competitive (and thus the RTA trade diverting) is the trade regime maintained by the importing country. When import tariffs are high, partners' imports are better protected against the competition from the more efficient world suppliers, triggering trade diversion.

Another cause for concern arises from the fact that most countries are involved in more than one regional trading initiative, and hence trade and welfare effects are also dependent on the developments taking place in other trade blocs involving members of individual RTAs. When relatively advanced members engage in preferential trading with other countries, weaker members in the original RTA are likely to face increased competition in their partners' home markets. These weaker countries may find that the trade preferences are not provided to them exclusively but rather comparable preferences are available to the suppliers outside of their original bloc. In South–South RTAs, relatively advanced developing countries are generally more inclined to explore new markets, striking more regional arrangement deals, as they might want to maximize gains resulting from their superior supply-side capacities. The third country imports can penetrate into weaker economies taking advantage of the trade preferences granted by one or some of the original RTA members. These trade deflections can be welfare improving.[7] However, if the weaker economies choose to prevent such flows, they can take recourse to rules of origin or other restrictive provisions. In fact, members' involvement in more than one regional bloc can activate more complicated trade regimes and rules of origin procedures, often known as spaghetti bowls, which may have adverse implications for trade and investment flows, particularly for the weaker economies.

3. EVIDENCE ON THE POTENTIAL CONSEQUENCES FOR WEAKER ECONOMIES IN SAFTA

3.1 Qualitative Evaluation

Table 16.1 provides some of the basic economic indicators of SAFTA members. These countries differ remarkably in respect to their size and economic characteristics. In fact, they are so heterogeneous that drawing conclusion about their relative strengths based on some aggregate indicators alone might be misleading. For example, LDCs such as Bhutan and Maldives have per capita incomes greater than that of India, which is regarded as a much more advanced country not only in the region but also among other global developing economies.[8] Along with India, Pakistan and Bangladesh are countries with large populations that have debilitating effects on their per capita incomes. However, India's enormous supply-side capacity is reflected in the volume of its absolute exports. Pakistan is considered to be another relatively advanced developing country in the region with a per capita income comparable to that of India's. Conversely, with a population of about 20 million, Sri Lanka is a smaller developing country that has the third highest per capita income after Maldives and Bhutan.

Even within the set of LDCs, one can notice widely diverging characteristics. Bangladesh has by far the largest economy, but its per capita gross national income (GNI) is just one-sixth of Maldives and one-third of Bhutan. Nepal has the lowest per capita income in the region. Merchandise exports from Bangladesh and Nepal are dominated by manufactured items, largely because of textile and clothing products, while Bhutan and Maldives mostly rely on primary goods.[9] Dependence on exports from commercial services (primarily tourism) is unusually high for Maldives with its total trade (exports plus imports of goods and services) registering 182 percent of gross domestic product (GDP)—much higher than any other south Asian countries.[10] Despite these widely varying characteristics, there is consensus to consider the LDCs as the weaker economies among the group of countries, Sri Lanka as a smaller developing economy, and India and Pakistan as the relatively advanced developing countries. This has been reflected in various SAFTA provisions as well, in which LDCs have been given some special and differential treatment by allowing them longer time frames to reduce or eliminate tariffs, greater flexibility in the number of products not to be liberalized, favorable terms for the

TABLE 16.1 SAFTA Members: Basic Indicators

Countries	GDP volume (in current US$ billion)	Population	Land area (square kilometers)	Gross national income per capita (current US$)	Exports of goods and services (US$ billion)	Share of manufacturing in GDP (percent)	Trade as percent of GDP
Bangladesh[a]	61.9	156.0	130,170	450	12.9	17.2	44.2
Bhutan[a]	0.94	0.6	47,000	1,430	0.23	7.4	76.7
India	911.8	1,109.8	2,973,190	820	199.0	16.3	48.7
Maldives[a]	0.93	0.3	300	3,010	0.7	n.a.	182.1
Nepal[a]	8.9	27.6	143,000	320	1.2	7.7	45.2
Pakistan	126.8	159.0	770,880	800	20.5	19.5	38.6
Sri Lanka	27.0	19.9	64,630	1,310	8.5	13.9	74.7

Source Most figures come from World Bank 2006a.

Notes GDP = gross domestic product; n.a. = not applicable.
[a]Indicates a least developed country.

elimination of quantitative restrictions, and consideration of special terms when non-LDC members pursue antidumping and countervailing measures (Raihan 2007). Similarly, "less than full reciprocity" was a salient feature of the India–Sri Lanka Free Trade Agreement (ISFTA) under which Sri Lanka received significant concessions on the grounds of asymmetries in the two economies (Weerakoon and Thennakoon 2007).

As discussed above, the depth of intraregional trade and members' trade regimes are important in understanding the potential effects of RTAs on weaker economies, Figures 16.1 and 16.2 and Tables 16.2 and 16.3 provide some useful information. As the intraregional trade involving the SAFTA members is known to be quite low, Figure 16.1 shows that only in the case of Nepal such trade is significant. On average, the intraregional trade has hovered around 4 percent of SAFTA members' global trade for the past 50 years or so (Baysan et al. 2006), but for Nepal the corresponding figure is about 50 percent. Being a landlocked country, Nepal's primary trade is with India, resulting in a high significance of regional trade. Maldives and Sri Lanka also have sizeable proportions of regional trade—their ratio of trade with South Asian countries to the rest of the world is about 17 percent. For the three large countries (that is, Bangladesh, Pakistan, and India), the importance of intraregional trade is less prominent as the corresponding ratios are about 11, 6, and 3 percent, respectively.

The importance of intraregional trade is exhibited in Figure 16.1. The data are based on official statistics, which do not account for informal border trade, which is a remarkable feature of the trade involving the South Asian countries. Some studies and analysis suggest substantial

FIGURE 16.1   Share of Intraregional Trade to Total Trade in 2005

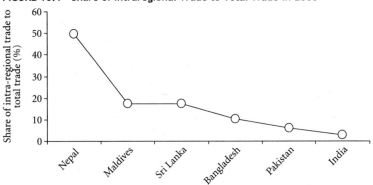

Source Based on the information provided in Sawhney and Kumar 2007.

magnitudes of informal trade with estimates of the ratio of informal to formal trade being 30 percent in the case of Indo–Sri Lankan bilateral trade, 103 percent between India and Nepal, and 138 percent between Bangladesh and India.[11] Such trade also exists between India and Bhutan, and India and Pakistan. Nevertheless, it is most sensible to conclude that weaker economies in South Asia rely more on the outside region for their international trade. Therefore the scope of trade diversion arises if, by taking the advantage of trade preferences, SAFTA members' exports replace more efficient supplies from outside the region.

In the above context, it is important to consider the growing significant of India as the source of imports for the individual weaker economies. Table 16.2 shows that between 2002 and 2006 imports from India into Maldives more than doubled and rose by a factor of three for Bangladesh; the corresponding Figures for Sri Lanka and Nepal are even higher (about 3.4).

Figure 16.2 shows that the share of India's total imports from Nepal rose rapidly from about 17 percent to more than 40 percent in about 3 years. In the cases of Bhutan, Sri Lanka, and Bangladesh the corresponding share has increased quite significantly as well. This growing significance of India as a source of imports in the region should not be a cause for concern. In fact, when these import flows take place under the Most Favored Nation (MFN) principle, they are potential sources of welfare gains. An important issue to be considered is whether, by taking advantage of regional tariff preferences, these imports are replacing the supplies originating outside the region. Bilateral free trade agreements (FTAs) involving India and Bhutan, India and Nepal, and India and Sri Lanka allow an exchange of tariff preferences to occur, although it is not known whether, and to what extent, these preferential arrangements have been trade diverting.

The overall insignificant level of intraregional trade seems to suggest a low probability of having the most efficient suppliers within the region, as observed by Baysan et al. (2006), which sets off the alarm of South Asian FTAs being trade diverting. In addition, by depicting the rapidly rising share of regionally sourced imports for the weaker economies, Figure 16.2 reinforces this concern. Even after implementing serious trade policy reforms, most South Asian countries still maintain considerable protective trade regimes, as evident in the simple average MFN tariff rates for such countries as Bangladesh, Bhutan, and Maldives (Table 16.3). If one goes beyond these simple average tariff rates, information provided in Table 16.3 would reveal that a large proportion of tariff lines attract duties

TABLE 16.2 Imports from India and the Rest of the World (US$ million)

Year	Bangladesh		Bhutan		Maldives		Nepal		Sri Lanka	
	Global imports	Imports from India	Global imports	Imports from India	Global imports	Imports from India	Global imports	Imports from India	Global imports	Imports from India
2002	8,592	1,002	196.5	7.6	391.7	26.8	1,419	250	6,105	630
2003	10,434	1,176	249.0	39	470.8	31.5	1,754	315	6,672	920
2004	12,036	1,740	411.0	89	641.8	42.3	1,870	669	7,973	1,319
2005	13,889	2,500	386.3	84	744.9	47.6	1,860	743	8,834	1,413
2006	16,086	2,990	320.0	99	926.5	67.5	2,100	859	10,258	2,024

Sources Author's compilation from World Bank *World Development Indicators* database (World Bank 2008) and Government of India sources.

382   Mohammad A. Razzaque

FIGURE 16.2   Significance of India in Sourcing Imports

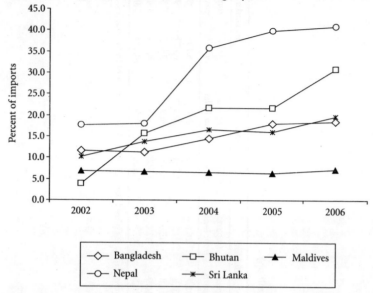

Source Author's estimates from the Direction of Trade Statistics of IMF, various years.

TABLE 16.3   Tariff Profiles of South Asian Countries

Countries	Simple average of MFN applied tariffs	Simple average applied tariffs in agriculture	Simple average applied tariffs in nonagricultural products	Share of duty-free tariff lines (% of tariff lines)	Share of tariff lines with duties more than 15 %	Maximum duty rate (MFN tariffs applied) (%)	Coefficient of variation (%)
Bangladesh	15.2	17.3	14.9	7.8	39.9	25	57
Bhutan	22.1	41.3	19.2	3.5	63.4	100	62
India	19.2	37.6	16.4	2.4	21.6	266	91
Maldives	20.2	18.4	20.5	0.1	59.5	200	62
Nepal	13.9	14.9	13.7	0.9	16.6	184	83
Pakistan	14.3	16.3	14.0	0	40.0	119	77
Sri Lanka	11.2	23.8	9.2	12.4	20.9	250	114

Source World Trade Organization 2007.
Note MFN = Most Favored Nation.

greater than 15 percent. Such lines constitute as high as 63.4 percent in Bhutan, 59.5 percent in Maldives, and 40.0 percent in Bangladesh. Therefore, these high MFN tariffs are likely to provide sufficient competitive advantage to partners to inflict trade diversions.

3.2 Results from Empirical Exercises

Although qualitative assessments provide important insights, quantitative evidence is perhaps more convincing. It is particularly of interest to know the potential implications of SAFTA arising from the empirical exercises. At the outset, three different techniques (that is, partial equilibrium analysis, econometric estimation of gravity equations, and computable general equilibrium [CGE] exercises) have been used in quantitative assessments. Each of these techniques has inherent limitations. Also, data limitations more often imply limited evidence for weaker economies.

The partial equilibrium models try to unearth the impact of tariff preferences by focusing on a specific sector, utilizing highly disaggregated data. However, they fail to capture the general equilibrium interactions, and thus cannot provide the intersectoral effects on the economy. Among the most important recent partial equilibrium studies that have tried to assess the effects for weaker economies of SAFTA, perhaps the most prominent one is a study by the World Bank (2006b). The study assessed the potential implications of a likely India–Bangladesh FTA for a few industries, including cement, light bulbs, sugar, and apparel. Using limited data from a few firms, the results suggest that in the case of cement, lights bulbs, and sugar, the likely FTA effects seem to provide an expansion of Indian exports to Bangladesh, but result in no exports from Bangladesh to India. This effect is mainly because Indian export prices for these products are substantially lower than ex-factory before-tax prices of the same or similar products in Bangladesh.[12]

The partial equilibrium model that has become most popular in undertaking the effects of regional trading arrangement is the World Integrated Trade Solution model, which has been developed jointly by the World Bank and United Nations Conference on Trade and Development (UNCTAD). This modeling system comes with the necessary database and an analytical tool that allows researchers to undertake simulation exercises to assess, among other things, the effects of tariff preferences exchanged between two countries. Using this framework, when all tariffs are abolished among the SAFTA member countries to postulate a regional free trade scenario in South Asia, the results reported in Figure 16.3 are obtained.

Figure 16.3 shows that SAFTA will lead to an increase in Bangladesh imports from the region of about US$400 million compared with a rise in regional exports of only US$33 million. The results show that only India stands to experience regional export gains higher than imports from regional sources. Bhutan, Nepal, and Sri Lanka individually appear to

FIGURE 16.3   Rise in Regional Exports and Imports

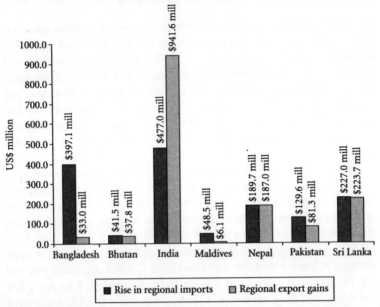

Source Estimates from the World Integrated Trade Solution (WITS) SMART simulations.

experience increases in exports and imports by similar magnitude; however, for Maldives, the imports are significantly greater than the exports. These intersectoral effects cannot be captured with this partial equilibrium framework, and the assessment of welfare effects from this model is not convincing.

Gravity models, on the other hand, aim to explain bilateral trade flows with a set of explanatory variables that are important in predicting the impact of the arrangement on bilateral trade flows. Gravity exercises are unable to capture the welfare effects, however, because they explain only the trade flows (that is, either exports, imports, or trade). Among the most recent gravity modeling exercises, Tumbarello (2006) and Hirantha (2004) found net trade creation from the South Asian Preferential Trading Arrangement (SAPTA), whereas Rahman (2003a) failed to detect any significant effect of the South Asian trading bloc. The two studies that have attempted to provide disaggregated results for individual South Asian countries include Rahman et al. (2006) and Rodríguez-Delgado (2007). In Rahman et al. (2006), Bangladesh, India, and Pakistan were expected to gain from joining the RTA, whereas Nepal, Maldives, and

Sri Lanka were found to be adversely affected. Rodríguez-Delgado (2007) evaluated the SAFTA within the global structure of overlapping regional trade agreements using a modified gravity equation. The simulation predicted that the SAFTA tariff liberalization program would have a minor effect on regional trade flows. The simulation results suggest that SAFTA would influence regional trade flows mainly by increasing India's exports and Bangladesh and Nepal's imports. Of every US$100 of new export trade (as Figure 16.4 shows), almost US$78 would accrue to India, whereas Bangladesh, Maldives, and Bhutan will have little to share. On the import side, Bangladesh and Nepal would be responsible for more 60 percent of new imports, whereas India would attract only 15 percent. For trade flows generated by SAFTA as a share of individual country's GDP, only the smallest countries would obtain significant increases: Bhutan and Maldives would experience increases in trade flows equivalent to 2 percent and 1 percent of GDP, respectively; India, Bangladesh, Pakistan, and Sri Lanka would find trade flows to increase by less than 0.25 percent of GDP. Among other countries, the study found that SAFTA would affect customs revenues in most of the weaker economies: for Bhutan the loss of revenue could amount to 2.5 percent of its GDP, while for Maldives and Nepal the corresponding figures could be 1.5 percent and 1.0 percent, respectively.

These results cannot determine whether or not the increased imports for Bangladesh, Nepal, and other countries are welfare enhancing. The results show only a rather weak export response emanating from the weaker economies and do not draw any inferences about the welfare implications.

Finally, the studies based on the CGE models, by considering intersectoral and intercountry interactions, predict the effects of the trading arrangement on a variety of variables of interest, including production, consumption, trade flows, and, most important, a convincing measure of welfare. One such model that has now become the most widely used analytical framework in assessing the likely effects of multilateral and bilateral or regional liberalization is the Global Trade Analysis Project model (best known as the GTAP model), which has been developed and is based at Purdue University (Hertel 1997). A key advantage of this model is that it combines analytical tool with a detailed database that includes intercountry trade flows, protection measures across countries, and numerical specifications of each of the economies using comparable sectors and factors of production.

FIGURE 16.4 Distribution of Changes in Regional Exports and Imports

Distribution of new exports

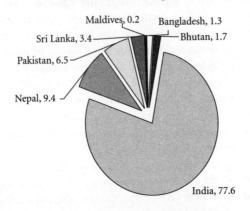

Distribution of new imports

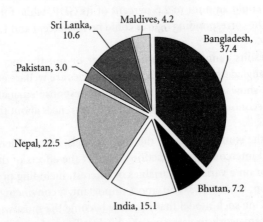

Source Based on the gravity model simulation results presented in Rodríguez-Delgado 2007.

The CGE or GTAP modeling approach to policy analysis is not free from limitations. Apart from its inherent characteristics and the nature of operation, which are often subjects of criticism, the simulation exercises using the GTAP model require adroit handling of data, database updates, and careful interpretation of results in line with economic theories. Therefore, to derive policy implications, it is important to focus only on judiciously designed and performed simulation results.

Among the recent GTAP studies, Bandara and Yu (2003) find that, in terms of real income, SAFTA would lead to 0.21 percent and 0.03 percent gains for India and Sri Lanka, respectively, while Bangladesh would stand to lose by 0.10 percent. The rest of South Asia, in which Pakistan, Nepal, Bhutan, and Maldives are lumped together, is found to gain by 0.08 percent. The researchers endorse the view that South Asian countries would gain much more from unilateral trade liberalization than from regional liberalization under SAFTA.

In a recent study, Raihan and Razzaque (2007) ran two different simulations using the GTAP model and database. In the first scenario, the authors depict a case in which all member countries eliminate their intraregional tariffs but keep their tariffs with the rest of the world intact. In the second scenario, in addition to SAFTA tariff cuts, the authors let Bangladesh slash its tariffs against the rest of the world by 50 percent. Consequently, the scenario comparisons provided an opportunity to examine the trade diversion effects when determining the overall welfare effects for Bangladesh. The results show that the full tariff liberalization under SAFTA alone leads to a net welfare loss of US$184 million for Bangladesh (Figure 16.5). India, Sri Lanka, and the rest of South Asia in this scenario register welfare gains, as trade creation effects dominate the trade diversion effects. However, when Bangladesh undertakes MFN tariff cuts by 50 percent along with the full tariff liberalization for SAFTA members, it stands to gain by US$84.1 million (Figure 16.6). In the latter exercise, the positive welfare gains of other countries were maintained as well.[13]

Raihan and Razzaque (2007) also explored the possible reasons for the large trade diversion effects for Bangladesh. From the simulation results, it appeared that under the first scenario, imports from China and other low-cost sources outside the region had declined, while those from India increased significantly. This indicated a replacement of the most efficient supplies with relatively expensive imports. Even when the advanced developing partners are globally efficient, it is possible that high MFN tariffs would prevent weaker economies from maximizing gains from trade creation, because the suppliers may decide not to reduce their prices by the full amount of tariff preferences granted under the regional arrangement.

FIGURE 16.5   Welfare Effects of SAFTA: General Equilibrium Effects

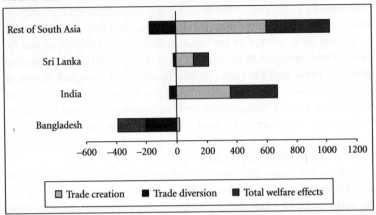

Source   Based on the results reported in Raihan and Razzaque 2007.

FIGURE 16.6   Welfare Effects of SAFTA When Bangladesh Reduces MFN Tariffs by 50 Percent

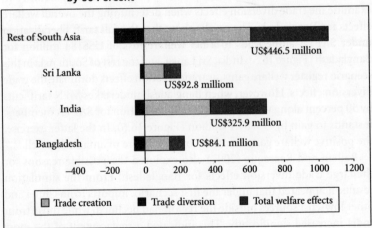

Source   Based on the results reported in Raihan and Razzaque 2007.

3.3 Loss of Regional Preference Resulting from Other Trading Blocs

Membership in more than one RTA has now become a reality, with an overwhelming majority of developing countries being involved in such a practice. The resultant overlapping membership creates numerous problems, requiring countries to enact different rules of origin provision. Another serious problem of these overlapping memberships is the loss of preference for some countries. Some of the South Asian members are in the process of forming new trading blocs that include extra SAFTA members (such as Thailand and Myanmar) but that exclude SAFTA members such as Pakistan (as in the case of Bay of Bengal Initiative for Multi-Sectoral Technical and Economic Cooperation [BIMSTEC]). As a result, the excluded members in the new initiative likely will experience competition from these new extra-SAFTA members in the markets of some of the original SAFTA members.[14] A recent initiative that is likely to be some serious cause for concern, particularly for weaker economies of SAFTA, is an FTA involving India and the European Union, for which the negotiations are currently under way.

Considering various traded goods across different tariff lines, one can identify four possible implications of the proposed European Union–India FTA on other SAFTA members, including the weaker members. First, there can be no negative or adverse effects. This will be the outcome in the products in which India already provides duty-free access to both SAFTA members and the European Union (that is, the sectors that are without any trade restrictions on an MFN basis). Second, a trade reorientation effect is likely to occur in sectors in which SAFTA members benefit from zero tariff access. The proposed FTA provides similar access to the European Union. If the European Union has the equal condition of providing access to the Indian market, a substitution across suppliers could lead to increases in market share at the expense of other exporters to India. Third, trade diversion effects can occur if the proposed preferential partner (the European Union) faces a tariff in the Indian market equal to that faced by SAFTA members. The preferential access of this tariff could lead to the proposed partner (again the European Union) becoming a less costly supplier solely because of preference. Fourth, a combined trade reorientation and diversion effect could be a possibility—for example, if, before preferences are granted, the proposed preferential partner faces a tariff in India greater than that faced by SAFTA members.

In a recent study, using the above four concepts, Winters et al. (2008) utilized highly disaggregated data to identify the scope of adverse consequences of the European Union–India FTA on different sets of countries, including the SAFTA members (see Tables 16.4 and 16.5). The authors show that a large proportion of tariff lines across SAFTA partners potentially suffer from increased competition from the EU in their access to the Indian market. For Bangladesh, the European Union would match the current access in approximately 5 percent of tariff lines. But, if there

TABLE 16.4 Tariff Lines and Value of Trade with India Affected by Improved Access by the European Union

	No change			Trade reorientation			Trade diversion			Trade reorientation/diversion			
	Quantity of tariff lines (% of tariff lines)	Value (US$ 1,000s)	Percent of total exports to India	Quantity of tariff lines (% of tariff lines)	Value (US$ 1,000s)	Percent of total exports to India	Quantity of tariff lines (% of tariff lines)	Value (US$ 1,000s)	Percent of total exports to India	Quantity of tariff lines (% of tariff lines)	Value (US$ 1,000s)	Percent of total exports to India	Percent share of exports to India (%)
Bangladesh	287 (2.5%)	685.2	0.5	481 (4.1%)	4,824.4	3.8	5,455 (46.7%)	47,051.8	36.9	5,470 (46.8%)	74,929.4	58.8	2.0
Bhutan	287 (2.5%)	72.6	0.1	291 (2.5%)	28,055.8	24.1	5,633 (48.2%)	29,272.8	25.2	5,482 (46.9%)	58,810.5	50.6	99.0
Maldives	287 (2.5%)	0	0	0	0	0	9,622 (82.6%)	1,968.6	99.3	1,744 (14.9%)	13.3	0.7	1.8
Nepal	287 (2.5%)	1,120.6	0.3	291 (2.5%)	30,009.4	7.3	5,633 (48.2%)	187,020.8	45.5	5,482 (46.9%)	193,073.4	47	63.0
Pakistan	287 (2.5%)	17.3	0	0	0	0	9,662 (82.6%)	52,731.5	29.3	1,744 (14.9%)	127,444.0	70.7	1.5
Sri Lanka	287 (2.5%)	3,404.3	0.3	9,121 (78.0%)	553,258	48.8	833 (7.1%)	13,991.0	1.2	1,452 (12.4%)	562,008.0	49.6	23.3

Source Compiled from Winters et al. 2008.
Note Trade values are for 2004.

TABLE 16.5 Tariff Lines and Value of Trade with the European Union Affected by Improved Access by India

	No Change			Trade Reorientation			Trade Diversion			Trade Reorientation/Diversion			Share of exports to EU (%)
	Quantity of tariff lines (% of tariff lines)	Value (US$ 1,000s)	Percent of total exports to EU	Quantity of tariff lines (% of tariff lines)	Value (US$ 1,000s)	Percent of total exports to EU	Quantity of tariff lines (% of tariff lines)	Value (US$ 1,000s)	Percent of total exports to EU	Quantity of tariff lines (% of tariff lines)	Value (US$ 1,000s)	Percent of total exports to EU	
Bangladesh	7,865 (55.6%)	101,782	2.5	6,276 (44.4%)	3,893,460	97.5	—	—	—	—	—	—	62.4
Bhutan	7,865 (55.6%)	581	94	6,276 (44.4%)	37	6	—	—	—	—	—	—	0.5
Maldives	7,865 (55.6%)	1,945	8.3	6,276 (44.4%)	21,627	91.7	—	—	—	—	—	—	20.9
Nepal	7,865 (55.6%)	20,643	39.1	6,276 (44.4%)	32,140	60.9	—	—	—	—	—	—	8.1
Pakistan	7,795 (55.1%)	634,075	21.3	—	—	—	6,346 (44.9%)	2,348,697	78.7	—	—	—	25.0
Sri Lanka	7,795 (55.1%)	606,006	41.2	—	—	—	6,346 (44.9%)	865,707	58.8	—	—	—	30.3

Source Compiled from Winters et al. 2008.

Note Trade values are for 2004; — = not available.

was complete liberalization of tariffs between the European Union and India, it would have improved market access in more than 95 percent of tariff lines.

In the case of Maldives and Pakistan, preferences are granted to only 1,744 tariff lines. Thus, the European Union is likely to surpass the South Asian Association for Regional Cooperation (SAARC) partner's market access in India in more than 97 percent of tariff lines. SAFTA LDCs benefit from a few more concessions in the form of 291 tariff lines gaining zero tariff entry to India, and from reduced tariffs in 4,029 products.[15] The European Union will improve its access to India over these countries in 95 percent of tariff lines. In the case of India's FTA with Sri Lanka, the predominant effect is trade reorientation, because the European Union will match its preferential access to the Indian market in nearly 78 percent of the tariff lines. Winters et al. (2008) suggest that the size of the effects on excluded countries of India granting preferences to the European Union will depend largely on the value of their exports to India and on the degree of comparative market access enjoyed by the European Union as a result of these preferences. Because countries like Bhutan and Nepal rely most heavily on the Indian market for their exports, granting EU exports preferential access to India is likely to negatively affect these countries. The amount of "affected trade" could be more than 90 percent of Bhutan's exports to India and 60 percent of Nepal's exports to India.

The European Union–India FTA could affect weaker SAFTA members in the EU market. Although this concerns economies outside the South Asian region, it nevertheless is important. Using the same four concepts as above, it is possible to identify the potential scope of adverse consequences as a result of India's gaining preferential access equal to what is available for SAFTA LDCs under the EU's Everything But Arms (EBA) initiative. These results from the Winters et al. (2008) study are summarized in Table 16.5. Respectively, 98, 92, and 61 percent of exports of Bangladesh, Nepal, and Maldives to the European Union could be subject to a trade reorientation effect as a result of India's better market access provision.

4. MITIGATING THE ADVERSE CONSEQUENCES AND BENEFITING FROM THE REGIONAL COOPERATION

As trade diversion is a dominant concern, there have been suggestions for SAFTA weaker members to reduce their MFN tariffs significantly. As illustrated above, unilateral tariff cuts along with regional trade liberalization provided welfare gains for Bangladesh, whereas regional liberalization alone resulted in welfare loss. For various reasons, the relatively weaker economies find this option to be difficult. These countries recognize the need to provide protection to some of their domestic industries, and they are dependent on these tariff revenues. It is also true that if tariff concessions are to be given to advanced regional partners, the revenue losses cannot be prevented. Conversely, opening trade to the region only could lead to significant competitive pressure for the domestic industries, particularly when countries like India and Pakistan have well-developed manufacturing bases and mimic the product range supplied by the rest of the world. Therefore, despite the associated difficulties, unilateral and multilateral liberalization is likely to remain a critical factor in mitigating some of the adverse welfare consequences.

The perceived need to support the domestic industries, along with the urgency of protecting tariff revenues, has resulted in developing a list of sensitive products that are not subject to tariff liberalization. While the rationale for such sensitive lists is well understood, it is not clear how judiciously these industries can be selected for protection. An essential feature of any dynamic industry is that eventually it should be able to compete with the rival suppliers without the need for any discriminatory policy support. The political economy factors might imply the selection of sectors for protection, because policymakers tend to select these sectors based on campaigns and pressure from lobbyists rather than from an informed analysis, which is rarely available.

Not only the LDCs have identified a range of products for not making concessions on them; other developing countries, too, have put a large number of items on the negative list. Around 25 percent of the items on the Harmonized Tariff Schedule for Bangladesh and Nepal are on the negative list, while the corresponding figures for India and Pakistan are 14 and 23 percent, respectively.[16] The inclusion of such large proportions of products on the sensitive list somewhat undermines the regional cooperation initiative in South Asia. The critical problem of LDCs is well known—that is, their export baskets lack diversity—in which case even a small number of goods on the negative list will obstruct any meaningful participation in regional trade.[17] Therefore, due consideration by relatively advanced SAFTA members that sectors of important export interest provided by weaker members not be kept on the sensitive list is important in ensuring gains of these countries from the regional trading arrangement.

Apart from the issue pertaining to negative lists, South Asian countries' trade regimes are characterized by nontariff and paratariff barriers. The cost of trading across borders, including the transaction costs for meeting the procedural requirements for exporting and importing, is excessive. Port facilities are poor and land border crossings suffer from a lack of harmonization of border procedures and a lack of transparency (World Bank 2006c). Improved trade facilitation measures alone can contribute to a significant rise in the intraregional trade in South Asia (Milner 2008).

Despite the current low level of intraregional trade and rather unimpressive quantitative evidence regarding the extent to which trade can be expanded among the SAFTA members, the potential scope of dynamic gains should not be undermined. Quantitative exercises base their predictions on the current levels of trade, and they cannot capture the possibility of dynamic trade gains that can emanate from increased cooperation. Therefore, while the concerns for trade diversion effects are genuine, new sectors triggering trade and welfare gains are not considered. One example in this regard is the trade in new products under the ISFTA, which could not be predicted in advance based on the then pattern of trade flows between these two countries. Between 2000 and 2006, merchandise exports from Sri Lanka to India rose from US$58 million to about US$489 million. Exports from India also increased rapidly. While critics point to a handful of items, mainly copper and vegetable oil, in which Sri Lanka's exports have been concentrated, for smaller developing countries and LDCs export growth from a wide range of products should not be expected. The argument that the growth in vegetable oil is due to Indian entrepreneurs setting up a processing plant in Sri Lanka to take advantage of duty-free access in India under the FTA does not constitute a convincing argument against trade gains. Extended cooperation can open up a number of avenues with different natures of trade expansion.[18] The increased trade relations between India and Sri Lanka have resulted in enhanced air travel linkages, with the flights from Colombo to different cities in India expanding enormously and the number of Indian tourists in Sri Lanka increasing significantly.

India's imposition of quantitative restrictions in the face of the rising imports of vegetable oil from Sri Lanka can be regarded as a step toward undermining the increased trade cooperation in the region. As already pointed out, smaller developing countries and other weaker economies are most likely to have a few items for export, and restrictions against them will greatly diminish trade potentials. The relatively advanced developing countries should consider this particular issue carefully before imposing any trade restrictions against these weaker economies.

The current SAFTA arrangement has been built primarily on trade in goods. Services, too, can provide significant opportunities for trade creation.

In services sectors, the neighboring countries (particularly India), are likely to have clear comparative advantage over the rest of the world. As such, opening up such areas as health, education, tourism, information technology, and other areas generally considered to be nontradable services (such as electricity generation and cross-border transmission) could lead to welfare gains for the weaker economies. It is widely recognized that much of the services trade involving education and health takes place through the informal channel.[19] Liberalization in these sectors will certainly enhance consumers' welfare with the current scope of trade diversion being extremely limited. Most of the South Asian countries are endowed with natural circumstances ideal for tourism. Particularly, Bhutan, India, Nepal, and Sri Lanka have been popular tourist destinations and an effective and extended cooperation on a regional basis may result in much larger gains for the region, including for countries like Bangladesh where tourism has not been a significant sector.

Another area of cooperation with high potential for gains is the transit trade. While transit through Bangladesh will help integrate north-eastern Indian provinces into the Indian economy, for landlocked countries like Bhutan and Nepal, access to ports in Bangladesh through Indian territory could promote their international trade. Geographic location is now considered to be an important determinant of international trade, and for landlocked countries, transport costs have been shown to be excessively high, thereby undermining their trading potentials.[20] In this backdrop, regional cooperation can lead to enormous benefits for the weaker economies in landlocked South Asia. When the issue of transit trade is kept out of the regional arrangement initiative, it implies that an important area of natural comparative advantage for these countries, particularly for the weaker economies in the region, is not exploited.

It is often argued that enhanced SAFTA cooperation will lead to a flow of investment from relatively strong countries to weaker economies. Investment flow may not necessarily take place, however, if the relatively advanced developing country suppliers make supplies available to the regional centers by producing goods from their own countries. Also, within the region, there could be a bigger tendency to concentrate investment in places traditionally known to be commercial centers, particularly when wages in different South Asian countries do not differ much. This is true both in the case of investment flows originating within the region and those coming from outside South Asia. Empirical evidence suggests that regional integration, on average, contributes to attracting foreign direct investment (FDI), but the benefits are unlikely to be distributed evenly

(Yeyti et al. 2003). Nonetheless, greater cooperation among these countries may result in FDI inflows from the relatively advanced developing countries to weaker economies. This has already taken place in the case of India–Sri Lanka trade. Bangladesh has witnessed India's investment in the health and information technology sectors along with investment proposals for other sectors.

Finally, regional cooperation in improving the infrastructure can have major beneficial effects for the weaker economies. Trade and cooperation in energy and water are important areas of common interest to most South Asian countries. As South Asia is a fast-growing region, developing uninterrupted sources of energy supplies will be crucial for future growth and economic activities. According to World Bank (2006c), regional cooperation in cross-border management of water resources, among other types of cooperation, may contribute to hydro and irrigation benefits to Nepal, flood control benefits in Bihar, India, and flood control and dry season water augmentation in Bangladesh. Developing better transport infrastructure is another area in which countries can cooperate and through which regional trade can be promoted. Cooperation is needed to create harmonization of standards and policies. Lack of harmonization of policies is currently a major nontariff barrier obstructing trade flows.

5. CONCLUSION

The existing literature and empirical evidence suggest that weaker economies within a South–South RTA are likely to lose, irrespective of whether or not the regional arrangement on a whole is welfare enhancing. Trade diversion is the principal cause of this adverse implication for the poorer countries. When the stronger economies tend to replace most imports from the rest of the world for a weaker economy, foregone revenues coupled with trade diversion become the worst consequences for these weak economies. While the protection of some domestic industries and the need for tariff revenues have resulted in a list of sensitive products for member countries, the depth of the product range not for liberalization along with the existing behind-the-border measures greatly restrict the scope of intraregional trade flows. Therefore, SAFTA, as it stands today, remains a paradoxical means for attaining development for the LDCs. Analysis of trade flows and tariff profile of the individual South Asian countries in this chapter suggests that the issue of unilateral liberalization is going to be important for weaker members to ensure overall trade creation effects of SAFTA. Weaker members of SAFTA may be challenged by other developments associated with the formation of trading blocs involving South Asian members and countries outside the region. This may create a loss of trade preferences not only in the regional market but also in other major global markets.

Despite all these grim assessments, the scope of dynamic gains arising from SAFTA can be substantial. Opening up the region can generate new exports, exerting trade effects much larger than what analytical exercises can predict based on the existing information on bilateral trade and protection structure. However, supportive policies in the relatively advanced developing countries will be required so that these new sectors do not become subject to restrictive trade measures. This is particularly important for LDCs, because they produce only a few items for export.

To exploit the maximum benefits of SAFTA, greater cooperation involving services, transit trade, investment, and regional infrastructure development should be seriously considered. Trade expansion can take place in these areas in the absence of adverse implications arising from trade diversion. These sectors cover the mutual interests of South Asian countries from the perspectives of their long-term growth and development, thereby creating a win–win situation for all members involved.

A political will is required on the part of the advanced developing members to ensure that the weaker economies benefit from the regional integration process. This political will requires providing generous treatment to all LDC goods immediately, including those included on the list of sensitive products. Advanced developing countries in collaboration with their weaker counterparts may devise fiscal and financial incentive packages so that regional and international investors find it attractive to invest in the weaker countries.

The LDC members of SAFTA should continue with their concerted efforts, in terms of reforms and addressing supply-side bottlenecks, so that they can benefit from a bigger regional market. In fact, South Asian countries will have to be involved in far more extended cooperation if the poorest countries can make use of SAFTA for their trade, economic growth, and development. It may be useful for LDC members to realize that regional cooperation may not depend on trade preferences alone. Mutual and extended cooperation are likely to augment trade irrespective of preferences exchanged.

398   Mohammad A. Razzaque

NOTES

1. The author is currently Economic Adviser, Economic Affairs Division, Commonwealth Secretariat, London, UK. Views expressed here are those of the author, and do not necessarily reflect those of the Commonwealth Secretariat or its Members.
2. Maldives is in the process of graduating out of the group of LDCs, but it will perhaps remain as a weaker economy. In fact, it is very difficult to define weaker economies precisely in the group of low-income countries. Based on manufacturing base, supply-side capacity, and overall economic dynamism, Sri Lanka also may be regarded as a weaker economy in the group that includes such countries as India and Pakistan.
3. The empirical literature seems to suggest that RTAs involving relatively high-income countries promote convergence of per capita income levels. Ben-David (1993, 1996), for example, showed that lower-income countries within the European Union (such as Ireland, Portugal, and Spain) registered more rapid growth than the larger and richer countries. On the other hand, Venables (2003), referring to the East African Common Market, among others, as an example of South–South integration, pointed out how the greater divergence within the member countries eventually led to the collapse of the cooperation scheme. In general, North–South trading blocs involving the rich industrial and poor countries are regarded as beneficial to the poorer countries.
4. A nice illustration of this can be found in Venables (2003), based on which the South Asian example in this chapter is drawn.
5. This is well-demonstrated in Panagariya (1998).
6. A numerical illustration of this point can be found in Hoekman et al. (2002).
7. But, it is not necessarily so. Most efficient exporters may remain outside the original and secondary RTAs.
8. It is the large population of India that makes its per capita income smaller.
9. However, Nepal's exports of textile and clothing items have declined substantially in the aftermath of the abolition of the Multi-fibre Arrangement (MFA) quotas in 2005.
10. Note that small countries, in terms of population, are likely to have greater trade-to-GDP ratios. Because of their small home markets, firms in small countries generally target the world market for production and export. In contrast, firms in a large domestic market may be more inclined to produce and sell to home consumers, even within a neutral trade regime, thereby exerting a negative influence on the degree of trade orientation (see Gylfason 1999).
11. Sawhney and Kumar (2007) provide a summary of the evidence on informal border trade in South Asia.
12. One interesting finding of the study is India's comparative advantage over Bangladesh in the production of apparel. Nevertheless, India has been reluctant to open its market to Bangladeshi apparel. Recently, under a tariff rate quota arrangement, India has allowed duty-free imports of 8 million pieces of apparel. Such a volume of exports appears to be small considering Bangladesh's total garment exports to the world market.
13. It should be noted that the original GTAP framework does not provide the decomposition of welfare effects into trade creation and trade diversion. To disentangle these two effects, the authors incorporated some necessary adjustments into the model. The GTAP model provides a net welfare estimate of the SAFTA simulation, which includes trade

creation and trade diversion effects. With a view toward isolating the trade creation effect from the total welfare effect, a separate simulation was run in which the relevant model closure was modified so that the imports to all South Asian countries from all regions (except from the South Asian countries) could be held fixed. The welfare effects from this scenario produced trade creation effects for individual SAFTA members. These trade creation effects were then deducted from the total welfare effects in the original simulation to get the estimates of trade diversion effects.

14. This is in addition to the problem of trade deflection that the excluded SAFTA members from the new initiative will have to face.

15. Tariff is above zero but below MFN level.

16. Countries in SAFTA make a distinction between sensitive items for LDC and non-LDC members. For example, India's sensitive items for non-LDC members account for about 17 percent of its Harmonised Trading System (HTS) lines as against 14 percent for LDCs. Among others, Bhutan and Maldives (LDCs) currently consider, respectively, 3 and 13 percent of their product range to be sensitive. The other developing country, Sri Lanka, has included about 20 percent of its tariff lines in the negative list (Raihan and Razzaque 2007).

17. This has particularly become evident since the conclusion of the WTO Hong Kong Ministerial, as many analysts are of the view that the duty-free access to 97 percent of tariff lines does not mean any meaningful market access given their exports' high concentration on a few items. In light of this, the depth in SAFTA member countries' list of sensitive goods is most likely to severely restrict LDCs' trading capacity.

18. However, note that tariffs in Sri Lanka are among the lowest in South Asia, which helps it protect from excessive trade diversion costs. For other South Asian countries with high MFN tariff barriers the scope of such adverse implications can be quite substantial, as discussed earlier.

19. Rahman (2003b) finds that annual payments made by Bangladeshi nationals to access education and health services in India could be about US$100 million, an overwhelming proportion of which goes unrecorded in the official balance of payments.

20. According to Redding and Venables (2004), *ad valorem* transport costs of 20 percent on both final output and intermediate goods can reduce the domestic value added by 60 percent when intermediate goods account for 50 percent of costs. The implication is that only because of unfavorable geography, some countries will experience much lower gains from trade, and foreign firms might be reluctant to move or relocate their production to those countries that are far from their main export markets, even when wages in those countries are low.

REFERENCES

Bandara, J. S. and W. Yu. 2003. "How Desirable is the South Asian Free Trade Area? A Quantitative Economic Assessment." In D. Greenaway (ed.), *World Economy: Global Trade Policy*. London: Oxford.

Baysan, T., A. Panagariya, and N. Pitigala. 2006. "Preferential Trading in South Asia." World Bank Policy Research Working Paper 3813. Washington, DC: World Bank.

Bhagwati, J., and A. Panagariya. 1996. "The Theory of Preferential Trade Agreements: Historical Evolution and Current Trends." *American Economic Review* 86: 82–87.

Ben-David, D. 1993. "Equalising Exchange, Trade Liberalisation and Income Convergence." *Quarterly Journal of Economics* 108: 653–79.

———. 1996. "Trade and Convergence among Nations." *Journal of International Economics* 40: 279–98.

Gylfason, T. 1999. "Exports, Inflation and Growth." *World Development* 27: 1031–57.

Hertel, T. W. 1997. *Global Trade Analysis: Modelling and Applications.* Cambridge: Cambridge University Press.

Hirantha, S. W. 2004. "From SAPTA to SAFTA: Gravity Analysis of South Asian Free Trade." Paper presented at the European Trade Study Group ETSG 2004. Available at http://www.etsg.org/ETSG2004/Papers/hirantha.pdf (accessed on March 2009).

Hoekman, B., M. Schiff, and J. Goto. 2002. "Benefiting from Regional Integration." In B. Hoekman, A. Mattoo, and P. English (eds), *Development, Trade and the WTO: A Handbook.* Washington, DC: World Bank.

Milner, C. 2008. *Trading on Commonwealth Ties: A Review of the Structure of Commonwealth Trade and the Scope for Developing Linkages and Trade in the Commonwealth.* London: Commonwealth Secretariat.

Panagariya, A. 1998. "Rethinking New Regionalism." In J. Nash and W. Takacs (eds), *Trade Policy Reform: Lessons and Implications.* World Bank Regional and Sectoral Studies Series. Washington, DC: World Bank.

———. 2000. "Preferential Trade Liberalization: The Traditional Theory and New Developments." *Journal of Economic Literature* 38: 287–331.

Rahman, M., W. Shadat, and N. C. Das. 2006. "Trade Potential in SAFTA: An Application of Augmented Gravity Model." Occasional Paper 61, Centre for Policy Dialogue, Dhaka.

Rahman, M. M. 2003a. "A Panel Data of Bangladesh's Trade: The Gravity Model Approach." Paper presented at the European Trade Study Group (ETSG) Programme in Madrid.

———. 2003b. "Bangladesh-India Bilateral Trade: An Investigation into Services." Paper prepared for South Asian Network of Economic Research Institutes (SANEI) Study Programme, Centre for Policy Dialogue, Dhaka.

Raihan, S. 2007. "SAFTA: Implications for Bangladesh." Paper prepared for the Commonwealth Secretariat, London.

Raihan, S., and A. Razzaque. 2007. "Regional Trading Arrangements in South Asia: Implications for Bangladesh." Chapter 6 in S. Raihan and A. Razzaque (eds), *WTO and Regional Trade Negotiation Outcomes: Quantitative Assessments of Potential Implications on Bangladesh.* Dhaka: Unnayan Shamannay and Pathak Shamabesh.

Redding, S., and A. J. Venables. 2004. "Economic Geography and International Inequality." *Journal of International Economics* 62: 53–82.

Rodríguez-Delgado, J. D. 2007. "SAFTA: Living in a World of Regional Trade Agreements." IMF Working Paper, 07/23, International Monetary Fund, Washington, DC.

Sawhney, A., and R. Kumar. 2007. "Why SAFTA." Paper prepared from the Commonwealth Secretariat, London.

Tumbarello, P. 2006. "Are Regional Trade Agreements in Asia Stumbling or Building Blocks? Some Implications for the Mekong Countries." Paper prepared for the seminar on Accelerating Development in the Mekong Region—the Role of Economic Integration, Siem Reap, Cambodia, June 26–27.

Venables, A. J. 2003. "Winners and Losers from Regional Integration Agreements." *The Economic Journal* 113: 747–61.

Weerakoon, D., and J. Thennakoon. 2007. "India-Sri Lanka FTA: Lessons for SAFTA." Paper prepared for the Commonwealth Secretariat, London.

Winters, L. A., M. Gasiorek, J. L. Gonzalez, P. Holmes, M. M. Parra, J. Rollo, and A. Shingal. 2008. "An EU-India Free-Trade Agreement: Reflections on the Implications for Excluded Countries." Paper prepared for the Commonwealth Secretariat, London.

World Bank. 2006a. *World Development Indicators*. Washington, DC: World Bank.

———. 2006b. *India & Bangladesh: Bilateral Trade and Potential Free Trade Agreement*. Dhaka and Washington, DC: World Bank.

———. 2006c. "South Asia's Growth and Regional Integration: An Overview." Chapter 1 in *South Asia: Growth and Regional Integration*. Washington, DC: World Bank.

———. 2008. *World Development Indicators*. Washington, DC: World Bank.

World Trade Organisation (WTO). 2007. *World Tariff Profile 2006*. Geneva, Switzerland: WTO.

Yeyti, E. L., E. Stein, and C. Daude. 2003. "Regional Integration and the Location of FDI." Inter-American Development Bank Working Paper No. 492. Washington, DC: IADB.

17

SAARC Programs and Activities

Assessment, Monitoring, and Evaluation

Mahendra P. Lama

The South Asian Association for Regional Cooperation (SAARC) established in 1985 includes Afghanistan, Bangladesh, Bhutan, India, Maldives, Nepal, Pakistan, and Sri Lanka. Since its inception, a range of activities has been carried out by the SAARC, which can be broadly categorized as follows:

- Creation of the SAARC Integrated Programme of Action (SIPA), including Agriculture and Rural Development; Communications and Transport; Social Development; Environment, Meteorology, and Forestry; Science and Technology; Human Resources Development; and Energy.
- Signing agreements and conventions, including an Agreement on Establishing the SAARC Food Security Reserve; Regional Convention on Suppression of Terrorism; Regional Convention on Narcotic Drugs and Psychotropic Substances; SAARC Convention on Preventing and Combating Trafficking in Women and Children for Prostitution; SAARC Convention on Regional Arrangements for the Promotion of Child Welfare in South Asia; Coordination of Positions on Multilateral Legal Issues; Agreement for Establishment of South Asian University.

- Initiation of SAARC programs, including poverty eradication; agreement on SAARC Preferential Trading Arrangement (SAPTA) and Transition from SAPTA to South Asian Free Trade Agreement (SAFTA); social charter; SAARC Development Fund (SDF); and regional connectivity program.
- Establishment of SAARC regional centers, including Agricultural Information Centre (Dhaka); Tuberculosis Centre (Kathmandu); Documentation Center (New Delhi); Meteorological Research Centre (Dhaka); Human Resources Development Centre (Islamabad); Energy Centre (Islamabad); Disaster Management Centre (New Delhi).
- Organization of People to People contact programs, including SAARC Audio-Visual Exchange (SAVE) Programme; SAARC Documentation Centre (SDC); SAARC Scheme for Promotion of Organized Tourism; SAARC Chairs, Fellowships, and Scholarships Scheme; SAARC Youth Volunteers Programme (SYVOP); SAARC Visa Exemption Scheme; South Asian Festivals; SAARC Consortium of Open and Distance Learning (SACODiL) and SAARC Awards.

Visible progress has been made in all these major spheres of activities. For instance, numerous regional institutions have been established and are functioning, and SAFTA has come into effect. A number of activities have been initiated under the rubric of the regional agreements and conventions, regional centers, and the broad framework of people-to-people contact. However, none of these activities and initiatives has had any major direct impact on strengthening the regional cooperation and integration process in South Asia. The heads of the states and the governments have had 15 summit meetings to date. A large number of meetings have taken place among the Council of Ministers (that is, the foreign ministers of these countries) and at the foreign secretary and various official levels. A series of special meetings have included home ministers, agriculture ministers, and finance ministers of the region.

There have been no institutionalized responses to the enthusiasm created by some of these activities in the region. The euphoria with which these activities are launched dies down in no time both in the absence of a proper monitoring and evaluation mechanism and because of the lack of involvement of people and nongovernmental institutions in the exercise. There is an increasing feeling that many of these activities are just initiated as summit rituals by the heads of states and governments. An array of literature calls SAARC "ritualistic," describes it as "suffocatingly slow," and criticizes it as a "magnificent paper tiger," "political white elephant," "talk shop of no consequence," "military convoy in a mountainous region," "a regional pastime," "a club of tongues," "bureaucratic den," and so on.

This chapter provides specific instances in which the SAARC process has failed in fulfilling its objectives and in meeting peoples' aspirations as the only regional body for almost 24 years.

1. POVERTY AND TERRORISM VERSUS RHETORIC AND ACTION

1.1 Poverty Alleviation

The 6th SAARC Summit (Colombo, 1991) for the first time accorded the highest priority to the alleviation of poverty in South Asia and established an Independent South Asian Commission on Poverty Alleviation (ISACPA), including eminent persons from member states. The commission conducted an in-depth study of the diverse experiences of member states and reported their recommendations on the alleviation of poverty to the 7th Summit. The 1992 Commission on Poverty Alleviation set rather formidable macroeconomic targets for the eradication of poverty in South Asia by 2002 (SAARC Secretariat 1992). The Commission provided a radical conceptual framework for poverty alleviation through social mobilization and empowerment in South Asia. To achieve this goal, it recommended that the region would require the following:

- An annual growth rate of 9.1 percent.
- Doubling of per capita income from US$300 to US$600.
- Lowering of incremental capital-output ratio from 4:1 to 3:1.
- Increasing the marginal savings rate from the current level to 27 percent or more.

The report elaborately discussed various micro-level interventions and lessons learned from the tedious delivery systems of the state mechanism. In most of the South Asian countries the delivery of services is carried out overwhelmingly by state agencies. Two very striking aspects of this delivery mechanism are found in this region. Firstly, the service delivery mechanism in critical areas like heath, food supplies, education, drinking water, electricity etc., has several layers of sub-institutions and sub-authorities and the actual delivery remains slow, tardy and cumbersome. And secondly, there is literal absence of monitoring and evaluation of the services delivered and poor accountability of the agencies and institutions involved in it. More seriously the leakages and corruption has become both rampant and deep rooted making the issues of transparency and accountability farfetched. This Report also mentioned the emergence of new trends at the grassroots level and discussed the shifting focus from macro interventions to participatory micro development organizations. On the basis of this report, the 7th SAARC Summit (Dhaka, 1993) for the first time committed to eradicate poverty in South Asia by 2002. The declaration stated that "the Heads of State or Government committed their Governments unequivocally to the eradication of poverty in South Asia, preferably by the year 2002 AD through an Agenda of Action" (SAARC Secretariat 1993) which would, among other things, embody the following:

- A strategy of social mobilization involving the building of organizations of the poor and their empowerment through appropriate national support mechanisms, with the assistance of respective governments.
- A policy of decentralized agricultural development and sharply focused household-level food security through the universal provision of *daal-bhaat* or basic nutritional needs.
- A policy of decentralized small-scale labor-intensive industrialization, with the choice of efficient and cost-effective technology.
- A policy of human development, including the enhancement of the social role and status of poor women, the provision of universal primary education, skill development, primary health care, shelter for the poor, and protection of children.
- A policy to support the above initiatives with adequate financial resources.

The Summit stressed that within the overall conceptual approach of *daal-bhaat*, the right to work and the right to primary education should receive priority. This 7th Summit also urged major actors in the world economic scene to create an enabling atmosphere supportive of poverty alleviation programs and expressed the need for a new dialogue with donors.

Despite this lofty and rather challenging declaration of poverty eradication in South Asia by 2002, the SAARC as a regional body undertook a meager number of inconsequential initiatives during the critical period from 1993 to 2002. These included calling for a new dialogue with donors, SAARC/World Bank Informal Workshop on Poverty Reduction in South Asia (Annapolis, Maryland, October 1993), United Nations Development Program (UNDP) and United Nations Economic and Social Commission for Asia and the Pacific (UNESCAP) proposals for cooperation with SAARC in poverty reduction, establishment of a three-tier mechanism for exchanging information on poverty eradication (8th SAARC Summit, New Delhi, 1995), and two rounds of meetings. The social mobilization strategy as envisaged by the first ISACPA has been put into practice across South Asia (except Bhutan) through the UNDP-sponsored South Asia Poverty Alleviation Program (SAPAP), which was launched in early 1996 and completed in March 2003. The Secretariat has been preparing a *SAARC Regional Poverty Profile* since 2003. The most recent profile was published in 2005, which highlighted regional dimensions based on the country-level profiles (SAARC Secretariat 2006b). However, the only concrete action has been the establishment of Three-tier Committees. Although these committees have met, nothing substantive has happened in terms of implementing the recommendations of both the Poverty Commission report and of the Three-tier Committees.

For many years, however, all the SAARC Summit declarations reiterated their stand of 1993 to eradicate poverty from the region by 2002. When it finally reached the year 2002, a new Poverty Commission was appointed. The goal of poverty eradication then shifted to the achievement of the SAARC Development Goals (SDGs), which would be done in the next five years starting from year 2007 (Table 17.1). Interestingly in the 13th Summit (Dhaka, 2005), the Heads of State or Government decided to declare the decade of 2006–2015 as the SAARC Decade of Poverty Alleviation. During this decade, endeavors—both at the national and regional level—will continue to be made with a sense of commitment and urgency to free South Asia from poverty.

The 11th SAARC Summit (Kathmandu, 2002) appointed another ISACPA to review the progress made on poverty alleviation and to suggest appropriate and effective measures for implementation. The Summit mandated a review of the Commission's report and suggested measures and strategies to downscale the incidence of poverty in the region. The second ISACPA submitted its report *Our Future Our Responsibility: A Road Map towards a Poverty Free South Asia* in 2004 (SAARC Secretariat 2004a).

TABLE 17.1   Poverty Alleviation-related Declarations in SAARC Summits since 1993

7th Summit, 1993, Dhaka	"The Heads of State or Government committed their Governments unequivocally to the eradication of poverty in South Asia, preferably by the year 2002 A.D. through an Agenda of Action."
8th Summit, 1995, Delhi	"The Heads of State or Government reaffirmed their commitment to the eradication of poverty in South Asia, preferably by the year 2002 A.D. through on Agenda of Action. In this context, they decided to declare 1995 as the *SAARC Year of Poverty Eradication*."[b]
9th Summit, 1997, Male	"The Heads of State or Government were unequivocal in their commitment to the eradication of poverty in South Asia at the earliest, preferably by the year 2002 A.D. through an Agenda of Action. They noted with satisfaction the establishment of a Three-tier Mechanism on Poverty Eradication and endorsed the recommendations of the two rounds of meetings under this mechanism hosted by India and Pakistan, respectively. They desired that the Ministers of Finance/Planning should meet again in the near future to give further impetus to this process."[c]
10th Summit, 1998, Colombo	"The Heads of State or Government reiterated the commitment of SAARC to the eradication of poverty in the Region at the earliest possible, preferably by the year 2002. They emphasized the need to encourage maximum participation by target groups in the formulation and implementation of poverty eradication programmes. The Heads of State or Government were of the view that such participation is essential for success of efforts in this field. They stressed the need for effective utilization of the SAARC Three-tier Mechanism on Poverty Eradication and in that context welcomed the offer of the Government of Pakistan to host the next meeting of the SAARC Finance/Planning Ministers under the Mechanism in October 1998."[d]
11th Summit, 2002, Kathmandu	"The Heads of State or Government acknowledged that investment in poverty alleviation programs contributes to social stability, economic progress, and overall prosperity. They were of the view that widespread and debilitating poverty continued to be the most formidable developmental challenge for the region. Conscious of the magnitude of poverty in the region, and recalling also the decision of the UN Millennium Summit 2000 to reduce world poverty in half by 2015, and also recalling the commitments made at the five-year review of the World Summit for Social Development

(Table 17.1 Continued)

(Table 17.1 Continued)

to reduce poverty through enhanced social mobilization, the Heads of State or Government made a review of the SAARC activities aimed at poverty alleviation and decided to reinvigorate them in the context of the regional and global commitments to poverty reduction.

The Heads of State or Government expressed their firm resolve to combat the problem of poverty with a new sense of urgency by actively promoting the synergetic partnership among national governments, international agencies, the private sector, and the civil society. They reaffirmed their pledge to undertake effective and sustained poverty alleviation programs through pro-poor growth strategies and social as well as other policy interventions with specific sectoral targets. The leaders also agreed to take immediate steps for the effective implementation of the programs for social mobilization and decentralization, and for strengthening institution building and support mechanisms to ensure participation of the poor, both as stakeholder and beneficiary, in governance and the development process.

The Leaders directed the Council of Ministers to coordinate efforts to integrate poverty alleviation programs into the development strategies of Member States. In this context, they agreed to reconstitute the Independent South Asian Commission on Poverty Alleviation, with Nepal as its Convener and Bangladesh as Co-convener, for reviewing the progress made in cooperation on poverty alleviation and for suggesting appropriate and effective measures."[e]

12th Summit, 2004, Islamabad

"We recognize poverty alleviation as the greatest challenge facing the peoples of South Asia and declare poverty alleviation as the overarching goal of all SAARC activities. It is imperative to relate regional co-operation to the actual needs of the people.

Provision of basic needs, promotion of literacy, and better health care are a regional priority. It is important to undertake effective and sustained poverty reduction programmes through pro-poor growth strategies and other policy interventions with specific sectoral targets.

The Plan of Action on Poverty Alleviation, prepared by the meeting of Finance and Planning Ministers in Islamabad in 2002, is hereby approved.

The reconstituted Independent South Asian Commission for Poverty alleviation (ISACPA) has done commendable work. An effective strategy should be devised to implement suggestions made in its Report *Our Responsibility*."[f]

(Table 17.1 Continued)

(*Table 17.1 Continued*)

13th Summit, 2005, Dhaka	"The Heads of State or Government decided to declare the decade of 2006–2015 as the SAARC Decade of Poverty Alleviation. During the Decade, endeavors—both at the national and regional level—will continue to be made with a sense of commitment and urgency to free South Asia from poverty... They entrusted the ISACPA to continue its advisory and advocacy role in this regard.... They decided to focus on formulation and implementation of concrete regional programmes and projects as well as forging partnerships among all stakeholders."[g]
14th Summit, 2007, New Delhi	"The Heads of State or Government appreciated the Independent South Asian Commission on Poverty Alleviation (ISACPA) for its elaboration of the SAARC Development Goals (SDGs), which reflect the regional determination to make faster progress toward attaining the Millennium Development Goals (MDGs). They agreed that the national plans for poverty alleviation should appropriately mirror the regional consensus reached in the form of the SDGs and the Plan of Action on Poverty Alleviation. Deciding that resource mobilization for achieving the SDGs would remain a high priority in the Decade of Poverty Alleviation, the Leaders directed translation of the highest regional level political commitment into action for creating opportunities for productive employment and greater access to resources for the poor that are essential for them to enhance their livelihood and realize their potentials. They entrusted the Two-tier Mechanism on Poverty Alleviation to monitor the progress and fine-tune the approaches toward pro-poor growth process."[h]
The New Goal	The Twenty-Seventh Session of the Council (Dhaka, 1–2 August, 2006) endorsed its recommendations that (*a*) SDGs would be achieved in the next five years starting from year 2007 and (*b*) a mid-term review on the attainment of SDGs would be undertaken toward the end of the third year.
15th Summit, 2008, Colombo	"The Heads of State or Government ... resolved to continue to combat poverty through all available means, including especially through people's empowerment. They committed themselves to continuing to share each other's experiences and success stories of pro-poor poverty reduction strategies such as micro-credit systems, community-driven initiatives and the raising of the consciousness of the poor on their right to resources and development ... They emphasized undertaking sustained efforts, including developing and implementing regional and sub-regional projects toward the attainment of

(*Table 17.1 Continued*)

(Table 17.1 Continued)

	SAARC Development Goals (SDGs). They noted the decision by the Ministers on Poverty Alleviation to obtain an inter-governmental mid-term review of the attainment of the SDGs to be completed by 2009."[i]

Source SAARC Secretariat 1993–2008.
Notes [a]SAARC Secretariat 2005a.
[b]Ibid., 96.
[c]Ibid., 113.
[d]Ibid., 138–39.
[e]Ibid., 53–154.
[f]Ibid., 169.
[g]SAARC Secretariat 2005b.
[h]SAARC Secretariat 2007a.
[i] Available at http://www.news.lk/index2.php?option=com_content&task=view& id=6621&Itemid=44&pop=1&page=0','win2' (accessed on 6 October 2009).

While providing a "Road Map towards a Poverty Free South Asia," the report highlighted the following strategic priorities:

- Mobilizing the Power of the Poor
- Prudent Macroeconomics
- Mainstreaming the Informal Economy
- Enhancing Gender and Other Equities
- Sustainable Development
- Effective, Harmonious, and All-round Cooperation among the Countries of the Region

The 12th Summit (Islamabad, 2004) provided continuity to ISACPA, giving it a special advocacy role to enable it to guide follow-up actions on its report. The Commission was given the task preparing the SDGs (SAARC Secretariat. For the first time, a SAARC Poverty Alleviation Fund (SPAF) was established with contributions to be voluntary or assessed, as may be agreed. India has already offered US$100 million (2005) for poverty alleviation projects with a regional dimension. The SPAF shall function within the SADF, which has been reconstituted, as the SAARC Development Fund (SDF). The three-tier mechanism on poverty alleviation has been replaced by a two-tier mechanism, comprising ministers and the secretaries dealing with poverty alleviation at the national level. In addition, the Secretariat published three regional poverty profiles.[1]

The 27th Session of the Council (Dhaka, 1–2 August 2006) endorsed its recommendations that *(a)* SDGs would be achieved in the next five years starting from year 2007 and *(b)* a mid-term review on the attainment of SDGs would be undertaken toward the end of the third year. ISACPA could play an overall oversight role on the SDG regional reporting process. However, how far these recommendations will be internalized by the member countries, what institutions they will involve, and in what way the SAARC process will be involved are of significant interest (SAARC Secretariat 2007b).

1.2 Suppression of Terrorism

Large-scale terrorist violence continues to beset South Asia today (Khatri and Kueck 2003; Lama 2006). The inclusion of Afghanistan as the eighth member of the SAARC adds a new dimension to this violence. The SAARC Regional Convention on Suppression of Terrorism was signed during the 3rd SAARC Summit (Kathmandu, November 1987). It came into force on 22 August 1988. This Convention provides for a regional approach to well-established principles of international law in respect of terrorist offenses. It includes such provisions as sharing of information on terrorist activities and extraditions. Article VIII of the Convention emphatically states that "contracting States shall cooperate among themselves, to the extent permitted by their national laws, through consultations between appropriate agencies, exchange of information, intelligence and expertise and such other cooperative measures as may be appropriate, with a view to preventing terroristic activities through precautionary measures" (SAARC 1988). This Convention led to the establishment of a SAARC Terrorist Offences Monitoring Desk (STOMD) in Colombo in 1990 primarily to collate, analyze, and disseminate information about the terrorist incidences, tactics, strategies, and methods.

Recognizing the distinct ominous link between terrorism, drug trafficking, money laundering, and other transnational crimes, the 12th SAARC Summit held in Islamabad in 2004 signed an Additional Protocol to the Convention to deal effectively with financing of terrorism. The additional protocol takes into account obligations falling on member states in terms of the United Nations Security Council resolution 1373 of 28 September 2001, and the International Convention for Suppression of Financing Terrorism in 1999.

It was 11 years since the first Summit before legal experts met in 1999 to formulate future guidelines and identify three key elements in the Convention as prerequisites for its successful implementation—namely, (a) creation of offenses listed in the Convention as extraditable offenses under the domestic laws of SAARC member states; (b) treatment of such offenses as "nonpolitical offences" for purposes of extradition; and (c) vesting of extraterritorial criminal jurisdiction in the event of extradition not being granted. The second meeting of legal advisers in 2002 emphasized the importance of the following to give practical effect to this Convention: *(a)* adoption of comprehensive domestic legislation by member states and *(b)* harmonization of the national legal regimes in the region. Following this second meeting, the SAARC Interior/Home Ministers met in 2007 in New Delhi.

Like any other SAARC activity, because of the sensitivity of this issue, the Convention on terrorism has been totally marginalized and made in redundant. Year after year since 1988 the SAARC Summits have passed the same resolution asking the member countries to make enabling laws compatible with the Convention (Table 17.2). Some member countries have consistently failed to enact enabling domestic legislation that is compatible with the Convention. The absence of this most fundamental action toward implementing the Convention has made it ineffective.

TABLE 17.2 Prevention and Combating Terrorism-related Declarations in SAARC Summits since 1988

4th Summit, 1988, Islamabad	"Thus reflecting the sincere desire on the part of the Member States to enter into meaningful cooperation to eliminate the scourge of terrorism from the South Asian region. They called for the adoption of **enabling measures** by Member States to implement the Convention at the earliest."
5th Summit, 1990, Male	"They called for expeditious enactment of **enabling measures** for the implementation of the SAARC Regional Convention on Suppression of Terrorism. They also urged Member States to continue to cooperate in accordance with the Convention."
6th Summit, 1991, Colombo	"They stressed in particular, the urgent need for the expeditious enactment of **enabling legislation** by those Member States which had not yet done so, for the implementation of the Convention and the need for a constant dialogue and interaction among the concerned agencies of Member States, including submission of periodic recommendations to the Council of Ministers."
7th Summit, 1993, Dhaka	"The Leaders reiterated the need to give high priority to the enactment of **enabling legislation** at the national level to give effect to the SAARC Regional Convention on Suppression of Terrorism, while urging the Member States which had not yet done so, to make every effort to finalize this matter before the Eighth SAARC Summit."

(Table 17.2 Continued)

(Table 17.2 Continued)

8th Summit, 1995, New Delhi	"The Heads of State or Government once again emphasised that highest priority should be accorded to the enactment of **enabling legislation** at the national level to give effect to the SAARC Regional Convention on Suppression of Terrorism. They urged Member States, which had not yet done so, to enact expeditiously enabling legislation at the national level to implement the convention."
9th Summit, 1997, Male	"They emphasised the urgent need to complete **enabling legislation** in order to implement the SAARC Regional Conventions on Suppression of Terrorism and on Narcotic Drugs and Psychotropic Substances."
10th Summit, 1998, Colombo	"They emphasized the urgent need to complete **enabling legislation** in order to implement the SAARC Regional Conventions on Suppression of Terrorism and on Narcotic Drugs and Psychotropic Substances."
11th Summit, 2002, Kathmandu	"They also reiterated their firm resolve to accelerate the enactment of **enabling legislation** within a definite time-frame for the full implementation of the Convention, together with strengthening of SAARC Terrorist Offences Monitoring Desk and the SAARC Drug Offences Monitoring Desk in an effective manner."
12th Summit, 2004, Islamabad	"We reaffirm our commitment to SAARC Regional Convention on Suppression of Terrorism, which, among others, recognizes the seriousness of the problem of terrorism as it affects the security, stability, and development of the region."
13th Summit, 2005, Dhaka	"The Heads of State or Government directed that **concrete measures** be taken to enforce the provisions of the Regional Convention on Narcotic Drugs and Psychotropic Substances through an appropriate regional mechanism."
14th Summit, 2007, New Delhi	"They reaffirmed their commitment to **implement** the SAARC Regional Convention on Suppression of Terrorism and the Additional Protocol to the SAARC Regional Convention dealing with the prevention and suppression of financing of terrorism."
15th Summit, 2008, Colombo	"The Heads of State or Government further emphasized the importance of completing all legislative and other relevant measures to implement within Member States, the provisions of the Regional Convention on Narcotic Drugs and Psychotropic Substances."

Source SAARC Secretariat 1988–2008.

Despite their determination to prevent and suppress terrorism in all its forms and manifestations, member countries have not been able to share even the basic information.

Terrorist activities both within a country and on a cross-border basis have sharply gone up despite the existence of this Convention.[2] Despite several reiterations and reaffirmation of their commitment to the Convention on Suppression of Terrorism by the heads of state or government, not a single action has been taken under this Convention. In almost every Summit the member states expressed

> ... serious concern on the spread of terrorism in and outside the region and reiterated their unequivocal condemnation of all acts, methods and practices of terrorism as criminal. They deplored all such acts for their ruinous impact on life, property, socio-economic development and political stability as well as on regional and international peace and cooperation. (SAARC 11th Summit Declaration, Kathmandu 2002)

The blatant absence of this most fundamental action toward implementing the Convention has made it ineffective. For instance, the Male Summit held in 1990 "called for expeditious enactment of enabling measures for the implementation of the Convention" and the Kathmandu Summit held 12 years later in 2002 "reiterated their firm resolve to accelerate the enactment of enabling legislation within a definite timeframe" (SAARC 11th Summit Declaration, Kathmandu 2002). The "enabling laws" are still not enacted by some member countries, thereby making implementation of the Convention impossible. Interestingly since 2004, this appeal has been dropped and the Summits held in New Delhi in 2007 instead asked the member states to implement this Convention. This is making SAARC "a talk shop of no consequence" (Mahendra P. Lama, "Cut the Rhetoric: Get Together," *Hardnews*, New Delhi, May 2007).

There is no harmonization of domestic legislation, including the sanction regime of the Convention. There is absence of bilateral agreement on extradition. There are differences on the very definition of terrorism. Except for some meetings, the STOMD has remained largely ineffective. Most of the information and knowledge base of terrorism in South Asia that are available in the public domain are generated by academic research, and civil society organizations spread over the subcontinent. The STOMD, which was supposed to be the fountainhead of such information, remains largely defunct and inaccessible.

After almost 20 years since the signing of the Convention, the 14th SAARC Summit (New Delhi, 2007) still talked about "working on the modalities to implement the provisions of the existing SAARC Conventions to combat terrorism; narcotics and psychotropic substances; trafficking of women, children and other crimes" (available at http://www.saarc-sec. org/data/summit14/ss14declaration.htm [accessed on 6 October 2009]). This has rather become a ritualistic practice. The increasing ineffectiveness and uselessness of this Convention is reflected in the attempts by various member states to pursue bilateral negotiations, the most recent being the "joint mechanism" framework being established between India and Pakistan.

The only way to come out of this rigmarole is to generate public pressure on the member states to seriously implement the Convention. Unfortunately, the overwhelming majority of South Asians do not even know that such convention exists. This is one of those many conventions that the SAARC member countries signed without consulting the diverse stakeholders in and outside the region. As a result, despite the serious need to regionally combat terrorism, literally no civil society action is conducted under this Convention. At the same time, given the size of the SAARC Secretariat in Kathmandu, the limited human resources, constricted mandate, and narrow autonomy given to it, not too much really can be expected from the already exasperated and overworked Secretariat.

Today, the South Asia region faces a formidable challenge. The region needs to focus on key actions—for example, domestic legislation to implement the regional conventions should be mandatory and should be completed within an established time frame. As an accountability measure, the inability to implement these conventions within a time frame should have the provision of dropping the defaulting concerned member from the convention or the convention should be abrogated within a stipulated time frame. The tendency of the member states to keep most of the conventions at the sublime level of a signed document only and their hesitation to implement any of them have become common practice in the SAARC process. This is an ominous trend for the future scope and for the confidence of obtaining regional cooperation.

A visible contradiction is evident on the essential SAARC provision that "no bilateral contentious issues will be discussed in the SAARC forum" and conventions such as the Regional Convention on Suppression of Terrorism. The very nature of terrorism in South Asia has a strong cross-border context and content. The cross-border facets have been the core debate and key tenor of discourse on terrorism in the subcontinent. In such a situation, not discussing terrorism from a bilateral perspective in the name of dislocating a regional forum like SAARC would mean sweeping core issues under the carpet. Additionally, signing an agreement without understanding and accepting the realities of its provisions would further mean pretension, hypocrisy, and public consumption. The option is to drop such provisions from the SAARC process and discuss the issues as openly and as candidly as possible and to sign an appropriate and realistic convention to address these issues.

2. DELIBERATE INACTION AND POOR ACCOUNTABILITY

2.1 Integrated Programme of Action

One can cite several instances of deliberate inaction. The Integrated Programme of Action (IPA) includes nine areas of cooperation that form the core of the SAARC process. The IPA provided the firm foundation from which regional cooperation could take off. Each IPA is conducted by a Technical Committee, which helps member states build up or reinforce their national capabilities and undertake coordinated programs and activities at national and regional levels. The Technical Committee could examine broad relationships at the policy level between IPA activities and economic and social development in a catalytic, promotional, and advisory capacity with a view toward incorporating various recommended programs into mainstream development.

Over the years, IPA has undergone several changes, including in the number of its activities. Under the reconstituted SAARC Integrated Programme of Action (SIPA) in 2000, the number of Technical Committees was reduced from 11 to 7 (that is, Agriculture and Rural Development; Communications and Transport; Social Development; Environment, Meteorology, and Forestry; Science and Technology; Human Resources Development; and Energy. As a whole, the SIPA activities have broadly led to personal contact among the experts of the region in their specific fields of specialization. It has facilitated the exchange of data and information and the creation of seminars, workshops, and training courses.

The nature, extent, and level of activities carried out under the IPA have been beneficial from the regional perspective only to a limited extent. SIPA activities have never converged toward the real critical priority areas and have failed to engage and involve the nongovernmental organization, experts, professionals, and real beneficiaries in the interactive game. No two member countries have initiated concrete cooperative ventures. The three major critical drawbacks are as follows: *(a)* resource crunch, *(b)* lack of intersectoral coordination and non-implementation of decisions taken that have stunted growth, and *(c)* effective performance of IPA activities.

The non-implementation of decisions generally can be seen at three different levels. First, within the Technical Committees, there has been a tendency not to follow up the decisions taken in the previous meeting. As a result, a particular issue like a "SAARC weather bulletin" has been discussed year after year, and fresh decisions are taken on the same issue as reminders or reiteration. This becomes particularly serious because in most cases a Technical Committee Meeting takes place after a one-year gap. Second, the non-implementation of decisions and recommendations can be seen at the workshop and seminar levels. Third, the decisions taken by the First Special Session of the Standing Committee and the First MCTC often are not implemented. For instance, the First MCTC had made broad suggestions and had recommended, *inter alia*, Universalization of Primary Education by AD 2000, Universal Immunization of Infants by 1995, Provision of Safe Drinking Water and Sanitation by AD 2000. All these targets have been missed one by one. Some of these targets do not figure in the various TC's documents. Fourth, region-wide attractive projects that go well with the recommendations made at the global level were defined, identified, and given shapes. These projects and programs also went slowly into oblivion and never appeared again. Fifth, even the plans and projects specifically recommended by various specific Ministerial group meetings have not been implemented.

The non-implementation of decisions in a prolonged manner leads to the repetition of the same activity. For instance, on the initiative of Transport (TC10), a study entitled "Transport Infrastructure and Transit Facilities in the SAARC Region" was completed by an independent agency in Nepal in 1993. For a long time, the report remained under the consideration of the Committee on Economic Cooperation (CEC), which requested member states to complete their examination of the report and send their comments. This process has run into so many official processes and grindings that even almost 14 years after its completion nothing has come out of it. This is appalling given the urgent need to improve the connectivity-related infrastructures in the region in the wake of massive economic liberalization. Instead, a new project, SAARC Regional Multimodal Transport Study (SRMTS), was carried out by the Asian Development Bank for the SAARC in 2006 (SAARC Secretariat 2006a). This study was the result of a decision at the 12th SAARC Summit (Islamabad, 2004) to strengthen transport, transit, and communication links across the region.

2.2 SAARC Food Security Reserve

The SAARC Food Security Reserve is another example of how inaction could lead to the erosion of confidence on the SAARC system. This reserve was established in 1988 primarily to provide for a reserve of food grains to meet emergencies in member countries. Reserves stood at 241,580 tons as of January 2002. In 2002, 14 years after its implementation, the 9th Meeting of the Board (Islamabad, December 2002) for the first time identified institutions and organizations in member states that could be contacted in case of emergency requirements for withdrawal from the reserve. Again after 20 years of sheer non-implementation of the SAARC Food Reserves, this program has been "revamped and renamed" into an "Agreement on Establishing the SAARC Food Bank" in 2007. This renamed institution discusses the establishment of a permanent headquarters of the food bank with a dedicated staff.

This food reserve has remained notional to date. No one knows its location. So far, the food reserves have never been used despite pressing demands in several disaster situations, including the wheat crisis in Pakistan, a cyclone hit in Orissa, a flood in Bangladesh, the tsunami in Sri Lanka, and Maoist violence leading to food insecurity in certain districts of Nepal. Even in the recent cyclone (Sidr) disaster in Bangladesh in November 2007, despite the unprecedented food insecurity in the affected areas, the SAARC Food Reserve was never invoked and utilized. There is no existence of a clear-cut transportation mechanism, border formalities, institutional mechanisms, and appropriate delivery method of the food grains to the recipient countries. The terms and conditions of operationalizing the reserves (that is, prices, mode of payment, conditions of payment, and so on) that remained undecided have now been broadly worked out. However, in the absence of the actual implementation, the efficacy of these guidelines is yet to be tested.

3. CONCLUSION

A serious criticism of the SAARC process has been on the issue of non-implementation and the dismal performance of action. The SAARC as a regional body has little to show in terms of matching with its foundational objectives and in terms of reaching its benefits to the people and institutions in the region. It started with avowed objectives like *(a)* promotion of the welfare of the people; *(b)* acceleration of economic growth, social progress, and cultural development; *(c)* strengthening of collective self-reliance; *(d)* contribution to mutual trust and understanding; and *(e)* collaboration and mutual cooperation in the economic, social, cultural, and technical front.

The SAARC process started facing such criticism in the early 1990s. The then leaders had started reacting to such public criticism of nonperformance by voicing such concerns in various SAARC meetings. For example, the 7th SAARC Summit (Dhaka, 1993) had stated in its declaration that:

> The Heads of State or Government approved the recommendations of the Eleventh Session of the Council of Ministers for adopting a more business-like and functional approach in the conduct of Summit meetings. They also noted with satisfaction the guidelines and procedures approved by the Eleventh Session of the Council in this respect relating to other SAARC meetings. They decided to meet informally whenever necessary, between Summits. (SAARC, Declarations of SAARC Summits 1985–1998, Kathmandu, 1999)

In fact, the 13th Summit (Dhaka, November 2005) "directed all SAARC institutions and mechanisms to work collectively towards a decade dedicated to implementation so that a visible and discernible impact can be felt across South Asia" (available at http://www.saarc-sec.org/?id=159&t=7.1 [accessed on 6 October 2009]). The secretary general's analytical report mentioned that "in view of the foregoing directive of the Thirteenth Summit, it is timely for the Technical Committees/Working Groups, their equivalents and other SAARC processes, including the sectoral Ministerial Meetings, to focus on identification of tangible projects" (SAARC, Secretary General's "Periodic Analytical Report," SAARC/SUMMIT.14/SC.33/3 April 2007). It recommended measures as to how SAARC should devote its third decade to implementation.

The SAARC process, notwithstanding its serious nonperformance at the regional level, has not only generated significant interest and enthusiasm in intergovernmental consultation on many areas of common relevance, but also has built confidence among the member states. It is the only forum in the region that brings together the leaders on an annual basis.

This has helped members build confidence, move ahead on many of the bilateral projects, and resolve a range of problems directly and indirectly. More important, the official SAARC process has triggered a large number of nonofficial interactions and contacts among various sets of people and institutions. Many do believe that today the nonofficial SAARC process is far more active and robust than the official process. They also believe that ultimately it is the nonofficial SAARC that will lead to a people's SAARC and the official process will be forced to be active and operational.

Given the current situations, if drastic measures are not taken to both enhance the capacity of the Secretariat to operationalize the announced projects and also ensure strong monitoring and evaluation mechanisms to verify implementation of the decisions taken at various SAARC meetings, a situation may emerge in which leaders will year after year talk about the need to have effective implementation, while progress remains stunted. However, a new pattern of introducing programs and implementing them is emerging. The key to this new trend is a member country taking a lead role. For instance, India has taken the lead in a number of concrete activities. The latest examples include the South Asian University, a Tele-medicine Network, and a SAARC Textiles and Handicrafts Museum. These three programs and projects were proposed by India in the 13th SAARC Summit (Dhaka, 2005). India, while taking up the lead role, prepared concept papers for all three projects in a short time and brought them to the SAARC forum for discussion and approval (Council of Ministers 2006). All three projects are located in India, where implementation has begun (SAARC Secretariat 2006c).

NOTES

1. SAARC/CM.27/19 for consideration.
2. For more details on the steady increase in terrorist activities and their impact on the societies and economies of South Asia, read Khatri and Kueck 2003 and Muni 2006.

REFERENCES

Council of Ministers. 2006. Twenty-Seventh Session, SAARC/CM.27/22, Dhaka August 1–2.
Khatri, Sridhar, and Gert W. Kueck (eds). 2003. *Terrorism in South Asia: Impact on Development and Democratic Process.* New Delhi: Shipra.

Lama, Mahendra P. 2006. "Political Economy of Terrorism: Sustenance Factors and Consequences." In S. D. Muni (ed.), *Responding to Terrorism in South Asia*. New Delhi: Manohar.

Muni, S. D. (ed.). 2006. *Responding to Terrorism in South Asia.* New Delhi: Manohar.

SAARC Secretariat. 1988–2008. *Declaration of Summits, 1988–2008.* Kathmandu: Secretariat of the South Asian Association for Regional Cooperation.

———. 1992. *Meeting the Challenge.* Report of the Independent South Asian Commission on Poverty Alleviation. Kathmandu: Secretariat of the South Asian Association for Regional Cooperation.

———. 1993–2008. *Declaration of Summits, 1993–2008.* Kathmandu: Secretariat of the South Asian Association for Regional Cooperation.

———. 2004a. *Our Future Our Responsibility: A Road Map towards a Poverty Free South Asia.* Report of the Independent South Asian Commission on Poverty Alleviation. Kathmandu: Secretariat of the South Asian Association for Regional Cooperation.

———. 2004b. *SAARC Documents: Milestones in the Evolution of Regional Cooperation in South Asia,* Vol. VII. Kathmandu: Secretariat of the South Asian Association for Regional Cooperation.

———. 2005a. *Declarations of SAARC Summits, 1985–2004.* Kathmandu: Secretariat of the South Asian Association for Regional Cooperation.

———. 2005b. *Dhaka Declaration,* Thirteenth SAARC Summit, November 13. Kathmandu: Secretariat of the South Asian Association for Regional Cooperation.

———. 2006a. *SAARC Regional Multimodal Transport Study* (SRMTS). Kathmandu: Secretariat of the South Asian Association for Regional Cooperation.

———. 2006b. *SAARC Regional Poverty Profile 2005: Poverty Reduction in South Asia through Productive Employment.* Kathmandu: Secretariat of the South Asian Association for Regional Cooperation.

———. 2006c. Document No. SAARC/CM.27/4. Kathmandu: Secretariat of the South Asian Association for Regional Cooperation.

———. 2007a. *New Delhi Declaration,* Fourteenth SAARC Summit, April 4. Kathmandu: Secretariat of the South Asian Association for Regional Cooperation.

———. 2007b. "Progress of Work of the Independent South Asian Commission on Poverty Alleviation." Note by the Secretariat: SAARC/SUMMIT.14/CM.28/12. Presented before the Council of Ministers, Twenty-eighth Session, 14th SAARC Summit, New Delhi, April 2.

About the Editors and Contributors

Ahmed, Sadiq
Vice Chairman
Policy Research Institute of Bangladesh
Dhaka
(Former Chief Economist and
Sector Director, South Asia Region
The World Bank
Washington, DC)

Amin, Khalid
Secretary General
Federation of Pakistan Chambers of Commerce and Industry
Karachi

Banerjee, Pritam
School of Public Policy
George Mason University
Arlington

Chaturvedi, Sachin
Senior Fellow
Research and Information System for Developing Countries
New Delhi

De Alwis, Renton
Chairman
Sri Lanka Tourism Development Authority and
Sri Lanka Tourism Promotions Bureau
Colombo

Jayakody, Savindi
Research Analyst
Sri Lanka Resident Mission
Asian Development Bank
Colombo

Jayaratne, Chandra
Former President
Ceylon Chamber of Commerce
Colombo

Kelegama, Saman
Executive Director
Institute of Policy Studies of Sri Lanka
Colombo

Khan, Abdur Rob
Research Director
Bangladesh Institute of International and Srategic Studies
Dhaka

Khatri, Sridhar K.
Executive Director
South Asia Centre for Policy Studies
Kathmandu

Lama, Mahendra P.
Vice Chancellor
Central University of Sikkim
Gangtok

Rahmatullah, M.
Transport Policy Advisor – Transport Sector Management Reform
Bangladesh Planning Commission
Dhaka

and

Former Director
UNESCAP
Bangkok

De Mel, Deshal
Research Economist
Institute of Policy Studies of Sri Lanka
Colombo

De, Prabir
Fellow
Research and Information System for Developing Countries
New Delhi

Dutz, Mark Andrew
Senior Private Sector Development Specialist
South Asia Finance and Private Sector Unit
The World Bank
Washington, DC

Ghani, Ejaz
Economic Advisor
South Asia Region
The World Bank
Washington, DC

Harun, Yussuf A.
Former President
Federation of Bangladesh Chambers of Commerce and Industry
Dhaka

Hussain, Akmal
Distinguished Visiting Professor
Beacon House National University
Lahore

and

Senior Fellow
Pakistan Institute of Development Economics
Islamabad

Jain, Sonu
Confederation of Indian Industry
New Delhi

Razzaque, Mohammad A.
Economic Adviser
Economic Affairs Division
Commonwealth Secretariat
London

Roy, Jayanta
Principal Adviser
Trade and Globalization Research
Confederation of Indian Industry
New Delhi

Vokes, Richard
Country Director
Sri Lanka Resident Mission
Asian Development Bank
Colombo

Weerakoon, Dushni
Deputy Director and Fellow
Institute of Policy Studies of Sri Lanka
Colombo

Index